WordPerfect® 5.1 QuickStart

Kathie-Jo Arnoff

WordPerfect 5.1 QuickStart

Copyright © 1992 by Que® Corporation.

Library of Congress Catalog No.: 89-64227

ISBN: 0-88022-558-0

94 93 92   6 5 4 3 2 1

Interpretation of the printing code: the rightmost double-digit number is the year of the book's printing; the rightmost single-digit number, the number of the book's printing. For example, a printing code of 92-4 shows that the fourth printing of the book occurred in 1992.

Publisher: Lloyd J. Short

Associate Publisher: Rick Ranucci

Product Development Manager: Thomas H. Bennett

Book Designer: Scott Cook

Production Team: Jeff Baker, Paula Carroll, Michelle Cleary, Christine Cook, Terri Edwards, Jerry Ellis, Brook Farling, Betty Kish, Joy Dean Lee, Laurie Lee, Jay Lesandrini, Cindy L. Phipps, Caroline Roop, Sandra Shay, Dennis Sheehan, Linda Seifert, Tina Trettin, Angie Trzepacz, Suzanne Tully, Sue Vandewalle, Mary Beth Wakefield, Kelli Widdifield, Lisa Wilson, Phil Worthington

Product Director
Kathie-Jo Arnoff

Production Editors
H. Leigh Davis
Cindy Morrow

Editor
JoAnna Arnott

Technical Editor
Gary Pickavet

*Composed in ITC Garamond and
MCPdigital by Que Corporation*

About the Author

Kathie-Jo Arnoff is a product development specialist at Que Corporation. She is the author of *WordPerfect QuickStart* and a contributing author to *Introduction to Business Software* and *1-2-3 Release 2.2 QuickStart*. Over the past several years, she has helped to develop and edit titles on WordPerfect, 1-2-3, dBASE, DOS, and Excel. Her editorial influence is particularly evident throughout Que's line of QuickStart books, workbooks, instructor's guides, and QueCards. For 10 years before coming to Que, she worked as a writer, editor, and public relations director for several national associations.

Dedication

For Terry, Rebecca, and Jason

Trademark Acknowledgments

Que Corporation has made every attempt to supply trademark information about company names, products, and services mentioned in this book. Trademarks indicated below were derived from various sources. Que Corporation cannot attest to the accuracy of this information.

1-2-3 and Lotus are registered trademarks of Lotus Development Corporation.

Adobe Illustrator is a trademark of Adobe Systems Incorporated.

HP and LaserJet are registered trademarks of Hewlett-Packard Company.

Harvard Graphics is a registered trademark of Software Publishing Corporation.

Helvetica is a registered trademark of Allied Corporation.

Hercules Graphics Card and Hercules InColor are trademarks of Hercules Computer Technology.

IBM, IBM PC AT, Personal System/2, and PS/2 are registered trademarks of International Business Machines Corporation.

MS-DOS and Microsoft Excel are registered trademarks of Microsoft Corporation.

PC Paintbrush is a registered trademark of ZSoft Corporation.

PageMaker is a registered trademark of Aldus Corporation.

Quattro and Quattro Pro are registered trademarks of Borland International, Inc.

WordPerfect, DrawPerfect, and PlanPerfect are registered trademarks of WordPerfect Corporation.

Contents at a Glance

Table of Contents

Introduction

WordPerfect 5.1 QuickStart is a step forward in the evolution of how a book can be organized and structured. The book takes you through WordPerfect step-by-step, describing all the fundamentals you need to know about the software. The text supplies essential information, provides comments on what you see, and describes ideas. Many illustrations help guide you through procedures or clarify difficult concepts.

What Is WordPerfect?

WordPerfect is one of the most popular word processing software programs in the world. Why is WordPerfect so popular? Because it has all the "basic" features you would expect in a word processing package, plus a full complement of advanced features. The program is suited to your needs, whether they entail short memos or complex documents.

"What makes WordPerfect attractive is that it gets out of your way," explains W. E. "Pete" Peterson, executive vice president of WordPerfect Corporation. "It's like a well-mannered house guest who is kind enough not to disrupt your life or the way you do things."

An editing screen uncluttered by menus or cryptic codes, an abundance of features, support for a wide range of printers, and unparalleled customer assistance are just a few of the reasons why WordPerfect enjoys the prominence it so rightly deserves.

What Does This Book Contain?

Each chapter in *WordPerfect 5.1 QuickStart* focuses on a particular WordPerfect operation or set of operations. Overall, the book's movement reflects the steps typical in the creation of any document, from entering text to editing, spell-checking, and printing. Later chapters concentrate on more specialized topics, such as macros, columns, and graphics.

Chapter 1, "Getting Started," shows you how to start WordPerfect and introduces you to the editing screen, keyboard, mouse, and Help system. You also learn the basics of using the program: typing text, moving the cursor, making a menu selection, printing and saving a document, clearing the screen, and exiting.

In Chapter 2, "Editing," you learn to retrieve a file and modify it by inserting and deleting text. You also investigate WordPerfect's hidden codes and two document windows. Chapter 3, "Working with Blocks," shows you how to highlight a block and manipulate it in several ways; for instance, you learn to move, copy, delete, print, and save a block of text.

Chapters 4 and 5 cover formatting. First you work with formatting lines and paragraphs: you change the left and right margins, insert boldface and italic codes, set tab stops, indent text, align text in various ways, and use hyphenation. Then you move to formatting pages: you choose the paper size, change the top and bottom margins, design headers and footers, number pages, control page breaks, and use redline and strikeout.

After you create a document, you will want to proofread it. Chapter 6, "Proofreading," introduces you to WordPerfect's built-in Speller and Thesaurus and demonstrates how to use Search and Replace features to find particular words or codes in a document.

You learn to print a document in Chapter 7. After you see how to select a printer, you learn to print from the screen or disk. Other features for controlling print jobs also are covered.

Chapter 8, "Managing Files," explains how to use WordPerfect's List Files screen to manage your files — for example, to copy a file or change directories. You also learn how to use the program's Document Summary feature, which helps you keep track of the contents of your documents.

The rest of the book deals with more specialized features of WordPerfect. You learn the basics of creating macros in Chapter 9, and you create a few macros you can include in your own macro library. Chapter 10 covers merging documents, guiding you carefully through the steps for creating personalized form letters, addressing envelopes, and printing mailing labels. Chapter 11 introduces sorting and selecting. Chapter 12 teaches you how to create styles for special document formats. In Chapter 13, you practice setting up text columns, and you learn how to set up math columns and perform simple math calculations. In Chapter 14, you learn how to create tables and enhance them with various alignments, font styles, grid lines, and shading. Chapter 15 teaches you how to customize WordPerfect for your particular needs. Chapter 16 shows you how to create special characters and use WordPerfect's equation editor for typing complex formulas.

Chapter 17, "Referencing," explains how to create footnotes and endnotes, insert the current date into documents, create an outline, number the lines of your text, and insert comments into documents. The chapter also presents an overview of WordPerfect's other referencing tools.

Chapter 18, "Creating Graphics," shows you how to illustrate a document with graphics, draw lines, import graphics images, and enclose text in a box.

Appendix A provides step-by-step instructions for installing WordPerfect on both a hard disk system and a dual floppy disk system. You also learn how to install printers and how to select various cartridges and fonts. Appendix B provides a reference to WordPerfect's keyboard commands and pull-down menus. A detailed index helps you quickly find the specific information you need.

Who Should Use This Book?

WordPerfect 5.1 QuickStart is an easy guide for anyone just starting with WordPerfect 5.1. The book is intended for new users or for people who have not yet mastered WordPerfect. Basic information is presented to help a first-time user get started quickly. And enough essential information is provided so that a more experienced user can use the book as a reference tool.

Where To Find More Help

After you learn the fundamentals presented in this book, you may want to learn more advanced applications of WordPerfect. Que Corporation has a full line of WordPerfect books you can use. Among these are *Using WordPerfect 5.1*, Special Edition; *WordPerfect 5.1 Tips, Tricks, and Traps*, 3rd Edition; *WordPerfect 5.1 Quick Reference*; *Look Your Best with WordPerfect 5.1*; and *WordPerfect Power Pack*.

If you find yourself stymied at a particular point, WordPerfect's Help feature may be able to answer your questions. Using Help is explained and illustrated in Chapter 1, "Getting Started."

WordPerfect Corporation provides toll-free telephone support: 1-800-541-5096. The phone staff is helpful and knowledgeable. The line is open from 7 a.m. to 6 p.m. Mountain Standard Time, Monday through Friday.

What Hardware Do You Need To Run WordPerfect?

You can run WordPerfect 5.1 on an IBM PC or compatible computer with a hard disk drive or dual floppy disk drives. WordPerfect requires DOS 2.0 or later and at least 404K of random-access memory (RAM). A minimum of 512K is recommended.

If you plan to run WordPerfect from disks, you must have either the high-density 5 1/4-inch drives (1.2M) or the 3 1/2-inch drives. Because WordPerfect comes on eleven 5 1/4-inch disks or six 3 1/2-inch disks, you must frequently swap disks in and out of your drives if you use WordPerfect with a dual floppy disk system. To run WordPerfect with fewer interruptions, you probably should invest in a hard disk. Although WordPerfect is already a speedy program, it runs faster and performs better on a hard disk system.

Although you can run WordPerfect on a monochrome system without a graphics card, you will not be able to see any graphics, font changes, or font attributes (such as superscript, italic, and small caps). With a CGA card and a color or monochrome monitor, you can see graphics in View Document mode. EGA and VGA systems provide better resolution in graphics mode and offer more options for changing the screen display colors. To take full advantage of WordPerfect's graphics capabilities, you need a graphics card, such as a Hercules Graphics Card or a Hercules InColor card. With these cards, while in editing mode, you can see on-screen the various attributes as they will appear when printed.

WordPerfect prints to a wide variety of printers, from dot-matrix to laser. See Appendix A for instructions on how to install the software to use various printers.

WordPerfect 5.1 supports a mouse, but you don't need the device in order to use the program. Even if you have a mouse, you may decide that you don't want to use it with WordPerfect. WordPerfect works with either a two- or three-button mouse.

Conventions Used in This Book

Certain conventions are used throughout the text and graphics of *WordPerfect 5.1 QuickStart* to help you understand the book.

Function-key commands are identified both by name and by keystroke(s) — for example, Spell (Ctrl-F2). To choose this command, you press and hold down the Ctrl key while you then press the F2 key. Menu options are referred to by the name of the option, usually followed by the number of the option in parentheses — for example, Line (**1**). You press L or 1 to select the Line option.

When you need to press a series of keys, the names of the keys are separated in the text by commas; you press and release each key in turn. For example, to move to the top of a document, you press and release Home, then Home again, and then the up-arrow key (Home, Home, up-arrow).

Text that you type and hidden codes, such as **[Tab]**, are displayed in **boldface**. Screen messages appear in a `special` typeface.

Within the step-by-step instructions, keys are shown similar to how they appear on the keyboard. Blue lines emphasize the most important areas of the illustrations.

Commands accessed through WordPerfect's pull-down menu system are identified by a ▱. An instruction marked by this icon provides an alternative to using WordPerfect's function-key commands. Although the icon used in this book is a mouse, you can access the pull-down menu commands with either the mouse or the keyboard.

1

Getting Started

This chapter begins with the basics of WordPerfect: starting the program, looking at the editing screen, learning the keyboard, and using the Help feature. You learn some fundamental skills, including how to move around the editing screen, make a menu selection, print and save a document, and exit WordPerfect.

Before you learn these basic skills, the chapter gives you a brief overview of WordPerfect's features. Because this book is a QuickStart for those just learning WordPerfect, some of the advanced features are not covered in this text. You will, however, quickly learn to perform a variety of word processing tasks with WordPerfect's many features.

Starting WordPerfect

Understanding the editing screen

Using the keyboard and mouse

Using the Help system

Typing text

Understanding WordPerfect's built-in settings

Moving the cursor

Making a menu selection

Using Cancel (F1)

Previewing and printing a document

Saving and naming a document

Exiting WordPerfect

1

Key Terms in This Chapter

Defaults   Standard WordPerfect settings that are in effect each time you start the program.

Status line   The bottom line on the WordPerfect editing screen. The status line indicates the disk drive, file name, and position of the cursor on-screen. From time to time, the WordPerfect status line displays system messages and prompts.

Cursor   An on-screen marker that indicates where a character would appear if typed. The cursor also marks the location where a hidden formatting code will be entered.

Word wrap   A WordPerfect feature that eliminates the need to press the Enter (Return) key each time you reach the right margin. With word wrap, you need to press Enter only when you come to the end of a paragraph, short line, or command.

Soft return   The code inserted at the end of each line when the text reaches the right margin and is automatically wrapped to the next line.

Hard return   The code for a carriage return, inserted when you press the Enter key at the end of a line.

File name   A descriptive title that you assign to a file before storing it in system memory.

An Overview of WordPerfect Features

WordPerfect offers a range of features for making your word processing tasks convenient and efficient. These features enable you to create and edit text documents, enhance the appearance of the text, check the spelling, print documents, and manage files.

The more specialized features that WordPerfect offers enable you to create documents more quickly with macros (prerecorded keystrokes that help automate repetitive tasks), merge text files, create mailing labels, sort and select data, format text into columns, perform simple math calculations, and create tables.

Among the valuable tools that WordPerfect offers are automated features for generating footnotes and endnotes, date and time entries, outlines, line numbers, document comments, indexes, tables of authorities (legal documents), lists, indexes, and tables of contents. Also among the specialized features are graphics capabilities and options for customizing WordPerfect.

Basic Features

One of the first features you notice when you start WordPerfect is the uncluttered editing screen. Many word processors display indicators and codes while you edit, but WordPerfect keeps these to a minimum — freeing most of the screen for text. In addition, the document shown on-screen looks much the way it will appear when printed.

WordPerfect commands are easily accessed with either the keyboard or a mouse. When you are using WordPerfect, you will appreciate WordPerfect's on-line Help feature, which provides context-sensitive information (help that is appropriate to what you are doing) about WordPerfect's commands and keys. Even though you can access all of WordPerfect's commands with the function keys, you also have the option of using WordPerfect's system of pull-down menus to access many of the same commands. The pull-down menus, particularly when accessed with the mouse, often are easier to use for those just learning WordPerfect.

With WordPerfect's two document windows (on-screen areas in which to work), you can view different parts of the same document at once or work on two different documents. You can shift between full-screen displays of the two windows, or you can split the screen to display both windows.

1

Using the program's Block feature, you can designate a specific portion of a document on which you want certain commands to have an effect. You can, for example, use Block to move or copy a sentence or paragraph, format a certain portion of text in boldface, or delete a particular passage.

Several formatting features enable you to change the appearance of text. You can adjust margins, use boldface and italic, center text, justify text, hyphenate words, change the line spacing and line height, instruct the printer to shift (left, right, up, or down) before printing, design headers and footers, choose page numbering positions, and control where pages break.

Some other WordPerfect features are useful in particular situations. The Redline and Strikeout features are excellent tools for marking editing changes in a manuscript. With the Compose and Overstrike features, you can create special characters that you might need for foreign languages or equations. A special equation editor enables you to produce sophisticated mathematical and engineering formulas.

WordPerfect's Styles feature is a powerful tool with which you can format one document or a group of documents. You specify the format and enhancement codes you want in a particular style, and then apply that style to any future documents. You even can create a library of styles for use in a variety of document formats.

The built-in Speller and Thesaurus give you access to a 115,000-word dictionary, as well as lists of synonyms and antonyms you can access from the editing screen. Be aware that the dictionary does not contain the meanings of the words. Among the special printing features is View Document, which enables you to preview a document on-screen before you print it.

File management is handled efficiently through the List Files screen. From that screen, you can manipulate files and directories from within WordPerfect much more than most word processors allow. With the Retrieve option from the List Files menu, you can import or link spreadsheet files from programs such as Lotus 1-2-3 and PlanPerfect. And with WordPerfect's Document Summary feature, you easily can keep track of a file's contents — the file name, the date the document was created, the author's name, the typist's name, and other descriptive information about the document.

Specialized Features

To help you perform repetitive tasks more efficiently, you can use Word-Perfect's Macro feature. The keystrokes and commands that you want to include in a macro easily are recorded and then "played back" whenever you need them. You can keep macros for many different operations and call on a macro with as few as two keystrokes.

WordPerfect's Merge feature enables you to merge text files and thereby save valuable time for other tasks. You can, for example, merge data from an address list into a form letter, or piece together complicated reports. Other tools for handling data are WordPerfect's Sort and Select features. With these features, you can, for example, sort phone lists or extract certain ZIP codes from a mailing list.

In WordPerfect, you can use the Columns feature to create two kinds of columns: text columns and math columns. With text columns, you can pre-pare text in newspaper-style format (for magazine articles or newsletters) or in parallel-column format (for inventory lists or duty schedules). With math columns, you can perform simple calculations. In addition, you can use WordPerfect's Table feature to organize tabular material.

WordPerfect's referencing features are quite broad in scope. You can supple-ment your documents with footnotes and endnotes, date and time codes, outlines, line numbers, document comments, indexes, tables of authorities, lists, and automatic references. You can piece together a large project by creating a master document to keep track of and merge all the subdocument files that make up the project. And you can use WordPerfect's Document Compare feature to compare a new version of a document with a previous version.

With WordPerfect's graphics capabilities, you can import graphics images; create boxes around text; and enhance a document with borders, rules, shading, and many other features. These options are ideal for creating news-letters, brochures, and fliers.

Although WordPerfect comes with certain default settings, such as those for formatting and screen display, you can customize the program by altering settings through the Setup menu. After you become familiar with Word-Perfect's standard settings, you may want to change a number of these options for your future documents.

1

Starting WordPerfect

This section shows you how to start WordPerfect on a hard disk system and on a dual floppy disk system. Before you start the program, you must install it. Refer to Appendix A for instructions on how to make working copies of your original program disks, as well as how to install WordPerfect 5.1 and the printers you will be using with the program.

Starting WordPerfect on a Hard Disk System

These instructions assume that you have installed WordPerfect on the C drive in a directory called WP51. If you have installed the program to another location, substitute as necessary.

Follow these steps to start WordPerfect on a hard disk system:

1. Make sure that the drive door is open for the floppy drive(s).
2. Turn on your computer.
3. If necessary, respond to the prompts for date and time.
4. When the C> prompt appears, type **cd \wp51** and press ⏎Enter.
5. Type **wp** and press ⏎Enter.

You should see the opening screen for a few seconds, and then the editing screen is displayed.

If you are running WordPerfect and the power fails, the following prompt appears at the bottom of the screen when you restart the program:

```
Are other copies of WordPerfect currently running?
(Y/N)
```

Press N in response to this prompt.

Starting WordPerfect on a Dual Floppy System

Follow these steps to start WordPerfect on a dual floppy disk system:

1. Insert your working copy of the Program 1 disk into drive A.

    Note: If you are using your computer's 3 1/2-inch disk drive, the main program files are combined on one 3 1/2-inch disk labeled *Program 1*.

2. Insert a formatted data disk into drive B.

3. Turn on your computer.

4. If necessary, respond to the prompts for date and time.

5. When the A> prompt appears, type **b:** and press ⏎Enter).

    Drive B is now the default drive, which means that any data you save to disk is saved to the disk in drive B.

6. Type **a:wp** and press ⏎Enter).

    WordPerfect's opening screen appears. This screen contains Word-Perfect copyright information, the version number of your copy, and an indication of the default directory used by the operating system.

    WordPerfect prompts you to insert the Program 2 disk.

7. Remove your working copy of the Program 1 disk from drive A and insert your working copy of the Program 2 disk into drive A.

8. Press any key.

Before you begin to use WordPerfect, you should take a few minutes to become familiar with WordPerfect's screen display and keyboard.

Understanding the Editing Screen

WordPerfect displays a document almost exactly as it will appear when printed. What you see on-screen is approximately one-half of a standard typed page. The main portion of the screen displays the document.

```
Mr. Franklin Abbot
Director
Michigan Department of Commerce
P.O. Box 36226
Lansing, Michigan  48909

Dear Mr. Abbot:

Thank you for your willingness to help with our public relations
efforts for the River Park in Indianapolis.  I have enclosed the
preliminary market research.  Also, I have added your name to our
WaterNotes mailing list.

Please send us a list of TV and radio stations in Michigan along
with any other information you think would be helpful.

I look forward to your valuable input.

Sincerely,


Charles Gosnell
```

```
Mr. Franklin Abbot
Director
Michigan Department of Commerce
P.O. Box 36226
Lansing, Michigan  48909

Dear Mr. Abbot:

Thank you for your willingness to help with our public relations
efforts for the River Park in Indianapolis.  I have enclosed the
preliminary market research.  Also, I have added your name to our
WaterNotes mailing list.

Please send us a list of TV and radio stations in Michigan along
with any other information you think would be helpful.

I look forward to your valuable input.

Sincerely,


Charles Gosnell

C:\WP51\BOOK\PARK.LTR                    Doc 1 Pg 1 Ln 1" Pos 1"
```

Status line

At the bottom of the screen is the *status line*, which contains information describing the cursor's status. The left side of the status line shows the current document's name. From time to time, the document name is replaced temporarily by system messages and prompts, such as the following:

    * Please wait *

    Save document? Yes (No)

You can respond to a prompt by pressing Enter or clicking the left mouse button to accept the displayed response, or by typing an alternative response.

14

Doc indicates which of two available documents is currently displayed on-screen. WordPerfect is capable of holding two documents in memory simultaneously. The documents are identified as Doc 1 and Doc 2.

Pg identifies the number of the page on which the cursor is currently located.

Ln indicates the cursor's vertical position in inches (the default) from the top edge of the paper. You can change this measurement to centimeters, points, *w* units (1/1200th of an inch), or *u* units (WordPerfect 4.2 lines and columns).

Pos tells you the cursor's horizontal position in inches (the default) from the left edge of the paper. You can change this unit of measurement also. The Pos indicator serves these additional functions:

- The Pos indicator appears in uppercase letters (POS) if the Caps Lock key is activated for typing in uppercase.

- When the Pos indicator blinks, the Num Lock key is activated so that you can use the numeric keypad to type numbers.

- When you move the cursor through text that has been enhanced, the Pos indicator number reflects the enhancement of the text. For example, it may reflect boldfaced, underlined, or double-underlined text.

Status line information appears only on-screen; the information does not appear in the printed document.

Note: Through the Setup menu, you can customize many aspects of Word-Perfect's screen display. You can, for example, change the appearance and color of normal text (if you have a color monitor), specify whether the current file name is displayed on the status line, change the way menu letter options are displayed on-screen, and specify whether comments are displayed or hidden. For more information about customizing WordPerfect, see Chapter 15.

Using the Keyboard

WordPerfect uses the following main areas of the keyboard:

- The function keys, labeled F1 to F12 at the top of an Enhanced Keyboard (or F1 to F10 at the left of some keyboards).

- The alphanumeric or "typing" keys, located in the center of the keyboard. (These keys are most familiar to you from your experience with typewriter keyboards.)

- The numeric and cursor-movement keys, found at the right side of the keyboard.

1

Personal
Computer
keyboard

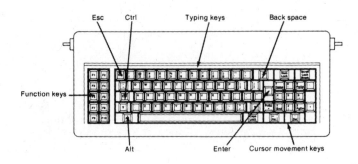

Personal
Computer AT
keyboard

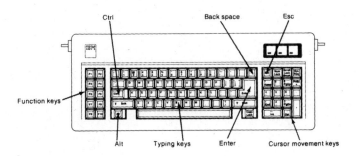

Enhanced
Keyboard (PS/2
computers and
others)

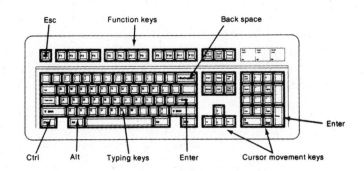

Function Keys

As the WordPerfect function-key template illustrates, each function key can accomplish four tasks when used by itself or in combination with another key. You routinely use the function keys to give instructions, called *commands*, to your computer. To activate a WordPerfect command, you press a function key alone or in combination with the Ctrl, Shift, or Alt keys.

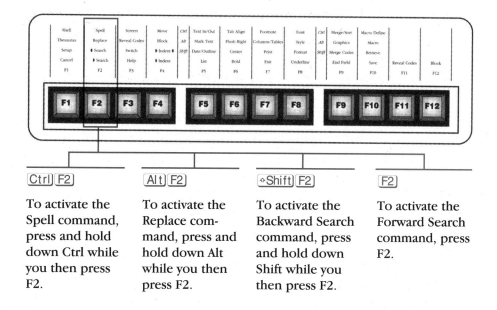

Ctrl-F2

To activate the Spell command, press and hold down Ctrl while you then press F2.

Alt-F2

To activate the Replace command, press and hold down Alt while you then press F2.

⇧Shift-F2

To activate the Backward Search command, press and hold down Shift while you then press F2.

F2

To activate the Forward Search command, press F2.

The commands on the WordPerfect template are color coded for easy use:

- Black means that the key is used by itself. Simply press the function key.
- Green means that you must press and hold down Shift while you press the function key.
- Blue means that you must press and hold down Alt while you press the function key.
- Red means that you must press and hold down Ctrl while you press the function key.

Note: An Enhanced Keyboard has 12 function keys. If your keyboard has only 10 function keys, you still can use all of WordPerfect's commands.

Some function keys are used as toggle switches to turn on and off a feature. To create boldfaced text, for example, first press F6 (to turn on Bold), and then type the text you want printed in boldface. To turn off Bold, press F6 again.

When you press some of the function keys, menus appear on-screen. When you press Ctrl-F7, for example, your system displays the Footnote and Endnote menu.

1

Other function keys start a feature that you end by pressing the Enter key. For instance, you begin the Center feature by pressing Shift-F6, and you end centering by pressing Enter.

Note: The commands assigned to the function keys when you first start WordPerfect are the default definitions for those keys. WordPerfect gives you the option of switching to other keyboard definitions so that the keys on your keyboard—the function keys as well as other keys—perform different commands or functions. You also can customize your keyboard by assigning alternate definitions to specified keys. In addition, you can display a map of any user-defined keyboard. To access WordPerfect's feature for alternate keyboard definitions, use the Keyboard Layout option on the Setup menu. For more information about customizing WordPerfect, see Chapter 15.

Alphanumeric Keys

The alphanumeric keys work similarly to those on a typewriter. Keep in mind a critical but easily overlooked difference between composing with a typewriter and composing with WordPerfect: when you type regular text in WordPerfect, you do not need to press the Enter key to end lines at the right margin. When you type text and reach the end of a line, the text that doesn't fit on the current line "wraps" automatically to the next line.

You can use the Enter key to force WordPerfect to move to the next line. You press Enter to insert blank lines in your text, such as the lines that separate paragraphs. You can use the Enter key also to initiate some commands in WordPerfect.

The Shift, Alt, and Ctrl keys are part of the alphanumeric keyboard. The Shift key creates uppercase letters and other special characters, just as it does on a typewriter keyboard. Shift also is used with the function keys to carry out certain operations in WordPerfect.

The Alt and Ctrl keys are used with other keys to provide WordPerfect capabilities that a single key cannot provide. The Alt and Ctrl keys don't do anything by themselves, but they work with function keys, number keys, or letter keys to operate various commands in WordPerfect.

18

Cursor-Movement Keys

The cursor is the blinking underline character that marks the location on the screen where the next character you type will appear. In addition, the cursor marks the location in your text where formatting codes will be entered (such as those used to change margin settings).

You use the keys marked with arrows at the far right of the keyboard to control cursor movement. When you press an arrow key, the cursor moves through the text in the direction indicated by the arrow on that key.

If you try to use an arrow key to move the cursor on a blank screen, nothing happens. WordPerfect doesn't permit the cursor to move where nothing exists. The cursor moves only through text, spaces, or codes.

When the Num Lock key is activated, the cursor-movement keys become the numeric keys, which can be used to type numbers.

Note: WordPerfect offers an option for changing the rate of speed at which the cursor moves. The Cursor Speed option is available through the Environment option on the Setup menu. For more information about customizing WordPerfect, see Chapter 15.

Using the Mouse

WordPerfect 5.1 supports a mouse, but you don't need the device in order to use the program. Even if you have a mouse, you may decide that you don't want to use it with WordPerfect. The mouse serves three main purposes:

- To make selections in most menus, including the pull-down menus.
- To mark text so that you can perform an action on the marked block (such as deleting, moving, underlining, or centering).
- To move the location of the cursor quickly without using the cursor-movement keys.

1

The mouse you are using has either two or three buttons; you can use either kind of mouse with WordPerfect.

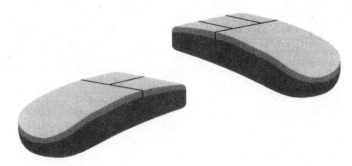

Mouse buttons can be used in four basic ways:

- You can press and then quickly release a button (this process is called *clicking*, as mentioned earlier).
- You can quickly press and release the button twice (this process is called *double-clicking*).
- You can press and hold down a button while you then move the mouse (this process is called *dragging*).
- You can press and hold down one button while you click another button.

Although you can position the mouse pointer (a block cursor) in blank areas of the screen where no text or codes exist, clicking on a blank area places the mouse pointer at the last text character or code.

Note: Many different types of mouse devices are available, and WordPerfect can work with most of them. However, you must specify what type of mouse you are using and how it is connected to your computer. In addition, you can change the way WordPerfect responds to some mouse operations. You can customize WordPerfect for your mouse and the options you want by selecting the Mouse option on the Setup menu. Refer to Chapter 15 for more information about customizing.

Using Help

WordPerfect has an on-line Help feature that you can access while working on WordPerfect documents. The screens in the Help system can help you learn more about WordPerfect commands and keys. Also included in the Help system are two valuable tools: an alphabetical listing of all WordPerfect features and an on-screen function-key template. Use these tools as reference aids for finding the WordPerfect command you need.

Accessing the Help Screens

If you have a question about a WordPerfect command or key, you can access
the Help system by pressing Help (F3).

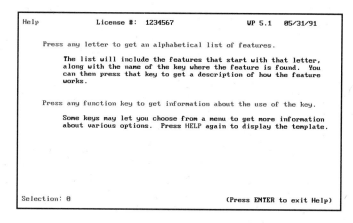

```
Help            License #:  1234567          WP 5.1   05/31/91

    Press any letter to get an alphabetical list of features.

        The list will include the features that start with that letter,
        along with the name of the key where the feature is found.  You
        can then press that key to get a description of how the feature
        works.

    Press any function key to get information about the use of the key.

        Some keys may let you choose from a menu to get more information
        about various options.  Press HELP again to display the template.




Selection: 0                            (Press ENTER to exit Help)
```

WordPerfect
displays the
opening Help
screen.

```
Format
    Contains features which change the current document's format. Options on
    the Line, Page and Other menus change the setting from the cursor
    position forward. Document Format options change a setting for the entire
    document. To change the default settings permanently, use the Setup key.

    If Block is On, press Format to protect a block.  You can use Block
    Protect to keep a block of text and codes together on a page (such as a
    paragraph which may change in size during editing).

        1 - Line
        2 - Page
        3 - Document
        4 - Other
Note: In WordPerfect 5.1, you can enter measurements in fractions (e.g., 3/4")
      as well as decimals (e.g., .75").  WordPerfect will convert fractions to
      their decimal equivalent.

Selection: 0                            (Press ENTER to exit Help)
```

Press the key
about which you
want more
information. For
example, press
Shift-F8 to display
the Format Help
screen. From that
screen, press 2 to
learn more about
page formats.

You can also access the Help system with the mouse. Click the right mouse
button to display WordPerfect's pull-down menu system across the top of the
screen. (You will learn more about the pull-down menus later in this chapter.)

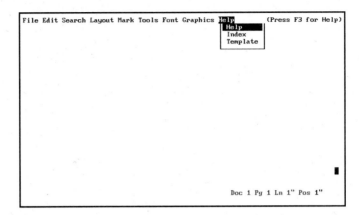

Place the mouse pointer on the Help option and click the left button to display the Help pull-down menu.

From anywhere in the program, you can press Help (F3) to access context-sensitive information about the feature you are using. WordPerfect's Help screens explain the function-key commands and menu options, as well as the Esc, Del, Ins, Backspace, Tab, Home, and arrow keys.

Using the Help Files

WordPerfect's Help files are located on the Program 1 disk. If you get an error message indicating that WordPerfect cannot find the Help files, insert the Program 1 disk into a floppy disk drive, close the drive door, type the drive letter and a colon (**a:**, for example), and press Enter. Help now should be displayed properly.

Displaying the Alphabetical Feature List

The alphabetical feature list provides the name of each feature along with the key name and keystroke(s) required to access that feature. After you access Help (F3), type any letter of the alphabet to view a list of the features that begin with that letter.

1

```
Features [A]

Absolute Tab Settings           Format          Shft-F8,1,8,t,1
Acceleration Factor (Mouse)     Setup           Shft-F1,1,5
Add Password                    Text In/Out     Ctrl-F5,2
Additional Printers             Print           Shft-F7,s,2
Advance (To Position, Line, etc.) Format        Shft-F8,4,1
Advanced Macro Commands (Macro Editor) Macro Commands Ctrl-PgUp
Advanced Merge Codes            Merge Codes     Shft-F9,6
Align/Decimal Character         Format          Shft-F8,4,3
Align Text on Tabs              Tab Align       Ctrl-F6
Alphabetize Text                Merge/Sort      Ctrl-F9,2
Alt/Ctrl Key Mapping            Setup           Shft-F1,5
Alt-=                           Menu Bar        Alt-=
Appearance of Printed Text      Font            Ctrl-F8
Append Text to a File (Block On) Move           Ctrl-F4,1-3,4
Append to Clipboard (Block On)  Shell           Ctrl-F1,3
ASCII Text File                 Text In/Out     Ctrl-F5,1
Assign Keys                     Setup           Shft-F1,5
Assign Variable                 Macro Commands  Ctrl-PgUp
Attributes, Printed             Font            Ctrl-F8
Attributes, Screen              Setup           Shft-F1,2,1
More... Press a to continue.

Selection: 0                           (Press ENTER to exit Help)
```

To display a list of features that begin with the letter A, press F3 and then press A.

Displaying the On-Screen Template

The on-screen template shows the command assignments for all the function keys and function-key combinations.

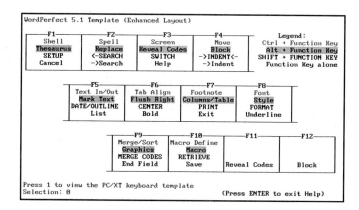

To display the on-screen template, press F3 twice.

If you lose your WordPerfect function-key template, you can display the on-screen template, press Print Screen or Shift-PrtSc to print the screen, and then use red, green, and blue highlighters to create your own function-key template.

Exiting Help

After you have reviewed the Help information, you can return to your file by using either of two methods. Press Enter or press the space bar.

1

Typing Text

With a word processor, you can get words on-screen as fast as you can type them. In a short time, you will realize that putting words on-screen can be far easier than putting them on paper. WordPerfect doesn't think or plan for you, of course, but it certainly simplifies self-expression.

At any stage of the writing process, you easily can revise your words on-screen. With a word processor, you can freely alter what you write; you can insert new words, delete ones you don't want, and move up and down through a document to see what you've written. Because you can alter text so effortlessly, you can first focus on getting words on-screen; you can later edit and revise the text. If you are a poor typist, you can leave spelling errors for WordPerfect's Speller to catch.

With WordPerfect's many formatting features, you can change the look of the text on the page, as you will see in subsequent chapters. You can, for example, change margins, indent text, vary line spacing, control word spacing, put text in columns, create headers and footers, and right-justify text. In this section, though, you examine the built-in settings that WordPerfect assumes most users want (at least initially). Later you learn how to modify these default settings to meet your needs.

Understanding WordPerfect's Built-In Settings

Before you even put fingers to keys and begin typing, WordPerfect has been at work for you. You will recall from your experience with a typewriter that you must do some formatting — for example, set margins, line spacing, and tabs — before you begin composing. With WordPerfect, you don't need to make any formatting decisions before you begin unless the preset values do not suit you.

WordPerfect comes with a number of default settings — for margins, tab settings, base font (basic character style), line spacing, and other features. Note that WordPerfect does not include page numbering as a default, nor does the program automatically use hyphenation. You should be familiar with the basic default settings before you begin writing. Subsequent chapters, especially those devoted to formatting and printing, offer many ways you can alter the look of a document.

Note: Through the Initial Settings option on the Setup menu, you can change a number of WordPerfect's built-in settings. For instance, you can change the

1

formatting specifications for all future documents, change the date format, and change the default repeat value (the number of times a character is repeated when you press Esc). For more information about customizing WordPerfect, see Chapter 15.

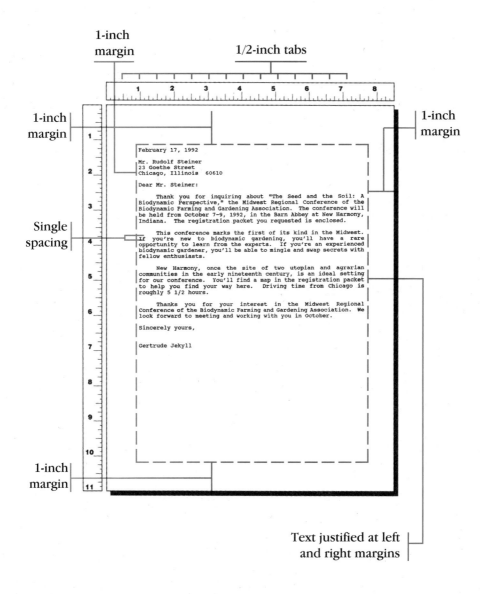

1-inch margin

1/2-inch tabs

1-inch margin

1-inch margin

Single spacing

1-inch margin

February 17, 1992

Mr. Rudolf Steiner
23 Goethe Street
Chicago, Illinois 60610

Dear Mr. Steiner:

Thank you for inquiring about "The Seed and the Soil: A Biodynamic Perspective," the Midwest Regional Conference of the Biodynamic Farming and Gardening Association. The conference will be held from October 7-9, 1992, in the Barn Abbey at New Harmony, Indiana. The registration packet you requested is enclosed.

This conference marks the first of its kind in the Midwest. If you're new to biodynamic gardening, you'll have a rare opportunity to learn from the experts. If you're an experienced biodynamic gardener, you'll be able to mingle and swap secrets with fellow enthusiasts.

New Harmony, once the site of two utopian and agrarian communities in the early nineteenth century, is an ideal setting for our conference. You'll find a map in the registration packet to help you find your way here. Driving time from Chicago is roughly 5 1/2 hours.

Thanks you for your interest in the Midwest Regional Conference of the Biodynamic Farming and Gardening Association. We look forward to meeting and working with you in October.

Sincerely yours,

Gertrude Jekyll

Text justified at left and right margins

1

Entering Text

As you type in WordPerfect, characters appear at the location of the cursor. After you type a few words, look at the Pos indicator on the status line. This value increases as you type and as the cursor moves horizontally across the line to the right. WordPerfect doesn't require you to press Enter to end a line, but inserts a *soft return* at the end of each line and wraps the text to the beginning of the next line. This feature is called *word wrap*.

To end a paragraph or insert blank lines in the text, use the Enter key. When you come to the end of the last sentence in a paragraph, press Enter twice.

```
Think of a place that you can either visit or remember quite
clearly, a place to which you have strong reactions.  Write a
personal description of it, attempting to re-create for your reader
the experience of seeing or entering the place you've chosen to
write about.

Details are essential in picturing whatever is described.  Try to
think of rich and suggestive words and phrases that will evoke
emotional responses in your readers.  Appeal to the senses.  Use
concrete nouns and active verbs.




C:\WP51\BOOK\DESCRIBE.TXT                        Doc 1 Pg 1 Ln 2.5" Pos 4.2"
```

When you press Enter the first time, WordPerfect inserts a *hard return*. When you press Enter the second time, WordPerfect inserts another hard return, creating a blank line in the text.

Moving the Cursor

You move the cursor through text in WordPerfect by using either the keyboard or the mouse. Keep in mind that WordPerfect does not allow the cursor to move where nothing exists. The cursor moves only through text, spaces, or codes.

Moving the Cursor with the Keyboard

You can move the cursor through a document with the cursor-movement keys on the numeric keypad: the up-, down-, left-, and right-arrow keys; the PgUp, PgDn, Screen Up, and Screen Down keys; GoTo (Ctrl-Home); and Esc (the Repeat key).

The Arrow Keys

When you press an arrow key, the cursor moves through the text in the direction indicated by the arrow on that key. Use the keys marked with arrows to control cursor movement as follows:

Keys	Movement
↑	Moves the cursor up one line.
↓	Moves the cursor down one line; when you press this key to move the cursor down through the text, the text automatically is reformatted.
←	Moves the cursor one position to the left.
→	Moves the cursor one position to the right.
Ctrl →	Moves the cursor one word to the right.
Ctrl ←	Moves the cursor one word to the left.
Home, → or End	Moves the cursor to the right end of the line.
Home, ←	Moves the cursor to the left edge of the screen.
Home, Home, ↑	Moves the cursor to the top of the document.
Home, Home, ↓	Moves the cursor to the bottom of the document.
Ctrl ↑	Moves the cursor up one paragraph.
Ctrl ↓	Moves the cursor down one paragraph.

PgUp *PgUp and* PgDn *PgDn*

Use the PgUp and PgDn keys to move the cursor a page at a time. When you press either of these keys, the message Repositioning appears on the status line.

PgUp moves the cursor to the top of the preceding page.

PgDn moves the cursor to the top of the next page. If there is no additional page, the cursor moves to the bottom of the current page.

1

-⃝ *Screen Up and* +⃝ *Screen Down*

Be sure to use -⃝ and +⃝ on the numeric keypad, not the keys at the top of the keyboard.

-⃝ or ⃝Home⃝, ↑⃝ moves the cursor to the top of the screen or, if you already are at the top, to the preceding screen.

+⃝ or ⃝Home⃝, ↓⃝ moves the cursor to the bottom of the screen or, if you already are at the bottom, to the next screen.

⃝Ctrl⃝⃝Home⃝ *GoTo*

Use GoTo (Ctrl-Home) with other keys to move to a specific page or character in a document. You can use GoTo also to move to the top or bottom of the page.

After pressing certain keys, you can press GoTo (Ctrl-Home) alone to move the cursor to its starting position. The cursor returns to its starting position only after you have used one of the following keys or key combinations: Esc, GoTo, Home and arrow keys, PgUp or PgDn, Forward Search or Backward Search, Replace, or Screen Up or Screen Down.

To move to a specific page in the document, press ⃝Ctrl⃝⃝Home⃝, the page number, and ⃝⏎Enter⃝.

To move to a specific character (for example, the letter *a*) in the document, press ⃝Ctrl⃝⃝Home⃝ and the character (non-numeric).

To move to the top of the page, press ⃝Ctrl⃝⃝Home⃝, ↑⃝.

To move to the bottom of the page, press ⃝Ctrl⃝⃝Home⃝, ↓⃝.

To return to the cursor's original position, press ⃝Ctrl⃝⃝Home⃝ twice.

⃝Esc⃝ *Esc*

Use ⃝Esc⃝ (the Repeat key) to repeat an operation *n* number of times. You can use Esc to move the cursor *n* number of characters (right or left), *n* number of words (right or left), *n* number of lines (up or down), *n* number of paragraphs (up or down), or *n* number of pages (forward or backward).

Usually, the value of *n* is 8; that is, WordPerfect repeats 8 times. But you can change this repeat value. Press Esc, enter the number of repetitions, and then press the key you want to repeat. For example, to move the cursor down 15 lines, press Esc, type **15**, and press the down-arrow key.

Some keys on the keyboard automatically repeat when you hold down the key. Many other WordPerfect features can be repeated only with the aid of the Esc key.

You can use the following keys or features with the repeat value:

- Cursor-movement keys
- Del, Delete to End of Line, Delete to End of Page, and Delete Word
- The Macro feature
- PgUp and PgDn
- Screen Up and Screen Down
- Word Left and Word Right
- Paragraph Up and Paragraph Down

To move the cursor n characters to the right or left, press Esc, enter the number of characters (n), and press → or ←. (Note that the default number of characters is 8.)

To move the cursor right or left n number of words, press Esc, enter the number of words, and press Ctrl→ or Ctrl←.

To move the cursor down or up n number of lines, press Esc, enter the number of lines, and press ↓ or ↑.

Moving the Cursor with the Mouse

You can use the mouse to position the cursor anywhere on the screen by placing the mouse pointer at a specific spot and clicking the left button. *Dragging* the mouse (pressing and holding down a button while you move the mouse) enables you to scroll the text up, down, left, or right to see more of the text on-screen. You cannot move the cursor through "dead space" (space with no text or codes) beyond where you stop typing. If you place the mouse pointer in dead space and click the left button, the cursor moves to the nearest text.

To move the cursor one character to the left, place the mouse pointer one space left and click the left button. To move the cursor one character to the right, place the mouse pointer one space right and click the left button.

To move the cursor from word to word, place the mouse pointer anywhere in the word to which you want to move, and click the left button.

To move the cursor up or down a line, place the mouse pointer on the line to which you want to move, and click the left button.

1

To scroll up line-by-line through a document, place the mouse pointer anywhere in the top line, press and hold down the right button, and drag the mouse to move the pointer upward. To scroll down line-by-line through a document, place the mouse pointer at the bottom of the screen, and simply press and hold down the right button. Scrolling stops when you reach the top or bottom of the document.

You can scroll left or right to see text not visible on-screen by holding down the right button and dragging the mouse to the left or right edge of the screen. Scrolling stops when you reach the beginning or end of the line.

Making a Menu Selection

WordPerfect uses three types of menus: one-line menus, full-screen menus, and pull-down menus. Many times when you press a function key or function-key combination, a one-line menu appears at the bottom of the screen. Other commands in WordPerfect display full-screen menus. WordPerfect's pull-down menus provide an alternative method of accessing most of the same commands you can activate from the one-line or full-screen menus.

One-Line and Full-Screen Menus

You can make a selection from a one-line or full-screen menu in any of three ways:

- Press the highlighted letter in the name of the menu option.
- Press the number that appears just before the menu option.
- Place the mouse pointer on the option and click the left mouse button.

For example, press Alt F7 to display the one-line Columns/Tables menu. To select **Tables (2)**, use any of these techniques:

1

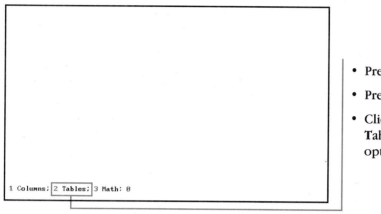

1 Columns; 2 Tables; 3 Math: 0

- Press T.
- Press 2.
- Click on the Tables (2) option.

When you press Format (Shift-F8), the full-screen Format menu appears. To select Line (1), use any of the same techniques:

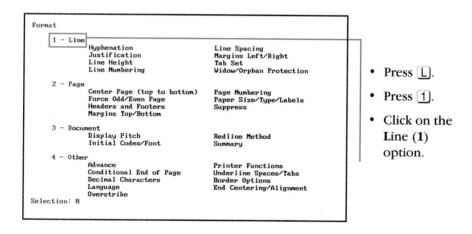

Format

1 - Line

Hyphenation	Line Spacing
Justification	Margins Left/Right
Line Height	Tab Set
Line Numbering	Widow/Orphan Protection

2 - Page

Center Page (top to bottom)	Page Numbering
Force Odd/Even Page	Paper Size/Type/Labels
Headers and Footers	Suppress
Margins Top/Bottom	

3 - Document

Display Pitch	Redline Method
Initial Codes/Font	Summary

4 - Other

Advance	Printer Functions
Conditional End of Page	Underline Spaces/Tabs
Decimal Characters	Border Options
Language	End Centering/Alignment
Overstrike	

Selection: 0

- Press L.
- Press 1.
- Click on the Line (1) option.

After you choose Line (1), the Format: Line menu is displayed.

1

From this menu,
you can choose
other options,
such as **Margins**
(7), the option for
adjusting the
margin settings.

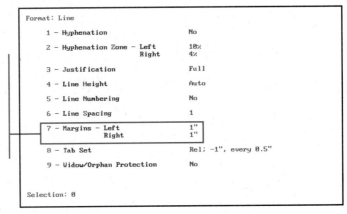

```
Format: Line

    1 - Hyphenation                    No

    2 - Hyphenation Zone - Left        10%
                          Right        4%

    3 - Justification                  Full

    4 - Line Height                    Auto

    5 - Line Numbering                 No

    6 - Line Spacing                   1

    7 - Margins - Left                 1"
                  Right                1"

    8 - Tab Set                        Rel; -1", every 0.5"

    9 - Widow/Orphan Protection        No


Selection: 0
```

Within menus, you click the left mouse button to select menu choices. If you
have turned on Assisted Mouse Pointer Movement from the Setup menu, and
if the menu list normally would place the cursor at the bottom of the screen
for either typed input or a menu choice, WordPerfect will move the mouse
pointer to the bottom of the screen. Otherwise, you need to reposition the
mouse pointer for each prompt. When a prompt line for entering values
appears, position the mouse pointer on the menu selection you want, and
click the left mouse button to select your choice.

If you change your mind and want to back out of a menu selection from a one-
line or full-screen menu, press Exit (F7). If you have a mouse, you can back
out of a menu by clicking the right mouse button.

Pull-Down Menus

Pull-down menus provide an alternative to using the function keys to access
WordPerfect menus. The pull-down menus, which group commands according to major categories of functions, make it easier for the occasional or new
user to become familiar and productive with WordPerfect. For those who
prefer to activate commands with the mouse instead of the keyboard, the pull-
down menus easily are accessed with the mouse.

The menu bar across the top of the screen offers nine main choices. Each of
these menu choices leads to a pull-down menu. Some of the options on pull-
down menus lead to further options, displayed in *pop-out* menus. If a menu
option contains a pop-out menu, an arrow appears to the right of the option.
If a menu option appears in brackets, it is not available for selection at this
time.

1

The File pull-down menu includes, for example, the Setup option, which leads to the Setup pop-out menu.

WordPerfect uses pull-down menus as a gateway to the regular menu system. For instance, if you want to print a document, you can use the function-key combination for Print (Shift-F7) to access the Print/Options screen from which you make your printing selection. Or you can choose **P**rint from the File pull-down menu to access the same Print/Options screen.

Because you can make so many selections with either the familiar function keys or the new pull-down menus, this book includes instructions for both methods. The book's emphasis, however, is on the function-key approach. Each time you see steps describing a procedure, the pull-down alternative, if available, is described after the function-key procedure. Even though you can access the pull-down menus without using a mouse, a mouse icon (⌨) will remind you that the procedure described uses the pull-down menus.

You access the pull-down menus in either of two ways:

- If you have a mouse, click the right button, and the menu bar (if you have not already set it up to be permanently visible) appears at the top of the screen.

- If you don't have a mouse (or don't want to use it), press Alt =.

After you have activated the menu bar, you can make choices with the mouse or the keyboard. To make a selection with the mouse, move the mouse pointer to the option you want, and then click the left mouse button. To make a selection with the keyboard, press the highlighted letter for your choice. As an alternative to pressing the highlighted letter, you can use the arrow keys; the right- and left-arrow keys move across the menu bar, whereas the up- and down-arrow keys highlight the menu selections. After you have highlighted your choice, press Enter to select it.

If you change your mind, you can back out of the pull-down menus one level at a time by pressing Esc, Cancel (F1), or the space bar. To back out of all the menus at once and remove the menu bar from the screen, press Exit (F7). If

1

you are using the mouse, you can click the right button to exit; if some of the menus have been pulled down, clicking either button outside a menu also enables you to exit.

Note: One of the ways you can customize the WordPerfect screen display is by making the pull-down menu bar visible at all times. From the Setup menu, you can choose to display the menu bar permanently, as well as display a separating line between the menu bar and the rest of the editing screen. For more information about customizing WordPerfect, see Chapter 15.

Accessing the pull-down menus is easier if you use the mouse rather than the keyboard. You easily can choose items from pull-down menus by moving the mouse and clicking (quickly pressing and releasing) the left button. Initially, moving the mouse makes the mouse pointer appear on-screen; further movements produce corresponding on-screen movements of the mouse pointer, enabling you to make menu selections and block text. Pressing any key makes the mouse pointer disappear.

When the pull-down menu bar is displayed, you can use the left mouse button to perform the following tasks:

- Make visible the menu items for one of the nine menu bar choices by either clicking the choice you want or dragging the mouse across the pull-down menu bar.

- Select a menu item by clicking it.

- Highlight each choice within a pull-down menu by dragging the mouse down the menu. If you highlight a menu item that has a pop-out menu, the menu will pop out. You can then drag the mouse down that menu to highlight your choice. Release the mouse button to select the highlighted choice.

From the editing screen, you can use the right mouse button to manage the pull-down menus in the following ways:

- If you have turned on Assisted Mouse Pointer Movement from the Setup menu and if the menu bar is not permanently visible, clicking the right mouse button makes the menu bar appear and places the mouse pointer on the word *File* on the menu bar.

- If you have turned on Assisted Mouse Pointer Movement from the Setup menu and if the menu bar is permanently visible, clicking the right mouse button places the mouse pointer on the word *File* on the menu bar.

Using the Cancel Command

The Cancel command (the F1 "oops" key) enables you to perform these tasks:

- Back out of a menu without making a selection.
- Restore text you have deleted.

When you use Cancel (F1) to back out of a menu, the most recent command is canceled, and you are returned to either the preceding menu or your document. When you use Cancel (F1) to restore text, WordPerfect retrieves one of the last three items you have deleted. An "item" in this case means the characters (letters, numbers, or punctuation) deleted before you moved the cursor. Cancel (F1) always acts as an "undelete" key when a menu is not visible.

Pressing more than one button on the mouse has the same effect as Cancel (F1). On a two-button mouse, holding down one button while clicking the other button is the same as pressing Cancel (F1). On a three-button mouse, clicking the middle button is the same as pressing Cancel (F1).

Backing Out of a Menu

With some one-line and full-screen menus, WordPerfect disregards your selections if you leave the menu by pressing Cancel (F1). These menus display a message that instructs you to leave the menu by pressing Exit (F7) if you want to save your selections in memory.

You can press Cancel (F1) to return to a preceding one-line or full-screen menu without making a choice from the current menu. When there is no preceding menu to which to return, you are returned to the current document.

Pressing Cancel (F1), Esc, or the space bar enables you to back out of the pull-down menus one level at a time. To back out of all the pull-down menus at once and remove the menu bar from the screen, press Exit (F7). With the mouse, you can click the right button to exit; if some of the menus have been pulled down, clicking either button outside a menu also enables you to exit.

Restoring Deleted Text

Press Cancel (F1) to restore deleted text to its original location or to another location. Remember, however, that WordPerfect stores only the last three deletions. When you make a fourth deletion, the oldest of the three preceding deletions is erased from memory.

1 Previewing a Document before Printing

Use the View Document feature to preview a document before printing it. You save costly printer paper and time by first previewing your document, making changes if needed, and then printing the document when you are certain that it's the way you want it. You learn more about the View Document feature in Chapter 7.

To view a document, follow these steps:

1. Display on-screen the document you want to preview.

2. Position the cursor anywhere on the page you want to view.

3. Press ⇧Shift F7 to activate the Print command and display the Print menu.

    ⌐◻ Access the File pull-down menu and choose Print.

4. From the Print menu that appears, select View Document (6).

5. Select 200% (2) to view the document at twice its actual size.

6. Press F7 (Exit) to return to the regular editing screen or press F1 (Cancel) to return to the Print menu.

A document viewed on-screen at twice its actual size.

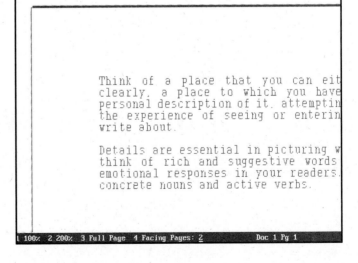

Think of a place that you can eit
clearly, a place to which you have
personal description of it, attemptin
the experience of seeing or enterin
write about.

Details are essential in picturing w
think of rich and suggestive words
emotional responses in your readers
concrete nouns and active verbs.

1 100% 2 200% 3 Full Page 4 Facing Pages: 2   Doc 1 Pg 1

1

You can press PgUp, PgDn, or GoTo (Ctrl-Home) to view other pages of the document. Note that you cannot edit the previewed document. You must return to the editing screen to make changes.

Printing an Unsaved Document

With WordPerfect, you can be flexible about printing. You may not want or need to save every document to disk. If you do not want to save a document, WordPerfect still enables you to print the document without requiring you to save it to disk first. Printing in this manner is called "printing from the screen," because you print what has been created on-screen and then stored in temporary memory (also known as random-access memory or RAM).

Before you print, you must be sure that your printer is installed and selected properly. See Appendix A for instructions on installing printers; see Chapter 7, "Printing," for instructions on selecting a printer after it is installed.

To print the document on-screen, follow these steps:

1. Press ⬆Shift F7 to activate the Print command.

Access the File pull-down menu and select Print.

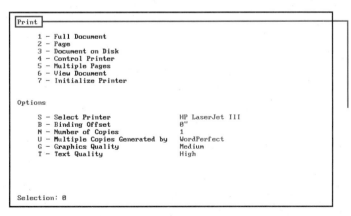

The Print menu is displayed.

2. To print the entire document, select Full Document (1). To print a single page, select Page (2).

WordPerfect displays a * Please wait * message on the status line as the program prepares to print the text. If the printer is properly configured and hooked up, and you are not printing graphics or downloading soft fonts, printing should begin almost immediately.

A document does not have to be on-screen for you to print it. With Word-Perfect, you can print any number of documents stored on disk (floppy or hard). You even can have documents in both windows and print a document stored on disk. The various ways of printing and managing print jobs are discussed in Chapter 7. But you know enough now to make a quick print of the text on-screen.

Saving, Exiting, and Clearing

What you see on-screen is a *temporary* display; only the documents you transfer to disk storage are secured for future use. Usually, you keep copies on disk of the documents you create. As a rule, you should save your work every 10 or 15 minutes. Use either of two methods to save a document to disk: (1) save the document with the Save (F10) command and remain in WordPerfect, or (2) save the document with the Exit (F7) command and either clear the screen or exit WordPerfect. To work on a new document or before you retrieve a document, clear the current document from the screen.

Note: WordPerfect offers two automatic backup features through the Environment option of the Setup menu: Timed Document Backup and Original Document Backup. With the Timed Document Backup option, at specified intervals WordPerfect automatically saves to disk the document displayed on-screen. With the Original Document Backup option, WordPerfect saves both the original file and the edited version. For more information about backups, see Chapter 15.

Saving a Document to Disk and Remaining in WordPerfect

The first time you save a document, WordPerfect prompts you for a file name. Suppose that you have created a document and you now want to save the file. With the document on-screen, follow these steps:

1

1. Press F10 to activate the Save command.

   ⌨ Access the **F**ile pull-down menu and select **S**ave.

   The following prompt appears on the status line:

   `Document to be saved:`

2. Type a file name for the document and press ↵Enter.

The document remains on-screen, and you can continue working.

A file name consists of a root name of one to eight characters, followed by an optional extension of one to three characters. If you use an extension, you must separate it from the root name by a period (.). When you name a file, you must observe the file-naming guidelines of your operating system (MS-DOS or PC DOS). After you name and save a file, the file name is displayed on the left side of the status line. You should choose a file name that is descriptive of the file's contents.

Naming a File

Valid	*Unacceptable*	
FILENAME	FILENAMES	(The name has too many charac- ters; the limit is eight. WordPerfect will shorten the name to FILENAME.)
A	"A"	(Quotation marks cannot be used in a file name.)
1-23-89	1/23/89	(/ cannot be used in a file name.)
december.90	december,90	(A comma cannot be used in a file name.)
ASSETS.DOC	ASSETS.FILE	(The extension is too long; the limit is three characters. WordPerfect will shorten the name to ASSETS.FIL.)
REPORT.NEW	REPORTNEW	(The period before the extension is missing. WordPerfect will shorten the name to REPORTNE.)
DEC_90	DEC 90	(Spaces are not allowed in file names. WordPerfect will shorten the name to DEC.)

1

Note: You can give a file a descriptive file name of up to 40 characters. For information on long file names, see Chapter 8.

WordPerfect responds a bit differently when you want to save a file that you have saved before. When you press Save (F10) or select **S**ave from the **F**ile pull-down menu, WordPerfect asks whether you want to replace the file on disk. If, for example, you have saved a document called REPORT.TXT, WordPerfect displays a prompt similar to the following:

```
Document to be saved: C:\WP51\BOOK\REPORT.TXT
```

If you want to keep this same file name for the new version of the document, press Enter. WordPerfect then displays the following prompt:

```
Replace C:\WP51\BOOK\REPORT.TXT? No (Yes)
```

Select **Y**es to replace the previous version with the new version. Or select **N**o, rename the file, and save it under a different name. If you want to save the document on-screen under a different file name, use the right-arrow key to move the cursor to the previous file name and change it accordingly. You can change any of the information following the Document to be saved: prompt.

Saving a Document to Disk and Exiting WordPerfect

If you want to save a document to disk and exit WordPerfect, follow these steps:

1. Press F7 to activate the Exit command.

   ▭ Access the **F**ile pull-down menu and select E**x**it.

   WordPerfect displays the following prompt:

   ```
   Save document? Yes (No)
   ```

2. To begin the saving process, select **Y**es.

   WordPerfect then displays this prompt:

   ```
   Document to be saved:
   ```

3. Type the file name and press ↵Enter.

4. If the document already exists, WordPerfect presents the following prompt:

   ```
   Replace C:\WP51\BOOK\REPORT.TXT? No (Yes)
   ```

1

Select Yes to save the document with the old name. Or select No, type a new file name, and press `⏎Enter`. The document is stored to disk under the name you select.

The following message appears:

```
Exit WP? No (Yes)
```

5. Select Yes to exit WordPerfect and return to DOS. Or, if you change your mind, press `F1` (Cancel) to return to the document.

Clearing the Screen

You should clear the current document from the screen before you start work on a new document — or before you retrieve an existing document. To clear the screen without saving the current document, you can either press Exit (F7) or select the Exit option from the File pull-down menu. Clearing the screen without saving your document is handy when you decide to discard what you have written. If you do not clear the current document before starting a new document or before retrieving a document from memory, the old and the new documents will merge to form a continuous (and confusing) document!

If you don't want to save the document you have created, or if you have saved the document previously but you want to clear the screen, follow these steps:

1. Press `F7` to activate the Exit command.

   🖰 Access the File pull-down menu and select Exit.

2. At the prompt `Save Document? Yes (No)`, select No.

   The following prompt then appears:

   ```
   Exit WP? No (Yes)
   ```

3. In response to the prompt, select No or press `⏎Enter` to clear the screen and stay in WordPerfect. If you press `F1` (Cancel) instead, you are returned to the document displayed on-screen.

Summary

In this chapter, you were introduced to the word processing features available in WordPerfect. The program's basic features are convenient and efficient for creating, editing, formatting, and printing documents. WordPerfect's specialized features give you a full range of tools for further supplementing your documents with such elements as spell checking, graphics, footnotes, tables, and lists.

1

You also learned how to start the program on a hard disk system and on a dual floppy disk system. You became familiar with the editing screen, from which you perform most of your work in WordPerfect. You learned how to use the keyboard and mouse, access the Help feature, type text, move the cursor, and make a menu selection. You learned also about WordPerfect's built-in settings that help you begin to create documents quickly. Finally, you learned to print and save your work, and to exit the document and the program.

Specifically, you learned the following key information about WordPerfect:

- To start WordPerfect on a hard disk system, at the C> prompt, type **cd \wp51** and press Enter. Then type **wp** and press Enter.

- To start WordPerfect on a dual floppy disk system, insert your working copy of the Program 1 disk into drive A. Insert a formatted data disk into drive B. At the A> prompt, type **b:** and press Enter. Then type **a:wp** and press Enter.

- The status line, at the bottom of the screen, contains information describing the cursor's status, file name, and messages from WordPerfect.

- The keyboard has three main areas: the function keys, the alphanumeric or "typing" keys, and the numeric or cursor-movement keys.

- You routinely use the function keys to give commands. To activate a WordPerfect command, you press a function key alone or in combination with the Ctrl, Shift, or Alt keys.

- The mouse serves three main purposes: to make menu selections, to mark text as a block, and to move the location of the cursor quickly.

- With WordPerfect's on-line help system, you can view an alphabetical list of all WordPerfect features, see an on-screen function-key template, and get context-sensitive help. Access the help feature with the Help (F3) function key.

- Because WordPerfect comes with built-in settings, you don't need to make any formatting decisions before you begin unless the preset values don't suit your needs.

- WordPerfect has *word wrap* — the program wraps text that doesn't fit on the current line to the beginning of the next line when you type.

- Move the cursor by using either the keyboard or the mouse. The cursor moves only through text, spaces, or codes.

- WordPerfect has three types of menus: one-line menus, full-screen menus, and pull-down menus.

1

- The Cancel command (the F1 "oops" key) lets you back out of a menu and restore text you have deleted.

- Use View Document to preview a document before printing it. Access View Document by selecting Print (Shift-F7) and then choosing **View Document (6)**.

- To print a document displayed on your screen, select Print (Shift-F7), and then choose either **Full Document (1)** or **Page (2)**.

- To save a document to disk, either use the Save (F10) command and remain in WordPerfect, or use Exit (F7) and either clear the screen or exit WordPerfect after saving the document.

In the next chapter, you examine WordPerfect's features for editing a document. You learn, for example, to retrieve files you have saved to disk, to insert and delete text in those files, and to restore the deleted text.

Editing

Revising a draft is an important part of polishing any document. Revision can consist of changing, adding, or deleting material; correcting grammar and punctuation; and making any other changes to your document. WordPerfect enables you to revise text easily with a number of built-in editing tools. This chapter focuses on the basic editing changes you can make with WordPerfect.

2

Retrieving files

Inserting text

Deleting text

Restoring deleted text

Using both document windows

Displaying and deleting hidden codes

2

Key Terms in This Chapter

Insert mode   The alternative to WordPerfect's Typeover mode. When you type in Insert mode (WordPerfect's default), new characters are inserted, and existing text moves forward.

Typeover mode   The alternative to WordPerfect's Insert mode. When you type in Typeover mode, the characters you type replace the original text.

Reveal codes   The WordPerfect command that displays the hidden formatting and other codes inserted in the text when you press certain keys. Hidden codes tell WordPerfect when to execute tabs, margin settings, hard returns, and so on.

Document window   An area in which to work. In WordPerfect, you can open two document windows: Doc 1 and Doc 2.

Retrieving Files

You can retrieve documents stored on disk in either of two ways:

- By issuing the Retrieve command and typing the file name. You can use this method if you know the exact name of the file.
- By displaying the List Files screen and choosing the file name from the list. This method is handy for locating any file, whether or not you remember the exact file name.

Before you retrieve a file with either method, be sure to clear the screen by pressing Exit (F7). If you do not clear the screen first, WordPerfect inserts the retrieved file into the document displayed on-screen.

Using the Retrieve Command

To retrieve a file with the Retrieve command, follow these steps:

1. Press ⬆Shift F10 to activate the Retrieve command.

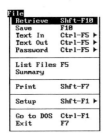

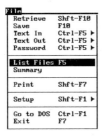

Access the
File pull-down
menu and select
Retrieve.

WordPerfect displays the following prompt:

`Document to be retrieved:`

2. Type the name of the document and press ⏎Enter.

If the message ERROR: File not found appears, either you have typed the name incorrectly or the file doesn't exist in the directory. Type the name again. If you cannot remember the name of the document you want to retrieve, use the List Files screen.

Suppose that after you press Retrieve (Shift-F10), you decide not to retrieve a file. You can press Cancel (F1) to cancel the command.

Using the List Files Screen

To access the List Files screen, follow these steps:

1. Press F5 to activate the List command.

Access the
File pull-down
menu and select
List Files.

WordPerfect displays in the lower left corner of the screen a file specification similar to the following:

```
Dir C:\WP51\*.*
```

2. To view the names of the files stored on the named drive, press ⏎Enter).

Or

To view file names stored on a drive other than the one designated, type the letter of the disk drive, a colon, and the path name (for example, type **c:\wp51\book**). Then press ⏎Enter).

The List Files screen and menu appear.

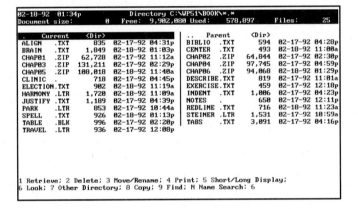

```
02-18-92  01:34p              Directory C:\WP51\BOOK\*.*
Document size:         0   Free:  9,902,080 Used:      578,897   Files:      25

     .  Current   <Dir>                   ..  Parent    <Dir>
   ALIGN    .TXT       835  02-17-92 04:31p  BIBLIO   .TXT      594  02-17-92 04:28p
   BRAIN    .TXT     1,849  02-18-92 01:03p  CENTER   .TXT      493  02-18-92 11:00a
   CHAP01   .ZIP    62,728  02-17-92 11:12a  CHAP02   .ZIP   64,844  02-17-92 02:30p
   CHAP03   .ZIP   131,211  02-17-92 02:29p  CHAP04   .ZIP   97,745  02-17-92 04:59p
   CHAP05   .ZIP   100,018  02-18-92 11:40a  CHAP06   .ZIP   94,068  02-18-92 01:29p
   CLINIC   .          718  02-17-92 04:45p  DESCRIBE .TXT      819  02-18-92 11:01a
   ELECTION .TXT       902  02-18-92 11:19a  EXERCISE .TXT      459  02-17-92 12:18p
   HARMONY  .LTR     1,720  02-18-92 11:09a  INDENT   .TXT    1,006  02-17-92 04:23p
   JUSTIFY  .TXT     1,189  02-17-92 04:39p  NOTES    .          650  02-17-92 12:11p
   PARK     .LTR       853  02-17-92 10:44a  REDLINE  .TXT      716  02-18-92 11:23a
   SPELL    .TXT       926  02-18-92 01:13p  STEINER  .LTR    1,531  02-17-92 10:59a
   TABLE    .BLK       996  02-17-92 02:20p  TABS     .TXT    3,091  02-17-92 04:16p
   TRAVEL   .LTR       936  02-17-92 12:00p


1 Retrieve; 2 Delete; 3 Move/Rename; 4 Print; 5 Short/Long Display;
6 Look; 7 Other Directory; 8 Copy; 9 Find; N Name Search: 6
```

The List Files screen displays a two-column alphabetical list of your files, including the file size and the date and time each file was last saved. The menu at the bottom of the screen shows the options you can choose.

Note: If you have the Long Distance Display feature on, your screen will look different. Refer to Chapter 8 for more information about this feature.

WordPerfect provides two ways to specify file names from the List Files screen. The first method is to use the arrow keys to move the highlight bar to the name of the file you want to retrieve.

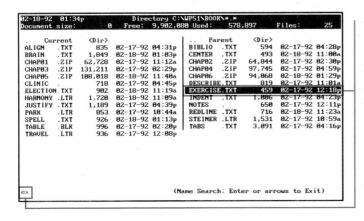

The second method is to press N for **Name** Search and type the file name. As you type the name, the highlight bar begins to move to the name of the file you want to retrieve.

Press Enter or an arrow key to end the name search and again display the menu at the bottom of the List Files screen.

If the document you want to retrieve is stored on another disk or in another subdirectory, select **Other Directory (7)** from the List Files menu and type a new subdirectory. That subdirectory automatically becomes the new default. Until you change the default again, documents are saved in this subdirectory; pressing List (F5) displays automatically the new default directory. If you want to display file names from another directory without changing the default, move the highlight bar to the name of the directory you want to display and press Enter twice. Directories are displayed at the top of the file list.

After you specify a file name, select **R**etrieve (**1**) from the menu displayed at the bottom of the screen. The file is then retrieved to the screen.

After you display the List Files screen, you might decide not to retrieve a file. You can press Cancel (F1) to cancel the command.

Inserting Text

Inserting text is a basic part of the editing process. This section shows how easily you can improve what you have written, by using Insert mode to insert additional text or by using Typeover mode to type over and thus replace the existing text with new text. The basic difference between Typeover mode and Insert mode is that Typeover mode replaces your original text; Insert mode adds new text to existing text.

2

Adding Text with Insert Mode

WordPerfect usually operates in Insert mode. As you type, the new characters are inserted on-screen; existing text moves forward and is automatically formatted. You may notice that sentences often push beyond the right margin and do not immediately wrap to the next line. Don't worry. The lines adjust as you continue to type. Or you can press the down-arrow key to reformat the text.

To add text in Insert mode, place the cursor where you want to insert new text. Then type the new text.

Typing Over Existing Text

You generally use Typeover mode if you have typed text incorrectly. For example, you probably would select Typeover mode to replace text if you had mistakenly typed the name *Jane* instead of *Dane*.

To type over existing text, place the cursor where you want the new text to begin. Then press Ins to change from Insert mode to Typeover mode. The Typeover mode indicator appears at the lower left of the screen. Next, type the replacement text, and then press Ins again to return to Insert mode.

Inserting Spaces

In either Insert or Typeover mode, you can create blank character spaces by pressing the space bar. In Insert mode, you can add blank spaces by pressing the space bar. In Typeover mode, however, if you press the space bar while the cursor is under a character, it is replaced with a blank space. Remember that Typeover mode is always destructive to the text on-screen.

Inserting Blank Lines

In either Insert or Typeover mode, you can insert blank lines by pressing the Enter key once for each blank line you want to insert. Inserting blank lines causes existing lines of text to move down the page.

Deleting Text

With WordPerfect, you can delete unwanted text of various lengths. For example, you can delete single characters, a word, a line, several lines, or part of a page. WordPerfect also has special options for deleting a sentence, paragraph, or page.

Deleting Single Characters

To delete a character at the cursor position, press the Del key if the cursor is under the character to be deleted. The text to the right of the deleted character moves in to fill the gap.

To delete a character to the left of the cursor, press the Backspace key if the cursor is one character to the right of the character to be deleted. (On some keyboards, the Backspace key is marked with a single left arrow at the top of the keyboard.) When you use the Backspace key, any text to the right moves one character position to the left.

Keep in mind that both the Del and Backspace keys are repeat keys. If you hold down either key (rather than press it once), multiple characters are deleted.

Deleting Words

To delete a word at the cursor position, press Delete Word (Ctrl-Backspace) if the cursor is anywhere in the word to be deleted. Note that, for WordPerfect, a "word" is the text of the word and the space following the text.

To delete a word to the left of the cursor, place the cursor in the blank space to the right of the word to be deleted, and then press Delete Word (Ctrl-Backspace). Or, place the cursor under the first character of the word following the word to be deleted, and then press Home and then press Backspace.

To delete a word to the right of the cursor, place the cursor under the first character of the word to be deleted. Press Home and then press Del.

2

Deleting Lines

To delete a single line of text or a portion of a line, position the cursor under the first character on the line, or on the first character in the portion you want deleted. Then press Delete to End of Line (Ctrl-End).

To delete several lines at a time, follow these steps:

1. Position the cursor under the first character on the first line to be deleted.

2. Count the number of lines you want to erase (including the line where the cursor is located).

3. Press Esc (the Repeat key).

   The message n=8 appears on the status line. The default repeat value is 8, but you can change that number to reflect the number of lines to be deleted.

4. If the number of lines to be deleted is more or less than 8, type the number you want.

5. Press Ctrl End to activate Delete to End of Line.

To delete a blank line, move the cursor to the left margin at the beginning of the blank line. Then press Del.

Deleting to the End of the Page

To delete text from the cursor position to the end of the page, follow these steps:

1. Position the cursor under the first character of the text to be deleted.

2. Press Ctrl PgDn to activate Delete to End of Page.

   WordPerfect prompts you to confirm that you want to delete the rest of the page:

   ```
   Delete Remainder of page? No (Yes)
   ```

3. Select Yes to delete the text or No if you have changed your mind.

To delete several pages at once, press Esc and enter the number of pages you want to delete. Then press Ctrl-PgDn.

Deleting a Sentence, Paragraph, or Page

To delete a sentence, paragraph, or page, follow these steps:

1. Position the cursor anywhere within the text you want to delete.
2. Press Ctrl F4 to activate the Move command.

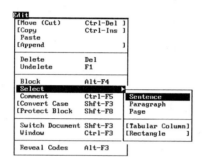

Access the Edit pull-down menu and choose Select.

3. Choose Sentence (1), Paragraph (2), or Page (3).

```
August 18, 1992

Dear Dane,

There's been a change in the location for this year's drivers
school for the Windy City Chapter, and I know you'll love this one!
Instead of going to Blackhawk Farms, we'll be going up to Road
America in beautiful Elkhart Lake, Wisconsin.

The dates will remain the same, September 12 and 13.  Lodging, as
always, will be available at Siebkens and Barefoot Bay in Elkhart
Lake, or at motels in Sheboygan or Fond du Lac.  Remember, you must
make your own reservations.

Driving directions to Elkhart Lake will be included with your
registration package, along with a map of the area.




1 Move; 2 Copy; 3 Delete; 4 Append: 0
```

The sentence, paragraph, or page to be deleted is highlighted.

4. Choose Delete (3).

The highlighted sentence, paragraph, or page is deleted. Press the down-arrow key to reformat the text.

2

Deleting Text with the Mouse

You can block text for deletion more quickly with the mouse than with the Block command (covered in Chapter 3). And using the mouse instead of the Select command from the Edit pull-down menu is not only faster, but also more powerful.

To delete text with the mouse, follow these steps:

1. Position the mouse pointer at either the upper left or lower right of the block (character, word, sentence, or paragraph) you want to delete.

2. Drag the mouse to the opposite corner of the block you are defining (the area is highlighted as you move the mouse).

3. Press the Del or ⬅Backspace key.

   Access the Edit pull-down menu and select Delete.

4. At the prompt `Delete Block? No (Yes)`, select Yes.

Restoring Deleted Text

To restore deleted text to its original location or another location, follow these steps:

1. Move the cursor to the place where you want to restore the deleted text.

2. Press ⬅Backspace to activate the Cancel command.

   Access the Edit pull-down menu and choose Undelete.

A block of high-lighted text—the most recently deleted text—appears at the cursor position.

WordPerfect displays the Undelete menu at the bottom of the screen.

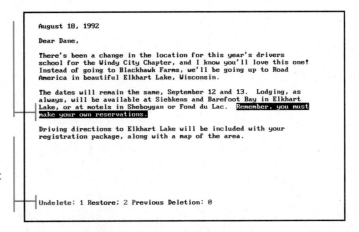

```
August 18, 1992

Dear Dane,

There's been a change in the location for this year's drivers
school for the Windy City Chapter, and I know you'll love this one!
Instead of going to Blackhawk Farms, we'll be going up to Road
America in beautiful Elkhart Lake, Wisconsin.

The dates will remain the same, September 12 and 13.  Lodging, as
always, will be available at Siebkens and Barefoot Bay in Elkhart
Lake, or at motels in Sheboygan or Fond du Lac.  Remember, you must
make your own reservations.

Driving directions to Elkhart Lake will be included with your
registration package, along with a map of the area.




Undelete: 1 Restore; 2 Previous Deletion: 0
```

3. Choose Restore (1) if the highlighted text is what you want to restore.

   Or

   Choose Previous Deletion (2) if you want to undelete previously deleted text. When the appropriate text appears on-screen, choose Restore (1).

Remember, however, that WordPerfect stores only the last three deletions. When you make a fourth deletion, the oldest of the three preceding deletions is erased from memory.

Adjusting the Screen after Editing

After you insert or delete text, you may need to adjust the alignment of the text. Press the down-arrow key to *rewrite* or *reformat* the text. As you move the cursor down, notice how WordPerfect adjusts the arrangement of the words. You may need to press the down-arrow key more than once to reformat the text.

Using Both Document Windows

WordPerfect gives you two "pads of paper" to work on at once if you like. The two document windows you can open are called Doc 1 and Doc 2. The status line indicates which window is the "active" work space. The cursor's position determines whether the window is active.

You can type in both windows and switch back and forth between them with ease. Initially, each window is the entire size of the screen. You can split the screen to look at two documents or at different parts of the same document at once.

Switching between Windows

To switch between document windows, press Switch (Shift-F3), or access the Edit pull-down menu and select Switch Document. The status line displays Doc 2, and the second document window is displayed in a full screen. Although any text in the first window is not visible now, that text is not lost. To display the Doc 1 window, press Switch (Shift-F3) again, or access the Edit pull-down menu and select Switch Document again.

55

The status line indicates the document in which you are working.

Doc 1, for example, can contain the text for a letter.

```
Mr. Franklin Abbot
Director
Michigan Department of Commerce
P.O. Box 36226
Lansing, Michigan  48909

Dear Mr. Abbot:

Thank you for your willingness to help with our public relations
efforts for the River Park in Indianapolis.  I have enclosed the
preliminary market research.  Also, I have added your name to our
WaterNotes mailing list.

Please send us a list of TV and radio stations in Michigan along
with any other information you think would be helpful.

I look forward to your valuable input.

Sincerely,


Charles Gosnell


C:\WP51\BOOK\PARK.LTR                              Doc 1 Pg 1 Ln 1" Pos 1"
```

Doc 2, for example, can contain notes for the letter.

```
Notes from letter to F. Abbot (8/08/92)

1.   Follow up in two weeks with phone call if we haven't received
     the list of TV and radio stations.

2.   Send him zoo's preliminary market research (get Elizabeth
     Ferguson's OK to send him this data).

3.   Put him on mailing list for WaterNotes.




C:\WP51\BOOK\NOTES                              Doc 2 Pg 1 Ln 2.33" Pos 5.4"
```

Splitting the Screen

You can split the screen so that WordPerfect's 24-line display is divided between two windows. When you display two documents at once, WordPerfect reserves two lines for its own use: an additional status line and a ruler line. If, for example, you display 12 lines in Doc 1, only 10 lines are displayed in Doc 2; the other two lines are taken up by the additional status line and the ruler line. When two windows are displayed on-screen, the triangles in the ruler line point to the active window.

Before you split the screen, you must decide how many lines you want to display in the current document (Doc 1). The other document will take what is left, less two lines. Sometimes, for example, you may want to split the screen in half. Other times, you may prefer to use two-thirds of the screen for the primary document, such as a letter or report, and the rest of the screen for supporting material, such as notes.

2

To split the screen, follow these steps:

1. Press ⌈Ctrl⌉ ⌈F3⌉ to activate the Screen command, and select Window (**1**).

   ▱   Access the **E**dit pull-down menu and select **W**indow.

   The following prompt is displayed:

   ```
   Number of lines in this window: 24
   ```

2. Type the number of lines you want in the first window, and then press ⌐Enter. For example, to split the screen in half, type **11** and press ⌐Enter.

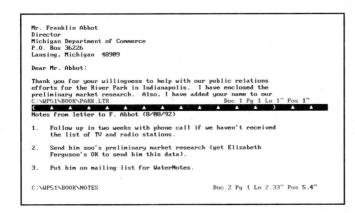

The screen is split in half, with WordPerfect's tab ruler line displayed across the middle.

If you are using a split screen and two windows, you can click the left mouse button on either window (Doc 1 or Doc 2) to move the cursor to the document in that window. Alternatively, you can switch documents by pressing Switch (Shift-F3), or you can access the **E**dit pull-down menu and select **S**witch Document.

Caution: If the same document is open in two windows, make all your changes in only one of the windows. Then be sure to save only the document in the window in which you have made changes. Otherwise, you may lose edits.

2

Resizing the Window to a Full-Screen Display

When you want to resize the window to a full-screen display, follow these steps:

1. Press `Ctrl` `F3` to activate the Screen command, and select Window (1).

   🖰 Access the Edit pull-down menu and select Window.

2. At the prompt asking for the number of lines in the window, type 24 and press `⏎Enter`.

The window is returned to a full-screen display.

Using the Reveal Codes Feature

Often when you press a key in WordPerfect, a hidden code is inserted into the text. The term *hidden* is used because you cannot see the code on-screen. By hiding the codes, WordPerfect keeps the editing screen uncluttered.

These hidden codes, which you can view with WordPerfect's Reveal Codes command, tell the program when to execute tabs, margin settings, hard returns, indents, and so on. Some codes—such as the codes for math and columns—turn those features on or off. Other codes—such as the codes for bold, underline, and italic—work in pairs. The first code in a pair acts as a toggle switch to turn on the feature; the second code serves to turn off the feature. When you press Reveal Codes (Alt-F3 or F11) the hidden codes appear on-screen. When you press Alt-F3 or F11 again, the hidden codes disappear from the screen.

Note: In the Reveal Codes screen, you cannot click the left mouse button or drag the mouse.

Displaying Hidden Codes

To display the hidden codes, follow these steps:

1. Turn on the Reveal Codes feature by pressing `Alt` `F3` or `F11`.

   🖰 Access the Edit pull-down menu and select Reveal Codes.

2

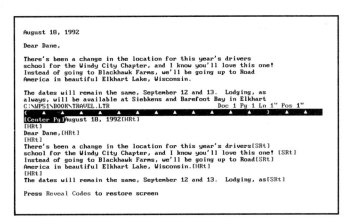

```
August 18, 1992

Dear Dane,

There's been a change in the location for this year's drivers
school for the Windy City Chapter, and I know you'll love this one!
Instead of going to Blackhawk Farms, we'll be going up to Road
America in beautiful Elkhart Lake, Wisconsin.

The dates will remain the same, September 12 and 13.  Lodging, as
always, will be available at Siebkens and Barefoot Bay in Elkhart
C:\WP51\BOOK\TRAVEL.LTR                              Doc 1 Pg 1 Ln 1" Pos 1"
[Center Pg]August 18, 1992[HRt]
[HRt]
Dear Dane,[HRt]
[HRt]
There's been a change in the location for this year's drivers[SRt]
school for the Windy City Chapter, and I know you'll love this one! [SRt]
Instead of going to Blackhawk Farms, we'll be going up to Road[SRt]
America in beautiful Elkhart Lake, Wisconsin.[HRt]
[HRt]
The dates will remain the same, September 12 and 13.  Lodging, as[SRt]

Press Reveal Codes to restore screen
```

The screen is split into two windows.

The same text is displayed in both windows, but the text in the bottom window includes the hidden codes; the codes are highlighted and appear in brackets. The ruler line between the windows displays the tab and margin settings for the line where the cursor is located.

2. To restore the regular editing screen, turn off Reveal Codes by pressing Alt F3 or F11 again.

⌨ Access the Edit pull-down menu and select Reveal Codes.

Editing in Reveal Codes

Editing in Reveal Codes is a little different from editing in the regular editing screen. The cursor in the upper window looks the same, but the cursor in the lower window is displayed as a highlight bar.

```
August 18, 1992

Dear Dane,

There's been a change in the location for this year's drivers
school for the Windy City Chapter, and I know you'll love this one!
Instead of going to Blackhawk Farms, we'll be going up to Road
America in beautiful Elkhart Lake, Wisconsin.

The dates will remain the same, September 12 and 13.  Lodging, as
always, will be available at Siebkens and Barefoot Bay in Elkhart
C:\WP51\BOOK\TRAVEL.LTR                              Doc 1 Pg 1 Ln 1" Pos 1"
[Center Pg]August 18, 1992[HRt]
[HRt]
Dear Dane,[HRt]
[HRt]
There's been a change in the location for this year's drivers[SRt]
school for the Windy City Chapter, and I know you'll love this one! [SRt]
Instead of going to Blackhawk Farms, we'll be going up to Road[SRt]
America in beautiful Elkhart Lake, Wisconsin.[HRt]
[HRt]
The dates will remain the same, September 12 and 13.  Lodging, as[SRt]

Press Reveal Codes to restore screen
```

When the cursor comes to a hidden code (in the lower window), the cursor expands to cover the entire code.

2

Deleting Hidden Codes

You can delete hidden codes in the regular editing screen or in the Reveal Codes screen. Because you can see the codes in the Reveal Codes screen, deleting them there is easier.

As you delete hidden codes from the Reveal Codes screen, notice that the effects of your changes are reflected in the upper window. With Reveal Codes turned on, you can enter commands and text and immediately observe the position of any new hidden codes.

To delete a hidden code, follow these steps:

1. Move the cursor to the place in the document where the code is likely to be located.

2. Turn on Reveal Codes by pressing $\boxed{Alt}\boxed{F3}$ or $\boxed{F11}$.

    🖮 Access the **E**dit pull-down menu and choose **R**eveal Codes.

3. Use the arrow keys to position the cursor on the hidden code.

For example, place the cursor on the **[TAB]** code.

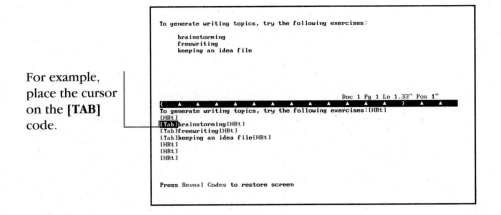

4. Press $\boxed{Del}$ to delete the hidden code.

    Your text reflects any editing changes you make in the Reveal Codes screen.

60

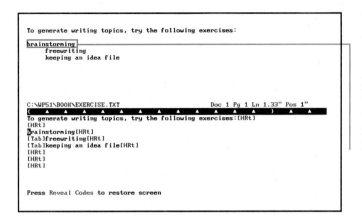

Because you deleted the **[TAB]** code, the text moves back to the left margin.

5. To return to the regular editing screen, turn off Reveal Codes by pressing [Alt][F3] or [F11].

   Access the Edit pull-down menu and choose Reveal Codes.

Note: You can adjust the size of the Reveal Codes screen by using the same procedure you use to resize document windows, as described in an earlier section. You can also resize the Reveal Codes screen permanently by customizing the program through the Display option of the Setup menu. For more information about customizing WordPerfect, see Chapter 15.

Summary

This chapter introduced WordPerfect's editing tools for revising your documents. You learned to retrieve files already saved to disk, and you learned to insert text, delete text, and restore deleted text in those files. You then examined WordPerfect's capability of displaying two document windows at the same time, and you learned to switch between the document windows, as well as to split the screen into two windows. Finally, you learned to display and delete WordPerfect's hidden codes.

Specifically, you learned the following information about WordPerfect:

■ Retrieve documents stored on disk in either of two ways: by issuing the Retrieve (Shift-F10) command, or by pressing List (F5) to display the List Files screen and choosing the file name from the list.

■ When you insert text, you can use Typeover mode to replace your original text, or you can use Insert mode to add new text to existing text.

61

2

■ Insert blank lines by pressing the Enter key once for each blank line you want to insert.

■ With WordPerfect, you can delete single characters, a word, a line, several lines, or part of a page. You also can use special options to delete a sentence, paragraph, or page.

■ Restore deleted text to its original location or another location with F1 (Cancel).

■ After editing, adjust the alignment of the text by pressing the down-arrow key to rewrite or reformat the text.

■ You can type in both of WordPerfect's document windows and use Switch (Shift-F3) or the mouse to switch back and forth between them.

■ You can split the screen with the Screen (Ctrl-F3) command to look at two documents or at different parts of the same document at once.

■ Use the Reveal Codes (Alt-F3 or F11) command to display Word-Perfect's hidden codes. The screen is split into two windows.

In the next chapter, you examine another of WordPerfect's editing tools: the Block feature.

Working with Blocks

3

The most powerful and flexible command in WordPerfect is the Block command. You use this command to block (mark) a segment of text so that only the blocked text is affected by the selected feature.

A block of text can be as short as a single letter or as long as the entire document. Flexibility is the Block command's strength. You define the size and shape of the block, and then you specify what to do with that selected text.

Defining a block

Moving or copying a block

Deleting a block

Saving a block

Printing a block

Appending a block

Underlining and boldfacing a block

Changing a block to uppercase or lowercase

Centering a block

Manipulating columns in a table

3

Key Terms in This Chapter

Block	A portion of text marked (highlighted) so that only it is affected by a WordPerfect feature you select. A block can be a single character, a single word, a phrase, a sentence, a paragraph, a page, a column, or an entire document.
Move	An operation that moves a block of text from one location to another. The text appears only in the new location.
Copy	An operation that duplicates a block of text. The text appears in both the original location and the location where the text is copied.

Defining a Block of Text

First, you must tell WordPerfect exactly what portion of the text you want affected. To define the block of text, you can use either the keyboard or the mouse. With the keyboard, you position the cursor at the beginning of the block of text, turn on the Block feature, and move the cursor to the end of the block. The block of text is highlighted. Using the mouse, you move the mouse pointer to the beginning of the block and drag the mouse to the end of the block. When you begin dragging the mouse, the Block feature is turned on automatically, and the block becomes highlighted.

When the Block feature is turned on, the Block on message flashes in the lower left corner of the screen.

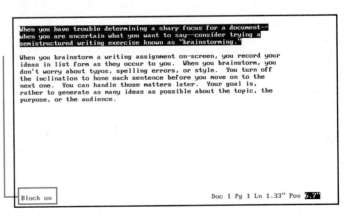

Highlighting text is the first step in any block operation. After you highlight a block of text, you can go on to perform any number of operations on the highlighted block. You can, for example, move or copy the block of text to another location, change the text to boldface, underline the text, or delete it.

Highlighting a Block with the Keyboard

To highlight a block of text with the keyboard, follow these steps:

1. Move the cursor to the character that begins the block of text to be highlighted.
2. Activate the Block command by pressing Alt F4 or F12.

   The Block on message flashes in the lower left corner of the screen.
3. Move the cursor until the last character in the block is highlighted.

As you highlight a block of text in this way, you can use any of the cursor-movement keys or key combinations—such as the PgDn and PgUp keys, the arrow keys, the End key, and GoTo (Ctrl-Home)—to move the cursor. To highlight an entire line, for example, turn on the Block feature and then press the End key. To highlight text from the cursor position to the bottom of the current screen, press Screen Down (+). To highlight multiple pages, press GoTo (Ctrl-Home) and type the number of the last page you want to highlight. You can move the cursor either forward or backward to highlight text. The highlighting moves with the cursor.

You also can use some shortcuts in highlighting text with the keyboard. To highlight a sentence, for example, you can turn on the Block feature at the beginning of the sentence and then press the period (.) key. The highlighting extends to the period at the end of the sentence. To highlight a paragraph, turn on Block and press Enter. The highlighting extends to the next hard return in the text.

Highlighting a Block with the Mouse

One of the most valuable uses of the mouse in WordPerfect is for highlighting a block of text. In the editing screen, dragging the mouse turns on Block automatically—as if you had pressed Block (Alt-F4 or F12).

3

To highlight a block of text with the mouse, follow these steps:

1. Place the mouse pointer on the character that begins the text you want to highlight.
2. Press and hold down the left mouse button as you drag the mouse over the block of text to be highlighted.
3. When you reach the end of the block, release the left mouse button.

If you drag the mouse beyond the top or bottom edge of the screen display, the text scrolls. You can increase or decrease the amount of text highlighted after you release the left mouse button by using the arrow keys to move the cursor.

Performing a Block Operation

After you highlight a block of text, you press the key or key combination that invokes the feature to be used on the block of text. The feature you select executes only on the highlighted block. If the feature will not work with the Block command, WordPerfect signals you with a beep. (Although the Block feature is flexible, it cannot be used with all WordPerfect features.)

Some features, such as Block Print or Block Delete, require confirmation. If a confirmation prompt, such as Delete Block? No (Yes), appears at the lower left of the screen, choose **Yes** or **No**.

Rehighlighting a Block

Block highlighting disappears automatically as soon as the task (such as move, copy, or bold) is completed. If you want to use the same block with another feature, or if you accidentally turn off the Block feature, you can easily rehighlight the block.

To restore highlighting with the keyboard, follow these steps:

1. Activate the Block command by pressing Alt F4 or F12.
2. Press Ctrl Home to activate the GoTo command.
3. Press Ctrl Home again to return to the beginning of the block.

If you have a mouse, you may prefer to rehighlight the block with the dragging method described earlier.

Backing Out of a Block Operation

To back out of the operation while the block is highlighted, you press either Cancel (F1) or Block (Alt-F4 or F12) to turn off the Block command.

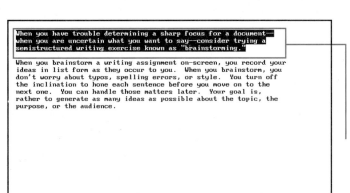   To turn off the Block command with the mouse, click the left mouse button; if you have a three-button mouse, click the middle mouse button.

The Block on message disappears, and the text no longer appears highlighted. The cursor remains at the end of the block (where the cursor was located when you finished highlighting).

Moving and Copying

Moving a block of text is a "cut and paste" operation—except that you don't fuss with scissors, paper, paste, and tape. With WordPerfect, you simply highlight the block, cut it from its current location, and paste it to a new location in the document. The block is erased from its previous location and appears in the new location. The new location can even be in another document.

When you copy (rather than move) a block of text, WordPerfect places into memory a duplicate of the text you have highlighted. You can then retrieve this block from memory and insert the block at another location in the same document or in another document.

When you have trouble determining a sharp focus for a document—when you are uncertain what you want to say—consider trying a semistructured writing exercise known as "brainstorming."

When you brainstorm a writing assignment on-screen, you record your ideas in list form as they occur to you. When you brainstorm, you don't worry about typos, spelling errors, or style. You turn off the inclination to hone each sentence before you move on to the next one. You can handle those matters later. Your goal is, rather to generate as many ideas as possible about the topic, the purpose, or the audience.

Block on   Doc 1 Pg 1 Ln 1.33" Pos 5.7"

A highlighted block ready to be moved or copied.

3

When you move a
block, the text is
deleted from the
original location
and appears in
the new location
you specify.

```
When you brainstorm a writing assignment on-screen, you record your
ideas in list form as they occur to you.  When you brainstorm, you
don't worry about typos, spelling errors, or style.  You turn off
the inclination to hone each sentence before you move on to the
next one.  You can handle those matters later.  Your goal is,
rather to generate as many ideas as possible about the topic, the
purpose, or the audience.

When you have trouble determining a sharp focus for a document—
when you are uncertain what you want to say—consider trying a
semistructured writing exercise known as "brainstorming."




C:\WP51\BOOK\BRAIN.TXT                          Doc 1 Pg 1 Ln 2.67" Pos 1"
```

When you copy a
block, the text
appears in both
the original
location and the
new location.

```
When you have trouble determining a sharp focus for a document—
when you are uncertain what you want to say—consider trying a
semistructured writing exercise known as "brainstorming."

When you brainstorm a writing assignment on-screen, you record your
ideas in list form as they occur to you.  When you brainstorm, you
don't worry about typos, spelling errors, or style.  You turn off
the inclination to hone each sentence before you move on to the
next one.  You can handle those matters later.  Your goal is,
rather to generate as many ideas as possible about the topic, the
purpose, or the audience.

When you have trouble determining a sharp focus for a document—
when you are uncertain what you want to say—consider trying a
semistructured writing exercise known as "brainstorming."


C:\WP51\BOOK\BRAIN.TXT                          Doc 1 Pg 1 Ln 1" Pos 1"
```

Moving a Block

To move a block of text, follow these steps:

1. Highlight the block by using [Alt][F4] or [F12] to activate the Block
   command, or by dragging the mouse.

2. Press [Ctrl][F4] to activate the Move command, select Block (1), and
   choose Move (1). Alternatively, press [Ctrl][Del].

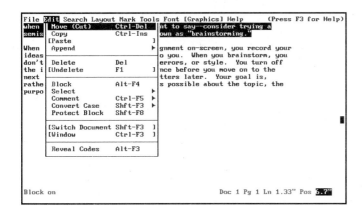

```
File Edit Search Layout Mark Tools Font [Graphics] Help      (Press F3 for Help)
when   Move (Cut)        Ctrl-Del  nt to say--consider trying a
senis  Copy              Ctrl-Ins  own as "brainstorming."
       [Paste                   ]
When   Append               ▶  gnment on-screen, you record your
ideas                             o you.  When you brainstorm, you
don't  Delete           Del       errors, or style.  You turn off
the i  [Undelete        F1     ]  nce before you move on to the
next                              tters later.  Your goal is,
rathe  Block            Alt-F4    s possible about the topic, the
purpo  Select                 ▶
       Comment          Ctrl-F5 ▶
       Convert Case     Shft-F3 ▶
       Protect Block    Shft-F8

       [Switch Document Shft-F3 ]
       [Window          Ctrl-F3 ]

       Reveal Codes     Alt-F3



Block on                          Doc 1 Pg 1 Ln 1.33" Pos 3.7"
```

Access the Edit pull-down menu and choose Move (Cut).

3

WordPerfect cuts the highlighted block, and it disappears from the screen. Don't worry; the block is stored in temporary memory.

WordPerfect displays the following message:

> Move cursor; press Enter to retrieve.

3. Move the cursor to the location in the document where you want the cut block to appear.

4. Press ⏎Enter to insert the block at the new location.

Copying a Block

To copy a block of text, follow these steps:

1. Highlight the block by using Alt F4 or F12 to activate the Block command, or by dragging the mouse.

2. Press Ctrl F4 to activate the Move command, select Block (1), and choose Copy (2). Alternatively, press Ctrl Ins.

3

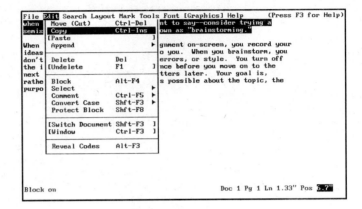

⌨ Access the
Edit pull-down
menu and choose
Copy.

3. Move the cursor to the location in the document where you want the duplicate text to appear.

4. Press ↵Enter.

You can retrieve the copied block as many times as you want. Generally, you use the Copy feature to repeat (without retyping) standard blocks of text in lengthy documents, such as legal, technical, or sales documents.

To retrieve the same block of text again, follow these steps:

1. Move the cursor to the location in the document where you want the block of text to appear.

2. Press Ctrl F4 to activate the Move command, select Retrieve (4), and choose Block (1).

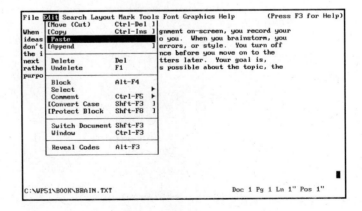

⌨ Access the
Edit pull-down
menu, choose
Paste, and select
Block (1).

Moving or Copying a Sentence, Paragraph, or Page

If the block you want to move or copy is a sentence, paragraph, or page, WordPerfect can highlight the block for you. Instead of using the Block command, follow these steps:

1. Place the cursor anywhere within the sentence, paragraph, or page to be moved or copied.

2. Press Ctrl F4 to activate the Move command; then choose Sentence (1), Paragraph (2), or Page (3).

   ▭ Access the Edit pull-down menu, choose Select, and select Sentence, Paragraph, or Page.

3. Select Move (1) or Copy (2).

4. Move the cursor to the location where you want the highlighted block of text to appear.

5. Press ⏎Enter.

Moving or Copying Text between Documents

WordPerfect's Block Move and Block Copy features make moving and copying text between documents easy. First you retrieve a document in each window, and then you move or copy the block between the documents with the help of the Switch (Shift-F3) command or Switch Document from the Edit pull-down menu.

To retrieve a second document, follow these steps:

1. Press ⇧Shift F3 to activate the Switch command.

   ▭ Access the Edit pull-down menu and choose Switch Document.

2. Retrieve a document by pressing ⇧Shift F10 to activate the Retrieve command, or press F5 to access the List Files screen. Or for a new document, begin typing the second document.

To move or copy text between the documents, follow these steps:

1. Highlight the block by using Alt F4 or F12 to activate the Block command, or by dragging the mouse.

3

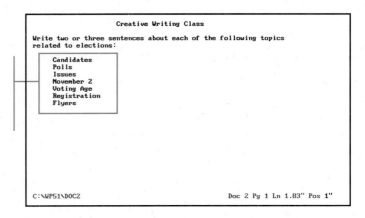

In this example, a list is highlighted.

```
When you have trouble determining a sharp focus for a document--
when you are uncertain what you want to say--consider trying a
semistructured writing exercise known as "brainstorming."

When you brainstorm a writing assignment on-screen, you record your
ideas in list form as they occur to you.  When you brainstorm, you
don't worry about typos, spelling errors, or style.  You turn off
the inclination to hone each sentence before you move on to the
next one.  You can handle those matters later.  Your goal is,
rather to generate as many ideas as possible about the topic, the
purpose, or the audience.

The following list shows some ideas that resulted from
brainstorming about elections:

        Candidates
        Polls
        Issues
        November 2
        Voting Age
        Registration
        Flyers
```

```
Block on                                    Doc 1 Pg 1 Ln 4.5" Pos 2.1"
```

2. Press Ctrl F4 to activate the Move command, select Block (1), and choose either Move (1) or Copy (2).

   ▭ Access the Edit pull-down menu and choose Move (Cut) or Copy.

3. Press Shift F3 (Switch) to display the second document.

   ▭ Access the Edit pull-down menu and choose Switch Document.

4. Move the cursor to the location in the second document where you want to move or copy the block of text.

5. Press Enter to retrieve the block.

The block appears in its new location—in the second document.

```
                        Creative Writing Class

Write two or three sentences about each of the following topics
related to elections:

        Candidates
        Polls
        Issues
        November 2
        Voting Age
        Registration
        Flyers
```

```
C:\WP51\DOC2                                 Doc 2 Pg 1 Ln 1.83" Pos 1"
```

Deleting a Block

In a few keystrokes, you can delete a sentence or several pages of text. To delete a block of text, follow these steps:

1. Highlight the block by using `Alt` `F4` or `F12` to activate the Block command, or by dragging the mouse. Then press `Del` or `◆Backspace`.

```
When you have trouble determining a sharp focus for a document--
when you are uncertain what you want to say--consider trying a
semistructured writing exercise known as "brainstorming."

When you brainstorm a writing assignment on-screen, you record your
ideas in list form as they occur to you.  When you brainstorm, you
don't worry about typos, spelling errors, or style.  You turn off
the inclination to hone each sentence before you move on to the
next one.  You can handle those matters later.  Your goal is,
rather to generate as many ideas as possible about the topic, the
purpose, or the audience.




Delete Block? No (Yes)
```

WordPerfect displays a confirmation prompt at the bottom of the screen.

2. To confirm the deletion, select **Y**es. (If you select **N**o, you are returned to the highlighted text.)

```
When you brainstorm a writing assignment on-screen, you record your
ideas in list form as they occur to you.  When you brainstorm, you
don't worry about typos, spelling errors, or style.  You turn off
the inclination to hone each sentence before you move on to the
next one.  You can handle those matters later.  Your goal is,
rather to generate as many ideas as possible about the topic, the
purpose, or the audience.




C:\WP51\BOOK\BRAIN.TXT                    Doc 1 Pg 1 Ln 1" Pos 1"
```

The block is deleted from the document.

73

You can delete as many as three blocks and restore all of them with Cancel (F1).

To restore deleted text, follow these steps:

1. Press ⌹F1⌹ (Cancel) to display the most recently deleted text.

   🖱 Hold down either button of a two-button mouse and click the other button. Or click the middle button of a three-button mouse.

The most recently deleted text reappears at the cursor position, and the Undelete menu appears at the bottom of the screen.

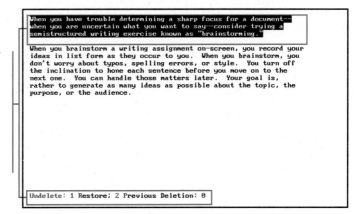

2. To restore the text you deleted most recently, select Restore (1).

   To restore a previous deletion, choose previous Deletion (2). Then select Restore (1) to restore that text.

   Select previous Deletion (2) to see the third deletion. Then select Restore (1) to restore that text.

Saving a Block

When you need to type the same block of text in one document several times, WordPerfect's Block Save feature helps reduce the amount of work. With Block Save, you first highlight the block of text you plan to use frequently, and then save the block as a separate file. Block Save enables you to build a timesaving library of frequently used blocks of text. You can even build an entire document from these files.

To save a block of text, follow these steps:

1. Highlight the block by using ⌜Alt⌟ ⌜F4⌟ or ⌜F12⌟ to activate the Block command, or by dragging the mouse.

2. Press ⌜F10⌟ to activate the Save command.

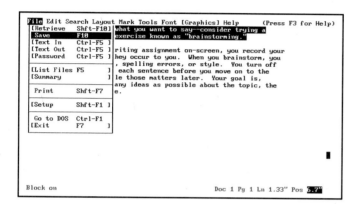

3

⊟◻ Access the File pull-down menu and choose Save.

WordPerfect displays the following prompt:

```
Block name:
```

3. Type the name of the file in which you want to save the block; then press ⌜↵Enter⌟.

Select a file name that clearly identifies the block you are saving. Be sure to include a drive letter and path name before the file name if you want to save the block to a directory other than the current directory.

Printing a Block

Sometimes you may want to print from a document just a single block of text—perhaps a page that lists sales quotas or a list of new personnel. You can use the Block Print feature to print part of the document.

3

To print a block of text, follow these steps:

1. Highlight the block by using [Alt][F4] or [F12] to activate the Block command, or by dragging the mouse.

2. Press [⇧Shift][F7] to activate the Print command.

   🖰 Access the File pull-down menu and choose Print.

   WordPerfect displays this prompt:

   ```
   Print block? No (Yes)
   ```

3. Select Yes.

Appending a Block

WordPerfect provides a simple way to add text to one document while you are working on another. With the Block Append feature, you can copy a block of text from the document on-screen to the end of another file on disk.

Note: If you want to copy or move text between documents retrieved into the two document windows, you can use the method described earlier in the section "Moving or Copying Text between Documents."

To append a block of text, follow these steps:

1. Highlight the block by using [Alt][F4] or [F12] to activate the Block command, or by dragging the mouse.

2. Press [Ctrl][F4] to activate the Move command, select Block (1), and choose Append (4).

🖰 Access the Edit pull-down menu, select Append, and choose To File.

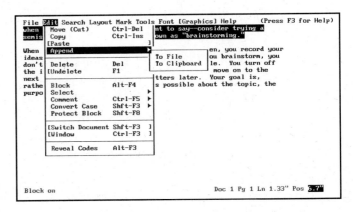

WordPerfect displays the following prompt:

```
Append to:
```

3. Enter the file name of the document to which you want the block appended.

The block remains in the current document and is appended (as a copy) to the end of the document in the specified file.

3

Enhancing a Block

WordPerfect offers a number of ways to add visual impact to your text. You can call attention to a section of text by boldfacing or underlining it. And you can change text to all uppercase (or all lowercase). For information about other enhancements, refer to Chapter 4.

Boldfacing or Underlining a Block

The appearance of your text on-screen depends on the type of monitor you are using. A color monitor can show boldfaced and underlined text in colors different from the color of regular text. You can change the way WordPerfect displays these enhancements on your monitor by customizing the program through the Display option on the Setup menu. For more information about customizing, refer to Chapter 15.

```
This is a line of plain text.

This line is in bold type.

This line is underlined.
```

When the text is printed, you can clearly distinguish the enhancements.

To boldface or underline a block of text you have already typed, follow these steps:

1. Highlight the block by using ⌈Alt⌉⌈F4⌉ or ⌈F12⌉ to activate the Block command, or by dragging the mouse.

2. Press ⌈F6⌉ to turn on the Bold feature, or press ⌈F8⌉ to turn on the Underline feature.

3

If you want the block to be both boldfaced and underlined, follow these steps:

1. Rehighlight the block by first pressing ⌈Alt⌉⌈F4⌉ or ⌈F12⌉, and then pressing ⌈Ctrl⌉⌈Home⌉ (GoTo) twice. Or rehighlight the block by dragging the mouse.

2. Press ⌈F6⌉ to turn on Bold, or press ⌈F8⌉ to turn on Underline (depending on which feature you used the first time).

Changing Uppercase and Lowercase

WordPerfect can automatically change whole words, sentences, paragraphs, or documents to uppercase or lowercase. This feature is useful when, for instance, you discover that you've typed a section of text with Caps Lock turned on.

To change a block of text to uppercase or lowercase, follow these steps:

1. Highlight the block by using ⌈Alt⌉⌈F4⌉ or ⌈F12⌉ to activate the Block command, or by dragging the mouse.

In this example, a list is highlighted.

```
When you have trouble determining a sharp focus for a document—
when you are uncertain what you want to say—consider trying a
semistructured writing exercise known as "brainstorming."

When you brainstorm a writing assignment on-screen, you record your
ideas in list form as they occur to you.  When you brainstorm, you
don't worry about typos, spelling errors, or style.  You turn off
the inclination to hone each sentence before you move on to the
next one.  You can handle those matters later.  Your goal is,
rather to generate as many ideas as possible about the topic, the
purpose, or the audience.

The following list shows some ideas that resulted from
brainstorming about elections:

        Candidates
        Polls
        Issues
        November 2
        Voting Age
        Registration
        Flyers

1 Uppercase; 2 Lowercase: 0
```

2. Press ⌨Shift F3 to activate the Switch command, and choose Uppercase (**1**) or Lowercase (**2**).

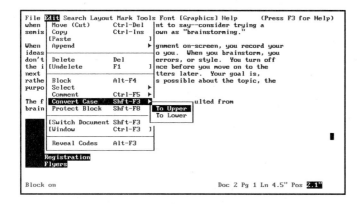

📟 Access the
Edit pull-down
menu, choose
Convert Case,
and select either
To Upper or To
Lower.

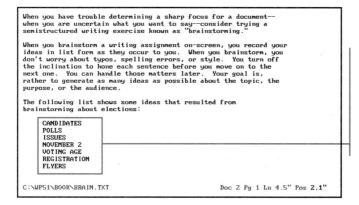

After you make
your selection,
the highlighted
text changes case.
In this example,
the text changes
to all uppercase.

WordPerfect recognizes that the pronoun *I* and the first letter of the first word
in a sentence should remain in uppercase. These letters, therefore, remain
capitalized when you change a block of text to lowercase. To ensure that
WordPerfect recognizes a block as a sentence, you can include the preceding
sentence's ending punctuation when you highlight the block of text.

Centering a Block between the Left and Right Margins

To center a block of text between the left and right margins, follow these steps:

1. Highlight the block by using Alt F4 or F12 to activate the Block command, or by dragging the mouse.

In this example, a list is highlighted.

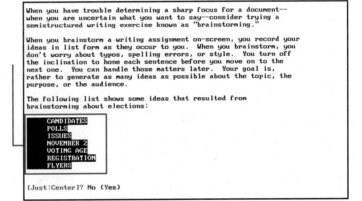

2. Press Shift F6 to activate the Center command.

Access the Layout pull-down menu, choose Align, and select Center.

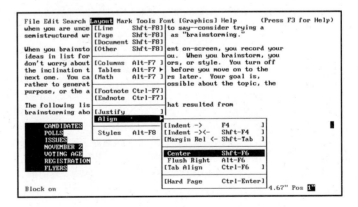

3. Select **Y**es to confirm that you want to center the block.

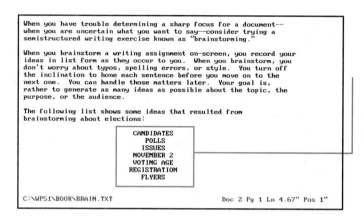

The block is centered between the left and right margins.

If the block contains full lines in paragraph form, not much blank space is left for centering between the margins. As a result, the effect of centering may not be readily apparent. To correct this problem, shorten the individual lines by ending each one with a hard return (by pressing Enter); then center the text.

Manipulating Columns in a Table Created with Tabs

In WordPerfect, you can move a grammatical block of text, such as a sentence or paragraph, or any text that falls within a defined rectangular block. Being able to move, copy, or delete lines, sentences, paragraphs, and other grammatical blocks of text is useful for editing text. But being able to move a column of text, even if the words are not contiguous, opens up many new creative possibilities. You can, for example, move, copy, or delete a single column of text or numbers from a table whose columns are separated by tabs. Note that the methods described here apply only to tables created with tabs; you learn about tables created with WordPerfect's Table feature in Chapter 13.

3

Moving or Copying a Column

When you move a column, you move the tab codes along with the text or numbers. The tab codes are included in the new location and are deleted from the original location. When you copy a column, the text or numbers remain in the original location, and the column and tab codes are duplicated in the new location.

To move or copy a column, follow these steps:

1. Place the cursor at the top left corner of the text to be moved or copied as a column, press [Alt] [F4] or [F12] to activate the Block command, and move the cursor to the bottom right corner of the column.

    [⌐] Place the mouse pointer at the top left corner of the text to be moved or copied as a column; then drag the mouse to the bottom right corner of the column.

The highlighted area of the screen initially includes some text that you do not want to move or copy.

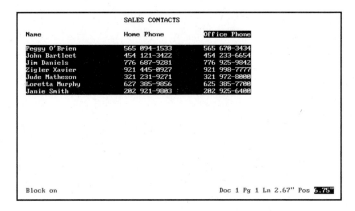

2. To highlight only the column you want to move or copy, press [Ctrl] [F4] to activate the Move command, and select Tabular Column (2).

    [⌐] Access the Edit pull-down menu, choose Select, and choose Tabular Column.

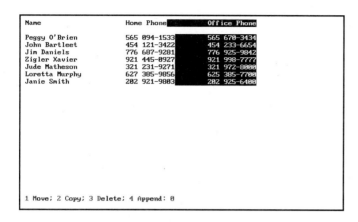

```
Name                Home Phone        Office Phone

Peggy O'Brien       565 094-1533      565 670-3434
John Bartleet       454 121-3422      454 233-6654
Jim Daniels         776 687-9281      776 925-9842
Zigler Xavier       921 445-0927      921 998-7777
Jude Matheson       321 231-9271      321 972-8000
Loretta Murphy      627 305-9856      625 305-7700
Janie Smith         202 921-9803      202 925-6400






1 Move; 2 Copy; 3 Delete; 4 Append: 0
```

Only the column to be moved or copied is highlighted.

3. Select Move (1) or Copy (2).

```
                SALES CONTACTS
Name                Home Phone

Peggy O'Brien       565 094-1533
John Bartleet       454 121-3422
Jim Daniels         776 687-9281
Zigler Xavier       921 445-0927
Jude Matheson       321 231-9271
Loretta Murphy      627 305-9856
Janie Smith         202 921-9803






Move cursor; press Enter to retrieve.        Doc 1 Pg 1 Ln 2.67" Pos 1"
```

The highlighted column temporarily disappears from the screen.

4. Move the cursor to the location where you want to retrieve the column, and press ⏎Enter).

```
                              SALES CONTACTS
          Name                 Office Phone      Home Phone

          Peggy O'Brien        565 670-3434      565 094-1533
          John Bartleet        454 233-6654      454 121-3422
          Jim Daniels          776 925-9042      776 687-9281
          Zigler Xavier        921 998-7777      921 445-0927
          Jude Matheson        321 972-0000      321 231-9271
          Loretta Murphy       625 385-7700      627 385-9856
          Janie Smith          202 925-6400      202 921-9803




          C:\WP51\BOOK\TABLE.BLK              Doc 1 Pg 1 Ln 1.33" Pos 3.55"
```

In this example, the Office Phone column is moved. Notice that the Home Phone column is shifted to the right.

Deleting a Column

You also can delete a column of text. You may, for example, want to delete a whole column of numbers from a table created with tabs.

To delete a column, follow these steps:

1. Place the cursor at the top left corner of the text to be deleted as a column, press Alt F4 or F12 to activate the Block command, and move the cursor to the bottom right corner of the column.

   ▭ Place the mouse pointer at the top left corner of the column to be deleted; then drag the mouse to the bottom right corner of the column.

   The highlighted area of the screen initially includes some text that you do not want to delete.

2. To highlight only the column you want to delete, press Ctrl F4 to activate the Move command and select Tabular Column (2).

   ▭ Access the Edit pull-down menu, choose Select, and choose Tabular Column.

3. Choose Delete (3).

84

```
┌─────────────────────────────────────────────────────────────┐
│                         SALES CONTACTS                        │
│                                                               │
│     Name                    Office Phone                      │
│                                                               │
│     Peggy O'Brien           565 670-3434                      │
│     John Bartleet           454 233-6654                      │
│     Jim Daniels             776 925-9842                      │
│     Zigler Xavier           921 998-7777                      │
│     Jude Matheson           321 972-8000                      │
│     Loretta Murphy          625 385-7700                      │
│     Janie Smith             202 925-6400                      │
│                                                               │
│                                                               │
│                                                               │
│                                                               │
│                                                               │
│                                                               │
│                                                               │
│                                                               │
│  C:\WP51\BOOK\TABLE.BLK                Doc 1 Pg 1 Ln 2.67" Pos 1" │
└─────────────────────────────────────────────────────────────┘
```

The Home
Phone column
is deleted.

3

Summary

Knowing how to use WordPerfect's Block feature gives you great versatility in editing documents. This chapter showed you how to define a block of text by highlighting the block. You learned how to move or copy the highlighted block, delete the block, save it, print it, and even append it to another file. You learned several ways to enhance your text by using the Block feature. And you learned how to manipulate columns in a table created with tabs.

Specifically, you learned the following key information about WordPerfect:

- A block is a portion of text marked (highlighted) so that only it is affected by a WordPerfect feature you select.

- To highlight a block of text, use either the keyboard or the mouse. With the keyboard, use the Block (Alt-F4 or F12) command. With the mouse, press and hold down the left mouse button as you drag the mouse over the block to be highlighted.

- After you highlight a block of text, you press the key or key combination that invokes the feature to be used on the block of text. The feature you select executes only on the highlighted block.

- When you move a block, it is erased from its previous location and appears only in the new location. When you copy a block, WordPerfect makes a duplicate of the highlighted text.

- To move a block, highlight it, select Move (Ctrl-F4), and choose Move (**1**).

- To copy a block, highlight it, select Move (Ctrl-F4), and choose Copy (**2**).

85

3

■ To move or copy a sentence, paragraph, or page, put the cursor anywhere within the text, select Move (Ctrl-F4), and then choose **Sentence (1)**, **Paragraph (2)**, or **Page (3)**. Next, select **Move (1)** or **Copy (2)**.

■ To move or copy text between documents, highlight the block, select Move (Ctrl-F4), and choose **Move (1)** or **Copy (2)**. Select Switch (Shift-F3), move the cursor to the location where you want to move or copy the block, and press Enter.

■ To delete a block, highlight it and press Del or Backspace.

■ To save a block, highlight it and press Save (F10).

■ To print a block, highlight it and press Print (Shift-F7).

■ To append a block, highlight it, select Move (Ctrl-F4), and choose **Append (4)**.

■ To boldface or underline a block, highlight it and choose Bold (F6) or Underline (F8).

■ To change a block of text to uppercase or lowercase, highlight it, select Switch (Shift-F3), and then choose **Uppercase (1)** or **Lowercase (2)**.

■ To center a block between the left and right margins, highlight it and choose Center (Shift-F6).

■ To move or copy a column in a table created with tabs, use the Block (Alt-F4 or F12), Move (Ctrl-F4), Tabular Column (2), and **Move (1)** or **Copy (2)** commands.

■ To delete a column in a table created with tabs, use the Block (Alt-F4 or F12), Move (Ctrl-F4), Tabular Column (2), and **Delete (3)** commands.

In the next chapter, you learn how to format lines and paragraphs of text so that you can perform such tasks as changing the left and right margins, setting tabs, indenting text, and centering a line of text.

Formatting Lines and Paragraphs

4

WordPerfect presets all initial or default settings for margins, tabs, and other basic features. If these settings do not fit your needs, you can change the settings for only the document on which you are working, or you can change the settings permanently through the Setup menu. Generally, this chapter tells you how to change the settings for the current document only.

This chapter discusses the formatting techniques that apply to lines and paragraphs. The next chapter covers the formatting of pages.

Changing left and right margins

Changing the unit of measurement

Enhancing text

Setting tab stops

Indenting text

Using Tab Align

Aligning text flush right

Centering text

Justifying text

Using hyphenation

Changing line height and line spacing

Key Terms in This Chapter

Initial font	The font in which text is normally printed, also called the *default base font* or *current font*. Often, font sizes and appearances are variations of the initial font.
Alignment character	The character on which you align numbers or text. In WordPerfect, you can choose any alignment character you want. The decimal point, comma, percent sign, dollar sign, and equal sign are commonly used alignment characters.
Line height	The vertical distance between the base of a line of text and the base of the line of text above or below. Printers call this distance *leading*.

Changing Left and Right Margins

WordPerfect's default margins are one inch for the left and one inch for the right—appropriate margins for 8 1/2-by-11-inch paper. WordPerfect measures margins from the left and right edges of the paper or from the perforation on pin-feed paper. You can change the margins for just the current document or permanently for all future documents. In addition, you can change the unit that WordPerfect uses to measure settings such as margins. If you want to change the margins, simply measure your stationery or paper and decide how many inches of white space you want as margins.

Changing Left and Right Margins for the Current Document Only

You can change the settings for left and right margins for only the current document by using either of two methods. The first method is to insert margin setting codes at the location in the document where you want those codes to take effect. If you insert the codes at the beginning of the document, they affect the entire document. If you insert the codes elsewhere, they affect only the portion from the codes to the end of the document or to the next codes.

The second method is to insert the codes in the Document Initial Codes screen. You can access this screen from anywhere in a document, and the settings you specify will affect the entire document. In addition, if you specify settings this way, they cannot be inadvertently deleted easily, as they might be if you use the first method. You may find that using this second method is advantageous for establishing many WordPerfect settings in addition to those for left and right margins.

To change the margin settings with the first method, you first place the cursor at the left margin of the line where you want the new margin settings to begin. If you want to change the margins for the entire document, move the cursor to the beginning of the document before setting the margins. After you position the cursor, follow these steps to change the left and right margins from this point until the next left and right margin code:

1. Press ⇧Shift F8 to activate the Format command. From the Format menu, select Line (**1**).

```
Format

    1 - Line
            Hyphenation                      Line Spacing
            Justification                    Margins Left/Right
            Line Height                      Tab Set
            Line Numbering                   Widow/Orphan Protection

    2 - Page
            Center Page (top to bottom)      Page Numbering
            Force Odd/Even Page              Paper Size/Type/Labels
            Headers and Footers              Suppress
            Margins Top/Bottom

    3 - Document
            Display Pitch                    Redline Method
            Initial Codes/Font               Summary

    4 - Other
            Advance                          Printer Functions
            Conditional End of Page          Underline Spaces/Tabs
            Decimal Characters               Border Options
            Language                         End Centering/Alignment
            Overstrike
Selection: 0
```

The Format menu is shown here.

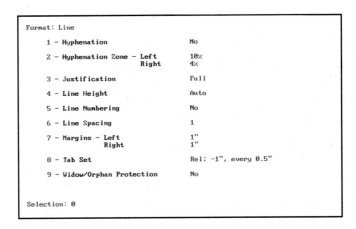

 Access the Layout pull-down menu and select Line.

4

Many of WordPerfect's formatting tasks begin at the Format menu or the Layout pull-down menu.

After you select Line (1), the Format: Line menu is displayed.

```
Format: Line

        1 - Hyphenation                    No

        2 - Hyphenation Zone - Left        10%
                             Right         4%

        3 - Justification                  Full

        4 - Line Height                    Auto

        5 - Line Numbering                 No

        6 - Line Spacing                   1

        7 - Margins - Left                 1"
                      Right                1"

        8 - Tab Set                        Rel; -1", every 0.5"

        9 - Widow/Orphan Protection        No


Selection: 0
```

2. Select Margins Left/Right (7).
3. Type a value for the left margin and press ⏎Enter.
4. Type a value for the right margin and press ⏎Enter.

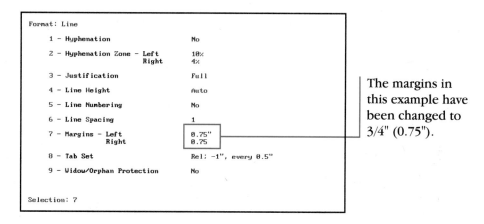

```
Format: Line

   1 - Hyphenation               No

   2 - Hyphenation Zone - Left   10%
                        Right     4%

   3 - Justification            Full

   4 - Line Height              Auto

   5 - Line Numbering            No

   6 - Line Spacing              1

   7 - Margins - Left          0.75"
                   Right       0.75

   8 - Tab Set                 Rel; -1", every 0.5"

   9 - Widow/Orphan Protection   No


Selection: 7
```

The margins in this example have been changed to 3/4" (0.75").

5. Press F7 (Exit) to return to the document.

These margin settings take effect from this point in the document until they are changed again.

If you change your mind about the new margin settings, pressing Cancel (F1) will not cancel the new settings. You can use Reveal Codes (Alt-F3, or F11) to display the **[L/R Mar:]** code, and then delete it.

To change left and right margin settings by using the second method, which affects the entire document (unless changed somewhere in the document), follow these steps:

1. Press ⇧Shift F8 to activate the Format command. From the Format menu, select Document (3).

   ▱ Access the Layout pull-down menu and select Document.

```
Format: Document

   1 - Display Pitch - Automatic  Yes
                        Width      0.1"

   2 - Initial Codes

   3 - Initial Base Font         Courier 10cpi

   4 - Redline Method            Printer Dependent

   5 - Summary




Selection: 0
```

The Format: Document menu is displayed.

2. Select Initial Codes (2).

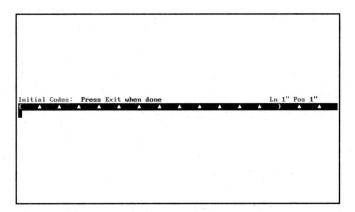

The Document
Initial Codes
screen is
displayed.

From this screen, you can change any settings you want, which will
govern the entire document (unless changed somewhere in the
document).

3. Press ⬆Shift F8 (Format) and select Line (1).

  ⌨ Access the Layout pull-down menu and select Line.

4. From the Format: Line menu, select Margins Left/Right (7).

5. Type a value for the left margin and press ↵Enter.

6. Type a value for the right margin and press ↵Enter.

7. Press F7 (Exit) to return to the Document Initial Codes screen.

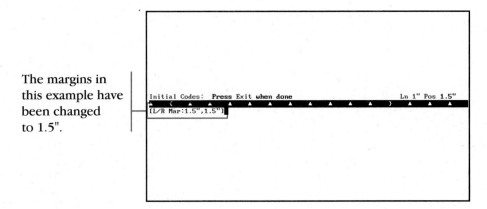

The margins in
this example have
been changed
to 1.5".

8. Press F7 (Exit) two more times to return to the document.

Changing Left and Right Margins Permanently

If you only occasionally produce a document with different margins (or other formatting options), you can change the settings for individual documents. You may, however, always use a specific setting—3/4-inch margins, for example. In this case, you can change the default margins, or other initial settings, through the Setup menu.

To change the margins permanently for all future documents, follow these steps:

1. Press ⇧Shift F1 to activate the Setup command.

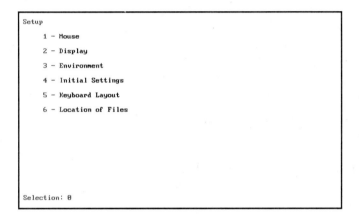

The Setup menu is displayed.

▱ Access the File pull-down menu and select Setup.

2. From the Setup menu, select Initial Settings (4).

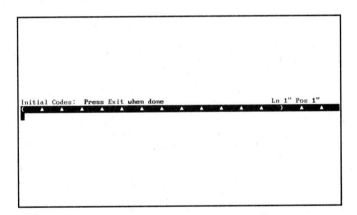

```
Setup: Initial Settings

    1 - Merge

    2 - Date Format                    3 1, 4
                                       March 18, 1992
    3 - Equations

    4 - Format Retrieved Documents     Yes
          for Default Printer

    5 - Initial Codes

    6 - Repeat Value                   8

    7 - Table of Authorities

    8 - Print Options




Selection: 0
```

The Setup: Initial Settings menu is displayed.

4

3. Select Initial Codes (**5**).

The Setup Initial Codes screen is displayed.

```
Initial Codes:   Press Exit when done                          Ln 1" Pos 1"
```

From this point, you follow the same steps for changing the margins for the current document only.

4. Press ⟨Shift⟩ ⟨F8⟩ (Format) and select Line (**1**).

   🖰 Access the Layout pull-down menu and select Line.

5. From the Format: Line menu, select Margins Left/Right (**7**).

6. Type a value for the left margin and press ⟨↵Enter⟩.

7. Type a value for the right margin and press ⟨↵Enter⟩.

8. Press ⟨F7⟩ (Exit) three times to return to the document.

Any new document you create in WordPerfect automatically will have this margin code placed in its Document Initial Codes screen.

Changing the Unit of Measurement

The default unit of measurement in WordPerfect is the inch. If you prefer, you can change this measurement to a centimeter, a point, a *w* unit (1/1200th of an inch), or a *u* unit (WordPerfect 4.2 line and column). You can change the unit of measurement for the settings you enter for menu selections such as left and right margins or tabs. And you can change the unit of measurement that appears in the status line.

4

Inches

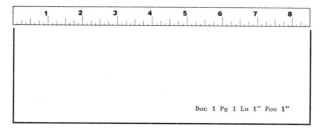

The status line showing the inch as the unit of measurement.

Points

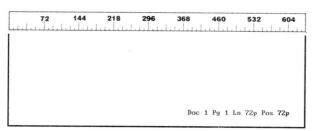

The status line showing the point as the unit of measurement.

Centimeters

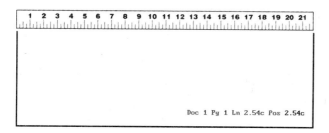

The status line showing the centimeter as the unit of measurement.

Inches

The status line showing the w unit (1/1200th of an inch) as the unit of measurement.

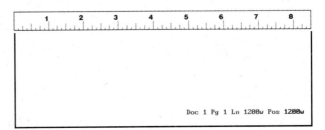

Doc 1 Pg 1 Ln 1200w Pos 1200w

Columns

The status line showing the u unit (line/column) as the unit of measurement.

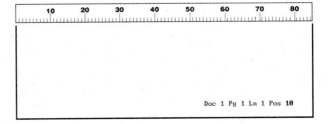

Doc 1 Pg 1 Ln 1 Pos 10

To change the default unit of measurement, follow these steps:

1. Press ⬆Shift F1 to activate the Setup command. From the Setup menu, select Environment (3).

   ⌨ Access the File pull-down menu, select Setup, and choose Environment.

WordPerfect displays the Setup: Environment menu.

```
Setup: Environment

        1 - Backup Options

        2 - Beep Options

        3 - Cursor Speed                      50 cps

        4 - Document Management/Summary

        5 - Fast Save (unformatted)           Yes

        6 - Hyphenation                       External Dictionary/Rules

        7 - Prompt for Hyphenation            When Required

        8 - Units of Measure

        9 - Alternate Keyboard                No
            (F1 - Help, Esc - Cancel, F3 - Repeat)



Selection: 0
```

2. Select Units of Measure (**8**).

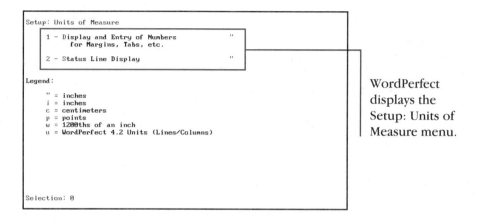

```
Setup: Units of Measure

    1 - Display and Entry of Numbers          "
            for Margins, Tabs, etc.

    2 - Status Line Display                   "

Legend:

    " = inches
    i = inches
    c = centimeters
    p = points
    w = 1200ths of an inch
    u = WordPerfect 4.2 Units (Lines/Columns)




Selection: 0
```

WordPerfect displays the Setup: Units of Measure menu.

3. Select Display and Entry of Numbers for Margins, Tabs, etc. (**1**), and then choose a new unit to use for menu selections. For example, press C to select centimeters.

4. Select Status Line Display (**2**) and choose a new unit to use in the status line. For example, press C to select centimeters.

5. Press F7 (Exit) to return to the document.

In any menu that requires specifying a measurement, as in changing left and right margins, you can force WordPerfect to use a nondefault measurement. If, for example, you have set the Units of Measure option to centimeters, but you want to enter left and right margins in inches, simply include " or *i* after the number; WordPerfect will convert the entry to the default setting of Units of Measure. In such menus, WordPerfect also converts fractions to decimals. For example, WordPerfect converts 6/7" to 0.857". For more about customizing the units of measure, refer to Chapter 15.

Enhancing Text

You can enhance a document by changing the size and appearance of the text. You accomplish some formatting tasks as you enter text simply by pressing the appropriate key, typing the text, and pressing the key again. For instance, from anywhere within the document, you can make text boldfaced or underlined as you type. You can apply other text enhancements by selecting them through the Font menu. For example, to make text italic, you choose that type style from the menu.

Enhancing Text from within a Document

A common text enhancement that you can make from within a document is to boldface or underline a portion of text. Although you can make either of these enhancements through the Font menu (as described in the next section), the simplest way to boldface or underline text that you are about to type is to press Bold (F6) or Underline (F8).

To boldface a portion of text that you are about to type, follow these steps:

1. Press F6 to turn on the Bold feature.

2. Type the text you want to boldface.

   The text that you type appears brighter (or in a different color) on-screen. The Pos number in the status line also changes in brightness or color.

3. Press F6 again to turn off the Bold feature.

To underline text, follow these steps:

1. Press F8 to turn on the Underline feature.

2. Type the text you want to underline.

3. Press F8 again to turn off the Underline feature.

Bold (F6) and Underline (F8) work as on/off toggle switches. You press the key once to turn on the feature; you press the key again to turn off the feature. If you press either Bold or Underline twice without entering text, the text you enter will not reflect bold or underline enhancements.

To enhance text that you have already typed, use the Block command as described in Chapter 3, "Working with Blocks." You first highlight the block of text with the Block command or the mouse. You then press either Bold (F6) or Underline (F8) once to enhance the highlighted block of text.

Enhancing Text with the Font Feature

With WordPerfect's Font feature, you can choose from the fonts (typefaces) available for use with your printer. The Font feature also controls size, color, and other variations of printed text, such as italics, outline and shadow printing, subscripts, and superscripts.

When you installed your printer, you selected an initial font, also called the default base font or the current font. The base font is the font in which text is normally printed. Other font sizes and appearance options usually are variations of the base font. If, for example, 10-point Helvetica is the base font, boldfaced text will be printed in 10-point Helvetica Bold, and italic text will be printed in 10-point Helvetica Italic.

Changing Font Attributes

Font *attributes* refer to the variations in a font's size and appearance that are available with your printer for a given base font. Size attributes include superscript and subscript, fine, small, large, very large, and extra large. Appearance attributes include boldface, underline, double-underline, italic, outline, shadow, small caps, redline, and strikeout. Remember that not all printers can print all attributes. Refer to your printer's manual for information about what size fonts and enhancements are available.

You can select the font attributes by pressing Font (Ctrl-F8) or accessing the Font pull-down menu. When you press Font (Ctrl-F8), WordPerfect displays the following menu:

1 Size; **2** Appearance; **3** Normal; **4** Base Font; **5** Print Color: **0**

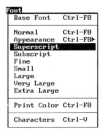

Slightly different options are displayed on the Font pull-down menu.

Changing the Font Size

WordPerfect offers a variety of font sizes through the Font menu. All the sizes are determined by the base font. If, for example, your base font is 10-point Helvetica, the large font may be 12-point Helvetica, the very large font may be 14-point Helvetica, and so on. Note that unless your graphics card supports it, you may not be able to distinguish the different sizes on-screen.

> This is 8 point type. It is hard to read
>
> This is 10 point type. Good for body text.
>
> This is 12 point type. Good for body text.
>
> This is 14 point type. Good for subheads.
>
> This is 18 point type. Good for subheads and some heads.
>
> This is 24 point type. Good for headlines.
>
> This is 36 point type. Good for mastheads.
>
> This is 72 pts.

4

How the various sizes appear in print depends on your printer.

To change the size of the font, use the following procedure:

1. Press Ctrl F8 to activate the Font command. From the Font menu, select Size (**1**). WordPerfect then displays the following attribute menu:

   1 Suprscpt; **2** Subscpt; **3** Fine; **4** Small; **5** Large; **6** Vry Large; **7** Ext Large: **0**

   ⌨ Access the Font pull-down menu.

2. Select any one of the attributes to change the size of the font.

When you select font size options such as **Fine**, **Large**, **Very Large**, and **Extra Large**, WordPerfect automatically chooses the correct line spacing (so that a large font will not overprint the preceding line, and fine print doesn't print with too much line spacing). If you later decide to print the same document with another printer or set of fonts, WordPerfect performs any required adjustments and sets the correct font, pitch, and line height automatically.

You can change a font attribute of existing text by first blocking the text with the Block command or the mouse, and then selecting the new font attribute with the procedure just described.

Changing the Font Appearance

WordPerfect offers a variety of font attributes for appearance through the Font menu. Note that you may not be able to distinguish the different appearance attributes on-screen.

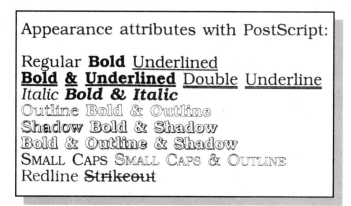

How the various attributes for appearance are printed depends on your printer.

To change the appearance of the font, follow these steps:

1. Press Ctrl F8 to activate the Font command. From the Font menu, select **A**ppearance (**2**).

   WordPerfect displays the following attribute menu:

   **1 Bold 2 Undrln 3 Dbl Und 4 Italc 5 Outln 6 Shadw 7 Sm Cap
   8 Redln 9 Stkout: 0**

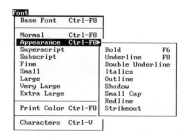

◱ Access the Font pull-down menu and select **A**ppearance.

2. Select any one of the attributes to change the appearance of the font.

Restoring Font Size and Appearance to Normal

To restore a single attribute for font size or appearance to normal after typing the text, press the right-arrow key one time to move the cursor past the attribute-off code. If more than one attribute is turned on, press the right-arrow key one time for each attribute you want to turn off.

Alternatively, after you have made several font attribute changes, you can restore the font size and appearance to normal by pressing Font (Ctrl-F8) and selecting Normal (3). Or you can access the Font pull-down menu and select Normal. Either method pushes the cursor beyond all attribute-off codes and ends all size and appearance attributes at that point in the document. If you have changed the font size or appearance using the Block command, WordPerfect automatically turns the attributes off at the end of the block.

Changing the Base Font

In addition to changing font attributes, you can change the base font that the printer uses—permanently (for all future documents), for the entire current document, or for a portion of the current document. To change the base font permanently, you use the Print menu, as explained in Appendix A. To change the base font for the entire current document, you change the Initial Base Font setting on the Format: Document menu or place the Base Font code at the beginning of the document. To change the base font for a portion of the current document, you use the Font menu.

Here are three categories of typefaces you might choose as your base font.

> This is Helvetica, a sans-serif typeface. Note the straight strokes. Helvetica looks good at larger point sizes.
>
> This is Times, a serif typeface. Note the tails on each letter. Good for body text and long stretches of smaller point sizes since it is easy to read.
>
> This is Cloister Black. A decorative typeface and not easy to read. It should be used only for impact.

102

To change the base font for the entire current document, follow these steps:

1. Press ⊙Shift F8 to activate the Format command, and select Document (3).

   🖱 Access the Layout pull-down menu and select Document.

2. Select Initial Base Font (3) from the Format: Document menu.

3. Highlight the font you want; then press ⏎Enter or choose Select (1).

The screen display adjusts to reflect for the new base font the number of characters that can be printed in a line with the current margin settings. If, for example, you select a 6-pitch font, the on-screen lines will be shorter than if you select a 10-pitch font. (Pitch indicates the number of characters per inch.)

To change the base font for a portion of the current document, follow these steps:

1. Move the cursor to the place in the document where you want to change the base font.

2. Press Ctrl F8 to activate the Font command, and select Base Font (4).

   🖱 Access the Font pull-down menu and select Base Font.

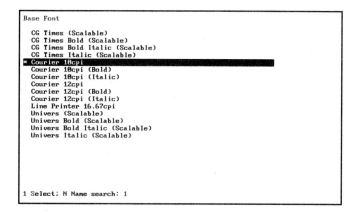

WordPerfect displays a list of the fonts available for use with your printer. The fonts listed are the printer's built-in fonts, plus any fonts you have selected with the Cartridges and Fonts feature.

3. Select Name Search and type the first letters of the font you want to select, or use the up-arrow and down-arrow keys to scroll through the list. When the name of the font is highlighted, press ⏎Enter or choose Select (1).

   🖱 Use the mouse pointer to highlight the font you want. Choose Select (1) or double-click the font to select it.

103

Setting Tab Stops

WordPerfect comes with tab stops predefined at one-half-inch intervals. Four basic types of tabs are available: left, center, right, and decimal. In addition, each type of tab can have a *dot leader* (a series of periods before the tab). You can establish tab stops in relation to the left margin or the left edge of the physical page.

4

A number of tab types are illustrated here. The hidden codes inserted to produce the tabs are displayed in the bottom window.

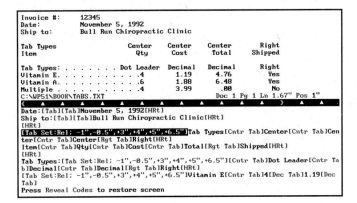

Displaying the Tab Ruler

To view current tab settings, you use the Window feature to display the tab ruler at the bottom of the screen. To display the tab ruler, follow these steps:

1. Press Ctrl F3 to activate the Screen command, and select Window (1).

   ▭ Access the Edit pull-down menu and select Window.

   WordPerfect displays the following prompt along with a number after the colon:

   `Number of lines in this window:`

2. Enter a number that is one less than the number displayed in the prompt. If, for example, the prompt displays 24, type **23** and press Enter.

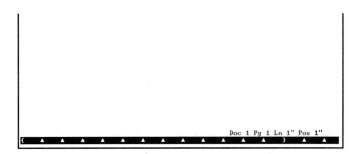

The tab ruler at the bottom of the screen indicates the left and right margins with curly braces, { and }. Tab stops are marked with triangles.

4

Instead of displaying curly braces, the tab ruler may display square brackets, [and]. Braces indicate margins and tabs at the same position; brackets indicate margins alone.

Hiding the Tab Ruler

To hide the tab ruler, you use almost the same procedure as for displaying the tab ruler. The only difference is that you type a number that is one greater than the number displayed in the prompt.

Changing Tab Settings

You can change tab settings for all documents or for only the document in which you are working. When you change the settings for just the current document, the settings affect the text only from that point forward.

You can set tab stops one at a time, or you can specify the increment and set several tab stops at once. Similarly, you can delete one tab stop, all tab stops, or only the tab stops to the right of the cursor. You can set multiple tab stops across 8 1/2 inches of a page. If you print on wider paper, you can extend tab stops from 8 1/2 inches to 54 1/2 inches, but you must set the tab stops at the far right individually. You can set a maximum of 40 tab stops.

Table 4.1 shows the various types of tabs available in WordPerfect.

4

Table 4.1
Types of Tabs Available in WordPerfect

Tab Type	Operation
Left (L)	Text is indented to the tab stop; then text continues to the right. A left tab (the default) is the most commonly used tab stop.
Center (C)	Text is centered at the tab stop. A center tab works much the same as Center (Shift-F6) except that a center tab can force centering anywhere on the line, not just the center between margins. Use center tabs to create column headings.
Right (R)	After a right tab stop, text continues to the left. A right tab works much the same as Flush Right (Alt-F6), except that a right tab can be placed anywhere on the line, not just at the right margin. Use right tabs to create headings over columns of numbers and dates.
Decimal (D)	After a decimal tab stop, text continues to the left until the alignment character is typed; then text continues to the right. Decimal tab stops work much the same as Tab Align (Ctrl-F6), except that you preset the alignment character as a tab stop. The default alignment character is a period (.), but you can change it to any character (for example, : or $). Use decimal tabs to line up columns of numbers.
Dot Leaders (.)	Any of the four tab types can be preceded by a dot leader (a series of periods). Use dot leaders for long lists that require scanning from left to right (phone lists, for instance).

To change tab settings, follow these steps:

1. Press ⌷Shift⌷ F8⌷ to activate the Format command, and select Line (1).

   ▭ Access the Layout pull-down menu and select Line.

2. From the Format: Line menu, select Tab Set (8).

106

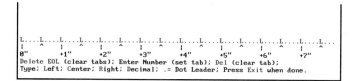

The bottom of the screen displays a graphical representation of the current tab stops.

After the tab ruler is displayed, you can delete or add single or multiple tab stops, and you can change the way tabs are measured (from the left margin or from the left edge of the physical page), as described in the text that follows. After you have changed the tab stops, press Exit (F7) twice to return to the document.

Deleting Tab Stops

To delete a single tab stop, use the cursor keys or mouse to move to the tab stop you want to delete, and press Del or Backspace to delete the tab stop.

To delete all tab stops, move the cursor to the left margin by pressing Home, Home, left arrow. Then press Ctrl-End.

To delete tab stops to the right of the cursor, type the number (in inches) of the first tab stop you want to delete, press Enter, or use the cursor keys or mouse to move to the tab stop, and then press Ctrl-End.

Adding Tab Stops

To add a single tab stop, use the cursor keys or mouse to move to the place where you want to add a tab stop, and press the letter for the appropriate tab type: L to add a left tab, C to add a center tab, R to add a right tab, or D to add a decimal tab. To add a dot leader, press the period (.) key. Alternatively, type the position for the tab and press Enter. For instance, type **3 1/8** and press Enter to place a tab at 3 1/8 inches. Note that WordPerfect automatically changes the number to its decimal equivalent of 3.125.

To add multiple left tab stops, first delete the existing tabs and then type the number of inches marking the location where the tabs are to begin, type a comma, and type the spacing increment. Then press Enter. For example, to space tabs one-half inch apart beginning at one inch, type **1,.5** and press Enter.

To add multiple center, right, or decimal tab stops and dot leaders, use the cursor keys or mouse to move the cursor to the place where you want the tab stops to begin. Or type the position for the first tab and press Enter. Then

107

press C (Center), R (Right), or D (Decimal). If you want a dot leader, press the period (.) key. Then type the number of inches marking the location where the tab stops are to begin, type a comma, and type the spacing increment. Finally, press Enter. For example, to space right-aligned tab stops one-half inch apart beginning at one inch, position the cursor at one inch, press R, type **1,.5**, and then press Enter.

When adding multiple tab stops that start at a position less than one inch, enter the number for the starting position as a decimal with a leading zero. For instance, if the tab stops start at one-half inch and are spaced at one-half-inch intervals, type **0.5,.5**.

Measuring Tabs

WordPerfect has two ways that tabs are measured in relation to the margin or physical page: Absolute and Relative to Margin (the default). Absolute tabs are set in relation to the left edge of the physical page. The hidden code for Absolute tabs looks similar to the following:

> **[Tab Set:Abs: 0", every 0.5"]**

Relative to Margin tabs are set in relation to the left margin setting. If the left margin is changed, the tabs adjust to the new margin setting. The hidden code for Relative to Margin tabs looks similar to the following:

> **[Tab Set:Rel: +1", +2", +3", +3.5"]**

With Relative to Margin tabs, if you want a tab stop to be one inch from the left margin, the tab will always be one inch in from the margin even if you later change the left margin setting.

To change the way tabs are measured, choose **T**ype and select either **A**bsolute (**1**) or **R**elative to Margin (**2**).

Indenting Text

Although WordPerfect's Tab and Indent features are similar, each has specific uses.

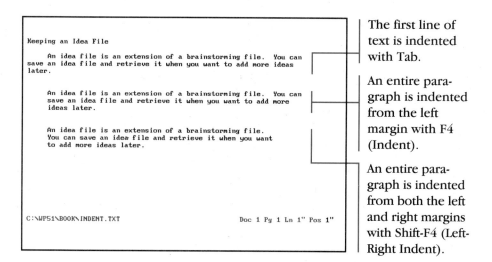

The first line of text is indented with Tab.

An entire paragraph is indented from the left margin with F4 (Indent).

An entire paragraph is indented from both the left and right margins with Shift-F4 (Left-Right Indent).

Never use the space bar for indenting or tabbing. If your printer supports proportional spacing, text will not align properly at the left indent or tab stop. Use instead the Tab key or the Indent key.

Tab⇥ Using the Tab Key

Use the Tab key to indent only the first line of a paragraph from the left margin. The Tab key, represented by left and right arrows at the left side of the keyboard, works like the Tab key on a typewriter. Each time you press Tab in WordPerfect, the cursor moves across the screen to the next tab stop.

F4 Using the Indent Key

Indent an entire paragraph from the left margin by using either the keyboard or the mouse.

With the keyboard, press Indent (F4) to indent an entire paragraph from the left margin.

109

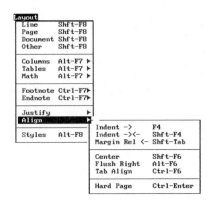

⌐□   With the
mouse, access the
Layout pull-down
menu, select
Align, and choose
Indent →.

The cursor moves one tab stop to the right, and the left margin is reset
temporarily. Everything you type, until you press Enter, is indented one tab
stop. To indent more than one tab stop, press Indent (F4) until the cursor is
located where you want to begin.

⇧Shift F4 Using the Left-Right Indent Key

Indent a paragraph from both the left and right margins by using either the
keyboard or the mouse.

With the keyboard, press Left-Right Indent (Shift-F4) to indent a paragraph
from both the left and right margins.

⌐□   With the mouse, access the **Layout** pull-down menu, select **Align**, and
choose **Indent** →←.

The cursor moves to the right one tab stop and temporarily resets both the left
and right margins. Everything you type, until you press Enter, is indented one
tab stop from the left margin and indented the same distance from the right
margin. To indent more than one tab stop from both margins, press Left-Right
Indent (Shift-F4) more than once.

Indenting an Existing Paragraph

You can use Indent (F4) or Left-Right Indent (Shift-F4) to indent an existing
paragraph. Follow these steps:

1. Move the cursor to the first character of the text you want to indent
   (or to the left of a tab indent at the beginning of a paragraph).

110

```
Keeping an Idea File

An idea file is an extension of a brainstorming file.  You can save
an idea file and retrieve it when you want to add more ideas later.










C:\WP51\BOOK\INDENT.TXT                    Doc 1 Pg 1 Ln 1.33" Pos 1"
```

Here, the cursor
is positioned at
the beginning of a
paragraph.

4

2. Press $\boxed{F4}$ (Indent) or $\boxed{\text{⇧Shift}}$ $\boxed{F4}$ (Left-Right Indent).

   ⌨ Access the Layout pull-down menu, select Align, and choose
   either Indent → or Indent →←.

3. Press $\boxed{↓}$ to reformat the screen so that the entire paragraph is
   indented.

```
Keeping an Idea File

      An idea file is an extension of a brainstorming file.  You can
      save an idea file and retrieve it when you want to add more
      ideas later.









C:\WP51\BOOK\INDENT.TXT                    Doc 1 Pg 1 Ln 1.33" Pos 1.5"
```

This paragraph is
indented from
both the left and
right margins.

Creating a Hanging Indent

A hanging indent is one in which the first line of the paragraph is flush with
the left margin, and the rest of the paragraph is indented to the first tab stop.

111

```
                          Bibliography
Sophocles, Oedipus the King.  Translated and adapted by Anthony
     Burgess, Minnesota Drama Editions, edited by Michael Langhan,
     No. 8, Minneapolis: University of Minnesota Press in
     association with Guthrie Theater Company, 1972.




C:\WP51\BOOK\BIBLIO.TXT                    Doc 1 Pg 1 Ln 1.83" Pos 6.2"
```

Hanging indents
are useful in re-
port formats such
as bibliographies.

4

To create a hanging indent, follow these steps:

1. Position the cursor at the left margin.

2. Press F4 (Indent) to move the cursor to the first tab stop.

   Access the **L**ayout pull-down menu, select **A**lign, and choose
   Indent →.

3. Press ⇧Shift Tab⇥ (Margin Release) to move the cursor back to its
   original position, at the left margin.

   Access the **L**ayout pull-down menu, select **A**lign, and choose
   Margin Rel ←.

4. Type your text.

5. To end the hanging indent, press ↵Enter.

Using Tab Align

Use the Tab Align feature to align text at the right on a specific character. For
example, you may want to use Tab Align to align names and addresses, or
numbers within columns.

112

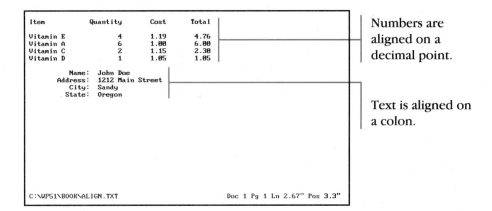

<table>
<tr><td>Item</td><td>Quantity</td><td>Cost</td><td>Total</td></tr>
<tr><td>Vitamin E</td><td>4</td><td>1.19</td><td>4.76</td></tr>
<tr><td>Vitamin A</td><td>6</td><td>1.00</td><td>6.00</td></tr>
<tr><td>Vitamin C</td><td>2</td><td>1.15</td><td>2.30</td></tr>
<tr><td>Vitamin D</td><td>1</td><td>1.05</td><td>1.05</td></tr>
</table>

Numbers are aligned on a decimal point.

```
       Name:   John Doe
    Address:   1212 Main Street
       City:   Sandy
      State:   Oregon
```

Text is aligned on a colon.

4

`C:\WP51\BOOK\ALIGN.TXT` Doc 1 Pg 1 Ln 2.67" Pos 3.3"

To align text at the right on a specific character, follow these steps:

1. Press Ctrl F6 to activate the Tab Align command.

   ⌨ Access the **L**ayout pull-down menu, select **A**lign, and choose **T**ab Align.

   The cursor jumps one tab stop to the right, and the following message appears:

   ```
   Align char = .
   ```

2. Type your text.

   All text that you type moves to the left of the tab stop until you type the alignment character (the default is a period).

3. Type the alignment character—in this case, a period (.).

   The text begins moving to the right of the tab stop.

If you want to align text at the right without typing the alignment character, you can repeat Step 1, type the text, and press Enter before pressing the alignment character. The typed text is right-justified at the tab stop.

The alignment character can be any character you want. The default is a period or decimal point (.), which works well with numbers. To align names and addresses, use a colon (:). To align numbers in an equation, an equal sign (=) is best. To align monetary amounts, use a dollar sign ($).

You can change the alignment character permanently for all future documents or for the current document only. To change the default alignment character, use the Setup menu.

113

To change the alignment character for a portion of the current document, first position the cursor at the place in the document where you want the setting to take effect. To change the alignment character for the entire document, first position the cursor at the top of the file. Then follow these steps:

1. Press ⬆Shift F8 to activate the Format command, and select Other (4).

   ⌨ Access the Layout pull-down menu and select Other.

2. From the Format: Other menu, select Decimal/Align Character (3).

3. Type a new alignment character and press ↵Enter twice.

4. Press F7 (Exit) to return to the document.

Using Justification

WordPerfect offers the following four types of justification:

- Full Justification aligns the text on the printed page along both the right and left margins. Use Full Justification (the default setting) when you have a printer capable of proportional spacing and you want a formal look.

- Left Justification leaves a ragged right margin.

- Center Justification centers all text.

- Right Justification aligns all text on the right margin, leaving the left margin ragged.

The four types of justification are used in this sample document. Notice that you cannot see on-screen the impact of Full Justification.

```
Left Justification:

This line has so many characters that the very next
extraordinarily long word wraps to the next line, creating a gap
at the right margin.

Full Justification:

This line has so many characters that the very next extraordinarily
long word wraps to the next line, creating a gap at the right
margin.

                    Center Justification:

      This line has so many characters that the very next
extraordinarily long word wraps to the next line, creating a gap
                    at the right margin.

                              Right Justification:

        This line has so many characters that the very next
 extraordinarily long word wraps to the next line, creating a gap
                              at the right margin.

C:\WP51\BOOK\JUSTIFY.TXT                  Doc 1 Pg 1 Ln 4.67" Pos 7.5"
```

```
Left Justification:

This line has so many characters that the very next
extraordinarily long word wraps to the next line, creating a gap
at the right margin.

Full Justification:

This line has so many characters that the very next extraordinarily
long  word  wraps  to  the  next  line,  creating  a  gap  at  the  right
margin.

                    Center Justification:

        This line has so many characters that the very next
extraordinarily long word wraps to the next line, creating a gap
                   at the right margin.

                              Right Justification:

        This line has so many characters that the very next
extraordinarily long word wraps to the next line, creating a gap
                                    at the right margin.
```

Because Full Justification is not visible on-screen, you must either use View Document or print the page to see the full effect.

4

Because text is justified by the addition of spaces between words and letters, the attractiveness of justified text depends on the capabilities of your printer.

You can change the justification setting through the Format menu. If the cursor is within the body of the document, the new setting affects only the portion of the document that follows the cursor position. If you want to change the justification setting for the entire document, either move the cursor to the beginning of the document or go to the Document Initial Codes screen before you complete the following steps.

To change the justification setting with the Format:Line menu, follow these steps:

1. Press ⇧Shift F8 to activate the Format command, and select Line (1).

   ▱ Access the Layout pull-down menu and select Line.

2. From the Format: Line menu, select Justification (3).

3. Select Left (1), Center (2), Right (3), or Full (4).

4. Press F7 (Exit) to return to the document.

If you are not sure whether justification is on or off, complete Steps 1 and 2 to check the setting. Then press Exit (F7) to return to the document.

115

Centering a Line

WordPerfect enables you to center text instantly, without laboriously counting characters. You can center a line of text between the left and right margins as you type the line or after you type it. You can center text also on a specific point.

4

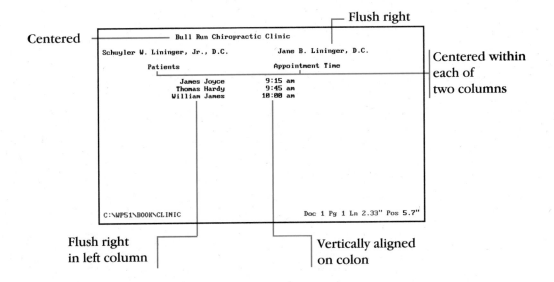

Centered

Flush right

Centered within each of two columns

Flush right in left column

Vertically aligned on colon

This screen illustrates centering, as well as other types of text alignment.

Centering between Margins

To center text that you are about to type, follow these steps:

1. Move the cursor to the left margin of a blank line on which you want to center text.

2. Press ⇧Shift F6 to activate the Center command.

    ▣▭ Access the Layout pull-down menu, select Align, and choose Center.

    The cursor is centered between the left and right margins.

116

3. Type your text.

   As you type, the text adjusts to the left and to the right, remaining centered.

4. Press ⏎Enter to end centering.

If you type more characters than will fit between the left and right margins, the rest of the text moves to the next line. Only the first line is centered. To center several lines, highlight the lines as a block, as described in Chapter 3, and select Center to change the justification, as described earlier in this chapter.

To center an existing line of text, follow these steps:

1. Press Alt F3 or F11 to turn on Reveal Codes.

   ▣ Access the Edit pull-down menu and select Reveal Codes.

2. Check to be sure that the line ends with a hard return code ([**HRt**]).

3. Press Alt F3 or F11 to turn off Reveal Codes.

   ▣ Access the Edit pull-down menu and select Reveal Codes.

4. Place the cursor at the left margin of the line of text to be centered.

5. Press ⇧Shift F6 to activate the Center command.

   The text moves to the center of the screen.

6. Press ↓ to reformat the screen.

Centering on a Specific Point

To center text on a specific point, follow these steps:

1. Use the **space bar** or Tab⇥ to move the cursor to the specific point on which you want to center the text.

2. Press ⇧Shift F6 to activate the Center command.

3. Type your text.

4. Press ⏎Enter.

The text is centered on the position of the cursor. You cannot center previously typed text on a specific point.

Aligning Text Flush Right

Use the Flush Right feature to align text with the right margin. This feature aligns the right edge of text flush (even) with the right margin.

4

You can align text flush right either before or after you type the text.

```
                                              900 Rose Garden Way
                                            New Harmony, IN  46003
                                               September 12, 1992

Mr. Rudolf Steiner
23 Goethe Street
Chicago, Illinois  60610

Dear Mr. Steiner:

    Thank you for inquiring about "The Seed and the Soil: A
Biodynamic Perspective," the Midwest Regional Conference of the
Biodynamic Farming and Gardening Association.  The conference will
be held from October 7-9, 1992, in the Barn Abbey at New Harmony,
Indiana.  The registration packet you requested is enclosed.

    This conference marks the first of its kind in the Midwest.
If you're new to biodynamic gardening, you'll have a rare
opportunity to learn from the experts.  If you're an experienced
biodynamic gardener, you'll be able to mingle and swap secrets with
fellow enthusiasts.

    New Harmony, once the site of two utopian and agrarian
communities in the early nineteenth century is an ideal setting
C:\WP51\BOOK\HARMONY.LTR                        Doc 1 Pg 1 Ln 1" Pos 1"
```

To create flush-right text as you type, follow these steps:

1. Move the cursor to a blank line.
2. Press Alt F6 to activate the Flush Right command.

   ⌨ Access the Layout pull-down menu, select Align, and choose Flush Right.

   The cursor jumps to the right margin.
3. Type your text.

   As you type, the cursor stays at the right margin, and the text moves to the left.
4. Press ⏎Enter to stop aligning text with the right margin.

To align existing text with the right margin, follow these steps:

1. Place the cursor at the left margin.
2. Press Alt F6 to activate the Flush Right command.

   ⌨ Access the Layout pull-down menu, select Align, and choose Flush Right.

   The line of text jumps past the right margin.
3. Press ↓ to reformat the screen.

When you use the Flush Right feature, some of the text may disappear past the right edge of the screen. Pressing the down-arrow key adjusts the screen display.

You can use the Block feature to right-align several lines at once. First highlight the block, using one of the methods described in Chapter 3, "Working with Blocks." Then follow the preceding steps to align the block of text flush right. An alternative is to use the Justification feature, as described earlier in this chapter.

Using Hyphenation

When a line of text becomes too long to fit within the margins, the last word in the line wraps to the next line. With short words, wrapping does not present a problem. With long words, however, the following problems can occur:

- If Justification is set to Left, a large gap can occur at the right margin, making the margin appear too ragged.
- If Justification is set to Full, large spaces between words become visually distracting.

Hyphenating a long word at the end of a line solves the problem and creates a visually attractive printed document. When you use WordPerfect's Hyphenation feature, the program fits as much of the word as possible on one line before hyphenating, and wraps the balance of the word to the next line.

Using Hyphenation Settings

To turn on the Hyphenation feature for the entire document, follow these steps:

1. Press ⬆Shift F8 to activate the Format command, select **D**ocument (**3**), and choose Initial **C**odes (**2**).

   ⌨ Access the **L**ayout pull-down menu, select **D**ocument, and choose Initial **C**odes (**2**).

   WordPerfect displays the Document Initial Codes screen.

2. Press ⬆Shift F8 (Format) and select **L**ine (**1**).

   ⌨ Access the **L**ayout pull-down menu and select **L**ine.

4

The Format:
Line menu is
displayed.

```
Format: Line

      1 - Hyphenation                      No (Yes)

      2 - Hyphenation Zone - Left          10%
                            Right          4%

      3 - Justification                    Full

      4 - Line Height                      Auto

      5 - Line Numbering                   No

      6 - Line Spacing                     1

      7 - Margins - Left                   1"
                    Right                  1"

      8 - Tab Set                          Rel; -1", every 0.5"

      9 - Widow/Orphan Protection          No


Selection: 1
```

3. Select Hyphenation (**1**).

4. Choose **Yes** to turn on hyphenation.

5. Press ⬚F7⬚ (Exit) three times to return to the document. Hyphenation is turned on for the document.

Hyphenation remains on until you turn off the feature. To turn it off, repeat the preceding steps, but select **No** instead of **Yes** in Step 4.

When hyphenation is on, as you type or scroll the document, WordPerfect may automatically hyphenate some words. At other times, WordPerfect may prompt you to make a decision regarding the hyphenation of a particular word.

When
WordPerfect
reaches a word,
such as *justifica-
tion*, the program
beeps and
displays a mes-
sage similar to the
one shown at the
bottom of this
screen.

```
      When you are planning your printed document, consider the
appearance you want to present.  With ragged text, you have an
uneven right margin and a less formal look.  With right-justification









Position hyphen; Press ESC justifica-tion
```

At this point, you have three options:

- You can press Esc to hyphenate the word as displayed.

- You can use the cursor keys to move the hyphen to another hyphenation point, and then press Esc to hyphenate the word.

- You can press Cancel (F1) to avoid hyphenating the word and wrap it to the next line. If you choose this option, a cancel-hyphenation code ([/]) is inserted before the word; you must delete this code manually if you later decide to hyphenate the word.

If you want to turn off hyphenation temporarily (for example, while scrolling a document or checking spelling), press Exit (F7). When WordPerfect finishes scrolling or checking spelling, hyphenation is automatically turned on again.

Note: To control hyphenation in the ways you prefer, you can customize WordPerfect with the Environment option on the Setup menu. You can choose to turn on hyphenation permanently, and you can choose the type of hyphenation you want. You might, for example, choose hyphenation based on an external dictionary, supplemented with internal rules when the word to be hyphenated is not in the dictionary. Or you can choose hyphenation based strictly on the rules. Although going by the rules is faster, the hyphenations are not as accurate. In addition, if you don't want WordPerfect to beep every time you are prompted for hyphenation, you can turn off the Beep option for hyphenation. For more about customizing WordPerfect, see Chapter 15.

Controlling Hyphenation

WordPerfect provides many features that enable you to control hyphenation of the text at the right margin. Among these features are a variety of hyphens, returns, and hard spaces.

Understanding the Types of Hyphens

At first glance, a hyphen looks simply like a hyphen, but WordPerfect uses—and enables you to use—several kinds of hyphens, including hard hyphens, hyphen characters, and soft hyphens.

A *hard hyphen* is part of the spelling of a word, as in father-in-law and jack-of-all-trades. A hard hyphen is displayed and printed at all times. The hard hyphen code appears on the Reveal Codes screen as [—]. If a hard hyphen appears in a word that needs to be hyphenated, WordPerfect uses the hard hyphen as the breaking point instead of prompting you for a hyphenation decision. To enter a hard hyphen, you press the hyphen key (located on the same key as the underline character).

The *hyphen character* appears in your text the same as a hard hyphen, but WordPerfect treats the hyphen character as if it were a character. A word containing a hyphen character is not necessarily split at the hyphen. You may be prompted for hyphenation. In Reveal Codes, the hyphen appears as an unhighlighted -. To enter a hyphen character, you press Home and then press the hyphen key. Be sure to use the hyphen key in the row of numeric keys, not the minus sign on the numeric keypad. (The minus sign is used in formulas.)

A *soft hyphen* is inserted between syllables during hyphenation. A soft hyphen is visible and prints only when it appears as the last character in a line; otherwise, a soft hyphen remains hidden. The soft hyphen appears in Reveal Codes as a highlighted -. You can insert soft hyphens at points where you want hyphenation to occur by pressing Ctrl-hyphen.

To insert a *dash* in the text, use a combination of two kinds of hyphens. For the first hyphen, you press Home and then press the hyphen key for the hyphen character. For the second hyphen, you press the hyphen key for a hard hyphen. WordPerfect will not separate the two hyphens at the end of a line.

If your printer is capable, you also can use the Compose feature to print an actual dash (printers call this an em dash). To print an em dash (—), you place the cursor where you want the dash to appear, press Ctrl-V, and press the hyphen key twice. WordPerfect places an em dash (character set 4, character 34) in the document.

Understanding Line Breaks

Another way you can control the text at the right margin is by specifying what kind of line break you want. In WordPerfect, a line can end with a soft return, a hard return, or an invisible soft return.

WordPerfect inserts a *soft return* code (**[SRt]**) at the end of each line when the text reaches the right margin and is automatically wrapped to the next line.

The program inserts a *hard return* code (**[HRt]**) when you press Enter to end a line. You can insert a hard return when you don't want a line to wrap automatically to the next line or when you want to insert a blank line.

WordPerfect inserts an *invisible soft return* code (**[ISRt]**) when you press Home and then press Enter. This feature is handy for dividing words without inserting a hyphen—for example, dividing words such as *and/or* or *either/or* after the slash or dividing words connected with an ellipsis (...).

WordPerfect inserts a *deletable soft return* code (**[DSRt]**) if hyphenation is off and a line doesn't fit between the left and right margins. This feature forces a line break without hyphenating in extremely narrow columns.

Keeping Words Together

If you want to keep two words together on a line, you can insert a hard space between them by pressing Home, space bar. For instance, you can keep the words *San Francisco* on one line by pressing first Home, and then the space bar after you type **San**. A hard space signals WordPerfect to treat the two words as a single unit. WordPerfect will not divide the words when they fall at the end of a line but will move both words to the following line. A hard space appears as **[ ]** in Reveal Codes.

Changing Line Height and Line Spacing

To format your text, you can change both the line height and the line spacing. *Line height* is the vertical distance between the base of a line of text and the base of the line of text above or below. Printers refer to this distance as *leading. Line spacing* controls the blank lines between lines of text; for example, double-spacing leaves one blank line between the lines of text.

Line Height

WordPerfect automatically controls line height. If the program did not adjust the line height and you changed to a larger type size, the vertical spacing would appear cramped on the printed page.

Because WordPerfect handles changes in line height automatically, you usually don't need to adjust it manually, except for special circumstances. If, for example, your document is one page plus two lines and you want the text to fit onto one page, you could change the line height to accommodate the extra lines.

Like many WordPerfect formatting features, line height can be changed for only the current document or permanently for all future documents. To change the line height for the entire current document, either move the cursor to the beginning of the document or go to the Document Initial Codes screen before you complete the following steps. If the cursor is within the body of the document, the new setting affects only the portion of the document that follows the cursor position. Note that the feature will not work if your printer can print only six lines per inch. Also note that changes in line height are not visible on-screen.

To change line height for the current document only, follow these steps:

1. Press ⌂Shift F8 to activate the Format command, and select Line (1).

   ▭ Access the Layout pull-down menu and select Line.

2. Select Line Height (4).

   WordPerfect displays the following menu:

   1 Auto; **2** Fixed: **0**

3. Select Fixed (2) to enter a fixed line height.

4. Type the line measurement you want (with up to three decimal places).

5. Press ↵Enter.

6. Press F7 (Exit) to return to the document.

To switch back to WordPerfect's automatic line height settings, repeat this procedure, but instead select Auto (1) from the menu.

Line Spacing

WordPerfect's line spacing default is single-spacing. To double-space or triple-space a document, you can change the line spacing default rather than enter hard returns as you type. You can make line spacing changes permanently or for the current document only. To change the line spacing for the entire current document, either move the cursor to the beginning of the document or go to the Document Initial Codes screen before you complete the following steps. If the cursor is within the body of the document, the new setting affects only the portion of the document that follows the cursor position. Although you can enter any number for the line spacing setting, you will not see changes in line spacing on-screen except when you enter a line height of 1.5 or larger.

To change line spacing for the current document only, follow these steps:

1. Press ⌂Shift F8 to activate the Format command, and select Line (1).

   ▭ Access the Layout pull-down menu and select Line.

2. Select Line Spacing (6).

3. Type a number for the amount of line spacing you want (with up to two decimal places); then press ⏎Enter.

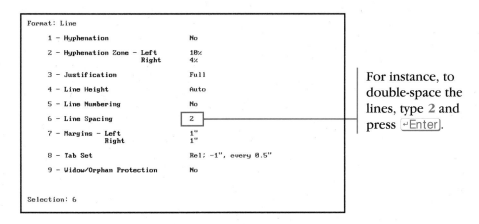

```
Format: Line

    1 - Hyphenation                    No

    2 - Hyphenation Zone - Left        10%
                          Right        4%

    3 - Justification                  Full

    4 - Line Height                    Auto

    5 - Line Numbering                 No

    6 - Line Spacing                   2

    7 - Margins - Left                 1"
                  Right                1"

    8 - Tab Set                        Rel; -1", every 0.5"

    9 - Widow/Orphan Protection        No


Selection: 6
```

For instance, to double-space the lines, type **2** and press ⏎Enter.

For one-and-one-half spacing, you would type **1.5** and press ⏎Enter.

Note that if you reduce the space between the lines too much, words may print on top of one another.

4. Press [F7] (Exit) to return to the document.

```
When you have trouble determining a sharp focus for a document--
when you are uncertain what you want to say--consider trying a
semistructured writing exercise known as "brainstorming."


When you brainstorm a writing assignment on-screen, you record your
ideas in list form as they occur to you.  When you brainstorm, you
don't worry about typos, spelling errors, or style.  You turn off
the inclination to hone each sentence before you move on to the
next one.  You can handle those matters later.  Your goal is,
rather to generate as many ideas as possible about the topic, the
purpose, or the audience.


C:\WP51\BOOK\BRAIN.TXT                      Doc 1 Pg 1 Ln 1" Pos 1"
```

This document is double-spaced.

Summary

This chapter presented many formatting options you can use to determine the format for the lines and paragraphs of your documents. You learned how to change the unit of measurement for various formatting options, change the settings for the left and right margins, and enhance your text with boldfacing and underlining. You also learned how to enhance text by changing the font attributes and the base font. And you learned ways to indent text, align text, and use hyphenation.

Specifically, you learned the following key information about WordPerfect:

- WordPerfect's default margins are one inch for the left and one inch for the right—appropriate margins for 8 1/2-by-11-inch paper.

- To change the left and right margins for a portion of or the entire document, select Format (Shift-F8), choose Line (**1**), choose **Margins Left/Right** (**7**), and type values for the left and right margins.

- To change the left and right margin settings for the entire document— regardless of your cursor position—select Format (Shift-F8), choose **Document** (**3**), and choose **Initial Codes** (**2**). Then select Format (Shift-F8), choose Line (**1**), choose **Margins Left/Right** (**7**), and type values for the left and right margins.

- To change the left and right margins permanently for all future documents, select Setup (Shift-F1), choose **Initial Settings** (**4**), and then choose **Initial Codes** (**5**). Then select Format (Shift-F8), choose Line (**1**), choose **Margins Left/Right** (**7**), and type values for the left and right margins.

- To change the default unit of measurement, select Setup (Shift-F1), choose **Environment** (**3**), and choose **Units of Measure** (**8**).

- To boldface a portion of text you are about to type, select Bold (F6), type the text, and then select Bold (F6) again.

- To underline a portion of text you are about to type, select Underline (F8), type the text, and then select Underline (F8) again.

- To change the size of a font, select Font (Ctrl-F8) and choose **Size** (**1**).

- To change the appearance of a font, select Font (Ctrl-F8) and choose Appearance (**2**).

- To change the base font for the entire current document, select Format (Shift-F8), select **Document** (**3**), and choose **Initial Base Font** (**3**).

4

- To change the base font for a portion of the current document, select Font (Ctrl-F8) and choose Base Font (**4**).

- To display the tab ruler, select Screen (Ctrl-F3), choose **Window** (**1**), and type a number that is one less that the number displayed in the prompt.

- WordPerfect has a variety of tab types: Left, Center, Right, and Decimal. Any of the four tab types can be preceded by a dot leader.

- To change tab settings, select Format (Shift-F8), select Line (**1**), and choose Tab Set (**8**). Then use the tab ruler at the bottom of the screen to delete or add tab stops.

- You can indent text in a variety of ways. Use Tab to indent the first line of text. Use Indent (F4) to indent an entire paragraph from the left margin. And use Left-Right Indent (Shift-F4) to indent and entire paragraph from both the left and right margins.

- To align text at the right on a specific character, select Tab Align (Ctrl-F6), type your text, and then type the alignment character.

- WordPerfect offers four types of justification: Full, Left, Center, and Right.

- To change the justification, select Format (Shift-F8), select Line (**1**), and choose **J**ustification (**3**).

- To center a line of text you are about to type, select Center (Shift-F6), type your text, and press Enter.

- To create flush-right text, use the Flush Right (Alt-F6) either before or after you type.

- To turn on the Hyphenation feature, select Format (Shift-F8), choose **D**ocument (**3**), and choose Initial Codes (**2**). Then select Format (Shift-F8), select **L**ine (**1**), and choose Hyphenation (**1**).

- WordPerfect used several kinds of hyphens—including hard hyphens, hyphen characters, and soft hyphens.

- You can control the text at the right margin by specifying what kind of line break you want. In WordPerfect, a line can end with a soft return, a hard return, an invisible soft return, or a deletable soft return.

- If you want to keep two words together on a line, insert a hard space between them by pressing Home, space bar.

- WordPerfect automatically controls line height. To change the line height for the current document only, select Format (Shift-F8), choose Line (**1**), and choose Line Height (**4**).

4

■ WordPerfect's line spacing default is single spacing. To change line spacing for the current document only, select Format (Shift-F8), choose Line (**1**), and choose Line **S**pacing (**6**).

In the next chapter, you examine formatting techniques that apply to pages as well as to the entire document.

4

Formatting Pages

5

Designing a document means making formatting choices at several levels. In the preceding chapter, you learned to format lines and paragraphs. In this chapter, you learn to format an entire document, or just a page or group of pages.

Formatting pages involves decisions such as changing the top and bottom margins, centering pages top to bottom, designing headers and footers, numbering pages, and controlling page breaks. While you work with the entire document, you also may want to take advantage of the Redline and Strikeout features as editing tools.

Key Terms in This Chapter

Header	Information that prints automatically at the top margin of every page.
Footer	Information that prints automatically at the bottom margin of every page.
Soft page break	A page break that occurs automatically. A soft page break appears on-screen as a dashed line.
Hard page break	A page break you insert to force a break at a certain spot. A hard page break appears on-screen as a line of equal signs.
Widow	In WordPerfect, a paragraph's first line at the bottom of a page.
Orphan	In WordPerfect, a paragraph's last line at the top of a page.

Choosing Paper Size and Type

To turn an on-screen document or an on-disk document into a printed document, WordPerfect must know the make and model of your printer and the characteristics of the paper on which you want the document printed. If the correct printer is not yet installed on your system, don't proceed with this section. First go to Appendix A and follow the procedure for installing a printer definition. Then refer to Chapter 7 for instructions on selecting a printer definition.

After you select a printer definition, you must define a form (sometimes called a *template*) for each type of sheet (page, envelope, or label) on which you want to print a document.

Note: The menus shown in the following exercise may differ from the menus displayed on your screen, depending on what kind of printer you are using. An assumption for this exercise is that you are using a laser printer. Some of these instructions, as indicated in the steps, do not apply to defining a form for a nonlaser printer (such as a dot-matrix or daisywheel printer).

5

In WordPerfect, a *form definition* includes the paper size and type, the location of the paper in the printer, and whether the orientation of the printing is portrait (vertical) or landscape (horizontal). When you first start WordPerfect, several forms—such as those for standard paper, legal paper, and business envelopes—already have been defined for you. If you need to define a new form, however, follow these steps:

1. Press ⇧Shift F8 to activate the Format command, and select Page (2).

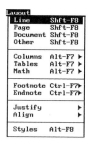

Access the Layout pull-down menu and select Page.

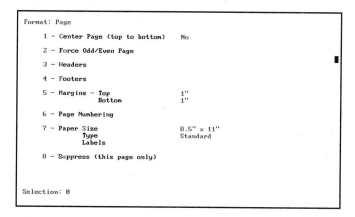

WordPerfect displays the Format: Page menu, offering a number of page formatting options.

2. Select Paper Size/Type (7).

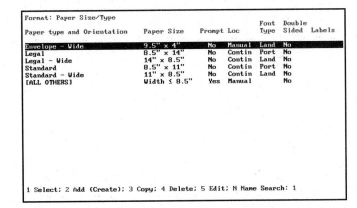

WordPerfect
displays the
Format: Paper
Size/Type menu.

```
Format: Paper Size/Type
                                                        Font  Double
Paper type and Orientation      Paper Size   Prompt Loc  Type  Sided Labels

Envelope - Wide                 9.5" x 4"    No   Manual Land  No
Legal                           8.5" x 14"   No   Contin Port  No
Legal - Wide                    14" x 8.5"   No   Contin Land  No
Standard                        8.5" x 11"   No   Contin Port  No
Standard - Wide                 11" x 8.5"   No   Contin Land  No
[ALL OTHERS]                    Width ≤ 8.5" Yes  Manual       No




1 Select; 2 Add (Create); 3 Copy; 4 Delete; 5 Edit; N Name Search: 1
```

This menu lists information about some standard forms already
defined by WordPerfect and ready to use. At the bottom of the screen
is a menu from which you can choose to select, add, copy, delete, or
edit a form.

3. Select Add (Create) (2).

```
Format: Paper Type
     1 - Standard
     2 - Bond
     3 - Letterhead
     4 - Labels
     5 - Envelope
     6 - Transparency
     7 - Cardstock
     8 - [ALL OTHERS]
     9 - Other


Selection: 1
```

WordPerfect
displays the
Format: Paper
Type menu.

The *paper type* is the name you choose for the form. When you choose
any of the first seven options from the Paper Type menu, you are
selecting that option's name as the paper type on the Format: Edit
Paper Definition menu (see Step 4 in this exercise).

Selecting [ALL OTHERS] (8) stops the form-definition process and
returns you to the Format: Paper Size/Type menu. Selecting Other (9)
causes WordPerfect to prompt you to enter a name for some other
form type. The name that you type becomes the form's paper type.

4. Select Standard (**1**).

```
Format: Edit Paper Definition

          Filename              HPLASIII.PRS

     1 - Paper Size             8.5" x 11"

     2 - Paper Type             Standard

     3 - Font Type              Portrait

     4 - Prompt to Load         No

     5 - Location               Continuous

     6 - Double Sided Printing  No

     7 - Binding Edge           Left

     8 - Labels                 No

     9 - Text Adjustment - Top  0"
                          Side  0"

Selection: 0
```

WordPerfect displays the Format: Edit Paper Definition menu.

On your screen, the [FILENAME] portion of [FILENAME].PRS will be the name of WordPerfect's definition for your printer.

5. Select Paper Size (**1**) from the Format: Edit Paper Definition menu.

```
Format: Paper Size           Width  Height

     1 - Standard             (8.5" x 11")

     2 - Standard Landscape   (11" x 8.5")

     3 - Legal                (8.5" x 14")

     4 - Legal Landscape      (14" x 8.5")

     5 - Envelope             (9.5" x 4")

     6 - Half Sheet           (5.5" x 8.5")

     7 - US Government        (8" x 11")

     8 - A4                   (210mm x 297mm)

     9 - A4 Landscape         (297mm x 210mm)

     o - Other

Selection: 0
```

WordPerfect displays the Format: Paper Size menu.

The *paper size* is the actual dimensions of the sheet on which WordPerfect will print the document. These dimensions can be a standard size, such as 8 1/2 by 11 inches, or a unique size, such as 4 by 9 inches.

If you choose any of the first nine options, WordPerfect uses the predefined dimensions listed for the option you select. If you select Other, WordPerfect prompts you to define the width and height for the form.

6. For this exercise, select Standard Landscape (2) to select a form 11 inches wide and 8 1/2 inches high.

WordPerfect displays the Format: Edit Paper Definition menu. The paper size has changed to 11" x 8.5". The paper type has changed to Standard - Wide.

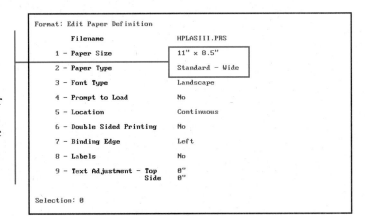

7. To define another form, select Paper Type (2).

   WordPerfect again displays the Format: Paper Type menu.

8. This time, select Other (9).

   WordPerfect displays the prompt `Other paper type:`. You can choose your own unique name for the form.

9. For this exercise, type **TEST** (in uppercase letters) and press ⏎Enter.

WordPerfect displays the Format: Edit Paper Definition menu. The paper type has changed to TEST - Wide.

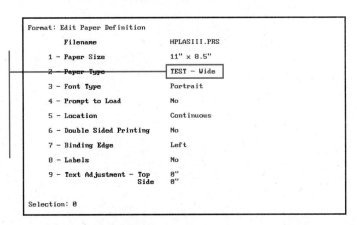

10. Select Font Type (3).

    The *font type* tells WordPerfect whether you want to print with
    characters in portrait (vertical) or landscape (horizontal) orientation,
    relative to the paper's insertion edge. This setting is meaningful only if
    you are using a laser printer. If you don't use a laser printer, you can
    omit this option when you define the form.

    WordPerfect displays the following menu at the bottom of the screen:

    Orientation: 1 Portrait; **2** Landscape: **0**

11. Regardless of whether you use a laser printer, choose Landscape (2).

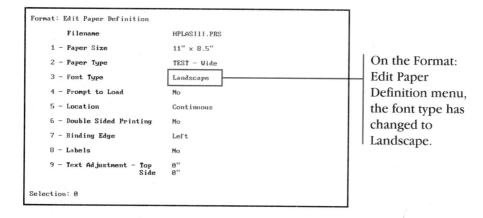

```
Format: Edit Paper Definition

        Filename              HPLASIII.PRS
   1 - Paper Size             11" x 8.5"
   2 - Paper Type             TEST - Wide
   3 - Font Type              Landscape
   4 - Prompt to Load         No
   5 - Location               Continuous
   6 - Double Sided Printing  No
   7 - Binding Edge           Left
   8 - Labels                 No
   9 - Text Adjustment - Top  0"
                       Side   0"

Selection: 0
```

On the Format:
Edit Paper
Definition menu,
the font type has
changed to
Landscape.

12. Select Prompt to Load (4).

    WordPerfect displays the No (Yes) prompt. Select Yes only if you
    want to hand-feed sheets into your printer. For this exercise, assume
    that you do not hand-feed sheets into the printer. Select No or press
    F1 (Cancel).

13. Select Location (5).

    The *location* indicates how the paper is inserted into the printer.
    WordPerfect displays the following menu at the bottom of the screen:

    Location: 1 Continuous; **2 B**in Number; **3 M**anual: **0**

The default setting is Continuous (1). Note the following options available:

Continuous (1)	Choose this option if the printer uses continuous-form paper inserted by a tractor feed or if the printer uses a paper tray.
Bin Number (2)	Choose this option if the sheets are inserted individually by a feeder from one or more cassettes. WordPerfect displays a Bin number: prompt.
Manual (3)	Choose this option if the sheets are inserted by hand.

For this exercise, assume that you have a sheet feeder and that the paper is being drawn from bin (cassette) number 1.

14. Select Bin Number (2), type 1, and press ⏎Enter .

On the Format: Edit Paper Definition menu, the location has changed to Bin 1.

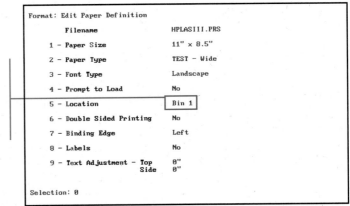

```
Format: Edit Paper Definition

        Filename                    HPLASIII.PRS

    1 - Paper Size                  11" x 8.5"

    2 - Paper Type                  TEST - Wide

    3 - Font Type                   Landscape

    4 - Prompt to Load              No

    5 - Location                   Bin 1

    6 - Double Sided Printing       No

    7 - Binding Edge                Left

    8 - Labels                      No

    9 - Text Adjustment - Top       0"
                          Side      0"

Selection: 0
```

15. Select Double Sided Printing (6).

WordPerfect displays the No (Yes) prompt. Select Yes if you have a laser printer capable of printing on both sides of the sheet (a process called *duplex printing*). If you don't use a duplex laser printer, you can omit this option when you define the form.

For this exercise, assume that your printer does not print on both sides of the sheet. Select No or press F1 (Cancel).

136

16. Select **B**inding Edge (**7**).

    WordPerfect displays the following menu at the bottom of the screen:

    Binding Edge: 1 Top; **2** Left: **0**

    The default selection is **L**eft (**2**). If you have a laser printer capable of duplex printing (printing on both sides of the sheet), this option controls the way the document prints on each side of the sheet.

    You select **T**op (**1**) to print the document with the second side upside-down so that the document can be bound on the top. You select **L**eft (**2**) to print the document in the same manner on both sides of the sheet so that the document can be bound on the side. Again, if you do not use a duplex laser printer, you can omit this option when you define the form.

    For this exercise, assume that your printer does not print on both sides of the sheet. Press [F1] (Cancel).

17. Select **L**abels (**8**).

    At the No (Yes) prompt, select **Y**es.

```
Format: Labels

   1 - Label Size
                Width           11"
                Height          8.5"

   2 - Number of Labels
                Columns         1
                Rows            1

   3 - Top Left Corner
                Top             0"
                Left            0"

   4 - Distance Between Labels
                Column          0"
                Row             0"

   5 - Label Margins
                Left            0.22"
                Right           0.25"
                Top             0.29"
                Bottom          0.25"

Selection: 0                        (Press F3 for Help)
```

WordPerfect displays the Format: Labels menu, which you use to enter specifications for printing labels.

Choose the Labels option only if you want to print a document in a label format. You learn more about labels in Chapter 10, "Merging Documents." Press [F1] to cancel this menu.

18. Select **T**ext Adjustment (**9**) if you need to move the printed image horizontally or vertically on the sheet.

    With this option, you can make minor changes (less than a quarter-inch) to fine-tune the placement of the printed image on the sheet. If

5

major changes (a quarter-inch or more) are needed, adjust the settings for your printer, according to your printer's manual, rather than use this option.

WordPerfect displays the following menu:

Adjust Text: 1 Up; **2 Down; 3 Left; 4 Right: 0**

If you choose any of these options, WordPerfect displays the prompt Text Adjustment Distance: 0". You then enter (in decimal inches or as a fraction) the amount of adjustment that you want to make, such as **0.1**, and press ⏎Enter. Or press F1 to cancel the selection.

19. Press F7 (Exit).

WordPerfect displays the Format: Paper Size/Type menu. The form definition has been added to the list of forms.

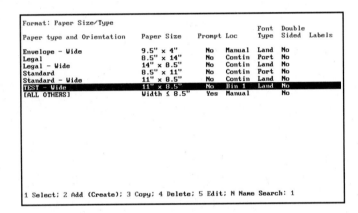

```
Format: Paper Size/Type
                                                  Font  Double
Paper type and Orientation    Paper Size  Prompt Loc   Type  Sided  Labels

Envelope - Wide               9.5" x 4"    No   Manual Land  No
Legal                         8.5" x 14"   No   Contin Port  No
Legal - Wide                  14" x 8.5"   No   Contin Land  No
Standard                      8.5" x 11"   No   Contin Port  No
Standard - Wide               11" x 8.5"   No   Contin Land  No
TEST - Wide                   11" x 8.5"   No   Bin 1  Land  No
[ALL OTHERS]                  Width ≤ 8.5" Yes  Manual       No





1 Select; 2 Add (Create); 3 Copy; 4 Delete; 5 Edit; N Name Search: 1
```

Note: Press Cancel (F1) or Esc three times to cancel all the settings you have entered and to return to the editing screen. To save your changes, press Exit (F7) twice.

To use one of the defined forms, follow these steps:

1. Press ⇧Shift F8 to activate the Format command, and select **P**age (**2**).

   ▭ Access the **L**ayout pull-down menu and select **P**age.

2. Select Paper **S**ize/Type (**7**).

   WordPerfect displays the Format: Paper Size/Type menu.

3. Use the arrow keys or mouse to move the highlight bar to the form you want to use.

4. Choose **S**elect (**1**) to accept the form definition or double-click the item with the mouse, and press F7 (Exit) to return to the editing screen.

Note: Press Cancel (F1) or Esc three times to exit the Format: Paper Size/Type menu and to return to the editing screen without selecting a form definition.

Changing Top and Bottom Margins

WordPerfect is preset to leave one-inch margins at the top and bottom of the page. Page numbers, headers, footers, and footnotes are placed within the allotted text area.

WordPerfect's default measurement is the inch; therefore, margins are measured in inches. The top margin is the distance between the top edge of the paper and the first line of text. The bottom margin is calculated from the bottom edge of the paper to the last line of text. A margin setting governs the placement of all text that follows the margin code—until a different setting changes the margins.

To change the top and bottom margins, follow these steps:

5

1. Move the cursor to the place in the document where you want to set margins. If you want to change the margins for the entire document, either move the cursor to the top of the document or go to the Document Initial Codes screen before performing the next steps. See Chapter 4 for more information about Document Initial Codes.

2. Press ⇧Shift F8 to activate the Format command, and select Page (2).

   ▭ Access the Layout pull-down menu and select Page.

3. From the Format: Page menu, select Margins Top/Bottom (5).

4. Type a new top margin and press ↵Enter. Then type a new bottom margin and press ↵Enter.

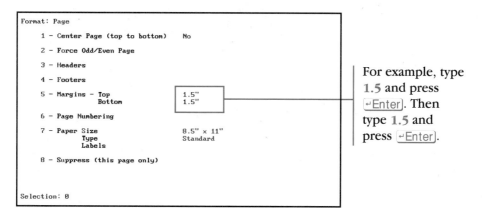

```
Format: Page

    1 - Center Page (top to bottom)    No

    2 - Force Odd/Even Page

    3 - Headers

    4 - Footers

    5 - Margins - Top              1.5"
                  Bottom           1.5"

    6 - Page Numbering

    7 - Paper Size                 8.5" x 11"
                  Type             Standard
                  Labels

    8 - Suppress (this page only)


Selection: 0
```

For example, type 1.5 and press ↵Enter. Then type 1.5 and press ↵Enter.

5. Press F7 (Exit) to return to the document.

Centering Pages Top to Bottom

When you center a page between the top and bottom margins, the setting applies to just one page—the page where you make the setting. You may, for example, want to center the title page of a sales report. The end of a centered page can be defined by either a soft page break or a hard page break. Ending the centered page with a hard page break ensures that the page never merges accidentally with the next page.

Before you insert the code to center a page, be sure that the cursor is located at the beginning of the page, before any other formatting codes or text. You can press Reveal Codes (Alt-F3, or F11 on an Enhanced Keyboard) to verify the cursor position.

5

To center a page top to bottom, follow these steps:

1. Press ⇧Shift F8 to activate the Format command, and select Page (2).

   ▭ Access the Layout pull-down menu and select Page.

2. Select Center Page (top to bottom) (1).

3. Select Yes.

4. Press F7 (Exit) to return to the document.

   WordPerfect inserts a **[Center Pg]** code.

Although the page doesn't appear centered on-screen, it will be centered when you print the document. If you change your mind about centering the page, delete the **[Center Pg]** code.

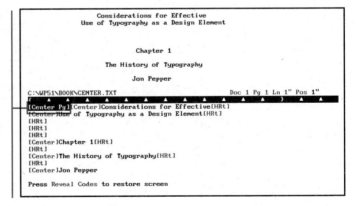

```
                    Considerations for Effective
                 Use of Typography as a Design Element


                            Chapter 1

                   The History of Typography

                          Jon Pepper

C:\WP51\BOOK\CENTER.TXT                              Doc 1 Pg 1 Ln 1" Pos 1"
[   ]  ▲    ▲     ▲     ▲    ▲    ▲    ▲    ▲    ▲  ]    ▲    ▲
[Center Pg][Center]Considerations for Effective[HRt]
[Center]Use of Typography as a Design Element[HRt]
[HRt]
[HRt]
[HRt]
[Center]Chapter 1[HRt]
[HRt]
[Center]The History of Typography[HRt]
[HRt]
[Center]Jon Pepper

Press Reveal Codes to restore screen
```

Note that the text is centered between the top and bottom margins of the page, not between the top and bottom edges of the paper. To adjust the centered text on the page, you can change the top and bottom margins, as described earlier in this chapter.

Using Advance

With WordPerfect's Advance feature, you can insert into your document a code that instructs the printer to move up, down, left, or right before printing. (Note that some printers cannot "advance" backward.) You also can use Advance to tell the printer to start printing at a specific location on the page. This option is used most often to help fill in preprinted forms.

To use the Advance feature, follow these steps:

1. Move the cursor to the place in the document where you want Advance to begin.

2. Press ⟨⇧Shift⟩⟨F8⟩ to activate the Format command, select Other (4), and choose Advance (1).

   ⌨ Access the Layout pull-down menu, select Other, and choose Advance (1).

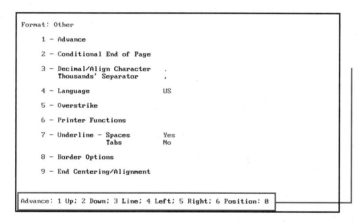

You can advance up, down, left, right, or to a specified line or position.

3. Select a menu option from the menu at the bottom of the screen.

4. Type the distance to advance; then press ⟨↵Enter⟩.

   The distance you enter for Advance Up, Down, Left, or Right is relative to the current position of the cursor. If you choose Position, the distance you enter specifies an absolute position on the page from the left edge of the paper. If you choose Line, the distance you enter specifies an absolute position on the page from the top edge of the paper.

5. Press ⟨F7⟩ (Exit) to return to the document.

141

When WordPerfect encounters an advance code, such as **[AdvDn:2"]**, the status line changes to reflect the new print position, but the cursor does not move.

Designing Headers and Footers

A *header* is information (text, numbers, or graphics) that prints automatically at the top margin of every page. A *footer* is information that prints automatically at the bottom margin of every page. Typical header and footer information may include chapter titles and page numbers, or revision numbers and dates.

You cannot see headers or footers on the editing screen; you can use either of two methods to see them. First, you can select Print (Shift-F7) and select View Document (**6**); or you can access the File pull-down menu, select **P**rint, and choose View Document (**6**). Second, you can press Reveal Codes (Alt-F3 or F11) to view header and footer text; or you can access the Edit pull-down menu and select **R**eveal Codes.

Creating a Header or Footer

To create a header or footer, follow these steps:

1. Press ⸢Shift⸥ ⸢F8⸥ to activate the Format command, and select **P**age (2).

    ⌨ Access the **L**ayout pull-down menu and select **P**age.

2. Choose **H**eaders (3) or **F**ooters (4).

You can create two headers (A and B).

```
1 Header A; 2 Header B: 0
```

And you can create two footers (A and B).

```
1 Footer A; 2 Footer B: 0
```

3. Select Header **A** (1) or Header **B** (2); or select Footer **A** (1) or Footer **B** (2).

```
Format: Page

    1 - Center Page (top to bottom)    No

    2 - Force Odd/Even Page

    3 - Headers

    4 - Footers

    5 - Margins - Top            1"
                   Bottom        1"

    6 - Page Numbering

    7 - Paper Size              8.5" x 11"
            Type                Standard
            Labels

    8 - Suppress (this page only)



 1 Discontinue; 2 Every Page; 3 Odd Pages; 4 Even Pages; 5 Edit: 0
```

A menu is displayed at the bottom of the screen.

5

4. From the menu, select one of three specifications:

   Select Every Page (2) if you want the header or footer to appear on every page.

   Select Odd Pages (3) if you want the header or footer to appear on odd pages only.

   Select Even Pages (4) if you want the header or footer to appear on even pages only.

5. Type the header or footer text, using any of WordPerfect's formatting features.

6. Press [F7] (Exit) twice to return to the document.

WordPerfect automatically skips one line between the header or footer and the first line (for headers) or last line (for footers) of text. If you want to insert more blank lines between the header or footer and the text, include blank lines when you define the header or footer.

Editing a Header or Footer

You can make changes to a header or footer. For instance, you can change the text or the appearance of the text in the header or footer.

To edit a header or footer, follow these steps:

1. Press [⇧Shift] [F8] to activate the Format command, and select Page (2).

   ⌨ Access the Layout pull-down menu and select Page.

2. Select Headers (3) or Footers (4).

3. Select Header **A** (**1**) or Header **B** (**2**); or select Footer **A** (**1**) or Footer **B** (**2**).

4. Select Edit (**5**).

   An editing screen with the header or footer text appears.

5. Edit the header or footer.

6. Press F7 (Exit) twice to return to the document.

Including Automatic Page Numbering in a Header or Footer

In addition to including text and formatting text in a header or footer, you can add automatic page numbering by including ^B (Ctrl-B) in the header or footer. You can, for example, specify the footer to read **Page** ^**B**, and the pages will be numbered consecutively as Page 1, Page 2, and so on.

You can include automatic page numbering in headers and footers when you first create them or when you edit them, using the procedures just described. To include automatic page numbering, type any text that will precede the page number. For example, type **Page** and press the space bar once; then press Ctrl-B.

Suppressing Headers and Footers

You can suppress any or all headers and footers so that they do not appear on a specific page. Suppose, for example, that you don't want to include headers and footers on a title page.

To suppress headers and footers, follow these steps:

1. Move the cursor to the beginning of the page where you want to suppress the header or footer.

2. Select Suppress (this page only) (**8**).

3. Select the header or footer you want to suppress:

   Suppress All Page Numbering, Headers, and Footers (**1**)
   Suppress Headers and Footers (**2**)
   Suppress Header A (**5**)
   Suppress Header B (**6**)
   Suppress Footer A (**7**)
   Suppress Footer B (**8**)

4. Select **Y** to suppress the header or footer.

5. Press F7 (Exit) twice to return to your document.

Numbering Pages

Numbering pages automatically, not as part of a header or footer, is as easy as telling WordPerfect how and where you want the numbers to appear on the page. Numbering begins with whatever number you select and appears in the style you specify. Be sure to move the cursor to the top of the document or go to the Document Initial Codes screen if you want page numbering to begin on the first page.

Page numbers print at the margin. Although page numbers don't appear on-screen, the status line indicates the current page number. You will not see the numbers on the pages until you print the document. You can preview the page numbers, however, with the View Document feature. To preview the page numbers, choose Print (Shift-F7) and select View Document (6). Or access the File pull-down menu, select **P**rint, and choose **V**iew Document (6).

5

Selecting a Page Number Position

You can select from a variety of page number positions. You can position the number at the top or bottom of the page—at the left, right, or center. Or you can have the page number appear at alternating positions—the left side of even pages and the right side of odd pages.

To select a page number position, follow these steps:

1. Press ⬆Shift F8 to activate the Format command, and select **P**age (2).

   ⌨ Access the **L**ayout pull-down menu and select **P**age.

2. Select Page **N**umbering (6).

```
Format: Page Numbering

    1 - New Page Number        1

    2 - Page Number Style      ^B

    3 - Insert Page Number

    4 - Page Number Position  No page numbering






Selection: 0
```

The Format: Page Numbering screen is displayed.

3. Choose Page Number Position (4).

The Format:
Page Number
Position screen is
displayed.

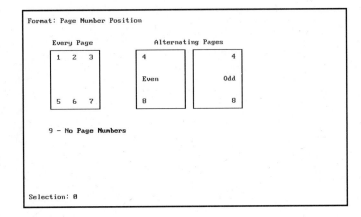

4. Type the number that corresponds to the position where you want
   page numbers to appear.

   For example, type 6 to center a page number at the bottom of every
   page.

   WordPerfect positions page numbers at the top or bottom margin and
   leaves a one-line space between the page number and the body of the
   text.

5. Press F7 (Exit) to return to the document.

If you turn on page numbering and later decide that you don't want page
numbers, you must delete the page-numbering code. To delete the code, first
move the cursor to the place where you invoked page numbering. Then press
Reveal Codes (Alt-F3 or F11) and delete the **[PgNumbering:]** code.

Changing the Starting Page Number

You can change page numbers at any point in a document; the change takes
effect from that point forward. Keep in mind that you can use Arabic numerals
(such as 1, 2, and 3) or upper- or lowercase Roman numerals (such as i and ii,
or I and II). If you want Roman numerals for the page numbers, you must use
the following procedure to change the starting page number, even if you plan
to start with Roman numeral i.

To change the starting page number, follow these steps:

1. Move the cursor to the top of the page where you want to start numbering.

2. Press ⬆Shift F8 to activate the Format command, and select Page (2).

    ▭▭ Access the Layout pull-down menu and select Page.

3. Select Page Numbering (6) and choose New Page Number (1).

4. Type the new starting page number (for example, 1 for Arabic, i for lowercase Roman, or I for uppercase Roman). Then press ↵Enter.

5. Press F7 (Exit) to return to the document.

Suppressing Page Numbering

You can turn off page numbering for an entire document or for a single page. To turn off page numbering for the entire document, follow these steps:

1. Press ⬆Shift F8 to activate the Format command, and select Page (2).

    ▭▭ Access the Layout pull-down menu and select Page.

2. Select Page Numbering (6).

3. Choose Page Number Position (4).

4. Select No Page Numbers (9).

5. Press F7 (Exit) to return to the document.

You can suppress page numbering for a single page so that no number appears for that page, but numbering continues on the following pages. For instance, you may not want the title page of a report to have a page number. To suppress page numbering for a single page, follow these steps:

1. Move the cursor to the top of the page where you want numbering suppressed.

2. Press ⬆Shift F8 to activate the Format command, and select Page (2).

    ▭▭ Access the Layout pull-down menu and select Page.

3. Select Suppress (this page only) (8).

```
Format: Suppress (this page only)

    1 - Suppress All Page Numbering, Headers and Footers

    2 - Suppress Headers and Footers

    3 - Print Page Number at Bottom Center   No

    4 - Suppress Page Numbering              No

    5 - Suppress Header A                    No

    6 - Suppress Header B                    No

    7 - Suppress Footer A                    No

    8 - Suppress Footer B                    No




Selection: 0
```

The Format:
Suppress (this
page only) screen
is displayed.

4. Choose Suppress Page Numbering (4).

5. Select Yes to confirm your choice.

6. Press F7 (Exit) to return to the document.

Inserting Page Number Styles and Page Numbers

With WordPerfect's Page Number Style option, you can insert a text string without having to go to the header or footer menu. And with WordPerfect's Insert Page Number option, you can insert the current page number, according to the page number style you have specified, at the cursor position in a document. You can, for example, insert the page number in a location on the page other than the standard positions that WordPerfect makes available.

To specify the page number style, complete the following steps:

1. Press ⬆Shift F8 to activate the Format command, select Page (2), and choose Page Numbering (6).

   ⌨ Access the Layout pull-down menu, select Page, and choose Page Numbering (6).

2. Choose Page Number Style (2) and type your text—for example, Jim's Report, Page or simply Page.

3. Press the space bar once.

4. Press ⏎Enter.

```
Format: Page Numbering

     1 - New Page Number        1

     2 - Page Number Style      Jim's Report, Page ^B

     3 - Insert Page Number

     4 - Page Number Position   No page numbering
```

WordPerfect puts the code for page numbering (^B) at the end of the text string.

5. Press F7 (Exit) to return to the document.

When the document prints, the text you entered precedes each page number.

To insert a page number anywhere on the page, complete the following steps:

1. Press Shift F8 to activate the Format command, select **Page** (2), and choose Page Numbering (6).

    ⌐ Access the **Layout** pull-down menu, select **Page**, and choose Page Numbering (6).

2. Choose Insert Page Number (3).

When you view or print the document, the current page number is inserted, according to the style you have specified, at the cursor position in the document.

Controlling Page Breaks

WordPerfect provides several ways to control where one page ends and the next one begins. You can use automatic page breaks (soft page breaks), hard page breaks, the Block Protect feature, the Conditional End of Page option, or the Widow/Orphan Protection option.

Using Automatic Page Breaks

WordPerfect automatically uses the current paper size and margins to determine where page breaks should go. In addition, WordPerfect automatically calculates the space needed for any headers, footers, page numbers, or footnotes when determining page breaks.

WordPerfect
inserts a dashed
line into the
document on-
screen wherever
an automatic page
break occurs.

```
┌─────────────────────────────────────────────────────────────────┐
│         This conference marks the first of its kind in the Midwest.│
│    If you're new to biodynamic gardening, you'll have a rare       │
│    opportunity to learn from the experts.  If you're an experienced│
│    biodynamic gardener, you'll be able to mingle and swap secrets with│
│    fellow enthusiasts.                                             │
│    ───────────────────────────────────────────────────────────── │
│         New Harmony, once the site of two utopian and agrarian    │
│    communities in the early nineteenth century is an ideal setting for│
│    our conference.  You'll find a map in the registration packet to│
│    help you find your way here.  Driving time from Chicago is roughly│
│    5 1/2 hours.                                                    │
│                                                                   │
│                                                                   │
│    C:\WP51\BOOK\HARMONY.LTR              Doc 1 Pg 2 Ln 1.67" Pos 2.2"│
└─────────────────────────────────────────────────────────────────┘
```

5

This soft page break produces a hidden **[SPg]** code. When you add or delete
text from a page, soft page breaks are recalculated automatically.

Inserting Hard Page Breaks

To force a page break at a certain spot—for example, at the beginning of a
new section in a report or after a title page—you enter a hard page break. The
page always ends at that point.

```
┌─────────────────────────────────────────────────────────────────┐
│                        Oedipus the King                           │
│                                                                   │
│                           Sophocles                               │
│                                                                   │
│                                                                   │
│              Translated and adapted by Anthony Burgess            │
│                                                                   │
│                                                                   │
│                       Minnesota Drama Editions                    │
│                    University of Minnesota Press                  │
│                            Minnesota                              │
│                                                                   │
│    ============================================================== │
│                                                                   │
│                                                                   │
│    C:\WP51\BOOK\BIBLIO.TXT               Doc 1 Pg 2 Ln 1" Pos 4.25"│
└─────────────────────────────────────────────────────────────────┘
```

A hard page break
appears on-screen
as a line of equal
signs.

To insert a hard page break, first move the cursor to the point where you want
the page break to occur. Then press Ctrl ↵Enter to insert a **[HPg]** code. To
delete a hard page break, use Reveal Codes (Alt F3 or F11) to find the
[HPg] code, and then delete it.

150

Using Block Protect

With the Block Protect feature, you can define a block of text that must not be split by a page break. If you later add or subtract lines from the block, WordPerfect keeps the block on the same page.

To use the Block Protect feature, follow these steps:

1. Highlight the block by using Alt F4 or F12 to activate the Block command, or by dragging the mouse.

   When you highlight the block, do not include the final return at the end of the paragraph.

2. Press ⇧Shift F8.

5

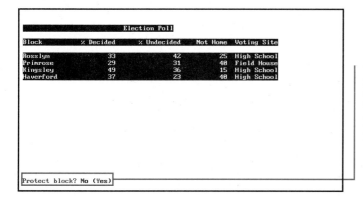

WordPerfect prompts you to indicate whether you want to protect the block.

3. Select Yes.

   ⌐⌐ Access the Edit pull-down menu and select Protect Block.

Now the protected block, when printed, will always appear on the same page.

Using Conditional End of Page

The Conditional End of Page option is similar to Block Protect, but instead of blocking the text, you specify the number of lines to keep together. When you use Conditional End of Page, WordPerfect groups a given number of lines so that they don't break between pages. Use this option, for example, when you want to be sure that a heading in a document is followed by at least three lines of text.

To use Conditional End of Page, follow these steps:

1. Count the lines that must remain together on the same page.

2. Move the cursor to the line above the lines you want to keep together.

3. Press ⸰Shift F8 to activate the Format command, and select Other (4).

   ▢ Access the Layout pull-down menu and select Other.

4. Select Conditional End of Page (2).

WordPerfect prompts you to enter the number of lines to keep together.

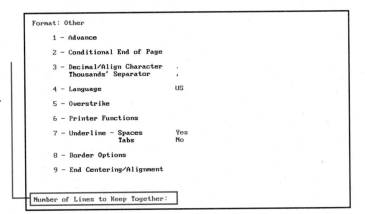

```
Format: Other

        1 - Advance

        2 - Conditional End of Page

        3 - Decimal/Align Character        .
                Thousands' Separator        ,

        4 - Language                        US

        5 - Overstrike

        6 - Printer Functions

        7 - Underline - Spaces              Yes
                        Tabs                No

        8 - Border Options

        9 - End Centering/Alignment


  Number of Lines to Keep Together:
```

5. Type the number of lines you counted; then press ⏎Enter.

6. Press F7 (Exit) to return to the document.

Using Widow/Orphan Protection

WordPerfect can automatically prevent single lines from being "stranded" at the top or bottom of a page. In WordPerfect, a paragraph's first line left at the bottom of a page is called a *widow*; a paragraph's last line left at the top of a page is called an *orphan*.

If you want to protect an entire document, either move the cursor to the beginning of the document or go to the Document Initial Codes screen before you complete the following steps. To protect only a portion of the document, move the cursor to the location where you want protection to begin.

To turn on Widow/Orphan Protection, complete these steps:

1. Press ⸰Shift F8 to activate the Format command, and select Line (1).

   ▢ Access the Layout pull-down menu and select Line.

```
Format: Line

     1 - Hyphenation                    No

     2 - Hyphenation Zone - Left        10%
                           Right        4%

     3 - Justification                  Full

     4 - Line Height                    Auto

     5 - Line Numbering                 No

     6 - Line Spacing                   1

     7 - Margins - Left                 1"
                   Right                1"

     8 - Tab Set                        Rel; -1", every 0.5"

     9 - Widow/Orphan Protection        No


Selection: 0
```

The Format: Line menu is displayed.

2. Select Widow/Orphan Protection (9).

3. Select Yes to turn on the feature.

4. Press $\boxed{\text{F7}}$ (Exit) to return to the document.

To turn off Widow/Orphan Protection, repeat the preceding steps but select **No** instead of **Yes** in Step 3.

Using Redline and Strikeout

Redline and Strikeout are tools for marking suggested editing changes in a manuscript. Redlining is a method of indicating segments of text where passages have been edited, added to, or deleted from a document. When several people work on a document, redlining is a useful way to let everyone know what changes are proposed. Redlining generally is used to identify text that has been modified; WordPerfect's Strikeout feature is used to identify text that the editor believes should be deleted.

In WordPerfect, you can choose how redlining appears on the printed page.

153

With many
printers, redlining
appears as a mark
in the margin
next to the
redlined text.
With other
printers, redlined
text appears
shaded or high-
lighted. If you
have a color
printer, redlined
text prints red.

> Brainstorming and freewriting at the keyboard are excellent strategies for warming up, generating ideas, and pushing your material toward a productive, critical mass. Out of chaos can come order; out of an inchoate sprawl of text on-screen--or on the printout--can come the key points and direction of your message. Brainstorming and freewriting can move you closer toward that first draft.

Strikeout appears
as characters
superimposed
over other
characters. The
text may be
marked out with a
series of hyphens
or an unbroken
line, depending
on your printer's
capabilities.

> Brainstorming and freewriting at the keyboard are excellent strategies for warming up, generating ideas, and pushing your material toward a productive, critical mass. ~~Out of chaos can come order; out of an inchoate sprawl of text on-screen--or on the printout--can come the key points and direction of your message.~~ Brainstorming and freewriting can move you closer toward that first draft.

Selecting the Redlining Method

To specify how you want redlined text to appear on the printed page, follow
these steps:

1. Press ⇧Shift F8 to activate the Format command, and select
   Document (3).

    ▭▭ Access the Layout pull-down menu and select Document.

2. Select Redline Method (4).

```
Format: Document

     1 - Display Pitch - Automatic Yes
                         Width     0.1"

     2 - Initial Codes

     3 - Initial Base Font        Courier 10cpi

     4 - Redline Method           Printer Dependent

     5 - Summary
```

WordPerfect displays the redlining options at the bottom of the screen.

```
Redline Method: 1 Printer Dependent; 2 Left; 3 Alternating: 1
```

3. Choose one of three redlining options:

   Select Printer Dependent (1) to have text marked according to your printer's definition of redlining.

   Choose Left (2) to have a vertical bar (or any other character) printed in the left margin.

   Select Alternating (3) to have a vertical bar (or any other character) printed in the outside margins of alternating pages.

4. If you chose Left (2) or Alternating (3) in the preceding step, type the character you want to use for redlining (such as |). Then press F7 (Exit).

   If you chose Printer Dependent (1), press F7 (Exit) to return to the document.

Marking Text with Redline or Strikeout

The procedures for marking text with redline and strikeout are the same, up until the last step. To mark text with redline or strikeout, follow these steps:

1. Highlight the block to be marked by using Alt F4 or F12 to activate the Block command, or by dragging the mouse.

2. Press Ctrl F8 to activate the Font command, and select Appearance (2).

   ⌨ Access the Font pull-down menu and select Appearance.

155

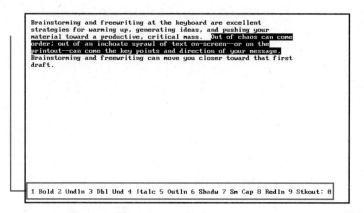

WordPerfect displays the appearance options at the bottom of the screen if you selected the commands from the keyboard.

```
Brainstorming and freewriting at the keyboard are excellent
strategies for warming up, generating ideas, and pushing your
material toward a productive, critical mass.  Out of chaos can come
order; out of an inchoate sprawl of text on-screen--or on the
printout--can come the key points and direction of your message.
Brainstorming and freewriting can move you closer toward that first
draft.
```

```
1 Bold 2 Undln 3 Dbl Und 4 Italc 5 Outln 6 Shadw 7 Sm Cap 8 Redln 9 Stkout: 0
```

3. Select Redln (8) or Stkout (9).

   ▭ Select Redline or Strikeout.

Removing Redline and Strikeout Markings

After you finish editing a document and the text is final, you can remove the redline and strikeout markings. When you remove the markings, only the redline markings are removed, not the text itself. When you remove the strikeout markings, however, you delete the actual text marked for strikeout, not just the strikeout characters. You can remove all redline and strikeout markings with one procedure. Follow these steps:

1. Press Alt F5 to activate the Mark Text command, and select Generate (6).

```
Brainstorming and freewriting at the keyboard are excellent
strategies for warming up, generating ideas, and pushing your
material toward a productive, critical mass.  Out of chaos can come
order; out of an inchoate sprawl of text on-screen--or on the
printout--can come the key points and direction of your message.
Brainstorming and freewriting can move you closer toward that first
draft.
```

The Generate (6) option appears at the bottom of the screen.

```
1 Cross-Ref; 2 Subdoc; 3 Index; 4 ToA Short Form; 5 Define; 6 Generate: 0
```

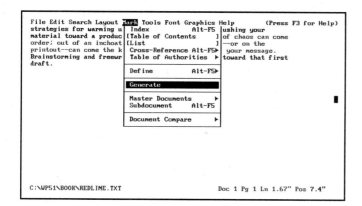

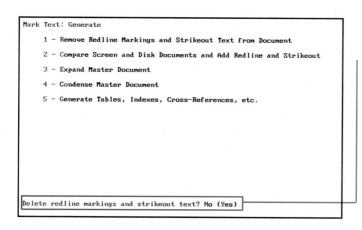

Access the **M**ark pull-down menu and select **G**enerate.

2. Select **R**emove Redline Markings and Strikeout Text from Document (**1**).

WordPerfect prompts you to indicate whether you want to remove redline markings and strikeout text.

3. Select **Y**es to confirm the deletion.

Summary

In this chapter, you learned about various formatting options for use with an entire document, or with just a page or group of pages. You learned how to change the top and bottom margins, center pages top to bottom, design headers and footers, number pages automatically, control page breaks, and mark text with the Redline and Strikeout features.

Specifically, you learned the following key information about WordPerfect:

■ WordPerfect comes with a number of form definitions for the paper size and type already defined. Some of the ready forms include standard paper, legal paper, and business envelopes.

■ To use a form definition, select Format (Shift-F8), choose **Page** (**2**), and choose **Paper Size/Type** (**7**).

■ WordPerfect is preset to leave one-inch margins at the top and bottom of the page. To change the top and bottom margins, select Format (Shift-F8), choose **Page** (**2**), and choose **Margins Top/Bottom** (**5**).

■ To center a page top to bottom—for a title page, for instance—select Format (Shift-F8), choose **Page** (**2**), and choose **Center Page (top to bottom)** (**1**).

■ Use the Advance feature to instruct the printer to move up, down, left, or right before printing. To use Advance, select Format (Shift-F8), choose **Other** (**4**), and choose **Advance** (**1**).

■ To create a header or footer, select Format (Shift-F8), choose **Page** (**2**), and choose **Headers** (**3**) or **Footers** (**4**).

■ To choose a page number position, select Format (Shift-F8), choose **Page** (**2**), choose **Page Numbering** (**6**), and choose **Page Number Position** (**4**).

■ Control where one page ends and the next one begins with automatic page breaks, hard page breaks, the Block Protect feature, the Conditional End of Page option, or the Widow/Orphan Protection option.

■ Use Redline and Strikeout as tools for marking suggested changes in a manuscript. You can specify how you want redlined text to appear, and then you can mark the text with redline and strikeout.

The next chapter introduces some of WordPerfect's utilities for checking your work.

Proofreading

WordPerfect makes two powerful tools available
every time you begin your editing tasks: Search and
Replace. If you have ever experienced the frustration of
searching, sentence-by-sentence, for a word you want to
change, you will welcome these time savers. In addition
to using the Search and Replace features, you can use
the Speller and Thesaurus to check and fine-tune your
work.

Caution: Don't rely on WordPerfect to correct all your
errors. WordPerfect finds only words that are misspelled, not words that are used incorrectly. Always give
your manuscripts a thorough check manually.

6

Key Terms in This Chapter

String	A set of characters—including codes and spaces—that WordPerfect uses in search and replace operations.
Synonym	A word with the same or nearly the same meaning as another word. You can use WordPerfect's Thesaurus to find synonyms.
Antonym	A word with the opposite or nearly opposite meaning of another word. WordPerfect's Thesaurus lists both synonyms and antonyms.
Headword	The word you look up with the Thesaurus. The headword has a collection of synonyms attached to it.

Using Search

The Search feature enables you to search for a single character, word, phrase, sentence, or code either forward or backward from the location of the cursor. A group of characters, words, or codes that you want to locate is called a *string*.

Suppose, for example, that you want to find where a particular topic, word, or phrase appears in a long document. Searching the document manually is time-consuming. But with WordPerfect's Search feature, you can find character strings, even codes, easily.

Launching a Search

You can search for text from any point in a document, and you can search in either direction—forward or backward. To search for text, follow these steps:

1. Press `F2` (Forward Search) to search from the cursor position to the end of the document.

   Or

   Press `⇧Shift` `F2` (Backward Search) to search from the cursor position to the beginning of the document.

```
Search
  Forward    F2
  Backward Shft-F2
  Next
  Previous

  Replace   Alt-F2

  Extended          ▶

  Go to     Ctrl-Home
```

Access the **S**earch pull-down menu and choose **F**orward or **B**ackward.

```
Brainstorming

When you have trouble determining a sharp focus for a document--
when you are uncertain what you want to say--consider trying a
semistructured writing exercise known as "brainstorming."

When you brainstorm a writing assignment on-screen, you record your
ideas in list form as they occur to you.  When you brainstorm, you
don't worry about typos, spelling errors, or style.  You turn off
the inclination to hone each sentence before you move on to the
next one.  You can handle those matters later.  Your goal is,
rather to generate as many ideas as possible about the topic, the
purpose, or the audience.

Keeping an Idea File

An idea file is an extension of a brainstorming file.  You can save
an idea file and retrieve it when you want to add more ideas later.

Using a Prewriting Template

Prewriting is everything you do up to the actual step of writing
that first draft.  It is very much a part of the planning stage.

-> Srch:
```

If you select Forward Search, a prompt appears at the lower left corner of the screen.

If you select Backward Search, the following prompt appears:

←Srch:

2. At the prompt, type the text string or code you want to find.

```
Brainstorming

When you have trouble determining a sharp focus for a document--
when you are uncertain what you want to say--consider trying a
semistructured writing exercise known as "brainstorming."

When you brainstorm a writing assignment on-screen, you record your
ideas in list form as they occur to you.  When you brainstorm, you
don't worry about typos, spelling errors, or style.  You turn off
the inclination to hone each sentence before you move on to the
next one.  You can handle those matters later.  Your goal is,
rather to generate as many ideas as possible about the topic, the
purpose, or the audience.

Keeping an Idea File

An idea file is an extension of a brainstorming file.  You can save
an idea file and retrieve it when you want to add more ideas later.

Using a Prewriting Template

Prewriting is everything you do up to the actual step of writing
that first draft.  It is very much a part of the planning stage.

-> Srch: prewriting
```

You can type as many as 60 characters in the string.

6

3. To begin the search, press ⟦F2⟧ (Forward Search) again or press ⟦Esc⟧.

   At this point, pressing ⟦F2⟧ works for both Forward Search and Backward Search.

   ⟦🖱⟧ Press the right mouse button or double-click the left button to begin the search.

When Word-Perfect finds the first occurrence of the search string, the search stops. You then can edit and move around in the document.

```
don't worry about typos, spelling errors, or style.  You turn off
the inclination to hone each sentence before you move on to the
next one.  You can handle those matters later.  Your goal is,
rather to generate as many ideas as possible about the topic, the
purpose, or the audience.

Keeping an Idea File

An idea file is an extension of a brainstorming file.  You can save
an idea file and retrieve it when you want to add more ideas later.

Using a Prewriting Template

Prewriting is everything you do up to the actual step of writing
that first draft.  It is very much a part of the planning stage.

A prewriting template is a set of prompts that force you to answer
some basic questions before you begin your document.  As you plan
the document, you may find it helpful to use a prewriting template
to refine your thinking about a particular writing task.  You can
ask the basic reporter's questions of "Who?" "What?" "Where?" "Why"
and "When?"

C:\WP51\BOOK\BRAIN.TXT                         Doc 1 Pg 1 Ln 4.17" Pos 2.8"
```

If you want to continue the search, press Forward Search (F2) again. You don't need to retype the text string or code because WordPerfect remembers your last search request. Press Forward Search (F2) or Esc again to find the next occurrence of the text string or code. If you use a mouse, repeat the search by accessing the **S**earch pull-down menu and choosing **N**ext or **P**revious.

If WordPerfect can't find the search string, a * Not found * message is displayed.

To return the cursor to its location before the search, press GoTo (Ctrl-Home) twice.

Guidelines for Defining a Search String

To use the Search feature effectively, you need to know how WordPerfect interprets a string. Here are the primary rules that WordPerfect follows:

- If you type a string in lowercase, WordPerfect looks for either upper- or lowercase characters. If, for example, you ask the program to find *search*, WordPerfect stops at *search*, *Search*, and *SEARCH*. But if you ask the program to find *Search*, WordPerfect stops at only *Search* and *SEARCH*.

- Be careful how you enter a search string. If you enter the string **the**, for example, WordPerfect matches the string to every occurrence of the word *the* as well as to words that contain the string, such as *anesthesia*. To locate only the word *the*, enter a space before and after the word: *<space>***the***<space>*.

- If you think that the string you're looking for might be in a header, a footer, a footnote, an endnote, a graphics box caption, or a text box, you must perform an *extended search*. This search is the same as a regular search except that you must press Home and then Forward Search (F2) for an extended forward search, or Home and then Backward Search (Shift-F2) for an extended backward search. You also can perform an extended search by selecting the **E**xtended option on the **S**earch pull-down menu.

- If you need to find a hidden code, such as a margin setting, use the normal search procedure, but when the search prompt appears, press the function key or key combination that creates the hidden code. When the hidden code is found, use Reveal Codes to view the code and perform any editing.

- When searching for paired codes, you can insert an ending code at the search (or replace) prompt by pressing the corresponding function key or key combination twice—for example, you can press Bold (F6) once to insert a **[BOLD]** code, or twice to insert a **[bold]** code. To remove the **[BOLD]** code, press the left-arrow key and then press the Backspace key to leave only the **[bold]** code in the search string.

- If you are searching for text that includes an element that changes from one occurrence to the next—for example, (1), (2), and (3)—or if you are uncertain about the correct spelling of a word, use the matching character ^X (press Ctrl-V and then Ctrl-X). This wild card character matches any single character within a character string. If you enter (^X) at the →Srch: prompt, the cursor stops at (1), (2), (3), and so on. When you are uncertain about the spelling, use ^X in the string. If, for example, you enter **c**^**Xt** at the →Srch: prompt, the cursor stops at such words as *cat, CAT, Cat, cot, cattle,* and *cutting.* Be as specific about the character string as you can.

- To find a word at the end of a paragraph, type the word at the search prompt, along with any following punctuation, and then press Enter to insert a hard return code (**[HRt]**). For example, type **Einstein**, press the period key (.), and press Enter. The search finds only occurrences of *Einstein* that are followed by a period and a hard return.

6

- At the search prompt, you can change the direction of the search with the up- or down-arrow key. Enter the search string, press the up- or down-arrow key, and then press Forward Search (F2) or Esc to begin the search.

- A common mistake is to press Enter instead of Forward Search (F2) or Esc to start the search. Pressing Enter inserts a **[HRt]** code in the search string, which may not be what you want.

Using Replace

WordPerfect's Replace feature automatically finds every occurrence of a string or code and replaces it with another string or code. You also can use the Replace feature to remove a string or code completely. For instance, if you complete a long sales report, and then need to remove all the boldfacing, you can use a replace operation to find all occurrences of the code and replace them with nothing.

Replacing a String

Sometimes you may want to replace the text that you find with different text. To replace a string, follow these steps:

1. Press [Alt] [F2] to activate the Replace command.

   ⌨ Access the **S**earch pull-down menu and select **R**eplace.

WordPerfect displays a confirmation prompt.

```
Brainstorming

When you have trouble determining a sharp focus for a document--
when you are uncertain what you want to say--consider trying a
semistructured writing exercise known as "brainstorming."

When you brainstorm a writing assignment on-screen, you record your
ideas in list form as they occur to you.  When you brainstorm, you
don't worry about typos, spelling errors, or style.  You turn off
the inclination to hone each sentence before you move on to the
next one.  You can handle those matters later.  Your goal is,
rather to generate as many ideas as possible about the topic, the
purpose, or the audience.

Keeping an Idea File

An idea file is an extension of a brainstorming file.  You can save
an idea file and retrieve it when you want to add more ideas later.

Using a Prewriting Template

Prewriting is everything you do up to the actual step of writing
that first draft.  It is very much a part of the planning stage.

w/Confirm? No (Yes)
```

2. Select **Yes** if you want to approve each replacement separately. Select **No** or press ⏎Enter if you want all occurrences replaced without confirming them.

3. At the →Srch: prompt, type your search string.

```
Brainstorming

When you have trouble determining a sharp focus for a document--
when you are uncertain what you want to say--consider trying a
semistructured writing exercise known as "brainstorming."

When you brainstorm a writing assignment on-screen, you record your
ideas in list form as they occur to you.  When you brainstorm, you
don't worry about typos, spelling errors, or style.  You turn off
the inclination to hone each sentence before you move on to the
next one.  You can handle those matters later.  Your goal is,
rather to generate as many ideas as possible about the topic, the
purpose, or the audience.

Keeping an Idea File

An idea file is an extension of a brainstorming file.  You can save
an idea file and retrieve it when you want to add more ideas later.

Using a Prewriting Template

Prewriting is everything you do up to the actual step of writing
that first draft.  It is very much a part of the planning stage.

-> Srch: pre[-]writing
```

The search string can contain up to 60 characters.

4. Press F2 (Forward Search) or Esc.

   ⌧ Press the right mouse button or double-click the left button.

5. At the Replace with: prompt, type the replacement string.

```
Brainstorming

When you have trouble determining a sharp focus for a document--
when you are uncertain what you want to say--consider trying a
semistructured writing exercise known as "brainstorming."

When you brainstorm a writing assignment on-screen, you record your
ideas in list form as they occur to you.  When you brainstorm, you
don't worry about typos, spelling errors, or style.  You turn off
the inclination to hone each sentence before you move on to the
next one.  You can handle those matters later.  Your goal is,
rather to generate as many ideas as possible about the topic, the
purpose, or the audience.

Keeping an Idea File

An idea file is an extension of a brainstorming file.  You can save
an idea file and retrieve it when you want to add more ideas later.

Using a Prewriting Template

Prewriting is everything you do up to the actual step of writing
that first draft.  It is very much a part of the planning stage.

Replace with: prewriting
```

If you want the search string deleted and not replaced with anything, don't enter anything in response to this prompt.

6. Press F2 (Forward Search) or Esc to begin the search.

   ⌧ Press the right mouse button or double-click the left button to continue the search operation.

   If you selected **No** at the w/Confirm? No (Yes) prompt in Step 2, WordPerfect replaces all occurrences automatically. If you selected **Yes**

6

at that prompt, the cursor stops at each occurrence of the search string, and WordPerfect displays the prompt `Confirm? No (Yes)`.

7. If you are prompted, select Yes to replace the string or No if you don't want to replace it. If you want to cancel the replace operation, press F1 (Cancel) or F7 (Exit); otherwise, WordPerfect continues to search the document.

   📧   Click the right mouse button to reject the change, or click the left button on Yes or No.

When all the occurrences have been found, the operation stops.

To return the cursor to its location before the replace operation, press GoTo (Ctrl-Home) twice.

Replacing Hidden Codes

You can use the Replace feature to replace hidden codes for any commands accessed through the function keys. You cannot use pull-down menus to enter replace codes.

To replace hidden codes, follow these steps:

1. Press Alt F2 to activate the Replace command.

   📧   Access the Search pull-down menu and select Replace.

2. At the prompt, select Yes if you want to confirm each replacement, or select No if you want all occurrences replaced automatically.

3. At the →Srch: prompt, press the function key or key combination that activates the desired command.

For example, to search for the bold codes, press F6 (Bold).

```
Brainstorming

When you have trouble determining a sharp focus for a document—
when you are uncertain what you want to say—consider trying a
semistructured writing exercise known as "brainstorming."

When you brainstorm a writing assignment on-screen, you record your
ideas in list form as they occur to you. When you brainstorm, you
don't worry about typos, spelling errors, or style. You turn off
the inclination to hone each sentence before you move on to the
next one. You can handle those matters later. Your goal is,
rather to generate as many ideas as possible about the topic, the
purpose, or the audience.

Keeping an Idea File

An idea file is an extension of a brainstorming file. You can save
an idea file and retrieve it when you want to add more ideas later.

Using a Prewriting Template

Prewriting is everything you do up to the actual step of writing
that first draft. It is very much a part of the planning stage.

-> Srch: [BOLD]
```

If the command accessed with a function key or key combination leads to a submenu, WordPerfect displays a list of menu items for entry into the search string. Press the number or letter of the menu item that represents the hidden code you want to replace. WordPerfect enters the appropriate code into the search string.

4. At the `Replace with:` prompt, type the replacement string and press ⏎Enter. Or, to delete the hidden code and replace it with nothing, don't enter anything in response to this prompt.

5. To begin the replace operation, press F2 (Forward Search) or Esc.

   ⌨ Press the right mouse button or double-click the left button to begin the replace operation.

Guidelines for Using Replace

To use the Replace feature effectively, you need to keep in mind the following basic guidelines:

- WordPerfect doesn't allow you to search for codes with specific settings, such as **[Margin Set:1,65]**, but you can find all occurrences of the command code **[Margin Set]**.

- To limit a replace operation to a specific section of a document, first define the text with the Block command, and then proceed with the replace operation.

- Use the Replace feature to enter a string of text that occurs frequently in a document. You might, for example, enter a backslash (\) wherever you want *methyl ethyl chloride* to appear. When you finish typing, replace the backslash with the chemical term.

- WordPerfect's Replace feature doesn't replace text in headers, footers, footnotes, endnotes, graphics box captions, or text boxes. To replace a character or string of characters in these locations, you must use an *extended replace* operation. The procedure is the same as for a replace operation, except that you initiate an extended replace operation by pressing first Home and then Replace (Alt-F2). You also can perform an extended replace operation by selecting the Extended option on the Search pull-down menu.

6

Using the Speller

WordPerfect's Speller contains a list of more than 115,000 words. You can use the Speller to search for spelling mistakes and common typing errors, such as transposed, missing, extra, or wrong letters—even typing errors, such as double words (*the the*) or irregular capitalization (*BOston* or *bOSTON*). You also can use the Speller when you know what a word sounds like but are unsure of its spelling. WordPerfect's Speller will check a single word, a page, a block of text, or an entire document.

The Speller compares each word in the document with the words in WordPerfect's dictionary. This dictionary contains a file that lists common words (words most frequently used) and main words (words generally found in dictionaries). WordPerfect checks every word against its list of common words, and if the program doesn't find the word there, WordPerfect looks in its dictionary of main words. If you have created a supplemental dictionary, the program looks there as well. Words found in any of the dictionaries are considered correct.

If your computer uses 3 1/2-inch disks, the Speller and Thesaurus files are stored on a single Speller/Thesaurus disk. If your computer uses 5 1/4-inch disks, the Speller and Thesaurus files are stored on two disks.

The main dictionary file, WP{WP}US.LEX, contains the main and common word lists. When you run the Speller for the first time and add words to the dictionary, a supplemental dictionary file, WP{WP}US.SUP, is created. You can use the Speller Utility, SPELL.EXE, to make changes to the main dictionary and to create or make changes to a supplemental dictionary.

If WordPerfect is loaded on a hard disk, the Speller files are immediately available. The standard installation procedure puts the Speller files in the C:\WP51 directory.

Before you use the Speller on a dual floppy disk system, remove the data disk from drive B and insert your copy of the Speller disk. (Do not remove the WordPerfect Program disk from drive A.) When you are finished checking spelling, put your data disk back into drive B and save the document.

Checking a Word, Page, or Document

You can check a word, a page, or an entire document. To check a word, page, or document, follow these steps:

1. Position the cursor anywhere in the word or page. When you check an entire document, the position of the cursor doesn't matter.

2. Press Ctrl F2 to activate the Spell command.

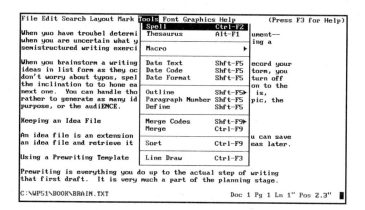

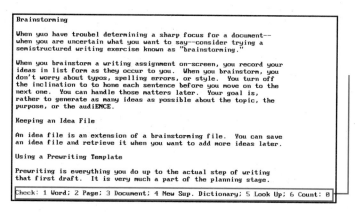

Access the Tools pull-down menu and choose Spell.

The Spell menu appears at the bottom of the screen.

3. Select the menu option you want.

The following options are available on the Spell menu:

- Choose **Word (1)** to check the word on which the cursor is located. If WordPerfect finds the word in its dictionaries, the cursor moves to the next word, and the Spell menu remains displayed. You can continue checking word-by-word or select another option from the Spell menu. If the word isn't found, WordPerfect offers alternative spellings.

- Choose **Page (2)** to check every word on the page. After the page is checked, the Spell menu remains displayed. Continue checking pages or select another option.

- Choose **Document** (**3**) to check every word in the document.

- Select **New Sup. Dictionary** (**4**), type the name of the supplemental dictionary you want to use, and press Enter. Generally, you create supplemental dictionaries to contain words pertaining to specialized or technical areas, such as medicine, law, or science.

- Choose **Look Up** (**5**) and at the prompt `Word or word pattern:`, type your "rough guess" of the word's spelling and then press Enter. You can type a word pattern that includes an asterisk (*) to represent several unknown letters, or a question mark (?) to represent a single unknown letter. WordPerfect offers a list of words that fit the pattern.

- Select **Count** (**6**) to count the number of words in the document. Note that after a spelling check, the number of words is displayed automatically.

When the Speller finds a word not in its dictionary, the Speller stops, highlights the word, usually provides a list of alternative spellings, and displays the Not Found menu.

Selecting from the Alternatives List

To select a word from the alternatives list, first look for the correct spelling from the list.

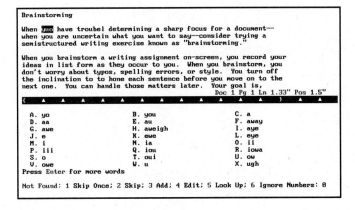

If you do not see the correct spelling and WordPerfect prompts you to `Press Enter for more words`, press Enter. When the correct spelling appears, type the letter next to the alternative you want to select.

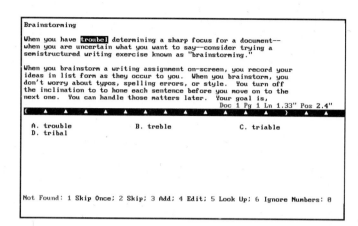

```
Brainstorming

When you have trouble determining a sharp focus for a document--
when you are uncertain what you want to say--consider trying a
semistructured writing exercise known as "brainstorming."

When you brainstorm a writing assignment on-screen, you record your
ideas in list form as they occur to you.  When you brainstorm, you
don't worry about typos, spelling errors, or style.  You turn off
the inclination to to hone each sentence before you move on to the
next one.  You can handle those matters later.  Your goal is,
                                        Doc 1 Pg 1 Ln 1.33" Pos 2.4"

   A. trouble            B. treble            C. triable
   D. tribal

Not Found: 1 Skip Once; 2 Skip; 3 Add; 4 Edit; 5 Look Up; 6 Ignore Numbers: 0
```

After you correct the word, the Speller continues checking the rest of the document.

Selecting Other Speller Options

Many correctly spelled words do not appear in WordPerfect's dictionary. Even though it contains 115,000 words, some words must be omitted. If the correct spelling is not displayed, you can choose from the options on the Not Found menu:

- Select Skip Once (**1**) to have the Speller ignore the word once but stop at every occurrence of the word thereafter. This option permits you to verify your spelling of the word; verification is a good idea if the word is a difficult technical term.

- Choose Skip (**2**) to skip all occurrences of what you know to be a correctly spelled word.

- Select Add (**3**) to add a frequently used word to your supplemental dictionary. WordPerfect stores the word in memory and ignores all future occurrences. At the end of the check, all words added are saved to the current supplemental dictionary.

- Select Edit (**4**) when the correct alternative is not offered and when you know that the spelling is incorrect. You must make the correction yourself. When you select Edit, the cursor moves to the word in question. Make the correction with the right- and left-arrow keys. Press Exit (F7) to continue the spelling check.

- Select Look Up (**5**) to look up a word. WordPerfect prompts you to enter a word or word pattern. Type your rough guess and press Enter. WordPerfect then displays all the possible matches. You can choose one of the alternative words. If you don't find the correct spelling, press Cancel (F1) twice; then select Edit (**4**) and enter the correction manually.

6

171

- Choose Ignore Numbers (**6**) if you want WordPerfect to ignore all words that contain numbers (such as RX7 or LPT1:).

Finding Double Words

In addition to identifying misspelled words, the Speller finds double words, such as *the the*.

When the Speller encounters a double word, the program doesn't offer alternatives. Instead, WordPerfect displays a differ-ent menu.

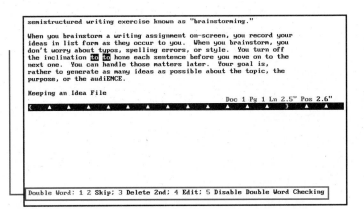

You can choose from these options:

- Select Skip (**1** or **2**) if the double word is legitimate.
- Select Delete 2nd (**3**) if you accidentally typed two words instead of one. The second word is deleted.
- Select Edit (**4**) and make the appropriate correction if one of the words is a typographical error.
- Select Disable Double Word Checking (**5**) if the document contains many legitimate double words and you are certain of your proofread-ing skill.

Correcting Irregular Case

The Speller checks also for some common errors in capitalization. For ex-ample, the Speller stops at words with irregular case and enables you to replace each word with the Speller's guess about the correct case or to edit the word. For instance, *cAse* is changed to *Case*, *CAse* to *Case*, *cASE* to *CASE*, and *caSE* or *caSe* to *case*.

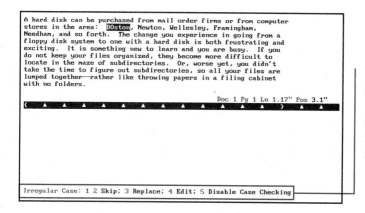

```
A hard disk can be purchased from mail order firms or from computer
stores in the area:  BOston, Newton, Wellesley, Framingham,
Needham, and so forth.  The change you experience in going from a
floppy disk system to one with a hard disk is both frustrating and
exciting.  It is something new to learn and you are busy.  If you
do not keep your files organized, they become more difficult to
locate in the maze of subdirectories.  Or, worse yet, you didn't
take the time to figure out subdirectories, so all your files are
lumped together--rather like throwing papers in a filing cabinet
with no folders.

                                  Doc 1 Pg 1 Ln 1.17" Pos 3.1"
```

```
Irregular Case: 1 2 Skip; 3 Replace; 4 Edit; 5 Disable Case Checking
```

The program stops at the word BOston and displays the Irregular Case menu.

If the unusual capitalization is actually correct for the word, select Skip (**1** or **2**). If you have many words with odd case selections, you may instead want to select Disable Case Checking (**5**). You can select Replace (**3**) to have the case for the word corrected. Note, however, that the Speller does not show you how it will correct the word. If you are not sure how the word will be corrected, select Edit (**4**) instead and correct the word yourself.

Checking a Block

To check the spelling of a block, follow these steps:

1. Highlight the block by using Alt F4 or F12 to activate the Block command, or by dragging the mouse.
2. Press Ctrl F2 to activate the Spell command.

    🖱 Access the Tools pull-down menu and choose Spell.

When you check a block, you skip the Spell menu because you have already told WordPerfect how much of the document you plan to check. Otherwise, the Speller operates as usual.

Using the Thesaurus

The Thesaurus is similar to the Speller except that the Thesaurus lists alternative word choices instead of alternative spellings. The Thesaurus displays synonyms (words with the same or nearly the same meanings) and antonyms (words with opposite or nearly opposite meanings) for the selected word. The Thesaurus only lists these words; you must decide which one best fits your meaning.

Displaying Synonyms and Antonyms

If you are using a hard disk system, the Thesaurus files are immediately available. WordPerfect's standard installation procedure puts those files in the C:\WP51 directory.

Before you use the Thesaurus on a dual floppy system, you must remove the data disk from drive B and insert the Thesaurus disk. The WordPerfect Program disk must remain in drive A. You then can start the Thesaurus. When you finish using the Thesaurus, you must remove the Thesaurus disk, replace it with your data disk, and save the document.

To use the Thesaurus, follow these steps:

1. Place the cursor anywhere in the word you want to look up.

2. Press Alt F1 to activate the Thesaurus command.

Access the Tools pull-down menu and select Thesaurus.

```
Tools
 Spell             Ctrl-F2
 Thesaurus         Alt-F1

 Macro                   ▶

 Date Text         Shft-F5
 Date Code         Shft-F5
 Date Format       Shft-F5

 Outline           Shft-F5▶
 Paragraph Number  Shft-F5
 Define            Shft-F5

 Merge Codes       Shft-F9▶
 Merge             Ctrl-F9

 Sort              Ctrl-F9

 Line Draw         Ctrl-F3
```

The word you look up is called the *headword* because it has a body of similar words attached to it. The headword appears at the top of the column. Synonyms and antonyms for the headword are noted also. Words are divided into numbered groups and parts of speech. The column of letters to the left of the words is called the Reference menu. Remember that words marked with a bullet are headwords too; you can look up any of these words.

If the columns are empty and the Word: appears at the bottom of the screen, either the cursor was not placed within the word, or the Thesaurus cannot find the word you want to look up. In either case, type the word you want to look up at the Word: prompt, and then press Enter.

Headword   Antonyms   Reference menu

Part of speech

Thesaurus menu

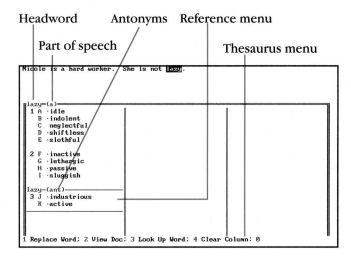

The word is highlighted, and the screen is split. The document text is displayed at the top; the Thesaurus menu and word list (in columns) are displayed at the bottom.

6

Selecting More Words

If you don't see a word that is exactly right or if you want to try other words, you can expand the word list. You can display more alternatives for any headword—a word with a bullet next to it.

Choose the headword that is close to the meaning of the word in question, and press the letter next to that word.

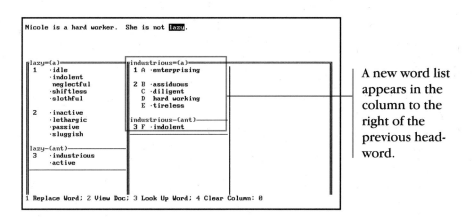

A new word list appears in the column to the right of the previous headword.

Use the right- or left-arrow key to move the letter choices to other columns.

175

Using the Thesaurus Menu

With the Thesaurus menu displayed, you can select from the following options:

- Select Replace Word (**1**) to replace the highlighted word. At the prompt `Press letter for word`, type the letter (from the Reference menu) that corresponds to the replacement word. The Thesaurus menu disappears, and the program inserts the word you selected into the text.

- Select View Doc (**2**) if you are unsure of a word's exact meaning in the context of your writing. The cursor moves back to the document, and you can use the cursor keys to move around and view the surrounding text. Press Exit (F7) to return to the Thesaurus menu.

- Select Look Up Word (**3**) to look up other words that come to mind. At the `Word:` prompt, type the word you want to look up. If the word is a headword, the Thesaurus displays the word with all its subgroups of synonyms and antonyms. If the word is not a headword, WordPerfect either looks up another similar word or displays the message `Word not found`.

- Select Clear Column (**4**) if you want WordPerfect to clear a column and make room for additional word columns.

Summary

This chapter introduced you to WordPerfect's features for checking a document. You learned how to use the Search feature to search for a string—a single character, word, phrase, sentence, code, or combination of these. You learned also how to use the Replace feature to replace a string with another string. You then explored the many options available through WordPerfect's Speller and Thesaurus.

Specifically, you learned the following information about WordPerfect:

- ■ The Search feature enables you to search for a string—which can be a single character, word, phrase, sentence, or code.

- ■ To search for text, select Forward Search (F2) or Backward Search (Shift-F2), type the string or code you want to find, and press Forward Search (F2) or Esc.

- ■ WordPerfect's Replace feature automatically finds every occurrence of a string or code and replaces it with another string or code.

■ To replace a string, select Replace (Alt-F2). Then select **Yes** if you want to approve each replacement or **No** if you want to make all the replacements without confirmation. Next, type the search string and press Forward Search (F2); and type the replacement string and press Forward Search (F2).

■ Use WordPerfect's Speller to check for spelling mistakes, typing errors, double words, and irregular capitalization. The Speller will check a single word, a page, a block of text, or an entire document.

■ To spell check a word, page, or document, use the Spell (Ctrl-F2) command.

■ WordPerfect's Thesaurus lists alternative word choices—displaying both synonyms and antonyms.

■ Select the Thesaurus (Alt-F1) command to access WordPerfect's Thesaurus.

The next chapter discusses WordPerfect's printing features.

6

Printing

7

You can install many printers at a time and select from among them for particular print jobs. This chapter shows you not only how to select your printer but also how to designate the many printing specifications, such as binding width, number of copies, and print quality.

You can print directly from the screen all or part of the document that currently appears. You can print all or part of a document you have previously saved to disk. WordPerfect can keep track of multiple print jobs and print them in the order you specify. If you suddenly have a rush job, you can interrupt the printing and bump the job to first place in the printing queue. Before you print, you can use WordPerfect's View Document feature to preview how the printed document will look and to avoid wasting time and paper.

Before you can select a printer for use, you must install the printer definition—tell WordPerfect the kind of equipment you have. You can have any number of printer definitions available at one time. Instructions on installing a printer definition are provided in Appendix A.

If you have a laser printer, you may want to refer to Appendix A for instructions on using font cartridges and soft (downloadable) fonts. With WordPerfect 5.1, you can take advantage of a variety of available fonts.

> ## Key Terms in This Chapter
>
> *Print queue*   An internal list of jobs to be printed.
>
> *Binding width*   The extra space added to the inside edge of each page when a document is printed on both sides. Setting a binding width shifts odd-numbered pages to the right and even-numbered pages to the left by the specified amount.

Selecting a Printer

After you have installed the printer definition for the printer you want to use (see Appendix A), you are ready to select it. To select a printer, follow these steps:

1. Press ⇧Shift F7 to activate the Print command.

   ⌨ Access the **File** pull-down menu and select **Print**.

WordPerfect displays the Print menu.

```
Print

    1 - Full Document
    2 - Page
    3 - Document on Disk
    4 - Control Printer
    5 - Multiple Pages
    6 - View Document
    7 - Initialize Printer

Options

    S - Select Printer
    B - Binding Offset              0"
    N - Number of Copies            1
    U - Multiple Copies Generated by   WordPerfect
    G - Graphics Quality            Medium
    T - Text Quality                High



Selection: 0
```

2. Choose **Select Printer** (**S**).

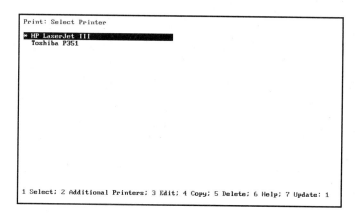

```
Print: Select Printer
► HP LaserJet III
  Toshiba P351




1 Select; 2 Additional Printers; 3 Edit; 4 Copy; 5 Delete; 6 Help; 7 Update: 1
```

WordPerfect displays the Print: Select Printer screen.

3. Move the highlight bar to the name of your printer, and then press ⏎Enter or choose Select (1) to make it the active printer.

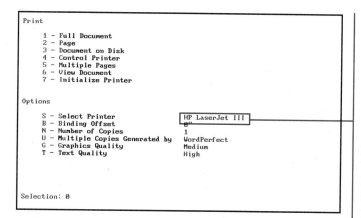

```
Print

    1 - Full Document
    2 - Page
    3 - Document on Disk
    4 - Control Printer
    5 - Multiple Pages
    6 - View Document
    7 - Initialize Printer

Options

    S - Select Printer          HP LaserJet III
    B - Binding Offset          0"
    N - Number of Copies        1
    U - Multiple Copies Generated by   WordPerfect
    G - Graphics Quality        Medium
    T - Text Quality            High


Selection: 0
```

WordPerfect returns to the main Print menu, which has been updated to show the printer you chose as the active one. Any print operation will use this printer until you select a different printer.

7

4. Press ⏎Enter to return to the document.

Note: You can select any printer you have installed. The documents you then create will be formatted for the selected printer. However, make sure that when you actually print, the selected printer is the one attached to your computer. Otherwise, you will get unpredictable printed results.

Printing the Test Document

Before you begin to print documents, you may want to test the printer definition you have just selected so that you can see what features your printer supports. For this purpose, WordPerfect includes a file named PRINTER.TST, which is installed with the WordPerfect Program files.

To print the test document, complete the following steps:

1. Retrieve the file PRINTER.TST to the screen by pressing ⇧Shift F10 to activate the Retrieve command, typing the file name **PRINTER.TST**, and pressing ↵Enter.

    ▱ Access the **F**ile pull-down menu, select **R**etrieve, type the file name **PRINTER.TST**, and press ↵Enter.

2. Press ⇧Shift F7 to activate the Print command. From the Print menu, select **F**ull Document (**1**).

    ▱ Access the **F**ile pull-down menu, choose **P**rint, and select **F**ull Document (**1**).

The test document is printed on the selected printer. Features that do not print properly are not supported by your printer.

Printing from the Screen

Printing a document from the screen is quicker than printing a document from disk—especially if the document is short. From the screen, you can print an entire document, a single page, selected pages, or a block of text.

Printing an Entire Document

To print an entire document from the screen, follow these steps:

1. Display the document.
2. Press ⇧Shift F7 to activate the Print command.

    ▱ Access the **F**ile pull-down menu and choose **P**rint.

3. Select **F**ull Document (**1**).

Printing a Single Page

To print a single page from a document on-screen, follow these steps:

1. Display the document and position the cursor anywhere within the page you want to print.
2. Press ⬆Shift F7 to activate the Print command.

   ⌨ Access the File pull-down menu and choose Print.
3. Select Page (2).

If the page you have selected doesn't appear near the beginning of the document, you may notice a short pause before the page prints. WordPerfect scans the document for the last format settings (such as margins and tabs) before printing the page.

Printing Selected Pages

To print selected pages from a document on-screen, follow these steps:

1. Display the document.
2. Press ⬆Shift F7 to activate the Print command.

   ⌨ Access the File pull-down menu and choose Print.
3. Select Multiple Pages (5). The Page(s): prompt appears.
4. Type the pages you want to print, and then press ↵Enter.

   Type the page numbers according to the following examples:

Example	Page(s) Selected for Printing
5	Page 5 only
2,25	Pages 2 and 25 only
3-	Pages 3 through the end of the document
1-10	Pages 1 through 10
-3	Pages from the beginning of the document through page 3

7

Printing a Block

Sometimes you may want to print only a single sentence, a paragraph, a page and a half, or five pages from a larger document. You can use WordPerfect's Block feature to specify what text you want to print.

To print a block of text from the screen, follow these steps:

1. Highlight the block by using [Alt][F4] or [F12] to activate the Block command, or by dragging the mouse.

2. Press [⇧Shift][F7] to activate the Print command.

   🖱 Access the File pull-down menu and choose Print.

WordPerfect prompts you for confirmation.

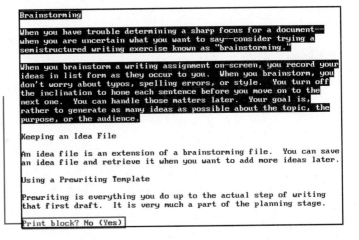

3. Select Yes to print the block.

Adding a Print Job to the Queue

You can continue working on the document (or another document) while you print. If you finish working on a second document before the first document has finished printing, you can print the second file just as you did the first. WordPerfect adds the print job to the queue.

Making a Screen Print

When you need a quick printout of whatever appears on-screen (for instance, a hard copy of a WordPerfect Help screen), you can press Print Screen (on an

Enhanced Keyboard) or Shift-PrtSc (on a PC keyboard). The printout will not show formatting codes, but it will include the information that appears on the status line.

Printing from Disk

With WordPerfect, you can print a document from disk without displaying the document on-screen. You can print from either the Print menu or the List Files screen. With both methods, you can specify which pages to print.

Note: If you want to reduce your printing time, you can turn off the Fast Save feature from the Setup: Environment menu. The Fast Save feature, which usually is turned on, enables WordPerfect to save a file quickly by storing an unformatted version of the file. At print time, however, WordPerfect must construct and format a temporary file before sending the job to the printer. For more information about customizing WordPerfect, see Chapter 15.

Printing from the Print Menu

When you print from the Print menu, you must know the complete file name before starting the operation. You cannot use the List Files screen to look up the file after you have pressed Print (Shift-F7).

To use the Print menu to print a document from disk, follow these steps:

1. Press ⌂Shift F7 to activate the Print command.

   ⌨ Access the File pull-down menu and choose Print.

2. From the Print menu, select Document on Disk (3).

3. Type the file name and press ↵Enter. (**Note:** If the document is stored in a directory other than the current directory, you must type the drive, path name, and directory name.)

   The prompt Page(s): (All) is displayed on the status line.

4. If you want to print the entire document, press ↵Enter. If you want to print particular pages only, type the pages you want to print, and then press ↵Enter.

   Type the page numbers according to the examples given in the earlier section "Printing Selected Pages."

WordPerfect reads the file from disk, creates a print job, and adds the document to the print queue.

Printing from the List Files Screen

In addition to printing from the Print menu, you can print from the List Files screen. Printing from this screen has two advantages: you don't need to remember the name of the file you want to print, and you can mark any number of files to print. The files are printed in the order in which they appear on the List Files screen.

To use the List Files screen to print a document from disk, follow these steps:

1. Press F5 to activate the List command.

   Access the File pull-down menu and choose List Files.

2. If the file resides in the current drive and directory, press ↵Enter. If the file is in a different directory, type the drive, path name, and directory name; then press ↵Enter.

   WordPerfect displays the List Files screen.

3. Use the cursor keys to highlight the name of the file you want to print.

   Or

   Select Name Search (N) and begin typing the file name. When the file you want is highlighted, press ↵Enter.

The Print (4) option is available from the menu at the bottom of the screen.

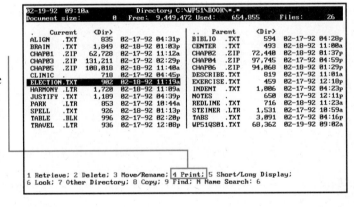

```
02-19-92  09:10a           Directory C:\WP51\BOOK\*.*
Document size:        0    Free: 9,449,472 Used:     654,855    Files:      26

.     Current  <Dir>                  ..    Parent   <Dir>
ALIGN    .TXT       835  02-17-92 04:31p   BIBLIO   .TXT       594  02-17-92 04:28p
BRAIN    .TXT     1,049  02-18-92 01:03p   CENTER   .TXT       493  02-18-92 11:00a
CHAP01   .ZIP    62,728  02-17-92 11:12a   CHAP02   .ZIP    72,440  02-18-92 01:37p
CHAP03   .ZIP   131,211  02-17-92 02:29p   CHAP04   .ZIP    97,745  02-17-92 04:59p
CHAP05   .ZIP   100,018  02-18-92 11:40a   CHAP06   .ZIP    94,868  02-18-92 01:29p
CLINIC   .          718  02-17-92 04:45p   DESCRIBE .TXT       819  02-17-92 11:01a
ELECTION .TXT       902  02-18-92 11:19a   EXERCISE .TXT       459  02-17-92 12:18p
HARMONY  .LTR     1,720  02-18-92 11:09a   INDENT   .TXT     1,006  02-17-92 04:23p
JUSTIFY  .TXT     1,189  02-17-92 04:39p   NOTES    .          650  02-17-92 12:11p
PARK     .LTR       853  02-17-92 10:44a   REDLINE  .TXT       716  02-18-92 11:23a
SPELL    .TXT       926  02-18-92 01:13p   STEINER  .LTR     1,531  02-17-92 10:59a
TABLE    .BLK       996  02-17-92 02:20p   TABS     .TXT     3,091  02-19-92 04:16p
TRAVEL   .LTR       936  02-17-92 12:08p   WP51QS01 .TXT    68,362  02-19-92 09:02a




1 Retrieve; 2 Delete; 3 Move/Rename; 4 Print; 5 Short/Long Display;
6 Look; 7 Other Directory; 8 Copy; 9 Find; N Name Search: 6
```

4. Select Print (4).

5. At the prompt Page(s): (All), press ↵Enter to print the entire document; or type the pages you want to print, and then press ↵Enter.

Marking Files To Print

From the List Files screen, you can mark several files to print. To mark each file, use the cursor keys to highlight the name of the file, and then press the asterisk (*) key. Or you can press Home and then press the asterisk (*) key to mark all the files on the List Files screen.

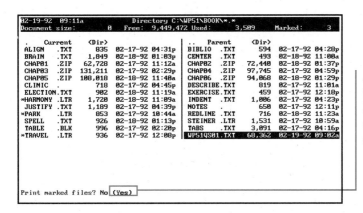

```
02-19-92  09:11a              Directory C:\WP51\BOOK\*.*
Document size:        0   Free: 9,449,472 Used:      3,509   Marked:      3

     .  Current     <Dir>              ..   Parent     <Dir>
    ALIGN   .TXT       835  02-17-92 04:31p  BIBLIO  .TXT      594  02-17-92 04:28p
    BRAIN   .TXT     1,849  02-18-92 01:03p  CENTER  .TXT      493  02-18-92 11:00a
    CHAP01  .ZIP    62,728  02-17-92 11:12a  CHAP02  .ZIP   72,440  02-18-92 01:37p
    CHAP03  .ZIP   131,211  02-17-92 02:29p  CHAP04  .ZIP   97,745  02-17-92 04:59p
    CHAP05  .ZIP   100,018  02-18-92 11:40a  CHAP06  .ZIP   94,068  02-18-92 01:29p
    CLINIC  .          718  02-17-92 04:45p  DESCRIBE.TXT      819  02-17-92 11:01a
    ELECTION.TXT       902  02-18-92 11:19a  EXERCISE.TXT      459  02-17-92 12:18p
   *HARMONY .LTR     1,720  02-18-92 11:09a  INDENT  .TXT    1,006  02-17-92 04:23p
    JUSTIFY .TXT     1,189  02-17-92 04:39p  NOTES   .         650  02-17-92 12:11p
   *PARK    .LTR       853  02-17-92 10:44a  REDLINE .TXT      716  02-18-92 11:23a
    SPELL   .TXT       926  02-18-92 01:13p  STEINER .LTR    1,531  02-17-92 10:59a
    TABLE   .BLK       996  02-17-92 02:20p  TABS    .TXT    3,091  02-17-92 04:16p
   *TRAVEL  .LTR       936  02-17-92 12:00p  WP51QS01.TXT   68,362  02-19-92 09:02a




Print marked files? No (Yes)
```

After you mark the files, select Print (4). To confirm printing, select Yes.

WordPerfect adds the marked files to the print queue and prints them in the order in which they appear on the List Files screen. To unmark all files, press Home and then the asterisk (*) key again.

Printing a Disk Directory

For a neatly formatted printout of a disk directory, follow these steps:

1. Press F5 to activate the List command.

    🖰 Access the File pull-down menu and choose List Files.

2. Press ⏎Enter .

3. Press ⇧Shift F7 to activate the Print command.

    🖰 Access the File pull-down menu and choose Print.

Controlling the Printer

WordPerfect's Control Printer feature is a powerful tool for managing your printing activities. With this feature, you can cancel print jobs, move a print job to the top of the list, display a list of jobs waiting to be printed, and suspend and then resume printing. You perform all these operations from the Print: Control Printer screen.

To access the Print: Control Printer screen, follow these steps:

1. Press ⟨⇧Shift⟩ ⟨F7⟩ to activate the Print command.

    ⌨️　Access the **File** pull-down menu and choose **Print**.

2. Select **Control Printer** (**4**).

    The Control Printer screen appears and is divided into three sections.

The Current Job portion of the screen gives you information about the job that is currently printing.

The Job List portion displays information about the next three print jobs.

The Control Printer menu gives you the options you need for managing your printing activities.

```
Print: Control Printer

Current Job

Job Number: 1                              Page Number:  2
Status:      Printing                      Current Copy: 1 of 1
Message:     None
Paper:       Standard 8.5" x 11"
Location:    Continuous feed
Action:      None


Job List

Job  Document              Destination       Print Options
 1   C:\...\WP51QS01.TXT   LPT 1
 2   C:\...\ELECTION.TXT   LPT 1
 3   C:\...\HARMONY.LTR    LPT 1

Additional Jobs Not Shown: 3


1 Cancel Job(s); 2 Rush Job; 3 Display Jobs; 4 Go (start printer); 5 Stop: 0
```

Canceling a Print Job

With the Print: Control Printer screen displayed, choose **Cancel Job(s)** (**1**) to cancel individual print jobs or all print jobs while they are printing. WordPerfect displays a message that tells you the number of the job currently printing. Press Enter to cancel the current job, or type the number of the job you want to cancel. Or cancel all jobs by pressing the asterisk (*) key and selecting **Yes** to confirm the cancellation.

Rushing a Print Job

Choosing **R**ush Job (**2**) from the menu at the bottom of the Print: Control Printer screen enables you to print a job in a hurry. You can use this option either to interrupt the current print job so that you can print another job in the queue, or to print the rush job after the current job is printed.

After you choose **R**ush Job (**2**), WordPerfect prompts you to specify which job to rush. Type the number of the print job you want to move up. Then select **Y**es to interrupt the current printing job, or select **N**o or press Enter to print the job after the current job is finished printing.

If you elect to interrupt the job currently printing, the interrupted print job automatically resumes printing after the rush job is done. If necessary, WordPerfect prompts you to change forms for the rush job and prompts you again to reinsert the original form for the interrupted job.

Displaying a List of Jobs

The Print: Control Printer screen can display only three of the jobs in the queue.

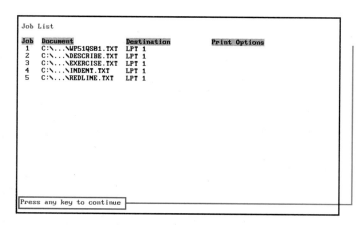

To display additional jobs in the print queue, choose **D**isplay Jobs (**3**) from the menu at the bottom of the Print: Control Printer screen.

Suspending Printing

If your printer has jammed or needs a new ribbon, you may need to suspend and then resume printing. In this case, choose **S**top (**5**) from the menu at the bottom of the Print: Control Printer screen. Then you can correct the problem.

Before you resume printing, you must position the print head at the top of the next page. Then press G to restart the printer. Printing resumes on page one if the document consists of only one page or if you stopped printing on page one.

Otherwise, WordPerfect prompts you to enter the page number where you want printing to resume. At the prompt Restart on page:, type the page number and press Enter.

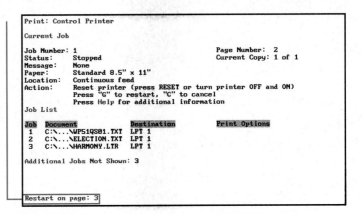

```
Print: Control Printer

Current Job

Job Number:  1                              Page Number:  2
Status:      Stopped                        Current Copy: 1 of 1
Message:     None
Paper:       Standard 8.5" x 11"
Location:    Continuous feed
Action:      Reset printer (press RESET or turn printer OFF and ON)
             Press "G" to restart, "C" to cancel
             Press Help for additional information
Job List

Job  Document              Destination       Print Options
  1  C:\...\WP51QS01.TXT   LPT 1
  2  C:\...\ELECTION.TXT   LPT 1
  3  C:\...\HARMONY.LTR    LPT 1

Additional Jobs Not Shown: 3


Restart on page: 3
```

7 Using View Document

Another option on the Print menu is **View Document** (**6**). Use this option to preview a document before you print it.

With the View Document option, you save costly printer paper and time by first previewing the document, making changes if needed, and then printing the document when you are certain that it's perfect. Document pages appear on-screen as they will appear when printed on paper, including graphics (if your system can display graphics), footnotes, page numbers, line numbers, headers, footers, and justification.

To preview a document, follow these steps:

1. Display the document you want to view in either the Doc 1 or the Doc 2 window.
2. Position the cursor anywhere on the page you want to view.
3. Press ⇧Shift F7 to activate the Print command.

   ⌨ Access the **F**ile pull-down menu and choose **P**rint.
4. Select **V**iew Document (**6**).
5. Choose one of the four options available.

Select 100% (1) to view the document at its actual size.

Select 200% (2) to view the document at twice its actual size.

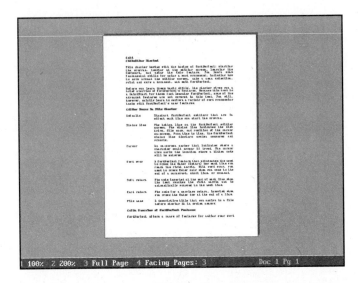

Select Full Page (3) to view the entire page.

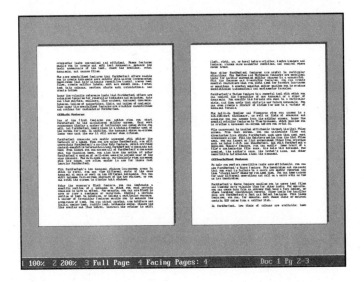

Select Facing Pages (4) to view the current page and its facing page (odd-numbered pages are displayed on the right side of the screen; even-numbered pages are displayed on the left).

6. Press PgUp, PgDn, or Ctrl Home (GoTo) to view other pages of the document.

   Note that you cannot edit this preview version of the document.

7. When you have finished previewing the document, press F7 (Exit) to return to the editing screen or F1 (Cancel) to return to the Print menu.

Selecting Print Options

From the options listed at the bottom half of the Print menu, you can set binding width, specify number of copies, print multiple copies, and select graphics or text quality.

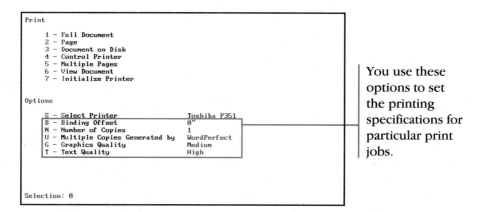

You use these options to set the printing specifications for particular print jobs.

Setting Binding Width

The binding width is the extra space added at the inside edge of each page when the document is printed on both sides. Setting a binding width shifts odd-numbered pages to the right and even-numbered pages to the left by the specified amount. The binding option provides an extra margin along the inside edge of the paper to allow for binding or three-hole drilling of the final copy.

To set the binding width, follow these steps:

1. Press ⬦Shift F7 to activate the Print command.

   ▱ Access the **File** pull-down menu and choose **Print**.

2. Select **Binding** Offset (**B**).

3. Type the amount of extra space you want added to the inside margin of each page; then press ↵Enter.

The binding width stays in effect until you change it again or exit WordPerfect.

Specifying Number of Copies

If you need more than one copy of a print job, you can change the number of copies through the Print menu. When you use the Number of Copies option, the pages in each copy of the print job are collated. Until you change the number back to one, the number of copies you specify on the Print menu will be printed for all print jobs.

To specify the number of copies to print, follow these steps:

1. Press ⬆Shift F7 to activate the Print command.

   ▭ Access the File pull-down menu and choose Print.

2. Select Number of Copies (N).

3. Type the number of copies you want to print, and then press ↵Enter.

Printing Multiple Copies of a Print Job

Some printers are capable of printing multiple copies after receiving the printer information only once. If your printer has that capability, you can use the Multiple Copies option to increase print speed. The copies, however, are not collated. Follow these steps to generate multiple copies of a print job:

1. Press ⬆Shift F7 to activate the Print command.

   ▭ Access the File pull-down menu and select Print.

2. Select Multiple Copies Generated by (U).

3. Choose Printer (2).

Changing Print Quality

The Graphics Quality option controls the degree of resolution (sharpness) your printer uses to print graphics images. Text Quality is identical to Graphics Quality except that Text Quality controls text only.

To change print quality, follow these steps:

1. Press ⬆Shift F7 to activate the Print command.

   ▭ Access the File pull-down menu and choose Print.

2. Select Graphics Quality (G).

3. Choose the desired setting from the Graphics Quality menu.

4. Select Text Quality (T).

7

5. From the Text Quality menu, select the desired print quality for text.

For both graphics and text, the following print qualities are available:

- Select Do Not Print (**1**) if you don't want either the graphics or the text to print. If your printer cannot print text and graphics in a single print run, select this option for Graphics Quality and print the text only. Then reload the paper, select this option for Text Quality, and print the graphics only.
- Select **Draft** (**2**) for a quick draft.
- Select **Medium** (**3**) for medium resolution.
- Select **High** (**4**) for high resolution. The higher the print resolution you select, the slower any pages containing graphics images will print.

Summary

In this chapter, you learned how to select a printer and how to print the printer test document. You examined some of WordPerfect's many printing features, learning how to print first from the screen and then from disk. You explored various ways to control your print jobs and specify the options you want, and you learned how to preview a document before printing.

7

Specifically, you learned the following key information about WordPerfect:

- After you have installed the printer definition, you must select it. Choose Print (Shift-F7) and select **Select Printer** (**S**). Then highlight the name of your printer and choose **Select**.
- To see what features your printer supports, print the test document. Select Retrieve (Shift-F10), type the file name **PRINTER.TST**, and press Enter. Then select Print (Shift-F7) and choose **Full Document** (**1**).
- To print from the screen, display the document, and then select Print (Shift-F7). To print the entire document, select **Full Document** (**1**). To print a single page, choose **Page** (**2**). To print selected pages, choose **Multiple Pages** (**5**) and specify the pages you want to print.
- To print a block from the screen, highlight the block, select Print (Shift-F7), and select **Yes** in response to the prompt.
- To print from disk using the Print menu, select Print (Shift-F7), choose **Document on Disk** (**3**), type the file name, and press Enter.

■ To print from disk using the List Files screen, select List (F5), highlight the file you want to print, and select **P**rint (4). To print multiple files, mark them with an asterisk (*).

■ With the Control Printer feature, you can cancel print jobs, move a print job to the top of the list, display a list of jobs waiting to be printed, and suspend and then resume printing. To access the Print: Control Printer screen, select Print (Shift-F7) and choose Control Printer (4).

■ To preview a document before printing, select Print (Shift-F7) and choose View Document (6).

■ From the options listed at the bottom of the Print menu, you can set binding width, specify number of copies, print multiple copies, and select graphics or text quality.

In the next chapter, you explore ways to manage your files through the List Files screen. You also learn how to create document summaries to keep track of your documents' contents.

7

Managing Files

8

In this chapter, you learn how WordPerfect can help you manage DOS and your computer system. With WordPerfect's List Files feature, you can manipulate files and directories much more than most word processing programs allow. You can use List Files to help you with common DOS and WordPerfect operations, such as deleting, moving, copying, and renaming files; making, changing, and deleting directories; and retrieving and printing documents. You also can use List Files to search for files with particular names or to search for phrases within groups of files.

Other file management tools offered in WordPerfect are the capability to lock files with passwords and to leave WordPerfect temporarily to go to DOS. Another tool for managing files is WordPerfect's Document Summary feature. That feature displays descriptive information about your files to help you keep track of their contents.

Using the List Files screen

Performing file operations

Displaying file names

Searching for particular files

Marking particular files for listing

Locking files

Exiting to DOS temporarily

Creating document summaries

Key Terms in This Chapter

DOS	An acronym for disk operating system. DOS is a collection of programs that gives you control of your computer's resources. DOS controls the use of disk drives for storing and retrieving programs and data.
Directory	A disk area in which information about files is stored. Displayed on-screen, a directory is a list of files.
Default directory	The directory WordPerfect currently is using to save and retrieve files. When retrieving a file, WordPerfect looks for the file in the default directory unless you specify a different directory. When saving a file, WordPerfect puts the file in the default directory unless you specify otherwise.
File specification	The drive and path name you enter for a file list.
Wild-card characters	Characters that can represent any single character (?) or any number of characters (*). Wild-card characters can be used to broaden or narrow an area of inquiry. You can, for example, use wild-card characters with the Find feature.

8

Using the List Files Screen

With the List Files feature, you can accomplish—from within WordPerfect—much of the file and directory management you ordinarily perform from DOS. To get to the List Files screen, follow these steps:

1. Press F5 to activate the List command.

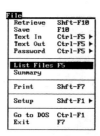

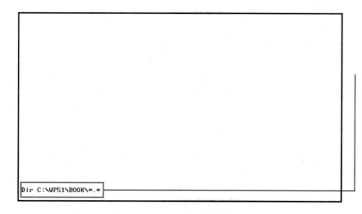

Access the File pull-down menu and select List Files.

WordPerfect displays the message Dir in the lower left corner, followed by a file specification for all files in the default directory, such as the following:

    Dir C:\WP51\BOOK*.*

This message says that WordPerfect is ready to give you a file list of all files in the default directory.

8

2. If this is the directory you want, simply press ↵Enter. If it is not the directory you want, change the specification, and then press ↵Enter.

Double-clicking the left mouse button is the same as pressing ↵Enter. For example, after choosing List Files from the File pull-down menu, you can double-click Dir C:\WP51\BOOK*.* to accept the default file specification.

If you type a new file specification, it replaces the original specification. You also can edit the file specification, just as you edit regular text—by using keys such as Del and ◆Backspace.

199

After you accept the current file specification or enter a new one, the List Files screen appears.

Heading

The three areas on the List Files screen are the heading, the file list, and the menu.

File list

Menu

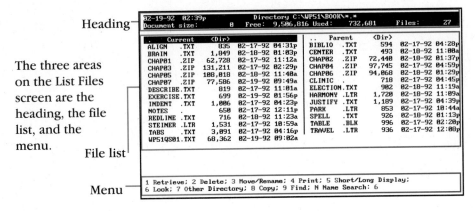

The Heading

The first line of the two-line heading on the List Files screen displays the date, the time, and the directory being listed.

The second line shows the size of the document currently being edited, the amount of free space left on the disk, the amount of disk space taken up by files in the current directory, and the number of files shown in the list.

The File List

The two-column file list on the List Files screen displays the names and directories in alphabetical order across the screen. Files whose names start with numbers are listed first. This list shows the complete file name, file size, and date and time the file was created or last modified. You can print this list, along with most of the information in the heading, by pressing Print (Shift-F7).

Notice that the top line of the file list contains the following information:

    .   Current <Dir>   ..   Parent <Dir>

<Dir> indicates that the items are directories. Other directories in the list are similarly labeled. The entry labeled Current refers to the currently listed directory. The other entry, labeled Parent, refers to the parent directory of the listed directory. The parent directory is one level higher than the current directory.

A highlight bar also appears on the top left entry. You can move this bar with the cursor keys or the mouse to highlight any name in the list. If you want to display files from a different directory, you can highlight the name of that directory and press Enter twice, or double-click the directory with the mouse.

Note: With the Location of Files option on the Setup menu, you can specify that certain types of files be stored automatically in separate directories. You can, for example, designate separate directories for dictionaries, backup files, and macros. Refer to Chapter 15 for more information.

The List Files Menu

From the List Files menu at the bottom of the screen, you can select from 10 menu items. Each operation, when selected, acts on the highlighted file or directory.

After you make a menu selection, WordPerfect often asks for confirmation. For instance, if you select **Delete (2)** to delete the file ELECTION.TXT, WordPerfect displays the following prompt:

```
Delete C:\WP51\BOOK\ELECTION.TXT? No (Yes)
```

Although WordPerfect displays the No response, you can select **Yes** to delete the file, or select **No** or press Enter to cancel the command.

8

Using the List Files Menu

You can use the options on the List Files menu to manage your files without leaving WordPerfect and going to DOS. The first step you perform for any operation is to highlight the name of the file or directory on which you want to operate. You can use the cursor keys to move to the entry or click the entry with the mouse, or you can use the Name Search option.

Name Search

With the **Name Search (N)** option on the List Files menu, you can move the highlight bar to a file name as you type the name. First press N and then type the first letter of the file name (for example, EXERCISE.TXT) for which you want to search.

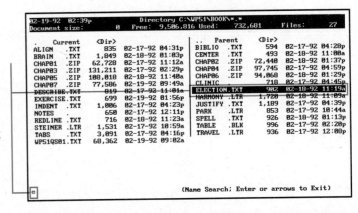

If you type **e**, for instance, the highlight bar jumps to the first file name starting with that letter.

8

If you type **x** as the second letter of the name, the highlight bar jumps to the first file name that starts with those two letters.

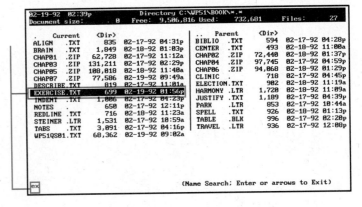

If you still don't find the file, type the third letter—in this case, **e**—and the highlight bar jumps to the first file name starting with those three letters.

If you make a mistake or change your mind, you can press Backspace; the last letter you typed is deleted, and the highlight bar jumps to its previous position. When the file name you want is highlighted, turn off Name Search by pressing Cancel (F1), Enter, or one of the arrow keys. Then you can perform on the highlighted file any of the List Files operations described in this chapter.

You can use Name Search to search for a directory name as well as a file name. Simply type a backslash (\) before the first character of the directory name. To find the LEARN directory, for example, type **\LEARN**.

In addition to using Name Search, you can use Forward Search (F2) and Backward Search (Shift-F2) to locate files within the List Files screen. These features are particularly useful with a long display of file names (discussed later in this chapter).

Retrieve

The **Retrieve** (**1**) option (discussed in detail in Chapter 2) works like Retrieve (Shift-F10) from the editing screen and like **Retrieve** from the File pull-down menu: the retrieve operation brings a file into WordPerfect for editing. Like Retrieve (Shift-F10), this option inserts the newly retrieved file at the cursor position.

If you already have a file on-screen, selecting **Retrieve** (**1**) from the List Files menu inserts the retrieved file into the document on-screen at the cursor position. Whenever you pick this option with a file already on-screen, WordPerfect displays the following prompt to prevent you from accidentally combining files:

```
Retrieve into current document? No (Yes)
```

Select **Yes** if you want to combine the new file with the file on-screen. Select **No** if you don't want to combine the files.

WordPerfect does not retrieve program files, nor does it retrieve any temporary or permanent WordPerfect system files.

The Retrieve option retrieves and automatically converts to WordPerfect 5.1 format any DOS text file or any file created with an earlier version of Word-Perfect. WordPerfect also automatically converts spreadsheet files created by PlanPerfect, Lotus 1-2-3 (Versions 1.0 through 3.0), Microsoft Excel Version 2.x, Quattro, or Quattro Pro for use in WordPerfect. In addition, you can perform many conversion operations through the Text In/Out (Ctrl-F5) feature. Such conversions, however, are beyond the scope of this book. For more information, refer to the Que book, *Using WordPerfect 5.1,* Special Edition.

Delete

The **Delete** (**2**) option on the List Files menu deletes files or directories. If the highlight bar is on a file name, that file is deleted. If the bar is on a directory name, the directory is deleted as long as it does not contain any files. If the directory contains files, WordPerfect displays an error message. Whether you are deleting files or directories, WordPerfect displays a prompt similar to the following:

8

203

```
Delete C:\WP51\BOOK\CHAP2? No (Yes)
```

Select **Yes** to confirm the deletion, or select **No** to cancel the deletion.

Move/Rename

To move or rename a file, first highlight the name of the file to be moved or renamed. Then press **Move/Rename (3)** from the List Files menu. If you are moving the file, type the directory or drive where you want to move the file, and press Enter. Moving a file means transferring it to a different directory or disk drive. If you are renaming the file, type the new name (the displayed name disappears) and press Enter. If the file you are moving already exists in the other directory, or if you select a name that is already in use, WordPerfect asks you to confirm that you want to replace the existing file. If you answer **Yes**, the existing file is erased.

Copy

Like the DOS COPY command, the **Copy (8)** option on the List Files menu copies the file. To copy a file, highlight the name of the file to be copied and select **Copy (8)**. WordPerfect displays the following prompt:

```
Copy this file to:
```

To copy the file to another disk or directory, type the drive or directory and press Enter. To make a copy of the file in the current directory, type a new file name and press Enter.

Print

The **Print (4)** option on the List Files menu prints the highlighted file on the currently selected printer. Unlike many programs, WordPerfect can print while you continue to edit another document. You can even tell the program to print more than one file. For a detailed discussion of WordPerfect's Print options, see Chapter 7, "Printing."

Short/Long Display

The **Short/Long Display (5)** option on the List Files menu enables you to toggle between the default (short) List Files display and a long display. The

204

long display includes from the document summary the first 30 characters of the file's descriptive name and the file type, provided that a summary exists for the file and includes those items. Document summaries are discussed later in this chapter. When you select this option, WordPerfect displays the following menu line:

1 Short Display; **2** Long Display: **2**

To choose the long display, press Enter twice to accept the default choice of 2.

```
02-19-92  02:52p          Directory C:\WP51\BOOK\*.*
Document size:       0    Free:  8,943,616 Used:      734,066    Files:     20
Descriptive Name              Type    Filename      Size    Revision Date

Current Directory                       .        <Dir>
Parent Directory                        ..       <Dir>
                                       ALIGN   .TXT     835   02-17-92 04:31p
Bibliography                  Report   BIBLIO  .TXT     967   02-19-92 02:52p
Brainstorming                 Essay    BRAIN   .TXT   1,982   02-19-92 02:48p
                                       CENTER  .TXT     493   02-18-92 11:00a
                                       CLINIC  .         718   02-17-92 04:45p
                                       DESCRIBE.TXT     819   02-17-92 11:01a
Election Poll                 Data     ELECTION.TXT   1,275   02-19-92 02:50p
                                       EXERCISE.TXT     699   02-19-92 01:56p
                                       INDENT  .TXT   1,006   02-17-92 04:23p
                                       JUSTIFY .TXT   1,189   02-17-92 04:39p
Midwest Regional Conference   Letter   HARMONY .LTR   1,853   02-19-92 02:49p
                                       NOTES   .         650   02-17-92 12:11p
                                       REDLINE .TXT     716   02-18-92 11:23a
River Park                    Letter   PARK    .LTR   1,226   02-19-92 02:51p
                                       SPELL   .TXT     926   02-18-92 01:13p
                                       STEINER .LTR   1,531   02-17-92 10:59a

1 Retrieve; 2 Delete; 3 Move/Rename; 4 Print; 5 Short/Long Display;
6 Look; 7 Other Directory; 8 Copy; 9 Find; N Name Search: 6
```

Unlike the short display, the long display lists each file on a separate row.

Each row's right half shows the same information found in the short display. The left half of each row, however, includes information from the document summary (covered later in this chapter), including the first 30 characters of the descriptive name as well as the file type—provided that the file has a document summary containing these two items. The files are listed in alphabetical order by their long descriptive file names. When descriptive file names are not available, the files are listed by their short file names.

Note: You can customize the program to display long file names permanently in the List Files screen by using the Environment option on the Setup menu. For more information about customizing WordPerfect, see Chapter 15.

Look

The Look (**6**) option on the List Files menu displays the highlighted file without retrieving it to the editing screen. Note that this option is the default menu choice. You don't have to select Look (**6**) to display a file (although you can if you want); you can just press Enter. Use Look to examine a number of files quickly—for example, if you forget which file you need to edit.

8

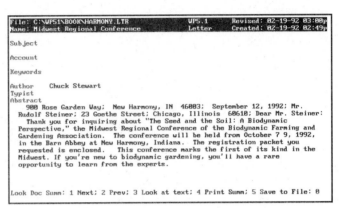 Double-clicking the left mouse button on a file name in the List Files screen causes the file to be displayed, as if you had highlighted the file and chosen Look (**6**).

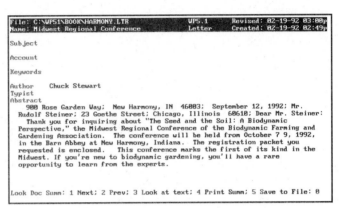

The file name is displayed at the top of the screen. If you have created a document summary for the file, that information is displayed.

You can use the up- and down-arrow keys to move the cursor through the file. You cannot edit the file. The Look option also continuously displays or scrolls each succeeding line of the document if you press S. Pressing S a second time stops the scrolling. Press Exit (F7) or Enter to cancel the Look option.

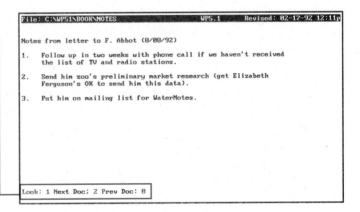

When you select Look (**6**) for a file that doesn't have a document summary, WordPerfect displays the Look menu at the bottom of the screen.

Selecting Next Doc (**1**) or PgDn moves the cursor to the first page of the next file in the file list. Selecting Prev Doc (**2**) or PgUp moves the cursor to the first page of the preceding file in the list. Use these options to scan quickly the document summaries and first pages of a list of files.

8

When a document is displayed with **Look (6)**, you can use Forward Search (F2) or Backward Search (Shift-F2) to search for text. You cannot, however, search for text in headers, footers, or footnotes.

Other Directory

Use the **Other Directory (7)** option on the List Files menu to change the default directory. Follow these steps:

1. Select Other Directory (7) from the List Files menu.

   WordPerfect displays in the lower left corner of the screen the message New directory = followed by the name of either the default directory or any directory you highlighted before starting this operation.

2. Type the name of the directory you want to make the default, or press ⏎Enter to use the currently listed directory as the default.

   WordPerfect displays Dir with the file specification for all the files in the selected directory—for example, Dir C:\WP51\LEARN*.*.

3. Press ⏎Enter to change to the new directory and display its listing.

If you decide that you don't want to change directories, press Cancel (F1) before pressing Enter the second time.

You can edit both the New directory = and the Dir messages. You can thereby change directly to any directory on your hard disk.

In addition, you can create a new directory by selecting **Other Directory (7)** and entering a unique name. If, for example, you enter **c:\wp51\essays**, WordPerfect displays the prompt Create c:\wp51\essays? No (Yes). Select **Yes** to create a new subdirectory called ESSAYS, or select **No** if that isn't what you want.

You also can use List (F5) to change the default directory or create directories from the editing screen. Press List (F5) and then type an equal sign (=). WordPerfect responds the same way as in the List Files screen.

If you want only to examine the contents of a directory without making it the default directory, simply highlight the directory name and press Enter twice.

Find

With the **Find (9)** option on the List Files menu, you can search for certain file names, or you can search through one or more files in the file list for a word

8

or phrase without retrieving the files into WordPerfect. You can, for instance, determine which documents are about a certain subject by searching for a word or phrase related to that subject.

To start a search, select Find (9) to display the Find menu at the bottom of the screen.

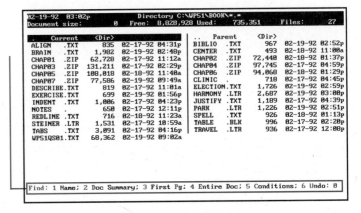

```
02-19-92  03:02p              Directory C:\WP51\BOOK\*.*
Document size:         0  Free:  8,828,928 Used:      735,351     Files:       27

      .     Current   <Dir>              ..    Parent    <Dir>
    ALIGN   .TXT      835  02-17-92 04:31p   BIBLIO  .TXT      967  02-19-92 02:52p
    BRAIN   .TXT    1,982  02-19-92 02:48p   CENTER  .TXT      493  02-18-92 11:00a
    CHAP01  .ZIP   62,728  02-17-92 11:12a   CHAP02  .ZIP   72,440  02-18-92 01:37p
    CHAP03  .ZIP  131,211  02-17-92 02:29p   CHAP04  .ZIP   97,745  02-17-92 04:59p
    CHAP05  .ZIP  100,018  02-18-92 11:40a   CHAP06  .ZIP   94,868  02-18-92 01:29p
    CHAP07  .ZIP   77,586  02-19-92 09:49a   CLINIC  .         718  02-17-92 04:45p
    DESCRIBE.TXT      819  02-17-92 11:01a   ELECTION.TXT    1,726  02-19-92 02:59p
    EXERCISE.TXT      699  02-19-92 01:56p   HARMONY .LTR    2,687  02-19-92 03:00p
    INDENT  .TXT    1,006  02-17-92 04:23p   JUSTIFY .TXT    1,189  02-17-92 04:39p
    NOTES   .         650  02-17-92 12:11p   PARK    .LTR    1,226  02-19-92 02:51p
    REDLINE .TXT      716  02-18-92 11:23a   SPELL   .TXT      926  02-18-92 01:13p
    STEINER .LTR    1,531  02-17-92 10:59a   TABLE   .BLK      996  02-17-92 02:20p
    TABS    .TXT    3,091  02-17-92 04:16p   TRAVEL  .LTR      936  02-17-92 12:00p
    WP51QS01.TXT   68,362  02-19-92 09:02a


Find: 1 Name; 2 Doc Summary; 3 First Pg; 4 Entire Doc; 5 Conditions; 6 Undo: 0
```

You can choose from the following options on the Find menu:

- Select **Name** (**1**) to locate a file or group of files in the list by searching for letter patterns that are part of the file name.

- Select options 2, 3, and 4 to search through one or more files in the file list for a particular word, word pattern, phrase, or logical expression. **Doc Summary** (**2**) restricts the search to only the document summaries. First **Pg** (**3**) restricts the search to each document's first page. **Entire Doc** (**4**) searches each document entirely.

- Select **Conditions** (**5**) to access additional options for limiting the scope of a search and specifying multiple search criteria.

- Select **Undo** (**6**) to reverse the results of the last search. You can undo up to three levels of searches with this option.

Searching for Specific File Names

Use the first option on the Find menu, **Name** (**1**), to locate a file or group of files in the list by searching for letter patterns that are part of the file name. WordPerfect searches the entire displayed list of file names regardless of the position of the highlight bar. WordPerfect displays the total number of files to be searched and a running tally of the number of files it has searched. When the search is finished, WordPerfect displays a new file list showing only the files that contain the search string.

8

To locate a file or group of files with **Name (1)**, follow these steps:

1. Press ⬚F5⬚ (List), and then press ⬚↵Enter⬚.

   ⌨ Access the **File** pull-down menu, select List **F**iles, and press ⬚↵Enter⬚.

2. Select **F**ind (9) from the List Files menu.

3. Select **N**ame (1).

   WordPerfect displays the prompt Word pattern:.

4. Enter a pattern of characters that is common in all the file names you want displayed. For example, to search for file names that contain the letters *chap*, type **chap** and press ⬚↵Enter⬚.

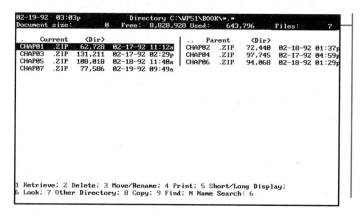

```
02-19-92  03:03p         Directory C:\WP51\BOOK\*.*
Document size:        0   Free: 8,828,928 Used:      643,796     Files:       7

    .   Current  <Dir>              ..    Parent    <Dir>
  CHAP01  .ZIP    62,728  02-17-92 11:12a   CHAP02  .ZIP    72,440  02-18-92 01:37p
  CHAP03  .ZIP   131,211  02-17-92 02:29p   CHAP04  .ZIP    97,745  02-17-92 04:59p
  CHAP05  .ZIP   100,010  02-18-92 11:40a   CHAP06  .ZIP    94,068  02-18-92 01:29p
  CHAP07  .ZIP    77,586  02-19-92 09:49a







1 Retrieve; 2 Delete; 3 Move/Rename; 4 Print; 5 Short/Long Display;
6 Look; 7 Other Directory; 8 Copy; 9 Find; N Name Search: 6
```

When you specify *chap* as the search string, WordPerfect finds such file names as CHAP1, CHAP2, and CHAP3. The upper right corner of the List Files screen shows the number of files found.

An alternative method to using **Name (1)** to locate particular file names is to use a specific file specification other than the default *.*. To give a specific file specification, follow these steps:

1. Press ⬚F5⬚ to activate the List command.

   ⌨ Access the **F**ile pull-down menu and select List **F**iles.

2. When the file specification appears, move the cursor to the end of it and replace the *.* with a more specific specification. To find all files that end with the extension LTR, for example, type **c:\wp51\book*.ltr** and press ⬚↵Enter⬚.

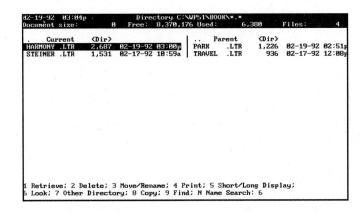

The List Files
screen appears,
displaying only
files with names
ending in LTR.

Searching for Specific Words or Phrases

You can use the **Find** (**9**) option on the List Files menu to search for a word or
phrase in one or more files in the file list without retrieving those files into
WordPerfect. To search a list of files for a specific word or phrase, follow these
steps:

1. Press F5 (List), and then press ↵Enter.

   ▱ Access the **File** pull-down menu, select List **Files**, and press
   ↵Enter.

2. Select **Find** (**9**) from the List Files menu.

3. Select one of the following options:

Doc Summary (**2**)	Searches only the document summary in each file.
First **P**g (**3**)	Searches only the first page of each document.
Entire Doc (**4**)	Searches an entire file.

   After you select an option, WordPerfect displays the `Word pattern:`
   prompt.

4. Type the word or phrase for which you are looking; then press
   ↵Enter.

WordPerfect displays the total number of files to be searched and a running
tally of the number of files it has searched. When the search is finished,
WordPerfect displays a new file list showing only the files that contain the
targeted word or phrase. The upper right corner of the List Files screen shows
the number of files found.

8

210

You can use the Look option to examine each file in turn by either pressing Enter or selecting **Look (6)**. Or you can retrieve each file individually into WordPerfect by selecting **Retrieve (1)**. To return to the same List Files screen, press List (F5) twice.

When WordPerfect prompts you to enter a word pattern, you can enter an exact word or phrase, or you can use special wild card characters and logical operators to make your search more general. A question mark (?) represents a single character, and an asterisk (*) represents any number of characters up to a hard return. Here are some examples of allowable word patterns:

Pattern Entered	WordPerfect Finds
duck	Files that contain the word *duck*
d?ck	Files that contain *duck, deck, Dick,* or *dock*
d*k	Files that contain *duck, damask,* and *Derek*
ducks can	Files that contain such phrases as *ducks can waddle* and *ducks cannot stand on their heads*
ducks*can	Files that contain such text as *Ducks have adapted to many environments. They can*
ducks;geese	Files that contain both the word *ducks* and the word *geese*
ducks,geese	Files that contain either the word *ducks* or the word *geese*

Uppercase and lowercase letters are treated the same. In this respect, the Find option differs from WordPerfect's Forward Search (F2) and Backward Search (Shift-F2) features, which match capitalized letters in a search string. If you enter **Duck**, neither Forward Search nor Backward Search will stop at *duck*, but Find will mark files that contain either *duck* or *Duck*.

Specifying Other Conditions

You can use the Conditions (5) option from the Find menu for even more flexible search options. To use Conditions (5), follow these steps:

1. Press F5 (List), and then press ⏎Enter.

   ⌨ Access the **F**ile pull-down menu, select List **F**iles, and press ⏎Enter.

2. Select Find (9) from the List Files menu.

3. Select Conditions (5).

WordPerfect displays the Find: Conditions screen.

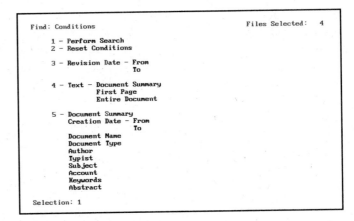

```
Find: Conditions                              Files Selected:    4

       1 - Perform Search
       2 - Reset Conditions

       3 - Revision Date - From
                           To

       4 - Text - Document Summary
                  First Page
                  Entire Document

       5 - Document Summary
           Creation Date - From
                           To

           Document Name
           Document Type
           Author
           Typist
           Subject
           Account
           Keywords
           Abstract

Selection: 1
```

4. Select from among the options to specify the search criteria you want.

5. Select Perform Search (1) to start the search.

The Find: Conditions screen offers the following options:

- Select Reset Conditions (2) to return all search conditions to WordPerfect's default values.

- Select Revision Date (3) to search files created within a specified range of dates. You can enter dates in single-digit form; for example, 9/2/92 is the same as 09/02/92. Or you can leave part of the date blank; for example, to search all files created in October, 1992, enter **10//92**.

- Select Text (4), and then enter one or more word patterns next to the sections of the documents you want to search: Document Summary, First Page, and Entire Document. WordPerfect searches for the word pattern(s) in the sections of the documents you indicate.

- Select Document Summary (5), and then enter one or more word patterns next to the document summary data lines you want to search: Creation Date, Document Name, Document Type, Author, Typist, Subject, Account, Keywords, and Abstract. The word pattern you enter in the Document Summary line will be the object of the search throughout the entire document summary. Word patterns entered on the other lines are searched for only in those specific lines.

When the search is completed, WordPerfect displays a file list containing only those files that match the search conditions.

8

Marking Files

To perform certain List Files operations on more than one file at a time, use
file marking. On the List Files screen, you mark any files you want to handle as
a group. Then you perform an operation, such as delete or print, on all the
marked files simultaneously.

To mark files, follow these steps:

1. Press F5 (List), and then press ↵Enter.

   ⌨ Access the File pull-down menu, select List Files, and press
   ↵Enter.

2. Move the highlight bar to the first file you want to mark, and then
   press * (the asterisk key).

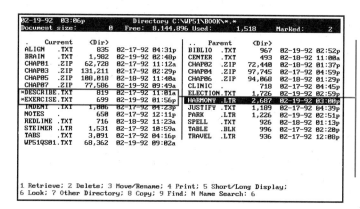

```
02-19-92  03:06p          Directory C:\WP51\BOOK\*.*
Document size:      0   Free:  8,144,896 Used:      1,518    Marked:      2

     Current     <Dir>                  Parent      <Dir>
 ALIGN   .TXT      835  02-17-92 04:31p  BIBLIO  .TXT      967  02-19-92 02:52p
 BRAIN   .TXT    1,982  02-19-92 02:48p  CENTER  .TXT      493  02-18-92 11:00a
 CHAP01  .ZIP   62,728  02-17-92 11:12a  CHAP02  .ZIP   72,440  02-18-92 01:37p
 CHAP03  .ZIP  131,211  02-17-92 02:29p  CHAP04  .ZIP   97,745  02-17-92 04:59p
 CHAP05  .ZIP  108,010  02-18-92 11:40a  CHAP06  .ZIP   94,060  02-18-92 01:29p
 CHAP07  .ZIP   77,586  02-19-92 09:49a  CLINIC  .        718  02-17-92 04:45p
*DESCRIBE.TXT      819  02-17-92 11:01a  ELECTION.TXT    1,726  02-19-92 02:59p
*EXERCISE.TXT      699  02-19-92 01:56p  HARMONY .LTR    2,687  02-19-92 03:00p
 INDENT  .TXT    1,006  02-17-92 04:23p  JUSTIFY .TXT    1,189  02-17-92 04:39p
 NOTES   .        650  02-17-92 12:11p  PARK    .LTR    1,226  02-19-92 02:51p
 REDLINE .TXT      716  02-18-92 11:23a  SPELL   .TXT      926  02-18-92 01:13p
 STEINER .LTR    1,531  02-17-92 10:59a  TABLE   .BLK      996  02-17-92 02:20p
 TABS    .TXT    3,091  02-17-92 04:16p  TRAVEL  .LTR      936  02-17-92 12:08p
 WP51QS01.TXT   68,362  02-19-92 09:02a


1 Retrieve; 2 Delete; 3 Move/Rename; 4 Print; 5 Short/Long Display;
6 Look; 7 Other Directory; 8 Copy; 9 Find; N Name Search: 6
```

WordPerfect puts
a bold asterisk (*)
next to the
highlighted file
name and moves
the highlight bar
automatically to
the next file name
in the list.

8

3. Move the highlight bar to each file name you want to include, and
   mark it with an asterisk (*).

If you want to mark all the files in the list, press Home and then the asterisk
(*), or press Mark Text (Alt-F5). To unmark all marked files, use the same
keys—press Home and then the asterisk (*), or press Mark Text (Alt-F5).

You can perform the following List Files operations on a number of marked
files simultaneously:

   Delete (2)
   Move (3) (but not Rename)
   Print (4) (on the currently selected printer)
   Copy (8) (to a different drive or directory)
   Find (9)

Locking Files

You can assign a password to files so that no one but you can retrieve them, examine them with the **Look (6)** option in List Files, or print them. Be sure to remember your password! If you forget it, the files will be inaccessible not only to others, but also to you.

To assign a password to a file, follow these steps:

1. Display the file on-screen.

2. Press Ctrl F5 to activate the Text In/Out command, select **Password** (**2**), and then select **Add/Change** (**1**).

Access the **File** pull-down menu, select **Password**, and then select **Add/ Change**.

3. At the Enter Password: prompt, type up to 24 characters for your password and press ↵Enter.

   WordPerfect prompts you to re-enter the password.

4. Type the password again and press ↵Enter.

   If you make a typing error or don't enter the correct password, you receive an error message and are prompted to go through the process again.

5. Save your document to complete the process.

To retrieve a locked file, follow these steps:

1. Clear the editing screen.

2. Use ⇧Shift F10 (Retrieve) or F5 (List) to retrieve the file.

   WordPerfect prompts you to enter the password.

3. Type the password and press ↵Enter.

8

214

To unprotect a file, follow these steps:

1. Retrieve the file (using the preceding steps).

2. Press [Ctrl] [F5] to activate the Text In/Out command, select Password (2) and choose Remove (2).

   ⌨ Access the File pull-down menu, select Password, and select Remove.

3. Save the file.

Exiting to DOS Temporarily

Although you can perform many file operations from within WordPerfect, you may need to exit WordPerfect and go to the DOS prompt to perform certain operations—such as formatting a disk. A convenient way to exit WordPerfect briefly is to use the Shell (Ctrl-F1) command.

To exit WordPerfect and go to DOS temporarily, follow these steps:

1. Press [Ctrl] [F1] to activate the Shell command.

⌨ Access the File pull-down menu and select Go to DOS.

2. Select Go to DOS (1).

3. Type a DOS command.

4. When you are ready to return to WordPerfect, type **exit** at the DOS prompt and press [↵Enter].

```
HP Vectra Personal Computer MS-DOS Version 4.01 - D.01.02

(C)Copyright Hewlett-Packard 1986-1989
(C)Copyright Microsoft Corp  1981-1988

Enter 'EXIT' to return to WordPerfect
C:\WP51>
```

WordPerfect
temporarily
disappears and a
DOS prompt,
such as C> or
C:\WP51 appears.

Using Document Summaries

With WordPerfect, you can place a document summary box at the beginning of
a file before you save the document to disk. Use the Document Summary
feature to display a descriptive document name, the dates the document was
created and revised, the author's name, the typist's name, and other information that may help you identify the document and its contents. You can view
document summaries on-screen or print them separately, but they are not
printed with documents.

Entering Document Summary Information

You can create and edit a document summary from anywhere in the document. To create a document summary, follow these steps:

1. Display the document.

2. Press ⌂Shift F8 to activate the Format command, and select
   Document (3).

   ⌨ Access the Layout pull-down menu and select Document.

3. From the Format: Document menu, select Summary (5).

   If you have previously saved the file, WordPerfect automatically enters
   the dates the file was created and revised. If you have not saved the
   file, the dates are added when you save the document.

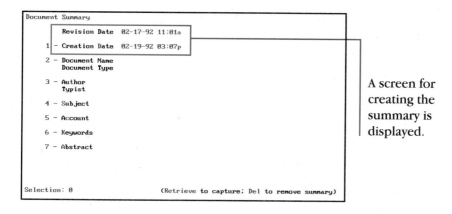

A screen for creating the summary is displayed.

4. Select each of the options in turn, type the requested information, and press ⏎Enter.

You can enter the document type, the names of the author and the typist, the subject, the account, and any keywords. For the abstract, type a summary of the document.

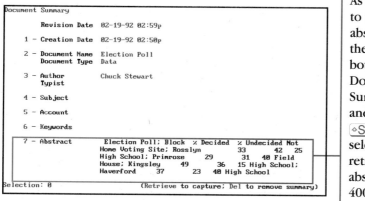

As an alternative to typing the abstract, position the cursor at the bottom of the Document Summary screen and press ⇧Shift F10. Then select Yes to retrieve as the abstract the first 400 characters of the document.

8

5. Press F7 (Exit) to return to the document.

Displaying a Document Summary

To look at a document summary, follow these steps:

1. Press F5 (List), and then press ⏎Enter.

   ▣ Access the File pull-down menu, select List Files, and press ⏎Enter.

2. Move the highlight bar to the document whose summary you want to see.

3. Select Look (6).

The document summary is displayed with a menu at the bottom of the screen. Up to 400 characters of the document are displayed under the heading Abstract.

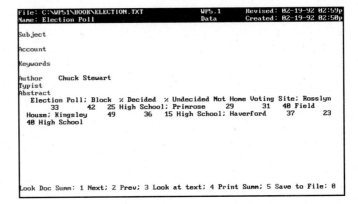

```
File: C:\WP51\BOOK\ELECTION.TXT          WP5.1    Revised: 02-19-92 02:59p
Name: Election Poll                      Data     Created: 02-19-92 02:50p

Subject

Account

Keywords

Author    Chuck Stewart
Typist
Abstract
    Election Poll; Block  % Decided  % Undecided Not Home Voting Site; Rosslyn
         33        42   25 High School; Primrose        29       31   40 Field
    House; Kingsley      49        36   15 High School; Haverford       37       23
    40 High School



Look Doc Summ: 1 Next; 2 Prev; 3 Look at text; 4 Print Summ; 5 Save to File: 0
```

The first and second options on the menu at the bottom of the screen let you view the next document or the previous document, respectively. From this menu, you also can choose Look at text (3) or press the down-arrow key to view the text as it appears on the editing screen, without the document summary information. You can choose Print Summ (4) to print the document summary, or Save to File (5) to save the document summary to a file.

Note: You can customize the Document Summary feature through the Environment option on the Setup menu. You can choose, for instance, to have WordPerfect prompt you to enter summary information the first time you save a document. For more information about customizing WordPerfect, see Chapter 15.

Summary

This chapter showed you how to manipulate files and directories with WordPerfect's List Files feature. You learned what types of information are displayed on the List Files screen, and how to use the List Files menu to perform such operations as retrieving a file, deleting a file, and moving or renaming a file. You learned how to lock files with passwords, and you

8

learned how to leave WordPerfect temporarily to go to DOS. You learned also how to use WordPerfect's Document Summary feature to keep track of your files' contents.

Specifically, you learned the following key information about WordPerfect:

■ With the List Files feature, you can accomplish—from within WordPerfect—much of the file and directory management you ordinarily perform from DOS. To access the List Files screen, first select List (F5). If this is the directory you want, press Enter; if you want a different directory, change the specification and press Enter.

■ The three areas of the List Files screen are the heading, the file list, and the menu.

■ With the **Name Search (N)** option on the List Files menu, you can move the highlight bar to a file name as you type the name.

■ The **Retrieve (1)** option on the List Files menu works like Retrieve (Shift-F10) from the editing screen to bring a file into WordPerfect for editing.

■ The **Delete (2)** option on the List Files menu deletes files or directories.

■ To move or rename a file, first highlight the file name on the List Files screen, and then select **Move/Rename (3)**. If you are moving the file, type the directory or drive where you want to move the file and press Enter. If you are renaming the file, type the new name and press Enter.

■ The **Copy (8)** option on the List Files menu copies the highlighted file.

■ The **Print (4)** option on the List Files menu prints the highlighted file on the currently selected printer.

■ The **Short/Long Display (5)** option on the List Files menu enables you to toggle between the default (short) List Files display and a long display.

■ The **Look (6)** option on the List Files menu displays the highlighted file without retrieving it to the editing screen.

■ Use the **Other Directory (7)** option on the List Files menu to change the default directory.

■ With the **Find (9)** option on the List Files menu, you can search for certain file names, or you can search through one or more files in the file list for a word or phrase without retrieving the files into WordPerfect.

8

■ To perform certain List Files operations on more than one file at a time, use file marking. To mark a file, move the highlight bar to a file on the List Files screen and press * (the asterisk key).

■ To assign a password to files so that no one but you can retrieve them, select Text In/Out (Ctrl-F5), choose **Password (2)**, and then select Add/Change (**1**).

■ To exit to DOS temporarily, select Shell (Ctrl-F1) and choose **G**o to DOS (**1**). Enter one or more DOS commands. To return to Word-Perfect, type **exit** and press Enter.

■ To create a document summary, select Format (Shift-F8), choose **Document (3)**, and select **S**ummary (**5**). Then type the requested information.

■ To look at a document summary, select List (F5), highlight the document whose summary you want to display, and select **L**ook (**6**).

In the next chapter, you learn the basics of creating a macro—a series of pre-recorded keystrokes that can save you time in performing repetitive tasks.

8

Creating
Macros

If you perform any task repeatedly, even one as simple as deleting a line, you can do it more quickly with a macro. Macros can automate simple tasks, such as typing *Sincerely yours* and your name. Macros also can perform complex operations that include both text and WordPerfect commands. After you create a macro, you press only one or two keystrokes to do almost instantly what would otherwise require many keystrokes.

You can create three types of macros. The first type you give Alt-letter names, such as Alt-C for a macro that centers text. Because only 26 letters are available for naming these macros, you should create this type for macros you use often. The second type you assign descriptive names, such as MEMO for a macro that enters a memo heading. You can create an unlimited number of this type of macro. The third type of macro is unnamed. If you have a repetitive task to perform that you aren't likely to do again later, you can create this type of macro. You can have only one unnamed macro at a time. As soon as you create an unnamed macro, that macro replaces any existing unnamed macro.

This chapter shows you how to create and run all three types of macros. At the end of the chapter are step-by-step instructions for creating some macros you can include in your own macro library.

Key Terms in This Chapter

Macro	A series of prerecorded keystrokes assigned to a single key or key combination. Macros greatly relieve the tedium of repetitive typing.
Alt-letter macro	A macro stored on disk, which has a name that consists of the Alt key plus a letter from A to Z. You can use an Alt-letter macro in any session of WordPerfect simply by pressing the macro's Alt-letter name.
Descriptive macro	A macro you store on disk, which has a name of one to eight characters. You can use a descriptive macro by issuing a special macro command and entering the macro's descriptive name.
Unnamed macro	A macro that works as you have defined it until you create another unnamed macro. Each unnamed macro you create replaces the preceding one.
Macro editor	A utility that enables you to modify a macro without recording it again.
Interactive macro	A macro that pauses and waits for the user to type information.

9

Note: In a macro, you cannot use the mouse to position the cursor or highlight text as a block. You can, however, use the mouse and pull-down menus to define a macro; the commands will be stored in the macro as normal keystrokes.

Using Alt-Letter and Descriptive Macros

You can create two kinds of macros that can be stored on disk and used in any WordPerfect session: Alt-letter macros and descriptive macros. An Alt-letter macro has a name that consists of the Alt key plus a letter from A to Z—for example, Alt-K or Alt-X. A descriptive macro has a name of one to eight characters—for example, TABS or MARGIN5.

Alt-letter macros are simpler to create and use. Choose Alt-letter names, therefore, for the macros you intend to use most often. Be sure to use macro names that will remind you of what your macros do; for instance, you might use the name Alt-C for a macro that centers text.

These two kinds of macros are saved to disk in a file with the macro name you have specified and the extension WPM—for example, ALTA.WPM or LTRHEAD.WPM. You don't have to provide the WPM extension for either of these two kinds of macros.

Note: When you create Alt-letter and descriptive macros, they are stored automatically in the \WP51 directory indicated on the Location of Files screen, which is accessed through the Setup menu. As you build your macro library, you will want to store your macros in their own directory rather than in the directory with your program files. To save your macros in their own directory, you can create a directory, such as \WP51\MACROS, and indicate that directory on the Location of Files screen. For more information about Location of Files, refer to Chapter 15.

Creating an Alt-Letter or Descriptive Macro

When you create a macro, you enter into the current document the keystrokes and commands you want the macro to "play back" when you run it. When you create a macro to change your tab settings, for example, you also change the tab settings at the cursor position in the current document. So that these macro keystrokes and commands do not interfere with any of your permanent files, you should save any document you are working on and clear the screen before you practice with macros. If you need some text for the macro to work on, you can type a few lines.

Suppose that you want to create a macro which inserts your return address, and you want to position each line of the address flush with the right margin. To create an Alt-letter or descriptive macro, follow these steps:

1. Press Ctrl F10 to activate the Macro Define command.

9

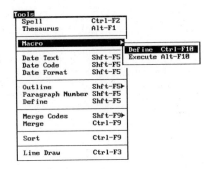

Access the Tools pull-down menu, select Macro, and choose Define.

The screen displays the following prompt:

```
Define macro:
```

2. Type the name of the macro.

   For an Alt-letter macro, press and hold down the [Alt] key, and then press a letter from A to Z.

For a descriptive macro, type one to eight characters (letters or numbers) and press [↵Enter]. For the return-address macro, type **ad** and press [↵Enter].

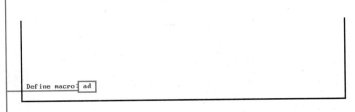

The screen displays this prompt:

```
Description:
```

3. Type a short description of what the macro does; then press [↵Enter].

   You can use any description, up to 39 characters, that will help remind you of the macro's commands. You should always provide a description of the macro. The description is the only part of the macro file that you can see when you use the Look option from the List Files menu.

9

For this example, type **Return address, flush right** as the description and press ⏎Enter.

`Macro Def` blinks at the bottom of the screen. This message tells you that the program is recording your keystrokes.

4. Type the keystrokes you want to record for the macro. Be sure to type them in the exact order in which you want them played back when you run the macro.

   For the return-address macro, press Alt F6 to activate the Flush Right command; or access the Layout pull-down menu, select Align, and choose Flush Right.

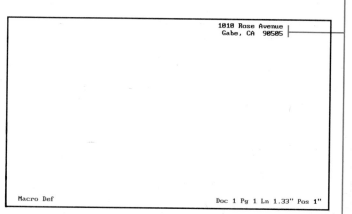

Type **1010 Rose Avenue** (or the first line of your actual address) and press ⏎Enter.

Press Alt F6 again; or access the Layout pull-down menu, choose Align, and select Flush Right.

Type **Gabe, CA 90505** (or your actual city, state, and ZIP code).

   Press ⏎Enter to position the cursor one line below the return address.

5. When you finish recording all the keystrokes for the macro, press Ctrl F10 (Macro Define) again.

   ▭ Access the Tools pull-down menu, select Macro, and choose Define.

Running an Alt-Letter or Descriptive Macro

When you run (play back) an Alt-letter or descriptive macro, the steps vary depending on which type of name you have assigned to the macro.

To run an Alt-letter macro you have created, simply press the Alt-letter key combination. If, for example, you have created an Alt-C macro to center a line of text, you invoke the macro by pressing and holding down the Alt key while pressing the letter C.

To run a descriptive macro you have created, follow these steps:

1. Press ⬚Alt⬚ ⬚F10⬚ to activate the Macro command.

   ⌨ Access the Tools pull-down menu, select Macro, and choose Execute.

2. Type the name of the macro (one to eight characters). For example, to run the return-address macro, type **ad**.

3. Press ⬚↵Enter⬚.

Notice that the command to run a descriptive macro—Macro (Alt-F10)—is different from the command to create a macro—Macro Define (Ctrl-F10). If you press Macro Define (Ctrl-F10) by mistake, you can press Cancel (F1).

Using Unnamed Macros

An unnamed macro works only until you create another one. You can have just one unnamed macro at a time because each unnamed macro you create replaces the preceding one. An unnamed macro can be useful, for instance, when you have a long or complicated name or title you must type repeatedly in a particular document.

An unnamed macro is preserved from one session to another. If you create an unnamed macro that types your name, for example, and then you exit WordPerfect before creating another unnamed macro, you still can use that unnamed macro the next time you use WordPerfect.

Creating an Unnamed Macro

You create an unnamed macro just as you create a descriptive macro, but instead of entering a macro name of one to eight characters and pressing Enter, you just press Enter.

Suppose, for example, that you want to create an unnamed macro that provides the title of an article, "Selma Stanislavsky and Modern Russian Theater," which appears a number of times in your document. To create an unnamed macro, follow these steps:

1. Press `Ctrl` `F10` to activate the Macro Define command.

   ▱ Access the **T**ools pull-down menu, select **M**acro, and choose **D**efine.

2. When the screen displays the prompt `Define macro:`, don't enter a name. Instead, press `⏎Enter`.

   WordPerfect automatically assigns the file name WP{WP}.WPM to the macro.

   Notice that you are not prompted for a description when you create an unnamed macro. The screen displays the blinking message `Macro Def`.

3. Type the keystrokes you want to record in the unnamed macro. For example, type the following:

   "Selma Stanislavsky and Modern Russian Theater"

4. Press `Ctrl` `F10` (Macro Define) to end the macro definition.

   ▱ Access the **T**ools pull-down menu, select **M**acro, and choose **D**efine.

Running an Unnamed Macro

Running an unnamed macro is a simple two-step procedure:

1. Press `Alt` `F10` to activate the Macro command.

   ▱ Access the **T**ools pull-down menu, select **M**acro, and choose **E**xecute.

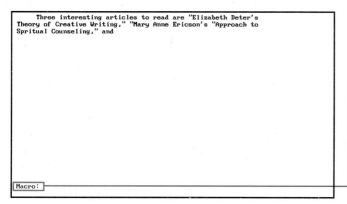

WordPerfect displays the prompt `Macro:`.

2. At the prompt, press ⏎Enter .

Notice that after
you run the
unnamed macro,
you need to add
punctuation
(a final period)
to the sentence.

> Three interesting articles to read are "Elizabeth Deter's
> Theory of Creative Writing," "Mary Anne Ericson's "Approach to
> Spritual Counseling," and "Selma Stanislavsky and Modern Russian
> Theater"

Although you could include the punctuation in the macro, you probably
would not want to do that because the punctuation throughout the document
may vary.

If you run an unnamed macro and it doesn't do what you expected, try
creating another unnamed macro. The new unnamed macro will replace the
existing one.

Stopping Macros

You use Cancel (F1) in many cases to "back out" of a process you started. You
can use this key also to back out of a definition you are creating for a macro or
to stop a macro in progress.

🖰   On a two-button mouse, holding down one button while clicking the
other button is the same as pressing Cancel (F1). On a three-button mouse,
clicking the middle button is the same as pressing Cancel (F1).

Backing Out of a Macro Definition

Before you name a macro, you can back out of a macro definition. If you start
to create a macro by using Macro Define (Ctrl-F10) and have not yet named it,
pressing Cancel (F1) cancels the macro definition and returns you to the
document.

After you name a macro, you cannot cancel it, but you can end the macro
definition either by pressing Macro Define (Ctrl-F10) or by accessing the **Tools**
pull-down menu, selecting **Macro**, and choosing **Define**. Although the macro
still is created with the name you assigned it, you can then delete, rename,
replace, or edit the macro.

Stopping a Macro in Progress

You can stop a macro while it is running by pressing Cancel (F1). If, for example, the macro is not doing what you expected, just press Cancel (F1).

After you cancel a macro, press Reveal Codes (Alt-F3, or F11 on an Enhanced Keyboard) to check the document for any unwanted codes. An incomplete macro can create codes you don't want in the document.

Replacing Macros

Imperfect macros, fortunately, are replaced easily. You may want to replace a macro for any of several reasons:

- You get an error message when you run the macro.
- The macro finishes but does not do what you want.
- You change your mind about exactly what you want the macro to do.

You can change what an Alt-letter or descriptive macro does in either of two ways:

- Replace the macro.
- Edit the macro.

When you replace a macro, you retain the macro name but create from scratch the description and contents of the macro. When you edit a macro, you use WordPerfect's macro editor to revise only the parts of the macro you want to change.

To replace a macro, follow these steps:

1. Press Ctrl F10 to activate the Macro Define command.

   ▣ Access the Tools pull-down menu, select Macro, and choose Define.

2. Enter the name of the preceding version of the macro.

9

For this example, type **ad** and press ⏎Enter).

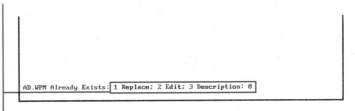

Define macro: ad

The program asks whether you want to **Replace** (**1**) the named macro, **Edit** (**2**) it, or simply change its **Description** (**3**).

AD.WPM Already Exists: 1 Replace; 2 Edit; 3 Description: 0

3. Select **Replace** (**1**).

4. At the prompt to confirm the replacement, select Yes.

    From this point in the procedure, replacing a macro is exactly the same as creating a macro from scratch.

5. Enter a description of the macro and press ⏎Enter).

6. Type the keystrokes you want the macro to record.

7. Press Ctrl F10 (Macro Define) to end the macro definition.

    ▭ Access the **Tools** pull-down menu, select Macro, and choose Define.

Remember that the procedure is exactly like creating a macro for the first time, except that you are prompted to replace the macro, edit it, or change the description.

Editing Macros

If you need to change an Alt-letter or descriptive macro you have created, you can start from scratch and create a revised macro with the Replace option. An alternative method is to edit the macro with WordPerfect's macro editor.

Note that within the macro editor, you can use the Enter key to rearrange the commands and text on-screen. Pressing Enter does not insert an {Enter} command. To insert an {Enter} command, you must first press Ctrl-V and then press Enter.

230

Suppose, for example, that you want to edit the AD macro so that it supplies and centers a new return address and the current date. To edit a macro with the macro editor, follow these steps:

1. Press Ctrl F10 to activate the Macro Define command.

   ▭ Access the Tools pull-down menu, select Macro, and choose Define.

2. Enter the name of the preceding version of the macro and press ↵Enter. In this case, type **ad** and press ↵Enter.

   The program asks whether you want to Replace (1) the named macro, Edit (2) it, or change its Description (3).

3. If you want to change the macro's description, select Description (3), edit the description, and press ↵Enter.

For this example, edit the description so that it states *Return address and date, centered*.

Or, if you want to retain the existing description, just select Edit (2).

9

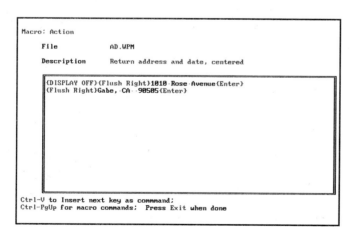

Whether you entered a new description or selected Edit (2) in this step, WordPerfect now displays the macro editor. This screen illustrates how the AD macro appears in the macro editor. From this screen, you easily can make changes and additions to the macro.

4. Make any editing changes you want to the commands or text. For this example, make the following changes:

   To change the address from flush right to centered, press → once to move the cursor to the first occurrence of the command {Flush Right}, and press Del to delete that command. With the cursor still positioned in the same spot, press ⇧Shift F6 to substitute the {Center} command.

   Move the cursor to the next occurrence of {Flush Right}, delete it, and press ⇧Shift F6 to substitute {Center}.

   To substitute a new return address, move the cursor to the text *1010 Rose Avenue*, delete it, and type in its place **333 Loop Rd.**

   Move the cursor to the text *Gabe, CA 90505*, delete it, and type in its place **Tucson, AZ 86023.**

   Press →, and then press ↵Enter to move the cursor to the beginning of the third line in the macro editor.

   To add the current date, press ⇧Shift F6 to insert the {Center} command that will center the date. Then press ⇧Shift F5 to enter the {Date/Outline} command, and type c to specify the code for the current date.

   Immediately after the *c* you just typed, press Ctrl V and then press ↵Enter to insert an {Enter} command.

   To move the cursor to a new line after you have entered the new address and current date, first press ↵Enter to move the cursor to the fourth line of the macro editor. Then press Ctrl V and ↵Enter to add an {Enter} command.

The AD macro is now edited so that it supplies and centers a new address and the current date.

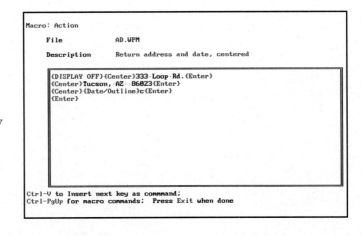

```
Macro: Action

   File           AD.WPM

   Description    Return address and date, centered

   {DISPLAY OFF}{Center}333 Loop Rd.{Enter}
   {Center}Tucson, AZ  86023{Enter}
   {Center}{Date/Outline}c{Enter}
   {Enter}




Ctrl-V to insert next key as command;
Ctrl-PgUp for macro commands;  Press Exit when done
```

```
┌─────────────────────────────────────────────────┐
│        333 Loop Rd.                              │
│     Tucson, AZ  86023                            │
│     February 19, 1992                            │
│                                                  │
│                                                  │
│                                                  │
│                                                  │
│                                                  │
│                                                  │
│                                                  │
│                                                  │
│                                                  │
│                                                  │
│                                                  │
│                                                  │
│                 Doc 1 Pg 1 Ln 1.67" Pos 1"       │
└─────────────────────────────────────────────────┘
```

When you run the revised AD macro on a clear screen, the result should look like this.

Creating a Macro Library

This section provides several macros you can create in starting your own macro library. Here you will find the step-by-step instructions for making the following macros:

- An interactive macro that creates memo headings
- A macro that changes margins
- A macro that italicizes the preceding word

Note: For these macros, you are instructed to make menu selections by pressing the appropriate letter for each menu item. This is good practice when you create any macro because you can then edit the macro easily.

An Interactive Macro That Creates Memo Headings

Suppose that you want to make a macro that creates standard memo headings. The macro will be interactive—that is, when you run the macro, it will pause and wait for your entries from the keyboard. After you type each entry, you must press Enter to continue the macro's operation.

Follow these steps to create a memo-headings macro:

1. Press Ctrl F10 to activate the Macro Define command.

   ⌨ Access the **T**ools pull-down menu, select **M**acro, and choose **D**efine.

2. Give the macro an Alt-letter name by pressing Alt M for *memo*. Or give the macro a descriptive name by typing **memo** and pressing ↵Enter.

3. For the macro description, type **Enter memo headings** and press
   ⏎Enter.

4. Press ⇧Shift F6 to activate the Center command.

5. Press F6 to activate the Bold command.

6. Type **MEMORANDUM**.

7. Press F6 again to end boldface for the title.

8. Press ⏎Enter four times to put enough blank lines between the title
   and the first heading.

9. Type **TO:** and press Tab⇆ twice.

10. To enter a pause in the macro, press Ctrl PgUp, P, and ⏎Enter.

11. Press ⏎Enter twice to insert a blank line between the first and second
    headings.

12. Type **FROM:** and press Tab⇆ once.

13. To enter a pause in the macro, press Ctrl PgUp, P, and ⏎Enter.

14. Press ⏎Enter twice to insert a blank line between the second and third
    headings.

15. Type **DATE:** and press Tab⇆ once.

16. Press ⇧Shift F5 to activate the Date/Outline command; then press C
    to insert today's date.

17. Press ⏎Enter twice to insert a blank line between the third and fourth
    headings.

18. Type **SUBJECT:** and press Tab⇆ once.

19. To enter a pause in the macro, press Ctrl PgUp, P, and ⏎Enter.

20. Press ⏎Enter four times to insert several blank lines between the last
    heading and the body of the memo.

The memo-
headings macro is
being created.

```
                              MEMORANDUM


        TO:

        FROM:

        DATE:        February 19, 1992

        SUBJECT:









 Macro Def                                    Doc 1 Pg 1 Ln 3.33" Pos 1"
```

9

21. Press `Ctrl` `F10` (Macro Define) to end the macro definition.

    🖰 Access the **T**ools pull-down menu, select **M**acro, and choose **D**efine.

A Macro That Changes Margins

You can create a macro to make any formatting command easier to use. Suppose, for example, that the default right and left margins are each 1 inch. Because you often may need to change each margin to 1 1/2 inches, you can create a macro that makes the changes quickly.

To create a macro that changes the margins, follow these steps:

1. Press `Ctrl` `F10` to activate the Macro Define command.

    🖰 Access the **T**ools pull-down menu, select **M**acro, and choose **D**efine.

2. At the `Define macro:` prompt, type **mar-15** and press `⏎Enter`.

3. At the `Description:` prompt, type **Change right and left margins to 1.5"** and press `⏎Enter`.

4. To go to the menu to edit margins, press `⇧Shift` `F8` (Format), and then press `L` to select **L**ine.

5. Press `M` to select **M**argins Left/Right from the full-screen menu that appears.

6. Type **1.5"** and press `⏎Enter`. Then type **1.5"** and press `⏎Enter` again.

7. Press `F7` (Exit) to return to the editing screen.

8. Press `Ctrl` `F10` (Macro Define) to end the macro definition.

    🖰 Access the **T**ools pull-down menu, select **M**acro, and choose **D**efine.

A Macro That Italicizes the Preceding Word

Italicizing text in WordPerfect requires several steps. When you need to italicize just one word, however, you can use a macro that italicizes the last word you typed.

Follow these steps to create a macro that italicizes the preceding word:

1. Type **Italicize the last word only**.

    The cursor is positioned immediately after the last word you want to italicize: the word *only*. Keep in mind that this is sample text used only

9

235

for the purpose of creating the macro. When you use the macro, the last word you type will be italicized, regardless of what word that is.

2. Press ⌈Ctrl⌉⌈F10⌉ to activate the Macro Define command.

   ▭ Access the **T**ools pull-down menu, select **M**acro, and choose **D**efine.

3. At the `Define macro:` prompt, press ⌈Alt⌉⌈I⌉ for *italicize* to name the macro.

4. At the `Description:` prompt, type **Italicize preceding word** and press ⌈⏎Enter⌉.

5. To highlight the text, press ⌈Alt⌉⌈F4⌉ or ⌈F12⌉ to activate the Block command, and then press ⌈Ctrl⌉⌈←⌉.

6. To italicize the block, press ⌈Ctrl⌉⌈F8⌉ to activate the Font command, press ⌈A⌉ (for **A**ppearance), and press ⌈I⌉ (for **I**talic).

   The word *only* is italicized.

7. Press ⌈Ctrl⌉⌈→⌉.

8. Press ⌈Ctrl⌉⌈F10⌉ (Macro Define) to end the macro definition.

   ▭ Access the **T**ools pull-down menu, select **M**acro, and choose **D**efine.

To use this macro, position the cursor immediately after the word you want to italicize. (The word can be the last word you typed or any word you have previously typed.) Then press Alt-I.

Summary

In this chapter, you learned the basics of creating a macro. You practiced the procedure by creating a return-address macro. You learned to name macros, run them, and stop them while they are running. You learned how to replace a macro and how to edit one in the macro editor. Finally, you learned to create several macros you can use in starting your own macro library.

Specifically, you learned the following key information about WordPerfect:

■ A macro is a series of prerecorded keystrokes assigned to a single key or key combination.

■ You can create three types of macros: Alt-letter, descriptive, and unnamed.

■ To create an Alt-letter or descriptive macro, select Macro Define (Ctrl-F10), type the name of the macro (either Alt-letter or a name from one to eight characters), and press Enter. Then type a short description and press Enter. Next, type the keystrokes you want to record. Finally, select Macro Define (Ctrl-F10) again.

■ To run an Alt-letter macro, press the Alt-letter key combination.

■ To run a descriptive macro, select Macro (Alt-F10), type the name of the macro, and press Enter.

■ An unnamed macro works only until you create another one. To create an unnamed macro, select Macro Define (Ctrl-F10), press Enter at the prompt, type the keystrokes you want to record, and select Macro Define (Ctrl-F10) again.

■ To run an unnamed macro, select Macro (Alt-F10) and press Enter at the prompt.

■ Use Cancel (F1) to back out of a macro definition you are creating or to stop a macro in progress.

■ When you replace a macro, you retain the macro name but create from scratch the description and contents of the macro. To replace a macro, select Macro Define (Ctrl-F10), enter the name of the macro, and choose the **Replace (1)** option. Answer **Yes** to the prompt. Then proceed as if you were creating a new macro.

■ When you edit a macro, you use WordPerfect's macro editor to revise only the parts of the macro you want to change. To edit a macro with the macro editor, select Macro Define (Ctrl-F10), enter the name of the macro, enter a description, and choose the **Edit (2)** option. Make the necessary changes with the macro editor.

■ Automate a number of tedious tasks you perform regularly and keep them in a handy macro library.

In the next chapter, you examine WordPerfect's Merge feature.

9

Merging Documents

The Merge feature, frequently referred to as *mail merge*, is one of WordPerfect's most versatile tools for increasing office productivity. You use Merge anytime you need to insert variable data into a fixed format. You can, for example, use Merge to create personalized form letters from an address list, produce phone lists, address envelopes, print mailing labels, piece together complicated reports, or fill in forms.

Key Terms in This Chapter

Merge	To assemble a document by inserting variable data into a fixed format.
Primary merge file	A skeleton document containing the fixed format into which pieces of data are merged.
Secondary merge file	A file containing the data (or variable information) that is merged into the primary merge file. The variable information is organized into records and fields.
Field	A unit of information that is part of a record. Each field contains the same type of information, such as a person's name; a street address; or a city, state, and ZIP code.
Record	A collection of fields with related information, such as a line of data, a paragraph, or a name and address in a secondary merge file.

Understanding the Basics

10

A merge operation requires a primary merge file, often in combination with a secondary merge file. The *primary merge file* is a skeleton document containing the fixed format into which pieces of data are merged. The *secondary merge file* contains data (or variable information) that is merged into the primary document.

This is the primary merge file.

```
{DATE}

{FIELD}FullName~
{FIELD}Company?~
{FIELD}Street~
{FIELD}City~

Dear {FIELD}FirstName~:

Simpson Travel and Tours want to help with all of your travel
plans.  Whether you are going across the state, across the country,
or around the world, give me a call.  I'll guarantee you the best
fares and the most convenient connections.

Enclosed is a brochure that describes some of this season's best
travel bargains.  Call me for additional details on prices and
schedules.

Sinderely,


Sally Oceans
Travel Agent
C:\WP51\BOOK\TRAVEL.PMF                        Doc 1 Pg 1 Ln 1" Pos 1"
```

```
{FIELD NAMES}FullName~Company~Street~City~FirstName~~{END RECORD}
================================================================
Ms. Katherine Haley{END FIELD}
Town Investments Company{END FIELD}
5 Waverly Place{END FIELD}
New York, NY  10022{END FIELD}
Kathy{END FIELD}
{END RECORD}
================================================================
Mr. Dave Acevedo{END FIELD}
Theatrical Productions{END FIELD}
1120 E. Broadway{END FIELD}
Sacramento, CA  95899{END FIELD}
Dave{END FIELD}
{END RECORD}
================================================================
Mr. John Quigley{END FIELD}
{END FIELD}
1423 So. Spencer St.{END FIELD}
Euclid, OH  46666{END FIELD}
John{END FIELD}
{END RECORD}
================================================================
C:\WP51\BOOK\ADDRESS.SMF                    Doc 1 Pg 1 Ln 1" Pos 1"
```

This is the secondary merge file.

```
February 20, 1992

Ms. Katherine Haley
Town Investments Company
5 Waverly Place
New York, NY  10022

Dear Kathy:

Simpson Travel and Tours want to help with all of your travel
plans.  Whether you are going across the state, across the country,
or around the world, give me a call.  I'll guarantee you the best
fares and the most convenient connections.
```

```
February 20, 1992

Mr. Dave Acevedo
Theatrical Productions
1120 E. Broadway
Sacramento, CA  95899

Dear Dave:

Simpson Travel and Tours want to help with all of your travel
plans.  Whether you are going across the state, across the country,
or around the world, give me a call.  I'll guarantee you the best
fares and the most convenient connections.
```

```
February 20, 1992

Mr. John Quigley
1423 So. Spencer St.
Euclid, OH  46666

Dear John:

Simpson Travel and Tours want to help with all of your travel
plans.  Whether you are going across the state, across the country,
or around the world, give me a call.  I'll guarantee you the best
fares and the most convenient connections.

Enclosed is a brochure that describes some of this season's best
travel bargains.  Call me for additional details on prices and
schedules.

Sinderely,
```

These letters resulted from merging the sample secondary merge file and the primary merge file.

10

The primary merge file contains fixed text, graphics, and merge codes. You place merge codes where you want to insert variable items into the fixed text. When a merge is completed, the codes are replaced with entries from a secondary merge file or from the keyboard.

241

The most typical and timesaving merge uses a secondary merge file that contains related variable data, such as an address list. All the information relating to one person makes up a *record*. Within each record, the separate items, such as a person's name or street address, are known as *fields*. WordPerfect inserts these items into the primary merge file by matching the codes in the primary and secondary merge files.

Fields, records, and certain merge operations are controlled by merge codes. You must put these codes in the right places and in the right order to ensure the success of a merge.

Merging Text Files

A text file merge combines two existing files—a primary merge file and a secondary merge file. Before you can execute such a merge, you must create these files. Create the secondary merge file first so that you know the field names and order before you create the primary merge file.

After you create the secondary merge file, such as an address list, you can merge the data in that file with several primary files. You can, for example, merge the data with a form letter for a mass mailing, and you can use the address data to print envelopes or mailing labels.

Creating a Secondary File

A secondary merge file, or secondary file, consists of records, each of which contains a number of fields. The structure must be uniform; otherwise, the merge won't work properly. Every record must have the same number of fields (although a field can be blank), and the fields must be in the same order in all records. If, for example, the first name is in the first field, but one record has the last name in the first field, WordPerfect will print a last name where the first name should be.

Suppose that you are creating a secondary file that contains address information. Each record in the file will contain the same units of information (or fields). The following is a list of the fields in each record:

FullName
Company
Street
City
FirstName

When you create a secondary file, you can name each of the fields and include at the top of the file a list of all the field names. You include also certain codes to indicate where each record ends and where each field ends.

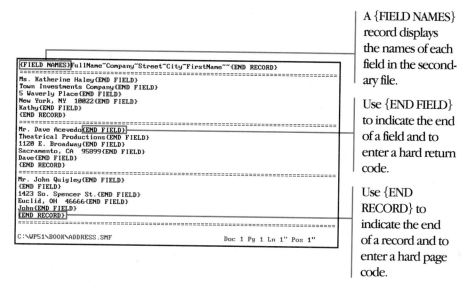

```
{FIELD NAMES}FullName~Company~Street~City~FirstName~~{END RECORD}
=================================================================
Ms. Katherine Haley{END FIELD}
Town Investments Company{END FIELD}
5 Waverly Place{END FIELD}
New York, NY  10022{END FIELD}
Kathy{END FIELD}
{END RECORD}
=================================================================
Mr. Dave Acevedo{END FIELD}
Theatrical Productions{END FIELD}
1120 E. Broadway{END FIELD}
Sacramento, CA  95899{END FIELD}
Dave{END FIELD}
{END RECORD}
=================================================================
Mr. John Quigley{END FIELD}
{END FIELD}
1423 So. Spencer St.{END FIELD}
Euclid, OH  46666{END FIELD}
John{END FIELD}
{END RECORD}
=================================================================
C:\WP51\BOOK\ADDRESS.SMF              Doc 1 Pg 1 Ln 1" Pos 1"
```

A {FIELD NAMES} record displays the names of each field in the secondary file.

Use {END FIELD} to indicate the end of a field and to enter a hard return code.

Use {END RECORD} to indicate the end of a record and to enter a hard page code.

To create the {FIELD NAMES} record for the sample secondary file, follow these steps:

1. Clear the screen and place the cursor at the top left margin.
2. Press ⇧Shift F9 to activate the Merge Codes command.

```
1 Field; 2 End Record; 3 Input; 4 Page Off; 5 Next Record; 6 More: 0
```

The Merge Codes menu is displayed at the bottom of the screen.

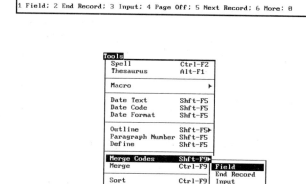

```
Tools
  Spell             Ctrl-F2
  Thesaurus         Alt-F1
  Macro                    ▶
  Date Text         Shft-F5
  Date Code         Shft-F5
  Date Format       Shft-F5
  Outline           Shft-F5▶
  Paragraph Number  Shft-F5
  Define            Shft-F5
  Merge Codes       Shft-F9▶
  Merge             Ctrl-F9  Field
                             End Record
  Sort              Ctrl-F9  Input
                             Page Off
  Line Draw         Ctrl-F3  Next Record
                             More
```

⌨ Access the Tools pull-down menu and select Merge Codes to display the Merge Codes pop-out menu.

10

243

3. Select More (6).

```
{END WHILE}~
{FIELD}field~                                    (^F)
{FIELD NAMES)name1~...nameN~~
{FOR}var~start~stop~step~
{GO}label~
{IF}expr~
{IF BLANK}field~
{IF EXISTS}var~
{IF NOT BLANK}field~
{INPUT}message~
```

The Merge Codes
selection box
appears.

```
field n                          (Name Search; Arrows; Enter to Select)
```

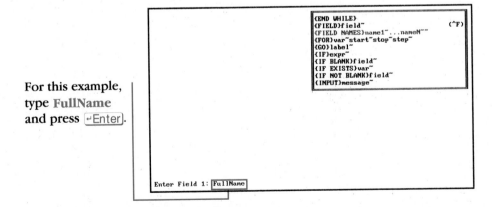

4. Highlight the {FIELD NAMES} code in the Merge Codes selection box. Either use the arrow keys or mouse to move the highlight bar to {FIELD NAMES}, or start typing the words *field names*.

   Move the mouse pointer to the Merge Codes selection box. Drag the mouse to move the highlight bar to the {FIELD NAMES} code.

5. With the highlight bar on the {FIELD NAMES} code, press ⏎Enter.

   Double-click the {FIELD NAMES} code.

6. At the Enter Field 1: prompt, type the name of the first field.

```
{END WHILE}~
{FIELD}field~                                    (^F)
{FIELD NAMES}name1~...nameN~~
{FOR}var~start~stop~step~
{GO}label~
{IF}expr~
{IF BLANK}field~
{IF EXISTS}var~
{IF NOT BLANK}field~
{INPUT}message~
```

For this example,
type **FullName**
and press ⏎Enter.

```
Enter Field 1: FullName
```

7. At the Enter Field 2: prompt, type the name of the second field. In this case, type **Company** and press ⏎Enter.

8. If you have more fields, continue to enter their names at the prompts. For this example, type **Street** for Field 3, type **City** for Field 4, and type **FirstName** for Field 5.

9. After you type the last field name, press ⏎Enter at the next prompt for a field name. Pressing ⏎Enter tells WordPerfect that you are finished entering field names.

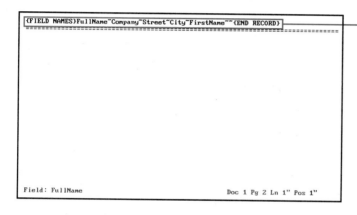

WordPerfect inserts a {FIELD NAMES} record at the top of the document.

To create the rest of the records for the secondary file, follow these steps:

1. Make sure that the cursor is at the top of page 2, immediately following the page break.

2. Type the name for the first record. For this example, type **Ms. Katherine Haley**. Do *not* press ⏎Enter.

3. Press F9 to activate the End Field command. WordPerfect inserts an {END FIELD} code and a hard return code after the name you have typed.

4. Notice that the field name indicator in the lower left corner has changed to Company. Type the name of the company. In this case, type **Town Investments Company**.

5. Press F9 again.

6. Type the rest of the information for the first record. Make sure that you press F9 at the end of each field, including the last one. Use the following data:

    5 Waverly Place
    New York, NY 10022
    Kathy

10

7. When you have entered all the fields for Katherine Haley's record, press ⟨⇧Shift⟩ ⟨F9⟩ (Merge Codes).

   ⌨️ Access the Tools pull-down menu and select Merge Codes to display the Merge Codes pop-out menu.

8. Select End Record (2).

An {END RECORD} code appears, followed by a hard page code.

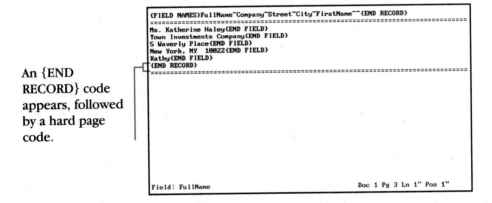

```
{FIELD NAMES}FullName~Company~Street~City~FirstName~~{END RECORD}
===============================================================================
Ms. Katherine Haley{END FIELD}
Town Investments Company{END FIELD}
5 Waverly Place{END FIELD}
New York, NY 10022{END FIELD}
Kathy{END FIELD}
{END RECORD}
===============================================================================




Field: FullName                                  Doc 1 Pg 3 Ln 1" Pos 1"
```

9. Repeat Steps 2 through 8 for each of the remaining records. Select End Record (2) after each set of fields in order to start each record on a separate page.

   Use the following data:

   > Mr. Dave Acevedo
   > Theatrical Productions
   > 1120 E. Broadway
   > Sacramento, CA 95899
   > Dave

   > Mr. John Quigley
   > {END FIELD}
   > 1423 So. Spencer St.
   > Euclid, OH 46666
   > John

   Note: If your records contain any blank fields, such as a field without an entry for the company name, you must acknowledge the presence of those fields. You do this by pressing ⟨F9⟩ (End Field) to insert an {END FIELD} code in the blank field.

10. When you finish entering records, press ⟨F7⟩ (Exit) and give the file a descriptive name, such as ADDRESS.SMF. The SMF extension can remind you that the file is a secondary merge file.

10

246

Creating a Primary File

A primary merge file, or primary file, contains fixed text and merge codes. Each merge code tells WordPerfect to insert a certain item from the secondary file into the primary file. The item is inserted at the location of the code. WordPerfect prepares a separate personalized document for each record in the secondary merge file.

Use a {DATE} code to insert the current date.

Use a {FIELD}*fieldname~* code to tell WordPerfect to insert an item from the secondary file into the primary file at the location of the code.

Use a {FIELD}*fieldname?~* code to prevent a blank line from appearing where an empty field exists in the secondary file.

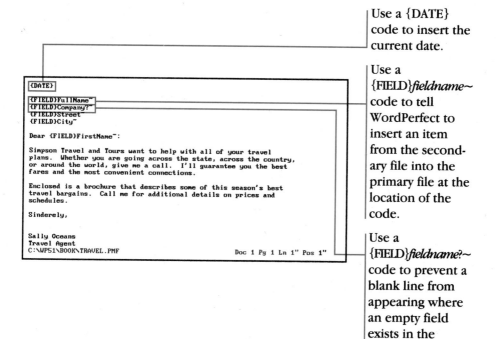

By splitting the screen, you can see the relationship between the two merge files. The field names in the primary file are evident in the top half, and the variable data fields in the secondary file are visible in the bottom half.

10

247

The most commonly used code is the field name code, {FIELD}*fieldname~*. The *fieldname* indicates the field name of each record in the secondary file. For example, when you specify {FIELD}Street~, you instruct WordPerfect to enter at that particular location the information found in the Street field.

If a record contains a blank field followed by a hard return, the empty field will be printed as a blank line. To prevent a blank line from appearing, add a question mark after the field name. For example, you might use the code {FIELD}Company?~ in your primary file because some records in your secondary file don't have a company name.

Make sure that you correctly enter the field names in the primary file. Each field name must match the appropriate field in the secondary file; otherwise, an incorrect item or no item will be merged.

To create the primary file, follow these steps:

1. Position the cursor at the place in the document where you want the current date entered.

2. Press ⬆Shift F9 to activate the Merge Codes command, and select **More** (6).

   ▭ Access the Tools pull-down menu, select Merge Codes, and choose More.

   The Merge Codes selection box appears.

3. Highlight the {DATE} code in the Merge Codes selection box. Either use the arrow keys to move the highlight bar to {DATE}, or start typing the word *date*.

   ▭ Move the mouse pointer to the Merge Codes selection. Drag the mouse to move the highlight bar to the {DATE} code.

4. With the highlight bar on {DATE}, press ↵Enter.

   ▭ Double-click {DATE}.

   A {DATE} code appears in the document.

5. Press ↵Enter twice to skip a line and to position the cursor where you want to begin entering the name and address.

6. Press ⬆Shift F9 (Merge Codes) and select Field (1).

   ▭ Access the Tools pull-down menu, select Merge Codes, and choose Field.

7. At the Enter Field: prompt, type the name of the field exactly as you have defined it.

10

For example, to enter the name of the first field, type **FullName**.

8. Press ⏎Enter.

WordPerfect inserts a {FIELD} code followed by the name of the field and a tilde (~).

9. Continue typing the sample letter, entering the {FIELD}*fieldname~* codes as they appear. Repeat Steps 6 through 8 to enter the codes. Be sure to add a question mark (?) when you enter the Company field. At the Enter Field: prompt for that field, type **Company?**

10. When you finish creating the primary file, press F7 (Exit) and save the file with a name that indicates the file's purpose. For example, use the name TRAVEL.PMF; the PMF extension serves as a reminder that this is a primary merge file.

Merging the Primary and Secondary Files

After you create the primary and secondary files, you are ready to start the merge. If you have a small secondary file, you can merge the files to the screen. If you have a large secondary file, you can merge directly to the printer.

Merging to the Screen

When you merge files to the screen, you can check for errors in the merge before you print. To merge the text files to the screen, follow these steps:

1. Clear the screen.

2. Press Ctrl F9 to activate the Merge/Sort command, and select **Merge** (**1**).

   ▱ Access the **Tools** pull-down menu and select **Merge**.

3. At the Primary file: prompt, type the name of the primary file and press ⏎Enter.

10

For this example, type **travel.pmf** and press ⏎Enter.

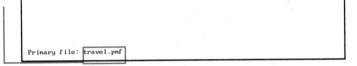

Primary file: travel.pmf

4. At the Secondary file: prompt, type the name of the secondary file.

In this case, type **address.smf** and press ⏎Enter.

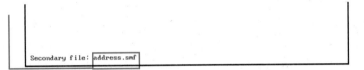

Secondary file: address.smf

WordPerfect merges the primary file with the secondary file. While this is happening, the program displays the message * Merging * in the lower left corner of the screen.

When the merging process reaches the {DATE} code, WordPerfect automatically replaces the code with the current date. If your computer has a battery-powered clock/calendar or if you have entered the correct date at the beginning of each session, the display shows the correct date; otherwise, an incorrect date may appear. At each of the {FIELD} codes, WordPerfect substitutes the appropriate information from the secondary file.

10

When the merge is completed, the screen displays the last letter in the merge operation.

```
February 28, 1992

Mr. John Quigley
1423 So. Spencer St.
Euclid, OH  46666

Dear John:

Simpson Travel and Tours want to help with all of your travel
plans.  Whether you are going across the state, across the country,
or around the world, give me a call.  I'll guarantee you the best
fares and the most convenient connections.

Enclosed is a brochure that describes some of this season's best
travel bargains.  Call me for additional details on prices and
schedules.

Sinderely,


Sally Oceans
Travel Agent

                                        Doc 1 Pg 3 Ln 4.67" Pos 2.2"
```

If you move the cursor to the beginning of the document, you will find the first completed letter. Notice that all the necessary items are filled in, and each letter is separated from the others with a hard page code. The letters are ready to print, and each letter will be printed on a separate page.

Merging to the Printer

When you are creating a large number of form letters, all the merged letters may not fit into memory. WordPerfect therefore won't be able to complete the merge and display the letters on-screen. To solve this problem—or simply to save time by eliminating the step of displaying the letters on-screen—you can send the results of a merge operation directly to the printer.

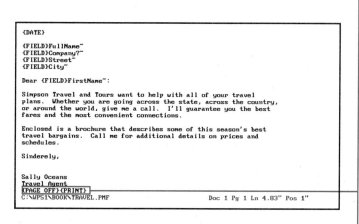

```
{DATE}

{FIELD}FullName~
{FIELD}Company?~
{FIELD}Street~
{FIELD}City~

Dear {FIELD}FirstName~:

Simpson Travel and Tours want to help with all of your travel
plans.  Whether you are going across the state, across the country,
or around the world, give me a call.  I'll guarantee you the best
fares and the most convenient connections.

Enclosed is a brochure that describes some of this season's best
travel bargains.  Call me for additional details on prices and
schedules.

Sinderely,


Sally Oceans
Travel Agent
{PAGE OFF}{PRINT}
C:\WP51\BOOK\TRAVEL.PMF                    Doc 1 Pg 1 Ln 4.83" Pos 1"
```

Create a merge to the printer by inserting into the primary file a {PRINT} code, which instructs WordPerfect to send to the printer any text merged up to that point.

You also must include a {PAGE OFF} code so that the printer properly prints consecutive sheets one at a time.

10

To add the codes for merging directly to the printer, follow these steps:

1. Press Home, Home, ↓ to move the cursor to the bottom of the primary file.

2. Press ⇧Shift F9 to activate the Merge Codes command, and select Page Off (4).

   Access the Tools pull-down menu, select Merge Codes, and choose Page Off.

   A {PAGE OFF} code appears at the bottom of the document.

3. Press ⬦Shift F9 again and select More (6).

   🖱 Access the Tools pull-down menu, select Merge Codes, and choose More.

4. Highlight the {PRINT} code in the Merge Codes selection box. Either use the arrow keys to move the highlight bar to {PRINT}, or start typing the word *print*.

   🖱 Move the mouse pointer to the Merge Codes selection box. Drag the mouse to move the highlight bar to the {PRINT} code.

5. With the highlight bar on {PRINT}, press ⏎Enter.

   🖱 Double-click the {PRINT} code.

   A {PRINT} code appears at the end of the document.

After you add the merge codes for printing, save the letter (again using the file name TRAVEL.PMF), turn on the printer, and merge the text files with the same procedure you used to merge the files to the screen. WordPerfect then prints your letters.

If your computer freezes while the screen displays the * Merging * message, don't panic—you probably forgot to turn on the printer. If you turn it on, the document starts to print, and the screen returns to normal.

Merging to the printer is an excellent way to automate certain tasks. If you have a fast printer, you can print many personalized letters with minimum effort.

10 | Merging from the Keyboard

The simplest form of merge is the keyboard merge. This kind of merge uses a special merge code that makes merge-printing pause so that you can enter information from the keyboard. Keyboard merges are useful for filling in preprinted forms, addressing memos, and entering frequently updated information in a form letter.

Preparing the Primary File for a Keyboard Merge

For a keyboard merge, you need only a primary file with text and a few merge codes. Suppose, for example, that you regularly send a memo announcing the time, date, and subject of a monthly meeting. Your primary file can contain the regular text of a letter and the merge codes that hold the places for the variable information.

Two kinds of merge codes are useful in the primary file for the memo:

- The {DATE} code to indicate where the current date is displayed.
- The {INPUT} code to indicate where an entry from the keyboard is placed.

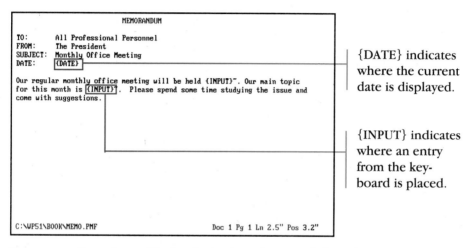

{DATE} indicates where the current date is displayed.

{INPUT} indicates where an entry from the keyboard is placed.

To prepare the primary file for the keyboard merge, follow these steps:

1. Begin typing the memo.

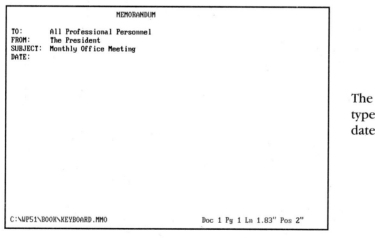

The memo is typed up to the date entry.

2. To enter the date merge code, press ⇧Shift F9 to activate the Merge Codes command.

253

☐ Access the Tools pull-down menu and select Merge Codes.

3. Select More (6).

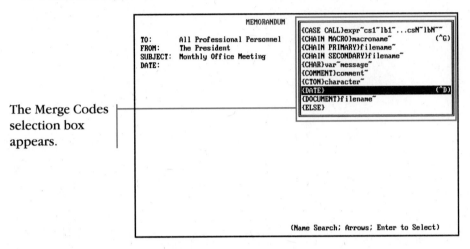

The Merge Codes
selection box
appears.

4. Highlight the {DATE} code in the Merge Codes selection box. Either use the arrow keys to move the highlight bar to {DATE} or start typing the word *date*.

☐ Move the mouse pointer to the Merge Codes selection box. Drag the mouse to move the highlight bar to the {DATE} code.

5. With the highlight bar on the {DATE} code, press ⏎Enter.

☐ Double-click the {DATE} code.

6. Continue typing the memo.

10

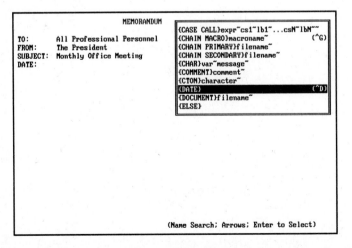

The memo is
typed up to the
point where the
{INPUT} merge
code will be
inserted.

7. To enter a merge code that pauses for keyboard input ({INPUT}), position the cursor at the first spot where you want the merge to pause.

8. To enter the first {INPUT} merge code, press ⬆Shift F9 to activate the Merge Codes command.

   ⌨️ Access the Tools pull-down menu and select Merge Codes.

9. Select More (6).

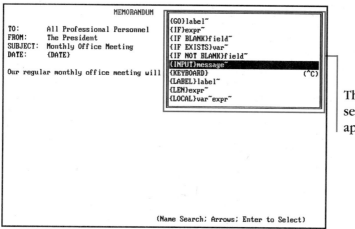

The Merge Codes selection box appears.

10. Highlight the {INPUT} code in the Merge Codes selection box. Either use the arrow keys to move the highlight bar to {INPUT} or start typing the word *input*.

    ⌨️ Move the mouse pointer to the Merge Codes selection box. Drag the mouse to move the highlight bar to the {INPUT} code.

11. With the highlight bar on the {INPUT} code, press ↵Enter.

    ⌨️ Double-click the {INPUT} code.

    At this point, you could enter a message to be displayed during the merge. But for this exercise, no message will be needed.

12. At the Enter Message: prompt, press ↵Enter.

13. Continue typing the memo, and repeat steps 7 to 12 to enter each of the other {INPUT} codes.

14. Finish typing the memo and save it. Name the memo MEMO.PMF, for example.

10

Running a Keyboard Merge

When you run the keyboard merge, WordPerfect pauses and waits for keyboard input whenever the program reaches an {INPUT} code.

To merge-print the memo, follow these steps:

1. Clear the screen.

2. Press `Ctrl` `F9` to activate the Merge/Sort command and select Merge (1).

    🖮 Access the Tools pull-down menu and select Merge.

3. Type the name of the primary file and press `⏎Enter`. For the example, type **memo.pmf** and press `⏎Enter`.

4. Because you are not using a secondary merge file, press `⏎Enter` again.

    The cursor replaces the {INPUT} code and is positioned at the appropriate place in your document.

5. Enter the first segment of the variable text. For the example, type **3:00 P.M., Thursday, August 25**.

6. Press `F9` (End Field) to continue the merge.

    The cursor goes to the position of the next {INPUT} code (which is no longer displayed) so that you can type the text for this code.

7. Enter the next segment of variable text. For the example, type **the company's sagging profit**.

8. Press `F9` (End Field).

9. Save and print the memo.

10

The example
memo is printed.

```
                        MEMORANDUM

        TO:       All Professional Personnel
        FROM:     The President
        SUBJECT:  Monthly Office Meeting
        DATE:     August 1, 1992

        Our regular monthly office meeting will be held 3:00 P.M.,
        Thursday, August 25.  Our main topic for this month is the
        company's sagging profit.  Please spend some time studying the
        issue and come with suggestions.
```

While the merge is in progress, WordPerfect displays the message `* Merging *` on the status line. When you enter the last item and press End Field (F9), the message disappears.

Automating Tasks with the Merge Feature

After you have created a secondary file, you can use that file to automate a number of other tasks. Two common tasks that you might want to automate are addressing envelopes and printing mailing labels.

Addressing Envelopes

The procedure for addressing envelopes begins with selecting the paper form. You must edit or create a form definition for envelopes (if your printer doesn't already have an appropriate definition). Next, you need to create a primary file that selects the envelope definition, specifies the location on the envelope where the address should be printed, and specifies which fields should be merged from the secondary file. Finally, you need to merge the secondary file of addresses directly to the printer to print your envelopes.

Creating an Envelope Form Definition

Depending on what kind of printer you are using, you may already have a form definition for envelopes. If you have one, you still may need to use the first procedure described here, showing how to edit your form definition so that it will work properly for printing envelopes. If you don't have an envelope definition, use the second procedure to create the definition. These procedures define a form for a standard 9 1/2-by-4-inch business envelope that you can feed manually into your printer. The printer will prompt you to insert each envelope. (This basic procedure is covered in detail in the section "Choosing Paper Size and Type" in Chapter 5.) Note that these procedures may vary according to your printer. The steps that follow are designed for an HP LaserJet Series II printer.

Follow these steps to edit a form definition for envelopes:

1. Press ⬆Shift F8 to activate the Format command, select Page (2), and choose Paper Size/Type (7).

   ▭ Access the Layout pull-down menu, select Page, and choose Paper Size/Type (7).

2. Use the arrow keys to highlight the envelope definition, and select Edit (5).

3. Select Location (5) and choose Manual (3).

4. Select Prompt to Load (4) and choose No.

10

5. Press [F7] (Exit) three times to return to the editing screen.

Follow these steps to create a form definition for envelopes:

1. Press [⇧Shift] [F8] to activate the Format command, select **Page** (2), and choose Paper Size/Type (7).

   ⌨️ Access the Layout pull-down menu, select **Page**, and choose Paper Size/Type (7).

2. Select **Add** (Create) (2), choose **Envelope** (5), and select Paper Size (1).

3. Select **Envelope** (5).

4. Select Font Type (3) and choose **Landscape** (2).

5. Select **Location** (5) and choose **Manual** (3).

6. Select **Prompt** to Load (4) and choose **No**.

The Format: Edit Paper Definition menu is displayed with your selections indicated.

```
Format: Edit Paper Definition

         Filename              HPLASIII.PRS

    1 - Paper Size             9.5" x 4"

    2 - Paper Type             Envelope - Wide

    3 - Font Type              Landscape

    4 - Prompt to Load         No

    5 - Location               Manual

    6 - Double Sided Printing  No

    7 - Binding Edge           Left

    8 - Labels                 No

    9 - Text Adjustment - Top  0"
                        Side   0"

    Selection: 0
```

7. Press [↵Enter] to return to the list of form definitions.

The definition you created for envelopes is highlighted.

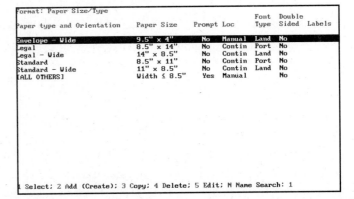

Paper type and Orientation	Paper Size	Prompt	Loc	Font Type	Double Sided	Labels
Envelope - Wide	9.5" x 4"	No	Manual	Land	No	
Legal	8.5" x 14"	No	Contin	Port	No	
Legal - Wide	14" x 8.5"	No	Contin	Land	No	
Standard	8.5" x 11"	No	Contin	Port	No	
Standard - Wide	11" x 8.5"	No	Contin	Land	No	
[ALL OTHERS]	Width ≤ 8.5"	Yes	Manual		No	

1 Select; 2 Add (Create); 3 Copy; 4 Delete; 5 Edit; N Name Search: 1

8. Press ⌗F7⌗ (Exit) twice to return to the editing screen.

Creating the Envelope Primary File

After you have defined the envelope form, you need to select the definition and then format your page for printing the address on the envelope. This section takes you step-by-step through the procedure for selecting the form and positioning the address on a standard 9 1/2-by-4-inch business envelope. The address will be printed 2 inches from the top of the envelope and 4 1/2 inches from the left side of the envelope. After you accomplish the formatting, you need to specify which fields should be used from the secondary file (in this example, ADDRESS.SMF) for merge printing the addresses.

To select the envelope definition, follow these steps:

1. Begin a new document. This document will become the primary file.

2. Access the Document Initial Codes screen by pressing ⌗Shift⌗ F8⌗ to activate the Format command, selecting Document (3), and choosing Initial Codes (2).

   ▭⌣ Access the Layout pull-down menu, select Document, and choose Initial Codes (2).

   Note: Putting the formatting codes for the primary document into Document Initial Codes is important. Otherwise, all formatting codes will be repeated at the top of every page in the final document.

3. Press ⌗Shift⌗ F8⌗ again and select Page (2).

   ▭⌣ Access the Layout pull-down menu and select Page.

4. Select Paper Size/Type (7).

5. Use the arrow keys or mouse to highlight the envelope definition, and choose Select (1).

6. Press ⌗F7⌗ (Exit) to return to the Document Initial Codes screen.

To enter the formatting codes for printing the address, follow these steps:

1. From the Document Initial Codes screen, press ⌗Shift⌗ F8⌗ (Format), select Line (1), and choose Margins Left/Right (7).

   ▭⌣ Access the Layout pull-down menu, select Line, and choose Margins Left/Right (7).

2. Type **4.5"** for the left margin and press ⏎Enter⌗. Then type **0.5"** for the right margin and press ⏎Enter⌗.

3. Press ⏎Enter⌗ to return to the Format menu.

4. Select Page (2) and choose Margins Top/Bottom (5).

10

5. Type 0 for the top margin and press ⏎Enter. Then type 0 for the bottom margin and press ⏎Enter.

   WordPerfect fills in the minimum values for the top and bottom margins.

6. Press F7 (Exit) three times to return to the editing screen.

7. Press ⇧Shift F8 (Format) and select Other (4).

   ⌨ Access the Layout pull-down menu and select Other.

8. Select Advance (1), choose Line (3), type 2", and press ⏎Enter.

9. Press F7 (Exit) to return to the editing screen.

To enter the merge codes for printing the envelopes, follow these steps:

1. Press ⇧Shift F9 to activate the Merge Codes command, and select Field (1).

   ⌨ Access the Tools pull-down menu, select Merge Codes, and choose Field.

2. At the Enter Field: prompt, type **FullName** (the name of the first field in the secondary file) and press ⏎Enter.

3. Press ⏎Enter to move the cursor to a new line.

4. Enter the rest of the fields from the secondary file for the envelope's address.

   At the next Enter Field: prompt, type **Company?** (the name of the second field in the secondary file) and press ⏎Enter. Remember that the question mark prevents the insertion of a blank line in an address. Press ⏎Enter to go to the next line.

   At the next Enter Field: prompt, type **Street** (the name of the third field in the secondary file) and press ⏎Enter. Press ⏎Enter again.

   At the next Enter Field: prompt, type **City** (the name of the fourth field in the secondary file) and press ⏎Enter.

5. Press ⏎Enter to move to a new line.

6. Press ⇧Shift F9 (Merge Codes) and select Page Off (4).

   ⌨ Access the Tools pull-down menu, select Merge Codes, and choose Page Off.

   A {PAGE OFF} code appears in the document, just below the field names.

7. Press ⇧Shift F9 again and select More (6).

   ⌨ Access the Tools pull-down menu, select Merge Codes, and choose More.

10

8. Highlight the {PRINT} code in the Merge Codes selection box. Either use the arrow keys to move the highlight bar to {PRINT}, or start typing the word *print*.

   ▧   Move the mouse pointer to the Merge Codes selection box. Drag the mouse to move the highlight bar to the {PRINT} code.

9. With the highlight bar on {PRINT}, press ⏎Enter.

   ▧   Double-click the {PRINT} code.

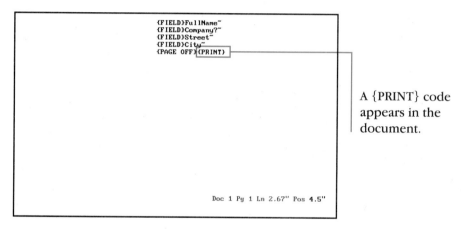

A {PRINT} code appears in the document.

10. Press F7 (Exit), and then save the file under the name ENVELOPE.PMF.

Merging Files To Print Envelopes

Now that you have created the envelope definition, selected it, and created a primary file for printing envelopes, you can merge the ENVELOPE.PMF file with the ADDRESS.SMF file. (**Note:** Be sure to open the back of your printer so that the envelopes can flow out easily.)

Follow these steps to merge the address and envelope files and to send the results directly to the printer:

1. Clear the screen.

2. Press Ctrl F9 to activate the Merge/Sort command, and select **Merge (1)**.

   ▧   Access the Tools pull-down menu and select **Merge**.

3. At the `Primary file:` prompt, type the name of the primary file. For this example, type **envelope.pmf** and press ⏎Enter.

4. At the `Secondary file:` prompt, type the name of the secondary file. In this case, type **address.smf** and press `⏎Enter`.

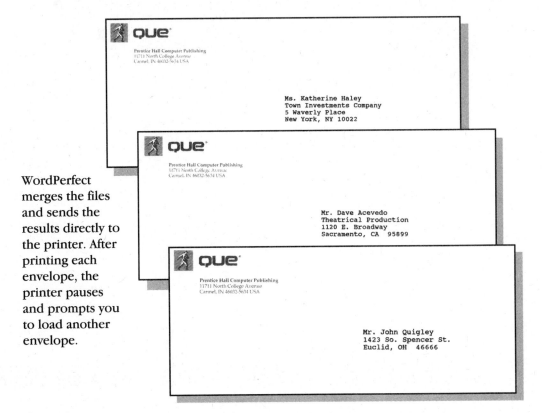

WordPerfect merges the files and sends the results directly to the printer. After printing each envelope, the printer pauses and prompts you to load another envelope.

10

Printing Mailing Labels

Mailing labels are one of the classic applications of merge capabilities. The first step is to create a label definition. You can do this through the Format: Labels menu by defining a paper size and type, showing the number of labels, the dimensions of each label, the arrangement of labels on the paper, and the margins you want to maintain on each label.

If you are using standard-sized labels, however, an easier method is to create the label definition with a macro. WordPerfect provides a macro, LABELS.WPM, that automatically creates label definitions for a variety of popular label sheets. You can run this macro and, if your labels are listed on the menu that appears, create the label definition you need. Refer to Chapter 9, "Creating Macros," for information on macros.

After you create the label definition, you need to create a primary file that selects the label definition and specifies which fields should be merged from the secondary file. Then you can merge the primary file with the secondary file of addresses and print your labels.

Suppose, for example, that you want to create mailing labels on a label sheet that is 8 1/2 by 11 inches and that holds 30 labels arranged in 3 columns. And you want to print the labels on an HP LaserJet Series II printer. Note that these instructions may vary depending on your printer.

To use the LABELS macro to create a label form definition, follow these steps:

1. Press ⎡Alt⎤ ⎡F10⎤ to activate the Macro command.

   ⌨ Access the Tools pull-down menu, select Macro, and choose Execute.

2. Type **labels** and press ⎡↵Enter⎤.

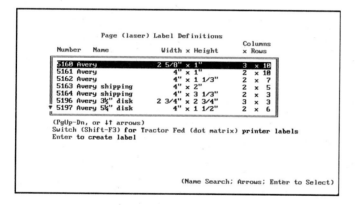

The macro displays a list of standard label sizes.

3. To select 3-up labels for this example, press ⎡↵Enter⎤.

4. At the Location: prompt, choose Continuous (1).

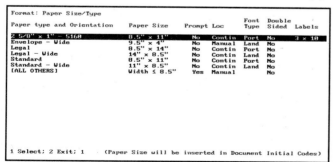

The definition you created for labels is highlighted.

10

5. Select **Exit** (**2**) to return to the editing screen.

Creating the Labels Primary File

After you have created the label definition, you need to create the primary file. In that file, you first must select the definition. You then can specify which fields should be used from the secondary file (in this example, ADDRESS.SMF) for merge printing the addresses.

To select the label form definition, follow these steps:

1. Begin a new document. This document will become the primary file.

2. Select [⇧Shift] [F8] to activate the Format command, choose **Document** (**3**), and select Initial **C**odes (**2**).

   ⌨ Access the **L**ayout pull-down menu, select **D**ocument, and choose Initial **C**odes (**2**).

3. Press [⇧Shift] [F8] again and select **P**age (**2**).

   ⌨ Access the **L**ayout pull-down menu and select **P**age.

4. Select Paper **S**ize/Type (**7**).

   The Format: Paper Size/Type menu appears.

5. Use the arrow keys to highlight the new definition for labels.

6. Choose **S**elect (**1**).

7. Press [F7] (Exit) three times to return to the editing screen.

Now you can enter the {FIELD} codes (and other merge codes as well) for your mailing-label merge. To enter the merge codes, follow these steps:

1. Press [⇧Shift] [F9] to activate the Merge Codes command, and select **F**ield (**1**).

   ⌨ Access the **T**ools pull-down menu, select **M**erge Codes, and choose **F**ield.

2. At the Enter Field: prompt, type **FullName** (the name of the first field in the secondary file) and press [↵Enter].

3. Press [↵Enter] to move the cursor to a new line.

4. Enter the rest of the fields from the secondary file for the envelope's address.

   At the next Enter Field: prompt, type **Company?** (the name of the second field in the secondary file) and press [↵Enter]. Remember that the question mark prevents the insertion of a blank line in an address. Press [↵Enter] to go to the next line.

10

At the next Enter Field: prompt, type **Street** (the name of the third field in the secondary file) and press ⏎Enter. Press ⏎Enter again.

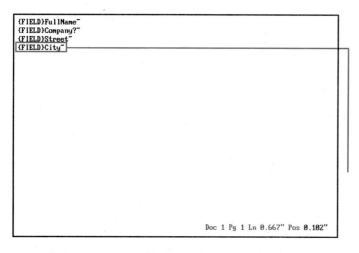

At the next Enter Field: prompt, type **City** (the name of the fourth field in the secondary file) and press ⏎Enter.

5. Press F7 (Exit) and then save the file under the name LABELS.PMF.

Merging Files To Print Labels

Now that you have created the primary file for printing labels, you can merge the LABELS.PMF file with the ADDRESS.SMF file.

Follow these steps to merge the labels and address files to the screen:

1. Clear the screen.

2. Press Ctrl F9 to activate the Merge/Sort command, and select **Merge (1)**.

   ⌨ Access the **Tools** pull-down menu and select **Merge**.

3. At the Primary file: prompt, type the name of the primary file. For this example, type **labels.pmf** and press ⏎Enter.

4. At the Secondary file: prompt, type the name of the secondary file. In this case, type **address.smf** and press ⏎Enter.

10

265

WordPerfect merges the files to the screen. On the editing screen, the records appear consecutively, separated by hard page breaks.

```
Mr. Zigler Xavier
Minds and Matters
456 Redwood Way
Petaluma, CA  95408
==================================================
Mr. Jude Matheson
Tots and Teens Furniture
515 Ross St.
Petaluma, CA  95408
==================================================
Ms. Loretta Murphy
Central Hardware
468 Mountain Ln.
Santa Rosa, CA  95401
==================================================
Mrs. Janie Smith
People's Drug Store
101 Saint St.
Petaluma, CA  95301

                                     Doc 1 Pg 10 Ln 0.667" Pos 0.102"
```

Now you are ready to print the labels. Before you do, however, a good practice is to preview the labels on-screen. Follow these steps to preview the labels and then print them:

1. Press ⇧Shift F7 to activate the Print command.

   📠 Access the **F**ile pull-down menu and choose **P**rint.

2. Select **V**iew Document (**6**).

To see the arrangement of the labels in this example, select 100% (**1**).

3. Press F7 to exit the View Document screen and return to the editing screen.

   If the labels are not arranged properly on-screen, check the primary and secondary files for possible errors in the codes or settings.

10

4. If the labels are arranged properly, load the label sheets face up into the paper tray.

5. Select ⟨⌂Shift⟩ ⟨F7⟩ (Print) and choose **F**ull Document (**1**) to print the labels.

    ▭ Access the **F**ile pull-down menu, choose **P**rint, and select **F**ull Document (**1**).

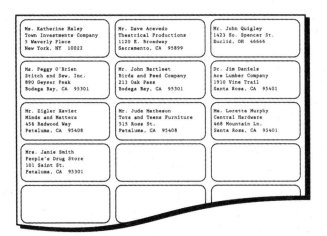

WordPerfect prints the labels.

Summary

This chapter introduced WordPerfect's powerful Merge feature. You learned how to use Merge by combining primary and secondary merge files. The text showed you how to merge these files to either the screen or the printer. You also learned how to merge from the keyboard. And you learned how to use Merge to create and print envelopes and mailing labels.

Specifically, you learned the following key information about WordPerfect:

- A text file merge combines two existing files—a primary merge file and a secondary merge file.

- A secondary merge file consists of records, each of which contains a number of fields.

- A primary merge file contains fixed text and merge codes.

- In a secondary merge file, a {FIELD NAMES} record displays the names of each field; an {END FIELD} code indicates the end of a field; and an {END RECORD} code indicates the end of a record.

10

■ In a primary merge file, a {DATE} code inserts the current date, and a {FIELD}*fieldname~* code tells WordPerfect to insert an item from the secondary file into the primary file at the location in the code.

■ To select Merge Codes, press Shift-F9.

■ If you have a small secondary merge file, you can merge the files to the screen. If you have a large secondary merge file, you can merge directly to the printer.

■ To merge files, select Merge/Sort (Ctrl-F9), choose **Merge**, and enter the primary and secondary file names.

■ For a keyboard merge, use the {INPUT} code in the primary merge field to indicate where an entry from the keyboard is placed.

■ After you have created a secondary merge file, you can use the file to automate a number of tasks—such as addressing envelopes and printing mailing labels.

In the next chapter, you are introduced to WordPerfect's Sort and Select features for handling record-keeping tasks and extracting particular data from a large database.

10

Sorting and Selecting

11

Using the Sort screen

Sorting lines and paragraphs

Sorting a secondary merge file

Selecting particular data

Although WordPerfect's Sort and Select features cannot compete with specialized database management programs in all respects, these features provide enough power and flexibility to handle many of your data management needs. When you combine Sort and Select with other WordPerfect features—such as Search, Replace, Merge, Math, and Macro—you create a powerful data management tool.

Examples of two simple applications of the Sort command are sorting lines to create alphabetical phone lists or rosters, and sorting mailing lists by ZIP code to conform with postal service rules for bulk mailings. An example of the use of the Select command is to find records that meet certain criteria—such as all the customers who live in Indianapolis and have a ZIP code of 46260. WordPerfect can work with four kinds of data: a line, a paragraph, a secondary merge file, or a table. This chapter shows you how to sort the first three kinds of records. Sorting tables is beyond the scope of this book.

11

> ## Key Terms in This Chapter
>
> *Sort keys*   The characters or numbers in a specific location in each record; WordPerfect uses sort keys to sort and select.
>
> *Record*   A collection of related information in a file: a line of data, a paragraph, or a name and address in a secondary merge file.
>
> *Fields*   The components that make up a record. Each field contains the same type of information, such as a person's first name, the name of a city, or a ZIP code.
>
> *Input file*   The file you intend to sort, which can be on the screen or on disk.
>
> *Output file*   The sorted (or selected) file, which you can display on-screen or save to disk.

Understanding the Sort Screen

You can sort files displayed on-screen or stored on disk, and you can return the sorted results to the screen or to a new file on disk. The Sort feature offers options for four types of sort operations based on the kind of data: a line, a paragraph, a secondary merge file, or a table. Use a line sort when records are lines (for example, a name or an item). Use a paragraph sort when records are paragraphs (as in a standard legal clause or a bibliography). Use a merge sort when records are in a secondary merge file (such as a list of names and addresses). And, finally, use a table sort for data arranged in rows and columns with the Table feature.

Note that the complex nature of a table may make sorting tabular data not worth the effort. And after you sort, the results may not be what you expected. For more information about sorting tables, refer to Que's *Using WordPerfect 5.1,* Special Edition.

Before you perform a sort, you must be sure that your data is set up properly. A line record must end with a hard or soft return, and records should be formatted with one tab per field. A paragraph record must end with two hard returns.

All the sort operations begin from the Sort screen.

```
Peggy O'Brien      890 Geyser Peak     Bodega Bay, CA     95301
John Bartleet      213 Oak Pass        Bodega Bay, CA     95301
Jim Daniels        1910 Vine Trail     Santa Rosa, CA     95401
Zigler Xavier      456 Redwood Way     Petaluma, CA       95408
Jude Matheson      515 Ross St.        Petaluma, CA       95408
Loretta Murphy     468 Mountain Ln.    Santa Rosa, CA     95401
Janie Smith        101 Saint St.       Petaluma, CA       95301
```

11

Before you display the Sort screen, you may want to retrieve to the screen the file containing the data to be sorted.

```
C:\WP51\BOOK\LINESORT.TXT                    Doc 1 Pg 1 Ln 2" Pos 7.5"
```

Then follow these steps to display the Sort screen:

1. Press ⌃Ctrl F9 to activate the Merge/Sort command, and select Sort (2).

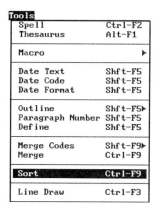

🖱 Access the Tools pull-down menu and select Sort.

2. At the prompt Input file to sort: (Screen), press ↵Enter if you want to sort the data already displayed on-screen. Or type the name of the input file on disk and press ↵Enter.

3. At the prompt Output file for sort: (Screen), press ↵Enter if you want the sorted results to replace the screen display. Or type the name of the output file and press ↵Enter if you want to save the results to disk in a new file.

11

Caution: If the input file and output file have the same names, the sorted data will replace the unsorted data.

The Sort screen is displayed. Notice that the screen is divided into five parts.

The heading ⎯⎯

The key definition area ⎯

The Select area ⎯

The Sort and Select menu ⎯

The Action, Order, Type area ⎯

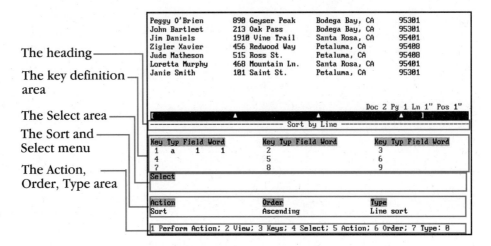

The heading displays the current Sort type. The default is Sort by Line.

The key definition area determines what criteria will control the sort. Note that you can specify criteria for nine sort keys.

In the Select area, you enter the formulas to select (extract) certain records from the data.

The area toward the bottom of the screen indicates the Action, Order, and Type area (which coincides with the heading) of the sort.

The seven options on the Sort and Select menu enable you to specify the type of sort, the order, and the sort criteria. After you enter this information, you start the sort from this menu.

The Sort and Select menu offers the following options:

Option	Action
Perform Action (**1**)	Instructs WordPerfect to begin sorting or selecting.
View (**2**)	Moves the cursor from the Sort screen into the document to be sorted. You can move the cursor to view the data,

Option	Action
	but you cannot edit it. You press Exit (F7) to return to the Sort screen.
Keys (3)	Moves the cursor into the key definition area so that you can define and change the sort keys (criteria) for the sort operation. When you select this option, the bottom of the screen displays the Type menu, from which you can select an alphanumeric sort or a numeric sort.
Select (4)	Moves the cursor to the Select area where you can enter the Select statement (a formula) containing the information you want to choose. This statement directs WordPerfect to choose certain records.
Action (5)	Is activated only when you choose Select (4). You can choose Select and Sort (1) to select and sort the data, or you can choose Select Only (2) to just select the data.
Order (6)	Offers a choice of **Ascending (1)**, A-to-Z order; or **Descending (2)**, Z-to-A order.
Type (7)	Displays a Type menu from which you can select sorting by line, paragraph, or secondary merge file.

Sorting Lines and Paragraphs

WordPerfect can sort the lines and paragraphs in any standard text file. The Sort feature is useful, for example, when you want to sort the data in office phone lists, personnel rosters, columns on charts, or dated paragraphs.

Display the Sort screen, using the procedure described earlier, and then continue with the procedure according to the text that follows.

Choosing the Sort Type

You can choose to sort by lines or paragraphs. Use a line sort when you want to sort rosters and lists. Use a paragraph sort for notes or reports.

Sorting Lines

Sort by Line is WordPerfect's default setting. If the heading on the Sort screen shows something other than Sort by Line, choose Type (7) and select Line (2).

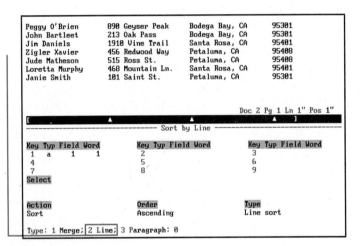

```
Peggy O'Brien      890 Geyser Peak     Bodega Bay, CA     95301
John Bartleet      213 Oak Pass        Bodega Bay, CA     95301
Jim Daniels        1910 Vine Trail     Santa Rosa, CA     95401
Zigler Xavier      456 Redwood Way     Petaluma, CA       95408
Jude Matheson      515 Ross St.        Petaluma, CA       95408
Loretta Murphy     468 Mountain Ln.    Santa Rosa, CA     95401
Janie Smith        101 Saint St.       Petaluma, CA       95301
```

```
                                              Doc 2 Pg 1 Ln 1" Pos 1"
[        .              ▲              ▲                  ▲    ]
─────────────────────── Sort by Line ───────────────────────
Key Typ Field Word       Key Typ Field Word       Key Typ Field Word
 1   a    1    1           2                         3
 4                         5                         6
 7                         8                         9
Select

Action                   Order                    Type
Sort                     Ascending                Line sort

Type: 1 Merge; 2 Line; 3 Paragraph: 0
```

Notice that the key definition area shows Field and Word. You identify the location of key words by their Field and Word positions in each line. Fields are separated by tabs, and words are separated by spaces.

Also notice the tab ruler above the heading Sort by Line. Because WordPerfect expects each field to be separated by one tab, the tab settings shown on the tab ruler must be set to one tab per field with no unused tabs between fields. If the tabs shown on the tab ruler do not reflect your one-tab-per-field setting, select View (2). When the cursor moves into the document, place the cursor in the middle of a line of data. The tab ruler changes to reflect your tab settings. Press Exit (F7) to return to the Sort screen.

Sorting Paragraphs

To sort by paragraph, choose Type (7) and select Paragraph (3). The title on the Sort screen displays Sort by Paragraph, and the key location headings are Line, Field, and Word. You identify the location of key words by their

Line, Field, and Word positions in each paragraph. Paragraphs are separated by two or more hard returns.

Selecting the Sort Order

Most of your sorts will be in ascending order—that is, from A to Z or from 0 to 9. At times, however, you may want to sort in descending order—from Z to A or from 9 to 0. To change the sort order, select **Order** (**6**) to display the Order menu.

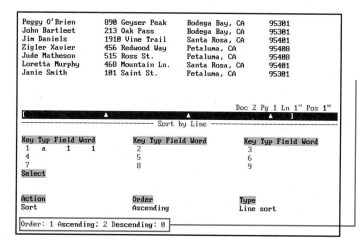

Choose either **Ascending** (**1**) for A-to-Z sort order or **Descending** (**2**) for Z-to-A sort order.

Defining the Sort Keys

WordPerfect uses sort keys to reorganize or select the information to be sorted. For example, to organize a list of names in alphabetical order, you would use the last name as the sort key. In performing sort operations, you will soon discover, however, that you often need more than one key to organize your data. If, for instance, you have several Smiths in your list, sorting by last name only will not be sufficient. You need a key to sort by first name as well. In that case, you can define the first key to be the last name, and the second key to be the first name. In WordPerfect, you can define nine sort keys.

Unfortunately, you cannot simply tell WordPerfect that a sort key is the "first name." You must instead specify the location of the key by telling WordPerfect which field, line, and word contains the information to sort by. When defining each key, you must specify also whether the information is alphanumeric or numeric.

275

11

In an alphanumeric sort, numbers are evaluated as normal text. If, therefore, you are sorting a column of numbers with an alphanumeric sort, all the numbers (such as ZIP codes or telephone numbers) must be the same length.

In a numeric sort, the information is evaluated as numbers only. Any text in the sort key is ignored. You use a numeric sort for numbers that are not the same length (in other words, for most of your sorts involving numbers).

To display the Keys menu, select Keys (3). The cursor moves under the **a** in the **Typ** column so that you can enter the location of each sort key.

Type **a** to specify an alphanumeric sort for Key 1, or type **n** to specify a numeric sort for Key 1.

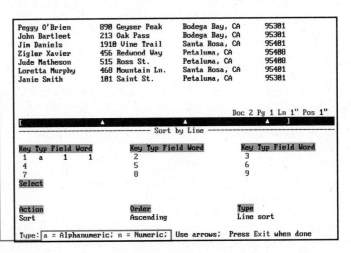

Enter the location of Key 1. The default values in Key 1 are preset at a 1 1. These values mean that the Sort type is alphanumeric and that the first word in the first field will be used as the basis for sorting. You can enter negative values in each key. For example, if you want to use the third word from the end of the field, enter -3 under Word.

If sorting by Key 1 results in ties (equal values, such as the same names or numbers), you can sort on more than one field by using Key 2, Key 3, and so on. Press the right-arrow key to move to Key 2, and then enter the values for this key.

Suppose, for example, that you want to sort the lines in the example by ZIP code and also by last name within each ZIP code.

Now suppose that you want to sort the bibliography shown in the next screen. Because some authors have the same last name, you will need to sort by the author's initials in addition to last name. Finally, because you have multiple works by some authors, you will want to sort the works by date. Notice that the bibliography is structured with the author's name on the first line and the date on the second line. This structure allows you to sort by paragraph on particular figures.

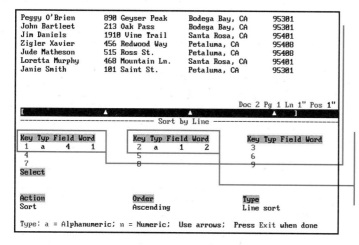

The ZIP code is specified by Key 1 as the first word in field number 4.

The last name is specified by Key 2 as the second word in the first field.

The lines are sorted by ZIP code. Within each ZIP code, the last names are listed alphabetically.

Note: Before you begin, make sure that you have changed the Sort type so that it is a paragraph sort.

277

11

The author's name is specified by Key 1 as the first word in the first field of the first line.

The author's initials are specified by Key 2 as the second word in the first field of the first line.

The work's date is specified by Key 3 as the last word in the first field of the second line.

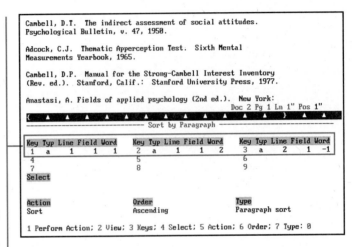

```
Cambell, D.T.  The indirect assessment of social attitudes.
Psychological Bulletin, v. 47, 1950.

Adcock, C.J.  Thematic Apperception Test.  Sixth Mental
Measurements Yearbook, 1965.

Cambell, D.P.  Manual for the Strong-Cambell Interest Inventory
(Rev. ed.).  Stanford, Calif.:  Stanford University Press, 1977.

Anastasi, A. Fields of applied psychology (2nd ed.).  New York:
                                          Doc 2 Pg 1 Ln 1" Pos 1"
```

```
----------------------------- Sort by Paragraph -----------------------------
Key Typ Line Field Word   Key Typ Line Field Word   Key Typ Line Field Word
 1   a   1    1    1       2   a   1    1    2        3   a   2    1    -1
 4                         5                         6
 7                         8                         9
Select

Action                    Order                     Type
Sort                      Ascending                 Paragraph sort

1 Perform Action; 2 View; 3 Keys; 4 Select; 5 Action; 6 Order; 7 Type; 0
```

The paragraphs are sorted alphabetically by the author's first name and initials and numerically by date.

```
Adcock, C.J.  Thematic Apperception Test.  Sixth Mental
Measurements Yearbook, 1965.

Anastasi, A. Fields of applied psychology (2nd ed.).  New York:
Macmillan, 1979.

Anastasi, A. Psychological testing (5th ed.).  New York:
Macmillan, 1982.

Cambell, D.P.  Manual for the Strong-Cambell Interest Inventory
(Rev. ed.).  Stanford, Calif.:  Stanford University Press, 1977.

Cambell, D.T.  The indirect assessment of social attitudes.
Psychological Bulletin, v. 47, 1950.




C:\WP51\BOOK\PARASORT.TXT                    Doc 1 Pg 1 Ln 1" Pos 1"
```

Performing the Sort

After you enter information for the sort keys, press Exit (F7). Then choose **P**erform Action (**1**) to sort the file. If you specified that the output goes to the screen, the results appear on-screen. If you specified that the output goes to the file, the results are sent to the file.

Sorting Secondary Merge Files

11

A secondary merge file is nothing more than a database with merge codes. WordPerfect can sort your secondary merge files so that the form letters, mailing lists, or labels you have previously typed will print in any order you choose.

Before you perform the sort, you must be sure that your data is set up properly. A secondary merge file contains records, each of which contains fields. Each field must end with an {END FIELD} code, and each record must end with an {END RECORD} code.

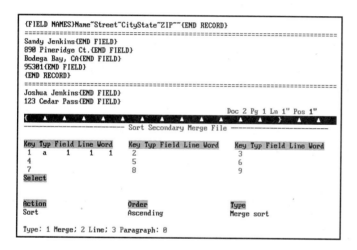

Begin by displaying the secondary merge file. Then display the Sort screen, using the procedure described earlier, and continue with the procedure according to the text that follows.

Choosing the Sort Type

From the Sort and Select menu, choose **Type** (**7**). Then select **Merge** (**1**) to sort a secondary merge file. The screen heading becomes `Sort Secondary Merge File`, and the location headings for each sort key become `Field`, `Line`, and `Word`.

Selecting the Sort Order

Select **Order** (**6**) to display the Order menu. Choose either **Ascending** (**1**) for A-to-Z sort order or **Descending** (**2**) for Z-to-A sort order.

11

Defining the Sort Keys

Select **Keys** (3) to display the Keys menu. The cursor moves under the a in the Typ column so that you can enter the location of each sort key. Type **a** to specify an alphanumeric sort for Key 1, or type **n** to specify a numeric sort for Key 1.

Enter the location of Key 1. The default values in Key 1 are preset at a 1 1 1. These values mean that the Sort type is alphanumeric and that the first word on the first line in the first field will be used as the basis for sorting.

If sorting by Key 1 results in ties (equal values, such as the same names or numbers), you can sort on more than one field by using Key 2, Key 3, and so on. Press the right-arrow key to move to the entry area for Key 2.

For this example, suppose that you want to sort the secondary merge file by state. You also want to sort entries for each state by last name and then by first name.

Key 1 is the state abbreviation (the first word from the right in the third field).

Key 2 is the last name (the first word from the right in the first field).

Key 3 is the first name (the first word in the first field).

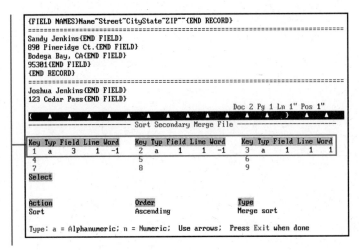

For all three keys, select alphanumeric sorting (**a**).

Performing the Sort

Press Exit (F7) to return to the Sort and Select menu. Then select **Perform Action** (**1**) to start the sort operation.

```
{FIELD NAMES}Name~Street~CityState~ZIP~~{END RECORD}
=============================================================
Joshua Jenkins{END FIELD}
123 Cedar Pass{END FIELD}
Bodega Bay, CA{END FIELD}
95301{END FIELD}
{END RECORD}
=============================================================
Sandy Jenkins{END FIELD}
890 Pineridge Ct.{END FIELD}
Bodega Bay, CA{END FIELD}
95301{END FIELD}
{END RECORD}
=============================================================
Pam Wagner{END FIELD}
309 South St.{END FIELD}
Bodega Bay, CA{END FIELD}
95301{END FIELD}
{END RECORD}
=============================================================



C:\WP51\BOOK\MERGE.SRT                    Doc 1 Pg 1 Ln 1" Pos 1"
```

11

WordPerfect sorts
the data based on
your sort criteria.

Selecting Data

When you are working with a large database, you often need to select particular data, and you need to be precise about your selection. Using the Select feature (accessed through the Sort and Select menu), you can choose only those paragraphs, lines, or secondary merge records that contain a specific combination of data—for example, the names of customers who live in California. The steps in selecting are the same as those used in sorting, but you must include a statement that describes the records you want to select.

Display the Sort screen, using the procedure described earlier, and then continue with the procedure according to the text that follows.

Choosing the Sort Type and Sort Order

Select **Type** (**7**) and specify whether you are selecting records from a line, paragraph, or secondary merge file. Then select **Order** (**6**) and choose **Ascending** (**1**) or **Descending** (**2**).

Defining the Sort Keys

Select **Keys** (**3**). Even though you may not want to sort your data, you must use sort keys to tell the program where to find the data you want.

Type **a** to specify an alphanumeric sort for Key 1, or type **n** to specify a numeric sort for Key 1. Then type the location for Key 1.

281

11

Use the right-arrow key to move to the Key 2 entry area and type the location for that key. Move to other Key entry areas and type their locations, if necessary.

In this example, a sort key has been entered as the specification for Key 1: Type = a (alphanumeric), Field = 3 (city and state), and Word = 1 (city). This information tells WordPerfect where to look for the select key.

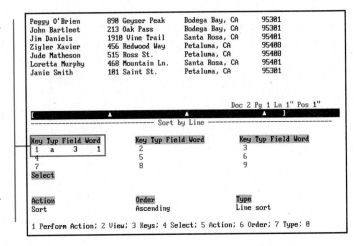

```
Peggy O'Brien      890 Geyser Peak    Bodega Bay, CA    95301
John Bartleet      213 Oak Pass       Bodega Bay, CA    95301
Jim Daniels        1910 Vine Trail    Santa Rosa, CA    95401
Zigler Xavier      456 Redwood Way    Petaluma, CA      95408
Jude Matheson      515 Ross St.       Petaluma, CA      95408
Loretta Murphy     468 Mountain Ln.   Santa Rosa, CA    95401
Janie Smith        101 Saint St.      Petaluma, CA      95301


                                         Doc 2 Pg 1 Ln 1" Pos 1"
[                 ▲                 ▲              ▲          ]
------------------------- Sort by Line -------------------------
Key Typ Field Word      Key Typ Field Word      Key Typ Field Word
1   a    3     1        2                        3
4                       5                        6
7                       8                        9
Select

Action                  Order                    Type
Sort                    Ascending                Line sort

1 Perform Action; 2 View; 3 Keys; 4 Select; 5 Action; 6 Order; 7 Type; 0
```

Entering the Selection Criteria

To return to the Sort and Select menu, press Exit (F7). Then choose Select (4).

You are now ready to provide the Select statement, which consists of the following items:

- A defined key in the form Key#. The # is replaced by the number of the key you want to use.

- A comparison operator indicating that the key must be one of the following in relation to the condition:

  Equal to (=)
  Not equal to (<>)
  Greater than (>)
  Less than (<)
  Greater than or equal to (>=)
  Less than or equal to (<=)

- A condition

After you choose Select (4), WordPerfect moves the cursor under the word Select and displays a list of comparison operators at the bottom of the screen.

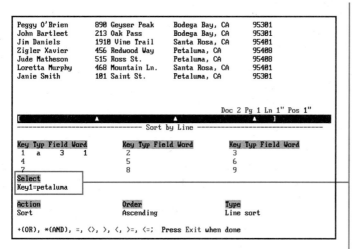

Under Select, enter **Key1 = petaluma**. This Select statement tells WordPerfect to select only those records in which the city is *petaluma* or *Petaluma*. (WordPerfect's Sort and Select features do not differentiate between upper- and lowercase.)

Press Exit (F7) to return to the Sort and Select menu. Then choose Action (**5**) to display the Action menu.

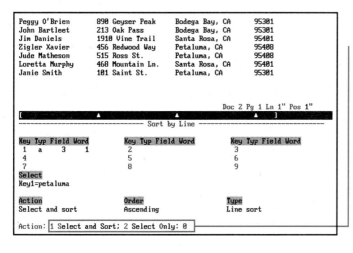

Choose Select and Sort (**1**) if you want to sort and select the records. Or choose Select Only (**2**) if you want to select records without sorting them.

WordPerfect returns you to the Sort and Select menu.

In the Select statement, you also can define multiple criteria. You must join the items with a logical operator to specify whether both conditions must be met or whether either condition is acceptable. To specify that both conditions must be met, use AND (indicated with an asterisk, *). To specify that either condition is acceptable, use OR (indicated with a plus sign, +).

11

Performing the Select

To perform the select, or select and sort, choose **Perform Action** (**1**).

```
Janie Smith      101 Saint St.     Petaluma, CA      95301
Jude Matheson    515 Ross St.      Petaluma, CA      95408
Zigler Xavier    456 Redwood Way   Petaluma, CA      95408
```

The selected
records are sent
to the screen or
to a disk file, as
you requested.

```
C:\WP51\BOOK\SELECT.TXT                    Doc 1 Pg 1 Ln 1" Pos 1"
```

Summary

In this chapter, you learned how to use WordPerfect's Sort feature to handle
some simple data management tasks. You explored WordPerfect's capabilities
to sort by line, paragraph, and secondary merge file. And you learned how to
use the Select feature to extract particular data from a large database.

Specifically, you learned the following key information about WordPerfect:

■ The Sort feature offers options for four types of sort operations based
on the kind of data: a line, a paragraph, a secondary merge file, or a
table.

■ You must be sure that your data is set up properly before you sort. A
line record must end with a hard or soft return, and records should be
formatted with one tab per field. A paragraph record must end with
two or more hard returns.

■ All the sort operations begin from the Sort screen, which is divided
into five parts: the heading, the key definition area, the Select area,
the Action/Order/Type area, and the Sort and Select menu.

■ To sort lines, select Merge/Sort (Ctrl-F9), choose **Sort** (**2**), press Enter
at each of the input and output prompts, choose **Type** (**7**), choose
Line (**2**), and select **Perform Action** (**1**).

11

■ To sort paragraphs, select Merge/Sort (Ctrl-F9), choose **S**ort (**2**), press Enter at each of the input and output prompts, choose **T**ype (**7**), choose **P**aragraph (**3**), and select **P**erform Action (**1**).

■ To sort a secondary merge file, select Merge/Sort (Ctrl-F9), choose **S**ort (**2**), press Enter at each of the input and output prompts, choose **T**ype (**7**), choose **M**erge (**1**), and select **P**erform Action (**1**).

■ To specify sort keys, choose the **K**eys (**3**) option from the Sort and Select menu, and then define the sort keys.

■ To select particular data, choose the **S**elect (**4**) option from the Sort and Select menu and enter the selection criteria.

In the next chapter, you will learn how to use WordPerfect's powerful Styles feature to control the format of one document or a group of documents.

Using Styles

12

Y ou can use WordPerfect's Styles feature as a powerful tool to control the format of one document or a group of documents. A *style* is a set of WordPerfect codes (you can include text also) that you turn on and off to control the format of a document. The Styles feature can save you time by reducing the number of keystrokes required for formatting tasks. For example, a style may contain all the codes needed to format a chapter heading, a long quotation, or a bibliography entry, or to set margins and tab stops. Moreover, by simply changing style definitions, you can easily make formatting changes to a document that was formatted with styles. Style definitions are saved with the current document, or you can save them to a *style library* file so that you can use the definitions with other documents.

WordPerfect's styles fall into two main categories: *open* and *paired*. Open styles remain in effect until you override the style codes, either by using another style or by inserting other formatting codes manually. Use open styles for formatting that affects an entire document. For instance, use open styles to set margins, tabs, line spacing, hyphenation, and so on. If you want the style to affect the entire document, move the cursor to the beginning of the document before turning on the style.

Creating a style

Using a style

Editing a style definition

Deleting a style definition

Saving definitions to a style library

Using the style library that comes with WordPerfect

Creating a style library

Managing style library files

12

Paired styles are turned on and off. For example, you can create a paired style called *Emphasized* that makes the text boldface and italic. When you use this style, you insert **[Style On: Emphasized]** and **[Style Off: Emphasized]** codes around the text to be formatted. Use paired styles for titles, section headings, tables—any text element that has a beginning and an end.

WordPerfect also has a third type of style: Outline. Outline styles organize and format hierarchical material. You can apply outline styles only through the Outline or Paragraph Numbering features. Outline styles are beyond the scope of this book. For more information about outline styles, refer to Que's *Using WordPerfect 5.1,* Special Edition.

Key Terms in This Chapter

Open style	A style that remains in effect until you use another style or insert other formatting codes manually. Use this type of style for formatting that affects an entire document.
Paired style	A style that is turned on and off. Use this type of style on any text element that has a beginning and an end.
Style library	A separate WordPerfect file that contains only style definitions, which can be used on any document.

Creating a Style

Use open styles for formatting that affects an entire document. Use paired styles for titles, section headings, tables—any text element that has a beginning and an end.

Creating an Open Style

Suppose, for example, that you want to create a style that formats your text for a draft style—with double spacing, a header that indicates the date of the draft, and a page number at the bottom.

To create an open style for a draft, follow these steps:

1. Press Alt F8 to activate the Styles command.

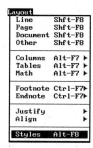

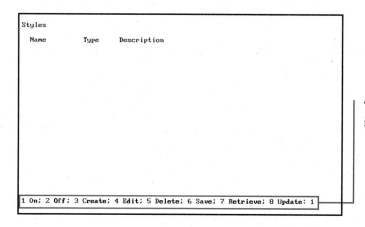

🖱 Access the Layout pull-down menu and select Styles.

The Styles menu is displayed.

2. Select Create (3) to create a new style.

The Styles: Edit menu is displayed.

12

3. Select Name (**1**), type a name for the style, and press ⏎Enter.

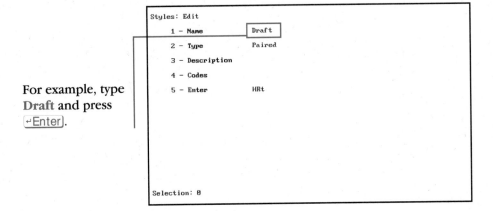

For example, type
Draft and press
⏎Enter.

4. Select Type (**2**).
5. Select Open (**2**) to create an open style.
6. Select Description (**3**), type a description of the style, and press
   ⏎Enter.

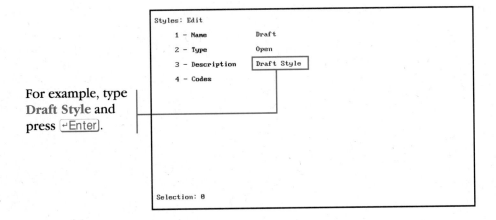

For example, type
Draft Style and
press ⏎Enter.

Descriptions can be up to 54 characters long. If you include the date, you can keep track of style revisions.

7. Select Codes (**4**).

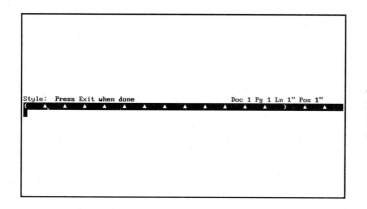

12

A screen that resembles the Reveal Codes screen appears.

8. Insert the formatting codes and text you want to include in the style just as if you were editing a normal WordPerfect document.

For a draft, press ⇧Shift F8 (Format), select **L**ine (**1**), choose Line **S**pacing (**6**), type **2**, and press ↵Enter. Then press ↵Enter again.

Select **P**age (**2**), choose **H**eaders (**3**), select Header **A** (**1**), choose Every **P**age (**2**), type **DRAFT**, and press F7.

Select **H**eaders (**3**), choose Header **B** (**2**), select Every **P**age (**2**), press Alt F6 (Flush Right), press ⇧Shift F5 (Date/Outline), choose Date **C**ode (**2**), and press F7 twice.

Press ⇧Shift F8 (Format), select **P**age (**2**), choose Page **N**umbering (**6**), select Page Number **P**osition (**4**), type **6**, and press F7.

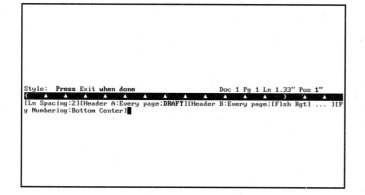

The codes for the draft style definition look like this.

9. Press F7 (Exit) three times to return to your document.

The style creation process for an open style is now complete. You can now use this style to prepare your manuscripts in draft style. See "Using a Style" later in this chapter.

Creating a Paired Style

Suppose that you want to create a style that formats headings with both italic and bold. To create a paired style, follow these steps:

1. Press Alt F8 to activate the Styles command.

   ▭◻ Access the Layout pull-down menu and select Styles.

   The Styles menu is displayed.

2. Select Create (3) to create a new style.

3. Select Name (1), type a name for the style, and press ↵Enter. For example, type **Headings** and press ↵Enter.

   Because paired style is the default, you do not have to specify the Type setting.

4. Select Description (3), type a description of the style, and press ↵Enter.

For example, type **Bold and italic** and press ↵Enter.

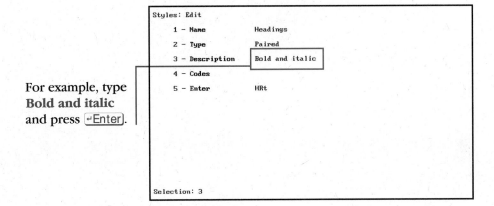

```
Styles: Edit

     1 - Name          Headings

     2 - Type          Paired

     3 - Description    Bold and italic

     4 - Codes

     5 - Enter          HRt




Selection: 3
```

Descriptions can be up to 54 characters long. If you include the date, you can keep track of style revisions.

5. Select Codes (4).

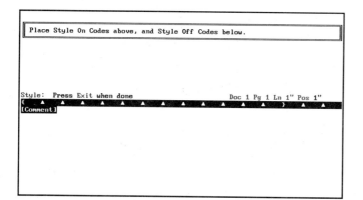

A screen with a comment box appears. The comment box represents the text you will type (and format) when you use this style.

6. Enter the beginning format codes (and any text), press → to move past the comment box, and then enter the ending format codes.

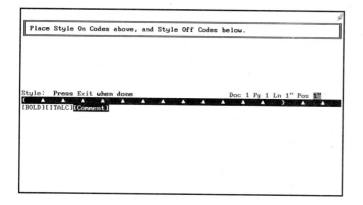

For the example, press F6 (Bold) and Ctrl F8 (Font), and then select Appearance (2) and Italc (4).

7. Press F7 (Exit).
8. Select Enter (5).

12

Your next selection determines the effect that pressing ⏎Enter has when you use a paired style.

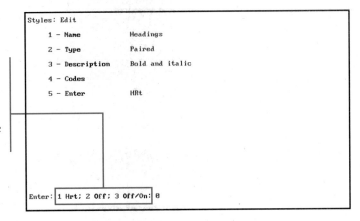

```
Styles: Edit

     1 - Name            Headings

     2 - Type            Paired

     3 - Description     Bold and italic

     4 - Codes

     5 - Enter           HRt




Enter: 1 Hrt; 2 Off; 3 Off/On: 0
```

9. Select **Hrt** (**1**) if you want the ⏎Enter key to function normally (insert hard returns). Use this style to format passages of text containing hard returns.

   Or

   Select **Off** (**2**) if you want WordPerfect to automatically turn off the style when you press ⏎Enter. Use this style to speed the use of styles with short sections of text, such as headings or titles.

   Select **Off/On** (**3**) if you want WordPerfect to automatically turn off and then immediately turn on a style. Use this style to quickly format several paragraphs (for instance, hanging paragraphs) in the same style.

   For this example, select Off (2); when you press ⏎Enter, you turn off the style.

10. Press F7 (Exit) twice to return to your document.

Using a Style

To use an open style, follow these steps:

1. Press Home, Home, Home, ↑ to move the cursor to the beginning of the document before any codes.

2. Press Alt F8 to display the Styles menu.

   🖰 Access the **L**ayout pull-down menu and select **S**tyles.

3. Use the cursor keys or mouse to highlight the style you want to use.

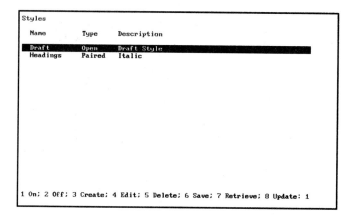

```
Styles

  Name         Type       Description

  Draft        Open       Draft Style
  Headings     Paired     Italic
```

12

For example,
highlight *Draft*.

```
1 On; 2 Off; 3 Create; 4 Edit; 5 Delete; 6 Save; 7 Retrieve; 8 Update: 1
```

4. Select **On** (**1**) or press ⏎Enter to turn on the style.
5. Type the text (if you are not using styles with existing text).

```
Brainstorming

When you have trouble determining a sharp focus for a document--
when you are uncertain what you want to say--consider trying a
semistructured writing exercise known as "brainstorming."

When you brainstorm a writing assignment on-screen, you record your
ideas in list form as they occur to you.  When you brainstorm, you
don't worry about typos, spelling errors, or style.  You turn off
the inclination to hone each sentence before you move on to the
next one.  You can handle those matters later.  Your goal is,
rather to generate as many ideas as possible about the topic, the
C:\WP51\BOOK\DRAFT.TXT                    Doc 1 Pg 1 Ln 1" Pos 1"
```

Here, the text
is formatted
for a draft.

12

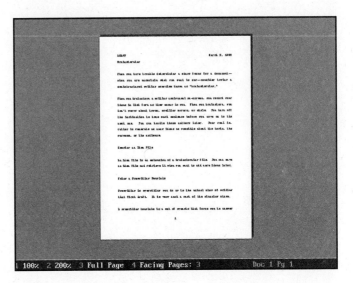

Press Shift-F7
(Print) and
choose View
Document (6) to
see the headers
and page number.

To use a paired style with existing text, press Block (Alt-F4 or F12) and
highlight the text. Or for text you are about to type, first move the cursor to
where you want the style to begin.

To use a paired style with existing text, follow these steps:

1. Highlight the block by using $\boxed{\text{Alt}}$ $\boxed{\text{F4}}$ or $\boxed{\text{F12}}$ to activate the Block
   command, or by dragging the mouse.

For example,
highlight a
heading you want
to emphasize.

```
 Brainstorming

 When you have trouble determining a sharp focus for a document--
 when you are uncertain what you want to say--consider trying a
 semistructured writing exercise known as "brainstorming."

 When you brainstorm a writing assignment on-screen, you record your
 ideas in list form as they occur to you.  When you brainstorm, you
 don't worry about typos, spelling errors, or style.  You turn off
 the inclination to hone each sentence before you move on to the
 next one.  You can handle those matters later.  Your goal is,
 rather to generate as many ideas as possible about the topic, the

 Block on                                     Doc 1 Pg 1 Ln 1.33" Pos 2.3"
```

12

2. Press ⌐Alt⌐F8⌐ to display the Styles menu.

⌐▭ Access the Layout pull-down menu and select Styles.

3. Use the cursor keys or mouse to highlight the style you want to use.

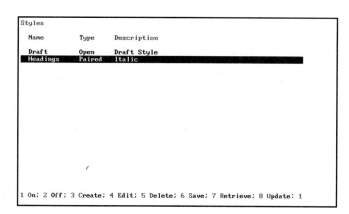

For example,
highlight
Headings.

4. Select On (1) or press ⌐Enter⌐ to turn on the style.

The heading now appears in bold and italic type.

To use a paired style with text you are about to type, follow these steps:

1. Press ⌐Alt⌐F8⌐ to display the Styles menu.

⌐▭ Access the Layout pull-down menu and select Styles.

2. Use the cursor keys or mouse to highlight the style you want to use. For example, highlight *Headings*.

3. Select On (1) or press ⌐Enter⌐ to turn on the style.

4. Type the text.

5. If you defined Enter as Off, press ⌐Enter⌐ to turn off the style.

Or

If you defined Enter as HRt or On/Off, turn off the style by pressing ⌐Alt⌐F8⌐, and then selecting Off (2).

Editing a Style Definition

Suppose that you want to change the Emphasized style so that headings appear in just italic rather than in bold and italic. To edit a style definition, follow these steps:

1. Press [Alt] [F8] to activate the Styles command.

   🖰 Access the **L**ayout pull-down menu and select **S**tyles.

   The Styles menu is displayed.

2. Use the cursor keys to highlight the style you want to edit. For example, highlight *Headings*.

3. Select **E**dit (4).

The Styles: Edit menu is displayed.

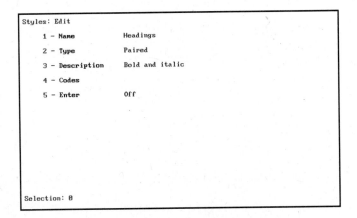

```
Styles: Edit

        1 - Name          Headings

        2 - Type          Paired

        3 - Description   Bold and italic

        4 - Codes

        5 - Enter         Off




Selection: 0
```

4. Select any options and make changes. For example, select **D**escription (2) and change the description to **I**talic. Select **C**odes (4) and delete the **[Bold]** code.

The style definition codes should now look like this.

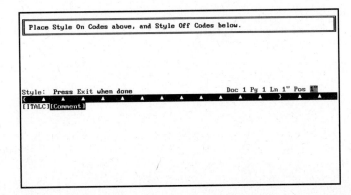

```
Place Style On Codes above, and Style Off Codes below.




Style:  Press Exit when done                    Doc 1 Pg 1 Ln 1" Pos
[ITALC][Comment]
```

5. Press F7 (Exit) three times to return to your document.

All occurrences of the style in your document automatically reflect the edits.
All the heads now appear in just italic instead of both bold and italic.

Deleting a Style Definition

Because all the styles are saved with a document regardless of whether you
used them, you should delete unused style definitions from the list.

To delete a style definition from the list, follow these steps:

1. Press Alt F8 to activate the Styles command.

   Access the Layout pull-down menu and select Styles.

   The Styles menu is displayed.

2. Use the cursor keys or mouse to highlight the style you want to delete.

3. Select Delete (5).

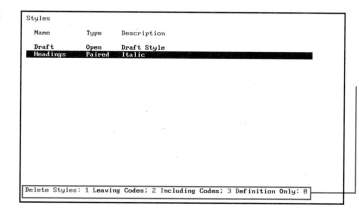

```
Styles

  Name       Type      Description

  Draft      Open      Draft Style
  Headings   Paired    Italic
```

```
Delete Styles: 1 Leaving Codes; 2 Including Codes; 3 Definition Only: 0
```

The Delete
Styles menu is
displayed.

4. Choose an option from the menu:

   Choose Leaving Codes (1) to delete the style definition and convert
   the corresponding style codes to regular WordPerfect codes.

   Choose Including Codes (2) to delete both the style definition and all
   corresponding style codes in the document.

   Choose Definition Only (3) to delete the definition without affecting
   the style codes in the document. Generally, this choice is not practical
   because you no longer control the text governed by the style codes.

12

Saving Definitions to a Style Library

When you save a document, you save the styles with it. So there is no need to save the styles if you want them for the current document only. If you want to use styles with other documents, then you must save them to a separate file.

To save style definitions to a style library, follow these steps:

1. Press [Alt] [F8] to activate the Styles command.

   ▭ Access the Layout menu and select Styles.

2. Select Save (6).

3. At the prompt, type a file name and press [↵Enter].

For example, type **business.sty** and press [↵Enter].

```
Styles
   Name          Type        Description

   Draft         Open        Draft Style
   Headings      Paired      Italic
```

```
Filename: business.sty
```

To help keep track of your files, use .STY as the file extension.

4. Press [F7] (Exit) to return to your document.

Using the Style Library That Comes with WordPerfect

WordPerfect comes with the LIBRARY.STY library file. This style library includes a number of style definitions you might be able to use *as is* or adapt for your specific needs. Among the style definitions in this library is one for a bibliography. Bibliography is a paired style for hanging paragraphs. The Enter key is defined as Off/On so that you can create a series of hanging paragraphs.

12

You can use the bibliography style either with existing text or before you type the text. If you use the style with existing text, use Block (Alt-F4 or F12) or the mouse to highlight the text before you complete the following steps. If you use the style before you type, move the cursor to the beginning of the document before you complete the following steps.

To use the bibliography style, follow these steps:

1. Press Alt F8 to display the Styles menu.

   Access the Layout pull-down menu and select Styles.

2. Select Retrieve (7).

3. At the prompt, type **library.sty** and press Enter.

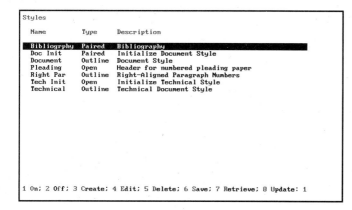

The Library style definitions are displayed.

4. Use the cursor keys or mouse to highlight the Bibliography style, if it isn't already highlighted.

5. Select On (1) or press Enter to turn on the style.

6. Type the text (unless you are using existing text).

Creating a Style Library

WordPerfect lists a number of built-in styles that come with the program and are available immediately for use. You can create additional styles to add to your style library. You can use any of WordPerfect's style libraries (with the STY extension), or you can create your own style library. Furthermore, you can set up one style library as the default; when you access the Styles feature, this style list appears.

When you save your document, the style definitions are saved with your document regardless of whether you used them or not. Whenever you edit this document, the styles are available for use. You also can save style definitions to a special file called a style library; then you can use these styles on other documents.

To use styles in more than one document, you must save the style to a style library. A style library is a WordPerfect document that consists solely of style definitions. You can make as many style libraries as you want, and each style library can contain as many styles as you want.

You can use any of WordPerfect's style libraries (with the .STY extension), found on the Conversion disk, or you can create your own style library. Moreover, you can set up one style library as your default; when you press Style (Alt-F8), this style list appears.

The text that follows shows you how to create some useful styles. You learn how to create styles for a title page, a numbered list, an envelope, and a letterhead. You can easily modify these styles to meet your specific needs.

Creating a Title Page Style

Suppose that you want to create a style for the title page of a term paper or report. The following open style centers your text top to bottom on the page and also centers the text between the left and right margins.

To create a title page style, follow these steps:

1. Press Alt F8 to activate the Styles command.

    Access the Layout menu and select Styles.

    The Styles menu is displayed.

2. Select Create (3) to create a new style.

3. Select Name (1), type the name Title, and press Enter.

4. Select Type (2).

5. Select Open (2) to create an open style.

6. Select Description (3), type Title Page Style, and press Enter.

7. Select Codes (4).

8. To center the text on the page top to bottom, press Shift F8 to activate the Format command. Select Page (2). Choose Center Page (1). Select Yes. Press Enter to return to the Format menu.

9. To center the text between the left and right margins, select Line (1). Choose Justification (3). Select Center (2). Press F7 to return to the style codes screen.

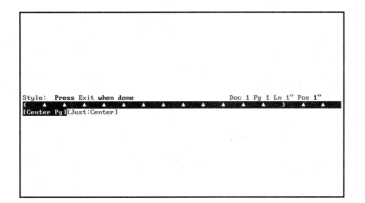

Style: Press Exit when done   Doc 1 Pg 1 Ln 1" Pos 1"
[Center Pg][Just:Center]

The codes for a title page are displayed.

10. Press F7 (Exit) three times to return to your document.

Generally, you will use this style before you type your text. If you use the style after you type the text, be sure to place the cursor at the beginning of the file before you use the style. Then press the down-arrow key to reformat the text.

Creating a Numbered List Style

You can create a paired style definition for a numbered list that automatically numbers a list of items.

To create a numbered list style, follow these steps:

1. Press Alt F8 to activate the Styles command.

   ▭ Access the **L**ayout pull-down menu and select **S**tyles.

   The Styles menu is displayed.

2. Select **C**reate (3) to create a new style.

3. Select **N**ame (1), type a name for the style, and press ↵Enter. For example, type **List** and press ↵Enter.

4. Select **D**escription (3), type a description of the style, and press ↵Enter. For example, type **Numbered List Style** and press ↵Enter.

5. Select **C**odes (4).

6. Press F4 (Indent) twice. Press ⇧Shift F5 (Date/Outline), select **P**ara Num (5) and press ↵Enter. Press F4 (Indent). Press → to move the cursor past the **[Comment]** code and press ↵Enter twice.

12

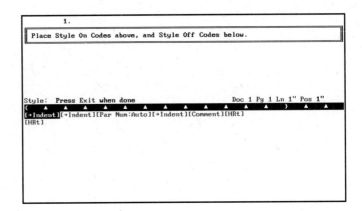

The codes for a numbered list are displayed.

7. Press F7 (Exit).

8. Select **Enter** (5).

9. Select **Off** (2).

10. Press F7 (Exit) twice to return to your document.

Creating an Envelope Style

Suppose, for example, that you want to create a style that formats the address for printing on a business envelope. (This example assumes that you already have created a form for an envelope. For more information about creating a paper form, see Chapter 5.)

To create an open style for a business envelope, follow these steps:

1. Press Alt F8 to activate the Styles command.

   ▭ Access the Layout pull-down menu and select Styles.

   The Styles menu is displayed.

2. Select **Create** (3) to create a new style.

   The Styles: Edit menu is displayed.

3. Select **Name** (1), type **Envelope**, and press ↵Enter.

4. Select **Type** (2).

5. Select **Open** (2) to create an open style.

6. Select **Description** (3), type **Business Envelope Style**, and press ↵Enter.

7. Select **Codes** (4).

8. For a business envelope, press ⇧Shift F8 (Format), select **P**age (**2**), and select Paper **S**ize/Type (**7**). Highlight the definition for a business envelope, choose **S**elect (**1**), and press ⏎Enter.

9. Select **L**ine (**1**). Then select **M**argins Left/Right (**7**), type **4.5** for the left margin and press ⏎Enter, type **0** for the right margin and press ⏎Enter. Press ⏎Enter again.

10. Then select **P**age (**2**) and choose **M**argin Top/Bottom (**5**). Type **0** for the top margin and press ⏎Enter; then type **0** for the bottom margin and press ⏎Enter. Press ⏎Enter again. If your printer definition will not allow 0-inch margins, WordPerfect automatically inserts the minimum allowed margins.

11. Select **O**ther (**4**) and select **A**dvance (**1**). Choose **L**ine (**3**), type **2**, and press ⏎Enter.

12. Press F7 (Exit).

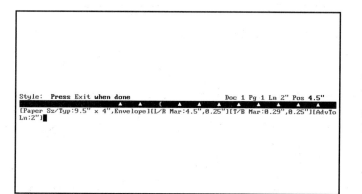

The codes for the business envelope style definition look like this.

13. Press F7 (Exit) three times to return to your document.

You can now use this style to select the envelope form and format text for a business envelope.

Creating a Letterhead Style

Suppose that you want to create a style for the Wheeling and Dealing company's letterhead. This style imports a graphic of a bicycle on the left and places the return address beside it on the right. You can modify the style by inserting your own address and importing an appropriate graphic.

1. Press Alt F8 to activate the Style command, and then select Create (3).

2. Select Name (1), type **Letterhead**, and press ↵Enter.

3. Select Type (2) and choose Open (2).

4. Select Description (3), type **Letterhead Style**, and press ↵Enter.

5. Select Codes (4).

6. Press ⇧Shift F8 to activate the Format command, select Page (2), choose Margins (5), type **.3** for the Top margin and press ↵Enter, and type **1** for the bottom margin and press ↵Enter. Then press F7.

7. Press Alt F9 to activate the Graphics command, select Figure (1), choose Options (4), select Border Style (1), and select None (1) four times. Press F7.

8. Press Alt F9 to activate the Graphics command, select Figure (1), choose Create (1), select Filename (1), type **bicycle.wpg**, and press ↵Enter. Then select Horizontal Position (6), choose Left (1), select Size (7), choose Set Width/Auto Height (1), type **2.5**, press ↵Enter, and press F7.

9. Press Ctrl F8 to activate the Font command, select Base Font (4), highlight Courier 12cpi, and choose Select (1).

10. Press ⇧Shift F8 to activate the Format command, select Other (4), choose Advance (1), select Down (2), type **.5**, press ↵Enter, and press F7.

11. Press ⇧Shift F8 to activate the Format command, select Line (1), choose Justification (3), select Right (3), and press F7.

12. Press Ctrl F8 to activate the Font command, select Size (1), choose Ext Large (7), type **Wheeling and Dealing**, press Ctrl F8, select Size (1), choose Ext Large (7), and press ↵Enter.

13. Press Ctrl F8 to activate the Font command, select Size (1), choose Vry Large (6), type **1001 West Wainwright Circle**, press ↵Enter, type **Wheeling, West Virginia 26003**, press Ctrl F8, select Size (1), choose Vry Large (6), and press ↵Enter.

14. Press Ctrl F8 to activate the Font command, select Appearance (2), choose Italc (4), type **Where There's a Wheel There's a Deal**, press Ctrl F8, select Appearance (2), choose Italc (4), and press ↵Enter.

15. Press ⬆Shift F8 to activate the Format command, select Line (**1**), choose Justification (**3**), select Left (**1**), and press F7.

16. Press ⬆Shift F8 to activate the Format command, select Other (**4**), choose Advance (**1**), select Line (**3**), type **2.75**, press ↵Enter, and press F7.

17. Press ⬆Shift F8 to activate the Format command, select Page (**2**), choose Margins (**5**), type **1** for the Top margin and press ↵Enter, type **1** for the Bottom margin and press ↵Enter, and press F7.

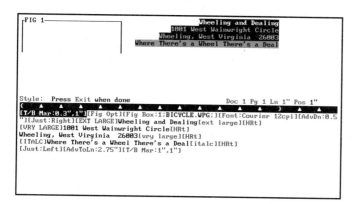

All the codes for producing the Wheeling and Dealing letterhead are stored in a style.

18. F7 (Exit) three times to return to the editing screen.

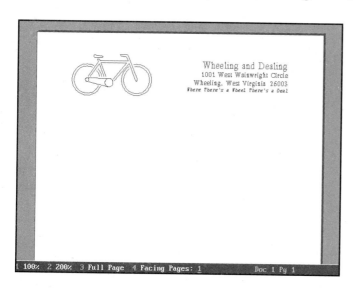

You can turn on the letterhead style, and then use View Document to see how the letterhead will look when printed.

Depending on your printer and the enhancements and fonts it supports, your document may look different from this example.

12 Managing Style Library Files

In this section, you learn how to retrieve a style library file, how to update a document with a style, and how to specify a default style library file.

Retrieving a Style Library File

To bring new styles into a document that already has styles, use the **Retrieve** (7) option. Keep two sets of documents with exactly the same style names— one for a draft, another for the final document. Then use Retrieve to update the draft into final form.

To retrieve a style library file, follow these steps:

1. Press `Alt` `F8` to activate the Styles command.

   ⌨️ Access the Layout menu and select Styles.

2. Select Retrieve (7).

3. Type a file name and press `⏎Enter`.

   If you have defined styles in your current document, you may be prompted:

   ```
   Styles already exist. Replace? (Y/N) No
   ```

4. Press `Y` to overwrite the style definitions with duplicate names in your document with the new style definitions.

   Or

   Press `N` to read in only the style definitions with different names from those in your document.

5. Press `F7` (Exit) to return to your document.

Updating Documents with a Style

If you change a style definition in the default style library and want to update the documents to which you've applied this style, you can use Update to reformat your documents with the modified style.

To update a document with the current style in the library file, follow these steps:

1. Retrieve the document.

2. Press ⟨Alt⟩ ⟨F8⟩ to activate the Styles command.

   ⌧ Access the Layout menu and select Styles.

3. Select Update (8).

4. Press ⟨F7⟩ (Exit) to return to your document.

5. Save your document.

   Unlike Retrieve, Update does not warn you before overwriting duplicate style names. WordPerfect assumes that you want to overwrite current styles with the styles in the default style library.

Specifying a Default Style Library File

If you use a single collection of styles regularly, you can use the Setup menu to make that collection the default style library file. If you switch among several style library files, leave the library file name blank in Setup.

To specify a default style library file, follow these steps:

1. Press ⟨⇧Shift⟩ ⟨F1⟩ to activate the Setup command.

   ⌧ Access the File pull-down menu and select Setup.

2. Select Location of Files (6).

```
Setup: Location of Files

     1 - Backup Files

     2 - Keyboard/Macro Files        C:\WP51

     3 - Thesaurus/Spell/Hyphenation
                      Main           C:\WP51
                      Supplementary  C:\WP51

     4 - Printer Files               C:\WP51

     5 - Style Files
             Library Filename

     6 - Graphic Files               C:\WP51

     7 - Documents                   C:\WP51

     8 - Spreadsheet Files



Selection: 0
```

The Setup: Location of Files screen appears.

3. Select Style Files (**5**).

4. Type a drive and directory, such as **c:\wp51**, and press ⏎Enter.

5. Type a file name, such as **business.sty**, and press ⏎Enter.

6. Press F7 (Exit) to return to your document.

Summary

In this chapter, you learned to create two types of styles: paired and open. You learned to apply those styles to existing text and to text you are about to type. You also learned how to use the style definitions that come with WordPerfect, how to create some new style definitions, and how to manage style library files.

Specifically, you learned the following key information about WordPerfect:

- Use open styles for formatting that affects an entire document or from a point in the document. For instance, use open styles to set margins, tabs, line spacing, hyphenation, and so on.

- Paired styles are turned on and off. Use paired styles for titles, section headings, tables—any text element that has a beginning and an end.

- To create an open style, select Styles (Alt-F8), and choose **Create** (**3**). Select **Name** (**1**), type a name for the style, and press Enter. Select **Type** (**2**), select **Open** (**2**), select **Description** (**3**), type a description of the style, and press Enter. Select **Codes** (**4**). Insert the formatting codes and text you want to include in the style.

- To create a paired style, select Styles (Alt-F8), and choose **Create** (**3**). Select **Name** (**1**), type a name for the style, and press Enter. Select **Codes** (**4**). Enter the beginning format codes (and any text), press → to move past the comment box, and then enter the ending format codes. Press Exit (F7). Select **Enter** (**5**). Then choose **Hrt** (**1**), **Off** (**2**), or **Off/On** (**3**).

- To use a paired style with existing text, press Block (Alt-F4 or F12) and highlight the text. For text you are about to type, first move the cursor to where you want the style to begin and turn the style on.

- To use a style, select Styles (Alt-F8), highlight the style you want to use, and select **On** (**1**).

- To edit a style definition, use the **Edit** (**4**) option.

- To delete a style definition, use the **Delete** (**5**) option.

■ To save style definitions to a style library, select Styles (Alt-F8) and choose **S**ave (6). At the prompt, type a file name and press Enter.

■ To bring new styles into a document that already has styles, use the **R**etrieve (7) option.

■ To update a document with styles from the default style sheet, use the Update (8) option.

■ To specify a default style library file, select Setup (Shift-F1), choose **L**ocation of Files (6), and select **S**tyle Files (5). Then enter a drive and directory and a file name.

In the next chapter, you learn about two types of text columns as well as math columns.

Using Columns

WordPerfect's versatile Columns feature provides options for displaying both text and numbers. When you display text, you can choose to arrange it in either newspaper-style or parallel columns. Newspaper-style columns are used for magazine articles, newsletters, lists, and indexes. Parallel columns are handy for inventory lists, personnel rosters, and duty schedules.

When you display columns of numbers, you can take advantage of WordPerfect's Math feature to execute simple math operations. You may want, for example, to perform some limited calculations when you prepare an invoice or develop a sales report.

13

Defining newspaper-style columns

Defining parallel columns

Entering text into columns

Calculating simple subtotals

Performing more complex math operations

Writing formulas that calculate numbers

13

Key Terms in This Chapter

Math operator   A symbol that tells WordPerfect the type of calculation you want to perform and where the result will be displayed.

Math definition   The instructions you enter on the Math Definition screen, defining the column type and format for math columns.

Text Columns

WordPerfect offers a powerful feature that enables you to put text in one of two types of columns: newspaper or parallel. Text in newspaper-style columns wraps from the bottom of one column to the top of the next column, and then wraps back to the first column on the left of the next page. Newspaper-style columns are read from top to bottom. Parallel columns are read from left to right; therefore, data is arranged across the page.

Newspaper-Style Columns

Johannes Gutenberg, the fifteenth-century inventor of movable type, brought the written word to the public, and thus is responsible for publishing as it has been known for five hundred years. In the last quarter century, Gutenberg's metal type has been replaced by electronic typesetting--faster, more flexible, but still very expensive, and still only part of the complex process of publishing. Today, personal computers bring a new generation of publishing to the individual. The technology is called "desktop publishing," and it represents a whole new approach to a very old art.

Desktop publishing starts with a personal computer. Your high-powered computer, along with the right software, gives you all the tools you need to design and publish a variety of printed materials at your own desk. Write a press release or create a simple letterhead with a word processing program like WordPerfect for IBM and compatible computers. Design a logo or business card with a graphics program like Adobe Illustrator or Aldus Freehand for the Macintosh. Create a newsletter and experiment with page layout with a page-design program like Aldus PageMaker for either IBM or Macintosh. Prepare graphs, illustrations, forms, applications, stationery, brochures, catalogs, reports, and much more--easily--with desktop publishing on a personal computer.

There are many software and hardware enhancements that can broaden your desktop publishing talents. Word processors give you powerful editing and document creation capabilities. Page-design software lets you shape your finished material into blocks or columns of text, and it lets you insert or outline illustrations. Graphics packages guide you in creating detailed illustrations or charts that you can add to a page you've already created. A scanner, video or optical, reproduces drawings of photos for you by electronically "reading" them with a camera or with a digitizer.

Newspaper-style columns are read from top to bottom. The text flows from the bottom of one column to the top of the next. You can define newspaper-style columns either before or after you type the text. Keep in mind that you can use the normal editing commands to modify text within a newspaper-style column.

13

Defining Columns Before You Type

To define newspaper-style columns before you type the text, follow these steps:

1. Move the cursor to the place where you want the columns to begin.

2. Press [Alt] [F7] to activate the Columns/Table command, and select Columns (**1**) to display the following Columns menu:

   Columns: 1 On; 2 Off; 3 Define: 0

13

⌨ Access the Layout pull-down menu and select Columns.

3. Select **Define** (3).

The Text Column Definition menu is displayed.

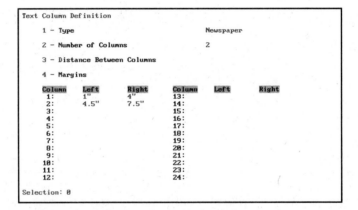

At this menu, you do not need to select **Type** (1) because Newspaper is WordPerfect's default setting.

4. Choose **Number of Columns** (2), enter the number of columns you want on the page (up to 24), and press ⏎Enter.

5. Select **Distance Between Columns** (3).

WordPerfect automatically calculates the margin settings with 0.5" (one-half inch) between columns, but you can space the columns as close together or as far apart as you want. In most cases, you will accept the default margin settings.

6. To accept the default settings, press ⏎Enter.

   Or

   To specify columns of different widths, choose **M**argins (**4**) and type the new settings for Left and Right column margins. Press ⏎Enter after each number.

7. Press ⏎Enter to return to the Columns menu.

8. Select **O**n (**1**) to turn on the Columns feature.

9. Begin typing. Typing with the Columns feature turned on is the same as typing in a regular WordPerfect document. Text wraps within the column until you reach the bottom of the page, and then wraps to the top of the next column. Notice that the column number appears in the status line.

10. To turn off the Columns feature, press Alt F7 (Columns/Table) again and choose **O**ff (**2**).

    ⌦ Access the **L**ayout pull-down menu, select **C**olumns, and choose **O**ff.

After you have turned off the Columns feature, any text you type is formatted in the usual way, and the column number disappears from the status line.

Creating Columns from Existing Text

```
Johannes Gutenberg, the fifteenth-century inventor of movable type,
brought the written word to the public, and thus is responsible for
publishing as it has been known for five hundred years.  In the
last quarter century, Gutenberg's metal type has been replaced by
electronic typesetting--faster, more flexible, but still very
expensive, and still only part of the complex process of pub-
lishing.  Today, personal computers bring a new generation of
publishing to the individual.  The technology is called "desktop
publishing," and it represents a whole new approach to a very old
art.

Desktop publishing starts with a personal computer.  Your high-
powered computer, along with the right software, gives you all the
tools you need to design and publish a variety of printed materials
at your own desk.  Write a press release or create a simple
letterhead with a word processing program like WordPerfect for IBM
and compatible computers.  Design a logo or business card with a
graphics program like Adobe Illustator or Aldus Freehand for the
Macintosh.  Create a newsletter and experiment with page layout
with a page-design program like Aldus PageMaker for either IBM or
Macintosh.  Prepare graphs, illustrations, forms, applications,
stationery, brochures, catalogs, reports, and much more--easily--
with desktop publishing on a personal computer.

C:\WP51\BOOK\COLUMN.TXT                    Doc 1 Pg 1 Ln 2" Pos 1"
```

Suppose that you want to create newspaper-style columns from text you have already typed.

13

To create newspaper-style columns from existing text, follow these steps:

1. Place the cursor at the beginning of the text you want to change to column format. If the text includes a centered heading, place the cursor on the line below the heading, unless you plan to include the heading in the first column.

2. Press [Alt] [F7] to activate the Columns/Table command, select Columns (**1**), define the columns according to the procedure described earlier, and press [↵Enter].

   ⌨ Access the **Layout** pull-down menu, select **Columns**, choose **Define**, define the columns, and press [↵Enter].

3. From the Columns menu, select **On** (**1**) to turn on the Columns feature.

4. Press the [↓] key.

<table>
<tr><td rowspan="2">WordPerfect automatically reformats your text into columns.</td><td>

```
Johannes Gutenberg, the fif-
teenth-century inventor of mov-
able type, brought the written
word to the public, and thus is
responsible for publishing as
it has been known for five hun-
dred years.  In the last quar-
ter century, Gutenberg's metal
type has been replaced by elec-
tronic typesetting--faster,
more flexible, but still very
expensive, and still only part
of the complex process of pub-
lishing.  Today, personal com-
puters bring a new generation
of publishing to the individu-
al.  The technology is called
"desktop publishing," and it
represents a whole new approach
to a very old art.           '

Desktop publishing starts with
a personal computer.  Your
high-powered computer, along
C:\WP51\BOOK\COLUMN.TXT
```

</td><td>

```
tions, stationery, brochures,
catalogs, reports, and much
more--easily--with desktop pub-
lishing on a personal computer.

There are many software and
hardware enhancements that can
broaden your desktop publishing
talents.  Word processors give
you powerful editing and docu-
ment creation capabilities.
Page-design software lets you
shape your finished material
into blocks or columns of text,
and it lets you insert or out-
line illustrations.  Graphics
packages guide you in creating
detailed illustrations or
charts that you can add to a
page you've already created.  A
scanner, video or optical, re-
produces drawings of photos for
you by electronically "reading"
them with a camera or with a
        Col 1 Doc 1 Pg 1 Ln 2" Pos 1"
```

</td></tr>
</table>

Displaying a Single Column

Instead of displaying all the columns on-screen at once, you can display only one column at a time. To display one newspaper-style column at a time, follow these steps:

1. Press [⬆Shift] [F1] to activate the Setup command, and select **Display** (**2**).

   ⌨ Access the **File** menu, select **Setup**, and choose **Display**.

2. Select **Edit-Screen Options** (**6**).

318

```
Setup: Edit-Screen Options

    1 - Automatically Format and Rewrite    Yes

    2 - Comments Display                    Yes

    3 - Filename on the Status Line         Yes

    4 - Hard Return Display Character

    5 - Merge Codes Display                 Yes

    6 - Reveal Codes Window Size            10

    7 - Side-by-side Columns Display        Yes




Selection: 0
```

The Setup: Edit-Screen Options menu is displayed.

13

3. Choose Side-by-side Columns Display (7).

4. Select No to tell WordPerfect to display just one column at a time.

5. Press F7 (Exit) to return to the editing screen.

```
Macintosh.  Create a newsletter
and experiment with page layout
with a page-design program like
Aldus PageMaker for either IBM
or Macintosh.  Prepare graphs,
illustrations, forms, applica-
─────────────────────────────────
                        tions, stationery, brochures,
                        catalogs, reports, and much
                        more--easily--with desktop pub-
                        lishing on a personal computer.

                        There are many software and
                        hardware enhancements that can
                        broaden your desktop publishing
                        talents.  Word processors give
                        you powerful editing and docu-
                        ment creation capabilities.
                        Page-design software lets you
                        shape your finished material
                        into blocks or columns of text,
                        and it lets you insert or out-
                        line illustrations.  Graphics
                        packages guide you in creating
C:\WP51\BOOK\COLUMN.TXT            Col 2 Doc 1 Pg 1 Ln 4.67" Pos 4.5"
```

The columns are separated and appear on-screen to be displayed one per page. Notice that in column 2, however, the cursor position still indicates that you are on page 1; column 2 will appear on page 1 in the printed document.

To return to multiple-column display, repeat the same procedure but select **Yes** instead of **No** in Step 4.

Parallel Columns

Parallel columns are read from left to right across the page. You may want to use parallel columns, for example, in an itinerary in which dates are typed in the first column and other information about the trip is typed in subsequent columns.

```
                           Tour Schedule

      Date      Location      Hotel      Sightseeing       Remarks

   Oct. 24    Luxembourg    Hotel       Tour of the     The Kasematten
                            Aerogolf    Kasematten      are an ancient
                                        and, if time    fortification;
                                        permits, a      the Luxembourg
                                        short visit     Swiss area is one
                                        to the          of the most
                                        Luxembourg      picturesque areas
                                        Swiss area.     of the country.

   Oct. 25    Trier         Dorint      Porta Nigra;    Supposedly
                            Hotel       Cathedral       founded in 2000
                                        and Imperial    B.C.
                                        Baths
```

You first define the columns you need, and then enter the headings and text. Keep in mind that you can use the normal editing commands to modify text within a parallel column.

Before you begin to define and type text in parallel columns, you may want to enter a heading for the document. Follow these steps:

1. Press ⇧Shift F6 to activate the Center command.

   ▭ Access the Layout pull-down menu, select **Align**, and choose **Center**.

2. Type the document's heading.

3. Press ↵Enter twice to move down the page.

Defining Columns

To define parallel columns, follow these steps:

1. Press Alt F7 to activate the Columns/Table command, select Columns (**1**), and choose **Define** (**3**).

   ▭ Access the Layout pull-down menu, select **Columns**, and choose **Define**.

2. Select **Type** (**1**).

320

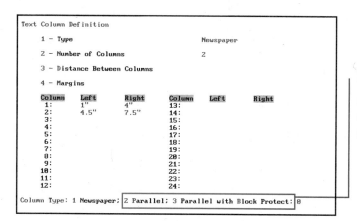

```
Text Column Definition

   1 - Type                          Newspaper

   2 - Number of Columns             2

   3 - Distance Between Columns

   4 - Margins

   Column   Left      Right    Column   Left      Right
     1:      1"        4"        13:
     2:      4.5"      7.5"      14:
     3:                          15:
     4:                          16:
     5:                          17:
     6:                          18:
     7:                          19:
     8:                          20:
     9:                          21:
    10:                          22:
    11:                          23:
    12:                          24:

Column Type: 1 Newspaper; 2 Parallel; 3 Parallel with Block Protect: 0
```

The Column Type
menu is displayed
at the bottom of
the screen.

13

3. Choose either Parallel (2) or Parallel with Block Protect (3).

   The Parallel with Block Protect option prevents a horizontal block of columnar text from being split by a soft page break. If a column reaches the bottom margin but is too long to fit on the page, the entire horizontal block of columns is moved to the next page.

4. Select Number of Columns (2), type the number of columns you want, and press ⏎Enter. For example, type 5 and press ⏎Enter.

5. Select Distance Between Columns (3).

   WordPerfect automatically calculates the margin settings with 0.5" (one-half inch) between columns, but you can space the columns as close together or as far apart as you want.

6. To accept the default settings, press ⏎Enter.

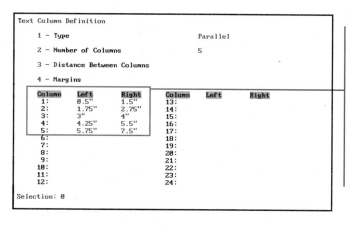

```
Text Column Definition

   1 - Type                          Parallel

   2 - Number of Columns             5

   3 - Distance Between Columns

   4 - Margins

   Column   Left      Right    Column   Left      Right
     1:      0.5"      1.5"      13:
     2:      1.75"     2.75"     14:
     3:      3"        4"        15:
     4:      4.25"     5.5"      16:
     5:      5.75"     7.5"      17:
     6:                          18:
     7:                          19:
     8:                          20:
     9:                          21:
    10:                          22:
    11:                          23:
    12:                          24:

Selection: 0
```

To specify columns of different widths, choose Margins (4) and type the new settings for Left and Right column margins. Press ⏎Enter after each number.

7. Press <kbd>↵Enter</kbd> to return to the Columns menu.

8. Select **On (1)** to turn on the Columns feature.

Entering Column Headings

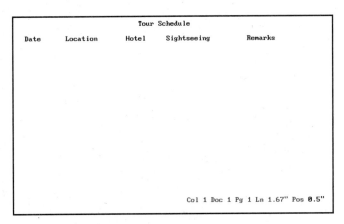

You can enter a centered column heading above each parallel column.

To enter a centered heading above each column, follow this procedure:

1. Press <kbd>⇧Shift</kbd> <kbd>F6</kbd> to activate the Center command.

    ⌨ Access the **L**ayout pull-down menu, select **A**lign, and choose **C**enter.

2. Type the first column heading.

3. To move to the next column, press <kbd>Ctrl</kbd> <kbd>↵Enter</kbd> (Hard Page).

4. With the cursor in that column, press <kbd>⇧Shift</kbd> <kbd>F6</kbd> (Center) again.

    ⌨ Access the **L**ayout pull-down menu, select **A**lign, and choose **C**enter.

5. Type the second column heading.

6. Repeat this procedure until you have entered all the column headings.

7. After you type the last column heading, press <kbd>Ctrl</kbd> <kbd>↵Enter</kbd> (Hard Page).

WordPerfect inserts a blank line and positions the cursor at the first column on the left of the page.

13

Entering Text

Type text into parallel columns by moving from column to column across the page. After typing the text in the first column, press Hard Page (Ctrl-Enter) to move the cursor to the next column. When you press Hard Page in the far right column, the cursor returns to the first column on the left.

```
                              Tour Schedule
         Date      Location      Hotel    Sightseeing        Remarks

      Oct. 24    Luxembourg    Hotel      Tour of the    The Kasematten are
                               Aerogolf   Kasematten     an ancient
                                          and, if time   fortification; the
                                          permits, a     Luxembourg Swiss
                                          short visit    area is one of the
                                          to the         most picturesque
                                          Luxembourg     areas of the
                                          Swiss area.    country.

      Oct. 25    Trier         Dorint     Porta Nigra;   Supposedly founded
                               Hotel      Cathedral      in 2000 B.C.
                                          and Imperial
                                          Baths




      C:\WP51\BOOK\PARALLEL.TXT              Col 5 Doc 1 Pg 1 Ln 3.33" Pos 6.95"
```

You can begin typing the next group of column entries. WordPerfect automatically inserts one blank line to separate the horizontal blocks of text.

To create an empty column, press Hard Page (Ctrl-Enter) twice.

Math Columns

WordPerfect's Math feature is designed to provide limited calculation capabilities for simple math operations. WordPerfect can calculate subtotals, totals, and grand totals down columns of numbers. The program can add, subtract, multiply, and divide, as well as calculate averages. The most common and simplest math operations calculate and display the totals of numbers down a column. More complex operations calculate and display the results of computations involving numbers in different columns on the same line.

Performing Simple Math Operations

Math operations that involve totals down a column of numbers are the simplest to perform. For these operations, you complete this set of procedures:

- Set tabs for math columns.
- Turn on the Math feature.
- Enter numbers and math operators in the columns.
- Calculate the results.
- Turn off the Math feature.

The steps required for each of these procedures are described in the text that follows.

Setting Tabs for Math Columns

To set tabs for math columns, use this procedure:

1. Position the cursor on the line following the column headings (if any).
2. Press ⬥Shift F8 to activate the Format command, and select **Line** (**1**).

   ⌨ Access the **Layout** pull-down menu and select **Line**.

3. From the Format: Line menu, choose **Tab Set** (**8**).
4. Press Ctrl End (Delete to End of Line) to remove all existing tab stops.
5. Move the cursor to the place where you want the first tab, and press L for **Left** to set the tab stop for the first column.
6. Repeat this procedure for the remaining columns.
7. Press F7 (Exit) twice to return to the editing screen.

Be sure that the columns are wide enough to accommodate the largest numbers you will use. Also keep in mind that the first math column begins at the first tab stop, not at the left margin. The left margin is reserved for labels, row headings, or other material not calculated.

Turning on the Math Feature

To turn on the Math feature, follow these steps:

1. Position the cursor after the tab settings for math columns but before the part of the document that is to contain the math operations.
2. Press Alt F7 to activate the Columns/Table command, select **Math** (**3**), and choose **On** (**1**).

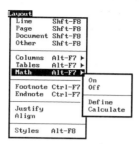

> ⌨ Access the Layout pull-down menu, choose Math, and select On.

13

The `Math` indicator appears at the lower left of the screen, showing that the cursor is in the math area.

Entering Numbers and Math Operators

To enter numbers and math operators in the columns, use this procedure:

1. Press `Tab⁺` or `Ctrl` `F6` (Tab Align) until the cursor is located in the correct column.

   ⌨ Access the Layout pull-down menu, choose Align, and select Tab Align to position the cursor in the appropriate column.

   WordPerfect displays the following prompt:

   `Align char = . Math`

2. In the column, type the number or math operator you want to appear.

   If you enter a number that contains a period, the number is aligned on the decimal point.

```
                    Loaf and Mug Cafe
                   Bank Reconciliation
                      June 31, 1992

Balance per bank statement              $2,345.77
Add: Deposit in transit                    644.26
                                               +

Less: Checks outstanding

    No. 2775 (Eden Foods)                  355.00
    No. 2776 (Elmer's Bakery)               30.00
    No. 2777 (Oldenburg Farms)             125.00
    No. 2778 (S.M. Dairy)                    N+

Adjusted balance                               =




Align char = . Math              Doc 1 Pg 1 Ln 3.67" Pos 6.5"
```

Here, the math operators +, N, and = are used.

3. Press Tab⁺ to move to the next column and enter data. Or press ↵Enter to go to the next line.

4. Type additional numbers or math operators in the columns.

You can use the following math operators to perform simple math operations down a column of numbers:

+	Subtotal
t	Extra subtotal
=	Total
T	Extra total
*	Grand total
N	Negative number

When you enter an operator, only the operator is displayed. The math results are not shown until you calculate the results.

Calculating the Results

To calculate the results, use this procedure:

1. Position the cursor anywhere in the math area.

2. Press Alt F7 (Columns/Table), select **Math** (3), and choose Calculate (4).

▭ Access the **Layout** pull-down menu, choose **Math**, and select Calculate.

WordPerfect calculates the results and inserts them next to the math operators; the results are aligned on the tabs.

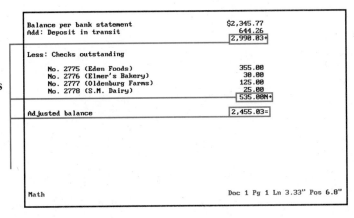

```
Balance per bank statement              $2,345.77
Add: Deposit in transit                    644.26
                                        ┌─────────┐
                                        │2,990.03+│
                                        └─────────┘
Less: Checks outstanding

   No. 2775 (Eden Foods)                   355.00
   No. 2776 (Elmer's Bakery)                30.00
   No. 2777 (Oldenburg Farms)              125.00
   No. 2778 (S.M. Dairy)                    25.00
                                        ┌─────────┐
                                        │535.00N* │
                                        └─────────┘
Adjusted balance                        ┌─────────┐
                                        │2,455.03=│
                                        └─────────┘




Math                          Doc 1 Pg 1 Ln 3.33" Pos 6.8"
```

Note that the math operators displayed on-screen do not appear in the printed document. Note also that if you make changes to the numbers or operators, you must recalculate.

Turning Off the Math Feature

Use the following procedure to turn off the Math feature:

1. Position the cursor after the math area.
2. Press [Alt] [F7] (Columns/Table), select **Math** (3), and choose Off (2).

   ▭ Access the **Layout** pull-down menu, choose **Math**, and select Off.

Performing More Complex Math Operations

More complex math operations in WordPerfect require you to use the Math Definition screen to "define" each column. Math columns that are defined require more planning than simple math columns. On the Math Definition screen, you must identify each column as numeric, total, text, or calculation. When you build complex math columns, you use the same procedure as for building simple math columns, but you add the step of defining the columns after you set the tab stops.

When you define the column type and format, you specify what calculations you want performed and how you want the results displayed. The instructions you provide are called the math definition.

You can define four types of columns in your math definition: numeric, total, text, and calculation.

13

Columns A and B are descriptions that do not involve math; therefore, they are defined as text columns. Although you can enter numbers or text in text columns, anything entered in these columns cannot be used in calculations.

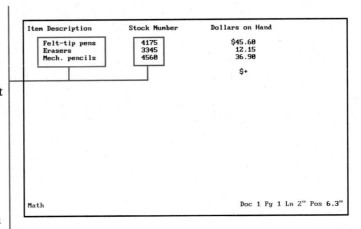

Column C is a numeric column, the default setting, which can be used in calculations. The text in the heading of column C does not affect the calculations. This type of column, the most common type used in math functions, is calculated and then displays the subtotals, totals, or grand totals below the other numbers in the column.

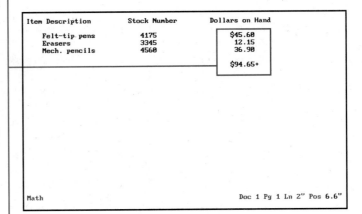

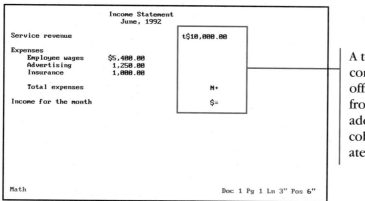

A total column is convenient for offsetting totals from the numbers added in the column immediately to the left.

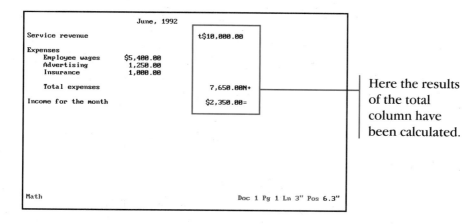

Here the results of the total column have been calculated.

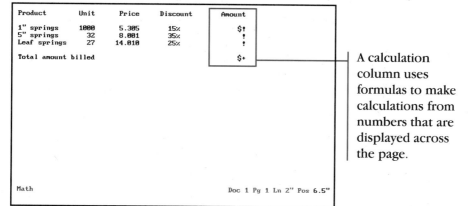

A calculation column uses formulas to make calculations from numbers that are displayed across the page.

```
Product        Unit      Price     Discount     Amount

1" springs     1000      5.305       15%       $4,509.25↑
5" springs       32      8.001       35%          166.42↑
Leaf springs     27     14.010       25%          283.70↑

Total amount billed                            $4,959.37+
```

13

Here the results
of the calculation
column have
been calculated.

```
Math                                    Doc 1 Pg 1 Ln 2" Pos 6.8"
```

To begin setting the math definition, follow these steps:

1. Set the tabs for the columns.

2. Position the cursor after the tab settings for math columns but before the part of the document that is to contain the math operations.

3. Press Alt F7 to activate the Columns/Table command, select Math (3), and choose Define (3).

   ⌨ Access the Layout pull-down menu, choose Math, and select Define.

WordPerfect
displays the Math
Definition screen.

```
Math Definition            Use arrow keys to position cursor

Columns                    A B C D E F G H I J K L M N O P Q R S T U V W X

Type                       2 2 2 2 2 2 2 2 2 2 2 2 2 2 2 2 2 2 2 2 2 2 2 2

Negative Numbers           ( ( ( ( ( ( ( ( ( ( ( ( ( ( ( ( ( ( ( ( ( ( ( (

Number of Digits to        2 2 2 2 2 2 2 2 2 2 2 2 2 2 2 2 2 2 2 2 2 2 2 2
  the Right (0-4)

Calculation      1
  Formulas       2
                 3
                 4

Type of Column:
     0 = Calculation    1 = Text      2 = Numeric     3 = Total

Negative Numbers
     ( = Parentheses (50.00)          - = Minus Sign  -50.00


Press Exit when done
```

The Math Definition screen is divided into three parts. The top part enables you to specify certain characteristics of the columns. WordPerfect uses the letters A through X to identify the 24 possible math columns. Notice in the third row of the screen that all the columns are preset to the numeric type.

330

Keep in mind that WordPerfect references columns in left-to-right order. The left margin is not a math column; numbers there cannot be added, but the left margin can be used for text and noncalculated numbers. Therefore, the first tab stop, not the left margin, is column A. The second tab stop is column B, the third tab stop is column C, and so on.

In the middle part of the Math Definition screen, you can specify calculation formulas for as many as four columns. The bottom part of the screen explains the codes used to indicate the type of column. You cannot insert information or make changes on the bottom part of the screen.

If you want to use the default settings (numeric columns, negative numbers displayed in parentheses, and two digits to the right of the decimal point), you do not need to define the math columns. Simply press Exit (F7) to complete the math definition.

If you are making setting changes, however, you need to perform some additional steps:

1. Use the arrow keys to position the cursor in the Type row (under the desired column letter in the Columns row).

2. Press the number for the Type of column:

    0 = Calculation
    1 = Text
    2 = Numeric
    3 = Total

3. Press (or - in the Negative Numbers row to specify how negative math results should be displayed.

4. For each column, type the number of digits you want displayed after the decimal point. Decimals are rounded to the degree of accuracy you specify.

5. When you finish defining the type and format for each column, press F7 (Exit) to return to the editing screen.

Using Calculation Columns

Calculation columns use formulas to calculate numbers across a row of a WordPerfect document. When you enter **0** for the column type on the Math Definition screen, WordPerfect automatically moves the cursor to the middle of the screen so that you can enter a formula for the calculation column. You can enter formulas in as many as 4 of WordPerfect's possible 24 math columns.

To build calculation columns, follow these steps:

1. Set tabs and display the Math Definition screen, using the procedures described earlier in this chapter.

2. Position the cursor in the Type row (under the appropriate letter in the Columns row) and press [0].

   The cursor jumps to the first available Calculation Formulas line.

3. Type the formula and then press [↵Enter] to leave the formula line and return to the top part of the Math Definition screen.

Here, the formula A*B*(-C/100+1) is entered.

```
Math Definition              Use arrow keys to position cursor

Columns                      A B C D E F G H I J K L M N O P Q R S T U V W X

Type                         2 2 2 0 2 2 2 2 2 2 2 2 2 2 2 2 2 2 2 2 2 2 2 2

Negative Numbers             ( ( ( ( ( ( ( ( ( ( ( ( ( ( ( ( ( ( ( ( ( ( ( (

Number of Digits to          0 3 2 2 2 2 2 2 2 2 2 2 2 2 2 2 2 2 2 2 2 2 2 2
   the Right (0-4)

Calculation    1      D     ┌─────────────┐
   Formulas    2           │ A*B*(-C/100+1) │
               3            └─────────────┘
               4

Type of Column:
      0 = Calculation    1 = Text      2 = Numeric    3 = Total

Negative Numbers
      ( = Parentheses  (50.00)        - = Minus Sign  -50.00
```

4. After you enter the formula, press [F7] (Exit) to return to the Math menu.

5. Select **On** (**1**) to turn on the Math feature.

6. Type the text and numbers in the columns.

WordPerfect inserts into the document an exclamation point (!) when you tab over to a column that is defined as a calculation column.

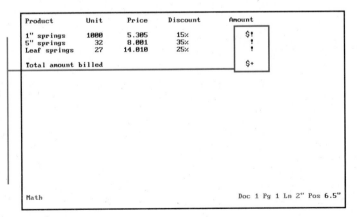

```
Product         Unit      Price     Discount      Amount

1" springs      1000      5.305       15%           $!
5" springs        32      8.001       35%            !
Leaf springs      27     14.010       25%            !

Total amount billed                                 $+




Math                                      Doc 1 Pg 1 Ln 2" Pos 6.5"
```

7. Press [Alt] [F7] (Columns/Table) and select Math (3).

    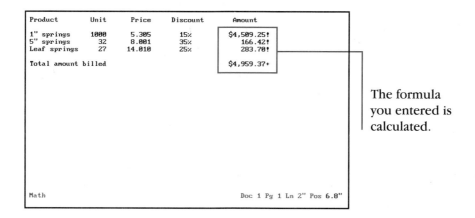 Access the Layout pull-down menu and choose Math.

8. Select Calculate (4).

```
Product        Unit      Price    Discount      Amount

1" springs     1000      5.305      15%       $4,509.25!
5" springs       32      8.001      35%          166.42!
Leaf springs     27     14.010      25%          283.70!

Total amount billed                           $4,959.37+




Math                                  Doc 1 Pg 1 Ln 2" Pos 6.8"
```

The formula you entered is calculated.

Formulas are composed of numbers, column identifiers, and math operators. If you include a column letter, such as A, the formula uses in the calculations the number in column A. When you type a calculation formula, don't include any spaces. And don't press Enter until you have finished entering the formula.

Note the following sample formulas:

Formula	Result
3*3-2	7
3*(3-2)	3
3*A+B	17 (if column A=4 and column B=5)
3*(A+B)	27

A calculation formula can include numbers in other columns (either to the left or right of the calculation column) in the same row of the document. In addition, a formula can include the number appearing in the calculation column on the preceding line of the document, and any numbers you type into the formula.

13

13

A formula can include the following standard arithmetic operators:

+	Adds
–	Subtracts
*	Multiplies
/	Divides

You must enter these special math operators by themselves on the formula line:

+	Adds the numbers in the numeric columns
+–	Averages the numbers in the numeric columns
=	Adds the numbers in the total columns
=/	Averages the numbers in the total columns

A formula is calculated from left to right. If you want a math expression to calculate before other items, place that expression in parentheses. However, you cannot use nested parentheses, such as (3+(3*A))-B, as you can in algebra. If you want to include a fraction, place it in parentheses or use its decimal equivalent—for example, (1/3) or 0.33.

Summary

This chapter described WordPerfect's feature for creating two types of text columns: newspaper and parallel. You learned to create newspaper-style columns that wrap from the bottom of one column to the top of the next. And you learned to create parallel columns that are read from left to right across the page. You also explored the use of math columns. First you examined WordPerfect's simple math capabilities for totaling numbers in a column. Then you looked at the Math feature for performing more complex calculations.

Specifically, you learned the following key information about WordPerfect:

- Newspaper-style columns are read from top to bottom. The text flows from the bottom of one column to the top of the next.

- To define newspaper-style columns, select Columns/Table (Alt-F7), choose Columns, select Define, choose Type, choose Newspaper, press F7, and choose On.

- To display a single newspaper-style column, choose Setup (Shift-F1), select Display, choose Edit-Screen Options, choose Side-by-side Columns Display, and select No.

■ Parallel columns are read from left to right across the page.

■ To define parallel columns, select Columns/Table (Alt-F7), choose **Columns**, choose **Define**, choose **Type**, select **Parallel** or **Parallel with Block** Protect, press F7, and select **On**.

■ WordPerfect's Math feature is designed to provide limited calculation capabilities for simple math operations. WordPerfect can calculate subtotals, totals, and grand totals down columns of numbers.

■ Math operations that involve totals down a column of numbers are the simplest to perform. For these operations, set tabs for math columns, turn on the Math feature, enter numbers and math operators in the columns, calculate the results, and turn off the Math feature.

■ More complex math operations in WordPerfect require you to use the Math Definition screen to "define" each column. You can define four types of columns: numeric, total, text, and calculation.

In the next chapter, you will learn about WordPerfect's Table feature.

13

Creating Tables

14

Although the Table feature is one of WordPerfect's most powerful features, tables are easy to create—even for a first-time user. You can create a table on a blank screen or in an existing document. You can create a table of any size, which can be located anywhere within the document.

The Table feature combines the best aspects of columns, math functions, and spreadsheets. For creating tabular material, you will find the Table feature easier to use than inserting tab stops. If you use a spreadsheet program—especially PlanPerfect 5.0—you already know approximately 90 percent of how the Table feature works.

With the Table feature, you can create parallel columns, create merge templates that function as fill-in forms, create mathematical formulas and perform math functions, sort data, import spreadsheet information into a table, place a table in a graphics box, and place a graphics box in a table. You can retrieve into a document a spreadsheet as a table. And you can use the Retrieve and Text In/Out features to bring text and numerical data into a table.

This chapter shows you how to create the structure for a table, enter text into the table, and edit the text within the table. You then learn how to use the table editor options. Specifically, you learn to edit the table structure—insert and delete rows and columns, join and split cells, change the grid lines, and shade certain cells. You learn also to format the cells—adjust the column widths, specify cell attributes (such as boldface type), and align text within cells. Finally, you learn how to use math in tables.

14

Key Terms in This Chapter	
Rows	Horizontal lines of cells, numbered from top to bottom beginning with 1.
Columns	Vertical stacks of cells, named from left to right with letters of the alphabet beginning with A.
Cell	The intersection of a row and a column in a table.
Spreadsheet	In computer terms, an electronic replacement for an accountant's pad.
Table structure	The physical layout of the rows and columns, the size, and the type of grid lines.
Cell format	The appearance of the text in the cells.
Table editor	A WordPerfect feature that enables you to define and change a table's structure and cell format.

Understanding Table Basics

When you create a table, a group of empty boxes, called *cells*, forms a grid on-screen. The grid is composed of columns and rows of cells. Columns are vertical stacks of cells, named from left to right with letters of the alphabet beginning with A. Rows are horizontal lines of cells, named from top to bottom with numbers beginning with 1.

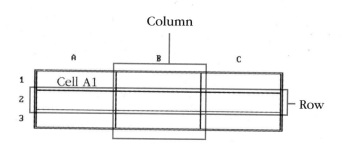

A cell is the intersection of a column and a row. The cell takes its name from the column and row. For example, the cell formed by the intersection of column A and row 1 is called cell A1.

14

Within a cell, you can use all of WordPerfect's font attributes for size and appearance to format text. In addition, text-editing keys and cursor-movement keys, with a few exceptions, function as they do in the main document.

WordPerfect's table editor enables you to define and change a table's structure and cell format. The table structure is the physical layout of the rows and columns, the size, and the type of grid lines. The cell format is the appearance of the text in the cells. You cannot enter or edit text while the table editor is active.

Creating a Table

With WordPerfect's Table feature, creating a basic table is reduced to a few simple steps. You don't need to bother setting tab stops or defining columns. Instead, you use the Table feature to create a column and row structure. Then you can move the cursor within that structure, enter text, and edit it.

Creating the Table Structure

Before you create the table structure, plan how many rows and columns the table will have. Although you can edit the structure later, planning will save you some time and effort.

Suppose that you want to create a table structure that is three columns wide and five rows deep. WordPerfect automatically calculates the space between the document's left and right margins, and formats the column widths to fill all available space.

To create the table structure, follow these steps:

1. Move the cursor to the left margin.

2. Press ⌑Alt⌑ ⌑F7⌑ to activate the Columns/Table command, and select Tables (**2**).

⌑⊡⌑ Access the Layout pull-down menu and select Tables.

WordPerfect displays a new menu:

Table: 1 Create; **2 Edit: 0**

3. Select Create (**1**).

WordPerfect displays the prompt `Number of Columns: 3`, showing a default of 3.

4. Type a value from 1 to 32 and press ⌑⏎Enter⌑. For this example, press ⌑⏎Enter⌑ to create a table with three columns.

WordPerfect displays the prompt `Number of Rows: 1`, showing a default of 1. By default, WordPerfect creates a single row that is one text line high.

5. Type a value from 1 to 32,765 and press ⌑⏎Enter⌑. For this example, type **5** and press ⌑⏎Enter⌑ to create a table with five rows.

WordPerfect creates a blank table and displays the table editor menu.

The status line at the bottom of the screen indicates the cell location of the cursor.

While the table editor is active, WordPerfect expands the cursor to highlight the cell in which the cursor is located. When you create a table, WordPerfect places the cursor in cell A1 (the upper left corner of the table).

At this point, you can use one or more of the table editor options to define the table's format, or you can exit from the table editor and return to the main document. You will learn more about the table editor and its options throughout this chapter.

6. For this example, press F7 (Exit) to leave the table editor.

   The cursor returns to its normal size and remains in the cell where it was located when you pressed F7.

7. Press F10 (Save) to save the table structure you have created.

   ⬚ Access the **File** pull-down menu and select **Save**.

8. Type **test.tbl** as the name of the file and press ⏎Enter.

Moving the Cursor within a Table

Moving the cursor within a table is as easy as moving the cursor in the main document. Within a table, when the table editor is not activated, most of the cursor-movement keys function as they do in the main document. Here are a few of the basic keys you can use for moving within a table:

Key(s)	Function
Tab	Moves the cursor forward to the next cell—from cell A1 to cell B1, for example, or from cell C1 to cell A2 if the cursor is in the last cell of the row.
Shift-Tab	Moves the cursor backward one cell.
↑	Moves the cursor up one cell in a column.
↓	Moves the cursor down one cell in a column.

You can use Home and Ctrl-Home with the arrow keys to move more quickly within the table. On an Enhanced Keyboard, you can use also the Alt key with the arrow keys, or Alt-Home-arrow key combinations to speed movement within the table.

The mouse moves the cursor within a table in the same way as in a regular document. Move the mouse pointer to the cell in which you want the cursor positioned, and click the left button.

Entering Text in a Table

You can enter, format, or edit text in a cell within a table in the same way that you accomplish these tasks in the main document. As you enter text in a cell, the cell expands downward as necessary. As you delete text, the cell contracts to the smallest height required by the largest cell in the row.

Suppose that you want to display gardening information within a table. With TEST.TBL displayed on-screen, follow these steps to add text to the table structure:

1. Position the cursor in cell A1.

2. Type **Plant Name**.

3. Press Tab↹ to move to cell B1, and type **Height (in.)**.

4. Press Tab↹ to move to cell C1, and type **Bloomtime**.

5. Press Tab↹ to move to cell A2, and type **Aster**.

6. Press Tab↹ to move to cell B2, and type **24-48**.

7. Press Tab↹ to move to cell C2, and type **Sept.-Oct.**

8. Move the cursor to each of the following cells and type the entry indicated:

Cell	*What You Type*
A3	**Columbine**
B3	**24-30**
C3	**May-June**
A4	**Coralbells**
B4	**12-24**
C4	**June-Aug**
A5	**Zinnia**
B5	**12-30**
C5	**July-Oct**

9. Press F10 (Save) to save the table you have created.

   ⌨ Access the **File** pull-down menu and select **Save**.

10. Type **garden.tbl** and press ↵Enter.

Plant Name	Height (in.)	Bloomtime
Aster	24–48	Sept.–Oct.
Columbine	24–30	May–June
Corabells	12–24	June–Aug.
Zinnia	12–30	July–Oct.

C:\WP51\BOOK\GARDEN.TBL   Cell C5 Doc 1 Pg 1 Ln 2.26" Pos 6.33"

The gardening information is displayed in the table.

14

Editing Text within a Table

With the Table feature, editing text within a table is as easy as editing text in the main document. Use the following keys to edit text within a table just as you use the keys for editing in a document:

Key(s)	Function
Del	Deletes a single character at the cursor position.
Backspace	Deletes a single character to the left of the cursor.
Ctrl-Backspace	Deletes a word at the cursor position.
Home-Backspace	Deletes a word to the left of the cursor.
Ctrl-End	Deletes text from the cursor to the end of the line (or to the end of the cell on an Enhanced Keyboard).
Ctrl-PgDn	Deletes text from the cursor to the end of the cell (or to the end of the table on an Enhanced Keyboard).

You can also block contiguous cells within the table and then delete them. You perform all these editing operations within the table while the table editor is turned off. WordPerfect deletes only the text within the cells, not the cells themselves. To delete an entire row or column of cells, you use the table editor.

Understanding the Table Editor

The table editor enables you to define or modify the structure or format of a table. Remember that the table structure is the physical layout of the rows and columns, the size, and the type of grid lines. The table format is the appearance of the text in the rows, columns, and cells. You can use the table editor whenever you edit a document containing a table. Keep in mind that text cannot be entered or edited while the table editor is active.

Note: After the table editor is active, you cannot access the pull-down menu bar. You can, however, use the mouse to select options on the table editor menu.

WordPerfect automatically starts the table editor in the following instances:

- You finish creating a new table's basic structure.
- You press Columns/Table (Alt-F7) when the cursor is located within a table.

If a document contains one or more tables and the cursor is *not* located within one of them, you can invoke the table editor with the following procedure:

1. Move the cursor within the table.
2. Press ⟨Alt⟩⟨F7⟩ to activate the Columns/Table command.

   ⌨ Access the Layout pull-down menu.
3. Select Tables (2).
4. Select Edit (2).

The margins and tab settings used for a table are the same as those used for the section of the document in which the table was created. The rest of the table's structure and format is defined by defaults you can change.

```
│
│
│
│
Table Edit:   Press Exit when done        Cell C5 Doc 1 Pg 1 Ln 2.26" Pos 5.43"
──────────────────────────────────────────────────────────────────────────────
Ctrl-Arrows Column Widths; Ins Insert; Del Delete; Move Move/Copy;
1 Size; 2 Format; 3 Lines; 4 Header; 5 Math; 6 Options; 7 Join; 8 Split: 0
```

Each option accessible from the table editor menu is listed in table 14.1. Also listed are options not shown on the menu.

Table 14.1
Table Editor Menu Options and Unlisted Options

Option	Function
⟨Ctrl⟩⟨→⟩	Expands the column containing the cursor one character width to the right each time you use the key combination.

continues

14

345

Table 14.1 Continued

Option	Function
Ctrl ←	Contracts the column containing the cursor one character width to the left each time you use the key combination.
Ins	Inserts one or more columns or rows.
Del	Deletes one or more columns or rows.
Ctrl Home, <*cell name*>	Moves the cursor to the specified cell location. This feature is not listed on the table editor menu.
Ctrl F4	Moves, copies, deletes, or retrieves a block, cell, column, or row. (**Note:** Text moved or copied with the table editor can be accessed only while you are using the table editor.)
Size (1)	Adds one or more columns or rows to a table, or deletes one or more columns or rows from the table.
Format (2)	Accesses additional submenus from which you can choose a variety of formatting options for a cell, a block of cells, or a column. For example, you can select font attributes (such as size and appearance), alignment, cell protection, and number of decimal places. In addition, you have options for designating whether rows include only one line of text or multiple lines.
Lines (3)	Displays a submenu that enables you to change the style of the grid lines, both within and outside the table. In addition, you can choose an option to turn off grid lines and another to shade specified cells.
Header (4)	Displays a submenu that enables you to designate the number of rows in the header. A header is repeated on every page of a multiple-page table.

Option	Function
Math (5)	Displays a submenu that enables you to designate the math operation to be performed in a cell.
Options (6)	Displays a submenu that enables you to designate the spacing between the text and grid lines; the display of negative results (minus sign or parentheses); the position of the table on the page; and the amount of shading (as a percentage of black).
Join (7)	Displays a submenu that enables you to combine two or more cells into a single cell, provided that the cells to be merged are highlighted with the Block feature.
Split (8)	Displays a submenu that enables you to create new columns or rows in the space occupied by a column or row. If you use Block to highlight more than one column or row before invoking this feature, all the highlighted columns or rows are split.
F1 (Cancel)	Restores the last block, column, or row deleted with the table editor. This feature is not listed on the table editor menu.

14

Editing the Table Structure

You can change the structure or format of a cell, a row, a column, or an entire table at any time. Whether the table contains text or is empty, the steps for editing the structure and format of the table are the same.

In this section, you learn to edit the table's structure. Specifically, you learn how to insert and delete rows and columns, to join and split cells, to change the grid lines, and to shade rows. The next section, "Formatting Cells," shows you how to change the cell format.

Inserting and Deleting Columns and Rows

With the table editor, you can either delete a column or row from a table, or insert a column or row. When you delete the column or row, you delete it from the table's structure, as well as the contents of that column or row. You can use Cancel (F1) to restore a deleted column or row, along with its contents.

To add a column or row at the top or left of a table, follow these steps:

1. Retrieve the file (in this example, GARDEN.TBL) if it isn't already displayed on-screen.

2. Press Home, Home, ↑ to move the cursor to the top of the document, *above* the table.

3. Press Alt F7 (Columns/Table), select Tables (2), and choose Edit (2).

   ▱ Access the Layout pull-down menu, select Tables, and choose Edit.

   WordPerfect automatically moves the cursor to cell A1 and displays the table editor menu.

4. Press Ins.

5. Select Rows (1) or Columns (2). For this example, select Rows (1).

6. Type the number of rows or columns you want to add, and then press ↵Enter.

In this case, just press ↵Enter to add one row (the default) to the top of the table.

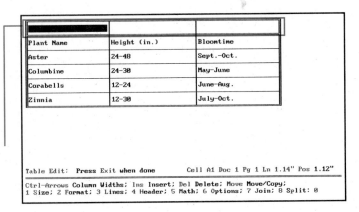

```
┌─────────────────────────────────────────────────────────┐
│  ██████████████                                          │
│  Plant Name          Height (in.)        Bloomtime       │
│  Aster               24-48               Sept.-Oct.      │
│  Columbine           24-30               May-June        │
│  Corabells           12-24               June-Aug.       │
│  Zinnia              12-30               July-Oct.       │
│                                                          │
│                                                          │
│                                                          │
│  Table Edit:  Press Exit when done    Cell A1 Doc 1 Pg 1 Ln 1.14" Pos 1.12" │
└─────────────────────────────────────────────────────────┘
Ctrl-Arrows Column Widths; Ins Insert; Del Delete; Move Move/Copy;
1 Size; 2 Format; 3 Lines; 4 Header; 5 Math; 6 Options; 7 Join; 8 Split: 0
```

To insert a row or column within a table, invoke the table editor and then follow these steps:

1. Press Home, ↓ to position the cursor at the bottom of the table.

2. Press [Ins].

3. Select **Rows** (**1**) or **Columns** (**2**). In this case, select **Rows** (**1**).

4. Type the number of rows or columns you want to insert, and press [↵Enter].

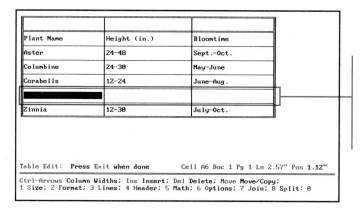

For this example, just press [↵Enter] to insert one row (the default) near the bottom of the table.

14

To delete a row or column from a table, follow these steps:

1. Place the cursor in the row or column you want to delete. For this example, move the cursor to the new row you inserted near the bottom of the table.

2. Press [Del].

3. Select **Rows** (**1**) or **Columns** (**2**). In this case, select **Rows** (**1**).

4. Type the number of rows or columns you want to delete, and press [↵Enter]. For this example, press [↵Enter] to delete a single row.

To restore a row or column you have deleted, follow these steps:

1. Position the cursor where you want to restore the row or column. In this case, position the cursor in the bottom left cell.

2. Press [F1] (Cancel).

3. Select **Yes** at the confirmation prompt.

After you insert a row or column, you must turn off the table editor before you can add text to that row or column. Follow these steps to turn off the table editor and add text to the row you have just restored:

1. Press [F7] to leave the table editor.

349

2. In the restored row near the bottom of the table, type the following information in the cells indicated:

Cell	What You Type
A6	Iris
B6	24-60
C6	April-May

14

Here, the new row of information has been added.

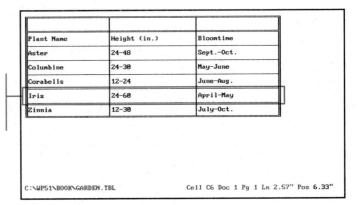

```
Plant Name      Height (in.)    Bloomtime
Aster           24-48           Sept.-Oct.
Columbine       24-38           May-June
Corabells       12-24           June-Aug.
Iris            24-68           April-May
Zinnia          12-38           July-Oct.



C:\WP51\BOOK\GARDEN.TBL               Cell C6 Doc 1 Pg 1 Ln 2.57" Pos 6.33"
```

3. Press F10 (Save) to save the table you have created.

   ⌨ Access the **F**ile pull-down menu and select **S**ave.

4. Type **garden.tbl** and press ⏎Enter.

Joining and Splitting Cells

You can join, or combine, cells to make a larger cell. Before you join the cells, however, you must highlight them with the Block feature. Suppose, for example, that you want to combine the cells in the first row of the gardening table so that you can add a heading there. Follow these steps to join cells:

1. With the cursor located within the table, press Alt F7 (Columns/Table) to turn on the table editor.

   ⌨ Access the **L**ayout pull-down menu, select **T**ables, and choose **E**dit.

2. Move the cursor to the first cell of the cells you want to join. For this example, press Home, Home, ↑ to move to cell A1.

350

3. Highlight the block of cells by pressing ⌊Alt⌋ ⌊F4⌋ or ⌊F12⌋ to activate the Block command. For this example, turn on the Block feature and press ⌊Home⌋, ⌊→⌋ to highlight cells A1 through C1.

4. Select Join (7) from the table editor menu.

   WordPerfect displays the following prompt:

   ```
   Join cells? No (Yes)
   ```

5. Select Yes.

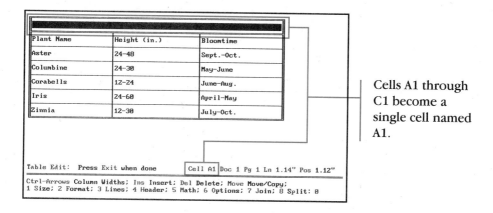

Cells A1 through C1 become a single cell named A1.

6. Press ⌊F7⌋ to leave the table editor.

7. Enter text into the cell. In this case, type the heading GARDEN PLANNING GUIDE in cell A1.

You can split a single cell or any number of cells in rows or columns. If you split the cells in an entire column, WordPerfect adds a complete column to the right of that column. If you split the cells in an entire row, WordPerfect adds a complete row below that row.

Suppose that you want to split the last column in the gardening table in order to add a column at the right of the table. To split the cells in a column, follow these steps:

1. With the cursor located within the table, press ⌊Alt⌋ ⌊F7⌋ (Columns/Table) to turn on the table editor.

   ⌐⌐ Access the Layout pull-down menu, select Tables, and choose Edit.

2. Position the cursor in the column or row you want to split. In this case, move the cursor to cell C2.

3. Highlight the column or row by pressing ⎡Alt⎤⎡F4⎤ or ⎡F12⎤ to activate the Block command.

For this example, turn on the Block feature and press ⎡Home⎤, ⎡↓⎤ to highlight cells C2 through C7.

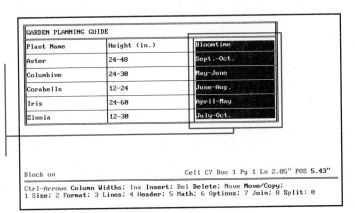

4. Select Split (8) from the table editor menu.

   WordPerfect displays the following menu:

   Split: 1 Rows; **2 C**olumns: **0**

5. Select **R**ows (**1**) or **C**olumns (**2**). In this case, select **C**olumns (**2**).

   WordPerfect displays the prompt Number of Columns: 1.

6. Type the number of rows or columns into which you want the highlighted row or column split, and then press ⎡↵Enter⎤. For this example, type **2** and press ⎡↵Enter⎤.

WordPerfect splits the column into two columns.

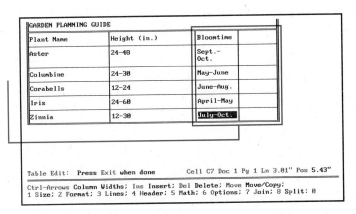

7. Press [F7] (Exit) to leave the table editor.

8. Enter text into the new cells created from the split operation.

    In the new column of the gardening table, type the following information in the specified cells:

Cell	What You Type
D2	**Light**
D3	**P. shade**
D4	**Sun/p. shade**
D5	**Sun/p. shade**
D6	**Sun**
D7	**Sun**

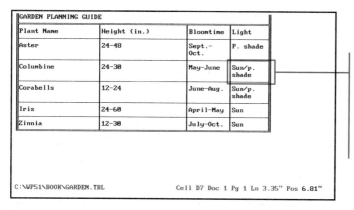

Notice that when you type an entry wider than the width of the cell, WordPerfect wraps the entry to a second line.

9. Press [F10] (Save) to save the table you have created.

    Access the **File** pull-down menu and select **S**ave.

10. Type **garden.tbl** and press [↵Enter].

Changing the Grid Lines

A table is visually defined by a grid of graphics lines. Grid lines print with a document only if your printer can print graphics images. The default line settings are the following:

- Double lines for the table's outside edges
- Single lines for the edges of each cell

14

The **Lines** (3) option on the table editor menu enables you to edit the type of lines and the shading that define the table. Suppose that you want to change the grid lines in the gardening table so that all the lines are single, except that a double line is at the bottom of the cells containing the table subheadings, and no outside lines surround the table heading.

With the cursor located within the table, activate the table editor. Then complete the procedures that follow.

To change all the lines in the table to single lines, follow these steps:

1. Press (Home), (Home), (↑) to position the cursor in cell A1.
2. Press (Alt)(F4) or (F12) to activate the Block command.
3. Press (Home), (Home), (↓) to highlight the entire table.

Here, the entire table is highlighted.

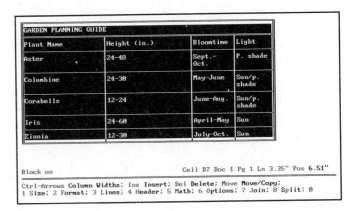

4. Select **Lines** (3).
5. Select **All** (7).
6. Choose **Single** (2).

To add a double underline under a particular row (in this example, the table subheadings), follow these steps:

1. Position the cursor in the first cell of the row for which you want to change the lines. In this case, move the cursor to cell A2.
2. Press (Alt)(F4) or (F12) to activate the Block command.
3. Press (Home), (→) to highlight the row.
4. Select **Lines** (3).

14

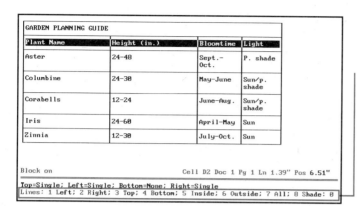

The Lines menu is displayed at the bottom of the screen.

5. To change only the line underneath the highlighted row, select Bottom (4).

6. To change that line to a double underline, choose Double (3).

To erase the outside lines around the table heading, follow these steps:

1. Press [Home], [Home], [↑] to position the cursor in cell A1.

2. Select Lines (3).

3. Select Outside (6).

4. Choose None (1).

5. Press [F7] to leave the table editor and display the table with modified grid lines.

```
GARDEN PLANNING GUIDE

Plant Name        Height (in.)     Bloomtime   Light

Aster             24-48            Sept.-      P. shade
                                   Oct.

Columbine         24-30            May-June    Sun/p.
                                               shade

Corabells         12-24            June-Aug.   Sun/p.
                                               shade

Iris              24-60            April-May   Sun

Zinnia            12-30            July-Oct.   Sun




C:\WP51\BOOK\GARDEN.TBL          Cell A1 Doc 1 Pg 1 Ln 1.1" Pos 1.00"
```

The lines around the table heading are erased.

Shading Rows

If your printer has graphics capabilities, you can emphasize the contents of a cell with the table editor's Shade option. When the Shade option and Block feature are used together, you can shade a row or column in a single operation. You can make the table easier to read by using the Shade option on alternating rows or columns. You can also adjust the density of the shading.

To shade alternating rows in a table, follow these steps:

1. With the cursor located within the table, press [Alt][F7] to activate the table editor.

   ⌨ Access the Layout pull-down menu, select Tables, and choose Edit.

2. Position the cursor in the first cell of the row you want to shade. For this example, move the cursor to cell A3.

3. Press [Alt][F4] or [F12] to activate the Block command.

4. Press [Home], [→] to highlight the row.

5. Select Lines (3).

The Lines menu appears at the bottom of the screen.

```
GARDEN PLANNING GUIDE

Plant Name       Height (in.)      Bloomtime   Light
Aster            24-48             Sept.-      P. shade
                                   Oct.
Columbine        24-38             May-June    Sun/p.
                                               shade
Corabells        12-24             June-Aug.   Sun/p.
                                               shade
Iris             24-68             April-May   Sun
Zinnia           12-38             July-Oct.   Sun


Block on                          Cell D3 Doc 1 Pg 1 Ln 1.7" Pos 6.51"
Top=Single; Left=Single; Bottom=None; Right=Single
Lines: 1 Left; 2 Right; 3 Top; 4 Bottom; 5 Inside; 6 Outside; 7 All; 8 Shade: 0
```

6. Choose Shade (8).

7. Select On (1).

8. Position the cursor in the first cell of the next row you want to shade. For this example, move the cursor to cell A5 and repeat Steps 3 through 7 to highlight that row. Then position the cursor in cell A7 and repeat Steps 3 through 7 to highlight that row.

9. Press ⌊F7⌋ (Exit) to leave the table editor.

10. To see the effect of the shading on-screen, press ⌊⇧Shift⌋⌊F7⌋ (Print) and select View Document (6). To get a clear view of the table's shading, select 200% (2).

    ⌨ Access the File pull-down menu, choose Print, select View Document (6), and select 200% (2).

```
              GARDEN PLANNING GUIDE
              ┌──────────────────┬──────────────┐
              │ Plant Name       │ Height (in.) │
              ├──────────────────┼──────────────┤
              │ Aster            │ 24-48        │
              ├──────────────────┼──────────────┤
              │ Columbine        │ 24-30        │
              ├──────────────────┼──────────────┤
              │ Corabells        │ 12-24        │
              ├──────────────────┼──────────────┤
              │ Iris             │ 24-60        │
              └──────────────────┴──────────────┘
 1 100%   2 200%   3 Full Page   4 Facing Pages: 2          Doc 1 Pg 1
```

Here, the table is shown enlarged to 200%.

11. Press ⌊F7⌋ (Exit) to return to the editing screen.

Formatting Cells

You can format cells in a table in several different ways. You can affect the display of a cell or column, or the height of a row; you can change the font attributes for the size and appearance of the text in a cell (for example, you can make the text boldfaced or underlined); and you can select the justification of the text in the cell.

Note: You won't be able to see on-screen the results of some attributes. To see the enhancements, you may have to leave the table editor and either use View Document or print the table.

You access the formatting features of the table editor by selecting Format (**2**) from the table editor menu. When you make that selection, WordPerfect displays a two-line menu at the bottom of the screen.

```
GARDEN PLANNING GUIDE

Plant Name      Height (in.)      Bloomtime    Light

Aster           24-48             Sept.-       P. shade
                                  Oct.

Columbine       24-30             May-June     Sun/p.
                                               shade

Corabells       12-24             June-Aug.    Sun/p.
                                               shade

Iris            24-60             April-May    Sun

Zinnia          12-30             July-Oct.    Sun


Table Edit:   Press Exit when done        Cell A1 Doc 1 Pg 1 Ln 1.1" Pos 1.08"

Cell: Top;Left;Normal                     Col: 6.5";Left;Normal
Format: 1 Cell; 2 Column; 3 Row Height: 0
```

Reading from the left, the information for the cell is its vertical alignment (Top), justification type (Left), and print/font attributes (Normal). The information for the column is its width (6.4"), justification type (Left), and print/font attributes (Normal).

The second line of the Format menu lists the format options.

You can use either of two methods to change a table's format:

- Use the function keys to insert the appropriate codes—such as those for tabs and font attributes—into a cell or a blocked group of cells while entering or editing text.
- Use the table editor (which also can change the table's structure).

The table editor's Format option enables you to define or change the formatting characteristics of a single cell or column. If you use the Block feature to highlight a section of the table, you can define or change the formatting characteristics of the cells in the area highlighted. The only way to change the formatting characteristics of a row in a single formatting action is to highlight the row before you choose the Format option.

Adjusting the Width of Columns

You can use the table editor to adjust the width of one or more columns within the table. Two methods for adjusting column widths are available. You can use [Ctrl]-[←] and [Ctrl]-[→] to adjust the widths one character at a time. Or you can use the table editor's Format option to set the column widths to specific measurements.

Suppose, for example, that you want to adjust the widths of the columns in the gardening table. Using the first method described, follow these steps:

1. Position the cursor within the table and press ⎇ F7 to turn on the table editor.

   ⌨ Access the Layout pull-down menu, select Tables, and choose Edit.

2. To make the first column narrower, move the cursor to cell A2, press and hold down Ctrl while you press ← repeatedly until the column is the width you want, and then release both keys.

3. To make the second column narrower, move the cursor to cell B2, press and hold down Ctrl while you press ← repeatedly until the column is the width you want, and then release both keys.

   Notice that the text moves down to adjust to the new width.

4. To widen the third column, move the cursor to cell C2, press and hold down Ctrl while you press → repeatedly until the column is the width you want, and then release both keys.

5. To widen the fourth column, position the cursor in cell D2, press and hold down Ctrl while you press → repeatedly until the column is the width you want, and then release both keys.

14

```
GARDEN PLANNING GUIDE

Plant Name    Height    Bloomtime    Light
              (in.)

Aster         24-48     Sept.-Oct.   P. shade

Columbine     24-30     May-June     Sun/p. shade

Corabells     12-24     June-Aug.    Sun/p. shade

Iris          24-60     April-May    Sun

Zinnia        12-30     July-Oct.    Sun



Table Edit:  Press Exit when done      Cell D2 Doc 1 Pg 1 Ln 1.38" Pos 4.71"
Ctrl-Arrows Column Widths; Ins Insert; Del Delete; Move Move/Copy;
1 Size; 2 Format; 3 Lines; 4 Header; 5 Math; 6 Options; 7 Join; 8 Split: 0
```

Here, the fourth column is widened.

With the second method, you use the Format (2) option on the table editor menu to change the column width to an exact measure. With the table editor activated, follow these steps to change the width of a column:

1. Position the cursor within the column you want to change.

2. Select Format (2).

3. Select Column (**2**).

4. Select Width (**1**).

5. Type an exact width and press `⏎Enter`.

Specifying Cell Attributes

You can change attributes for a single cell, a highlighted block of cells, or a column. Suppose that you want to make the gardening table's subheadings appear in boldface type. With the table displayed and the table editor activated, follow these steps:

1. Position the cursor in the first cell of the row or column in which you want to change the attribute, or in any cell of an entire column in which you want to change the attribute. For this example, move the cursor to cell A2.

2. To change the attribute for the cells in a row or for only some cells within a column, press `Alt` `F4` or `F12` to activate the Block command, and then highlight the cells you want to change. In this case, turn on Block and press `Home`, `→` to highlight the row.

3. Select Format (**2**).

4. Select Cell (**1**) to modify a single cell or a block of cells in a high-lighted area, or select Column (**2**) to modify all the cells in a column. For this example, select Cell (**1**).

5. Select Attributes (**2**).

6. Select Size (**1**) or Appearance (**2**). In this case, select Appearance (**2**) and choose Bold (**1**).

7. Press `F7` to leave the table editor.

8. To see the effect of the attribute change, press `⇧Shift` `F7` (Print) and select View Document (**6**). To get a clear view of the table's boldfaced subheadings, select 200% (**2**).

   ▭ Access the File pull-down menu, select Print, choose View Document (**6**), and select 200% (**2**).

14

```
GARDEN PLANNING GUIDE
┌─────────────┬─────────┬───────────┐
│ Plant Name  │ Height  │ Bloomtime │
│             │ (in.)   │           │
├─────────────┼─────────┼───────────┤
│ Aster       │ 24-48   │ Sept.-Oct │
├─────────────┼─────────┼───────────┤
│ Columbine   │ 24-30   │ May-June  │
├─────────────┼─────────┼───────────┤
│ Corabells   │ 12-24   │ June-Aug  │
├─────────────┼─────────┼───────────┤
│ Iris        │ 24-60   │ April-May │
├─────────────┼─────────┼───────────┤
│ Zinnia      │ 12-30   │ July-Oct  │
└─────────────┴─────────┴───────────┘
1 100%  2 200%  3 Full Page  4 Facing Pages: 2        Doc 1 Pg 1
```

Here, you can see that the subheads are boldfaced.

14

9. Press `F7` (Exit) to return to the editing screen.

Aligning Text within Cells or Columns

You can align text within cells or columns in one of five ways: right, left, center, full, and on the decimal character. For the gardening table, you will center the heading, align the text at the right of the first column, and center the text in the second column. To make these alignment changes, follow these steps:

1. With the cursor located within the table, press `Alt` `F7` to activate the table editor.

   ▭ Access the Layout pull-down menu, select Tables, and choose Edit.

2. To center the table's heading, position the cursor in cell A1, select Format (2), choose Cell (1), select Justify (3), and select Center (2).

3. To align the text at the right of the first column, position the cursor in cell A2, select Format (2), select Column (2), choose Justify (3), and select Right (3).

4. To center the text in the second column, position the cursor in cell B2, select Format (2), select Column (2), choose Justify (3), and select Center (2).

361

5. Press [F7] (Exit) to leave the table editor.

6. Press [F10] (Save) to save the table you have created.

   ⌨ Access the **File** pull-down menu and select **S**ave.

7. Type **garden.tbl** and press [↵Enter].

14

Here, you can see on-screen the alignment of text within the cells and columns.

```
                    GARDEN PLANNING GUIDE
        ┌───────────┬────────┬──────────┬──────────────┐
        │Plant Name │Height  │Bloomtime │Light         │
        │           │(in.)   │          │              │
        ├───────────┼────────┼──────────┼──────────────┤
        │     Aster │24-48   │Sept.-Oct.│P. shade      │
        ├───────────┼────────┼──────────┼──────────────┤
        │  Columbine│24-30   │May-June  │Sun/p. shade  │
        ├───────────┼────────┼──────────┼──────────────┤
        │  Corabells│12-24   │June-Aug. │Sun/p. shade  │
        ├───────────┼────────┼──────────┼──────────────┤
        │      Iris │24-60   │April-May │Sun           │
        ├───────────┼────────┼──────────┼──────────────┤
        │    Zinnia │12-30   │July-Oct. │Sun           │
        └───────────┴────────┴──────────┴──────────────┘



C:\WP51\BOOK\GARDEN.TBL            Cell B2 Doc 1 Pg 1 Ln 1.55" Pos 3.16"
```

To see the results of your formatting changes, as well as all the other changes you have made to the sample table, print the document on-screen. Follow these steps:

1. Press [⇧Shift] [F7] to activate the Print command. The Print menu is displayed.

   ⌨ Access the **File** pull-down menu and choose **P**rint.

2. Select **F**ull Document (**1**).

Here, you can see how the formatting changes look when the table is printed.

GARDEN PLANNING GUIDE			
Plant Name	**Height (in.)**	**Bloomtime**	**Light**
Aster	24-48	Sept.-Oct.	P. shade
Columbine	24-30	May-June	Sun/p. shade
Corabells	12-24	June-Aug.	Sun/p. shade
Iris	24-60	April-May	Sun
Zinnia	12-30	July-Oct.	Sun

Using Math in Tables

While WordPerfect doesn't offer as much as a dedicated spreadsheet program, the Table math features are more powerful than found in other word processors. In addition to the math features described in Chapter 13, you can perform basic math operations within the Table feature. You can add, subtract, multiply, and divide, as well as calculate a subtotal, total, and grand total. You can create formulas that perform a combination of these operations, and you can reference cells within those formulas.

Suppose, for example, that you want to find the average of a list of numbers in a table. To find an average, follow these steps:

1. Retrieve the table and move the cursor to the cell in which you want to enter the formula for the average.

Yellow Acre	$25,000.00
Brown Acre	$15,000.00
Orange Acre	$2,000.00
Purple Acre	$11,500.00
Gray Acre	$22,300.20
Average:	

C:\WP51\BOOK\TABMATH.DOC   Cell B6 Doc 1 Pg 1 Ln 2.54" Pos 4.38"

For example, position the cursor in cell B6.

2. Press Alt F7 to activate the table editor.

   ⌨ Access the **Layout** pull-down menu, select **Tables**, and choose **Edit**.

3. Select **Math** (**5**).

14

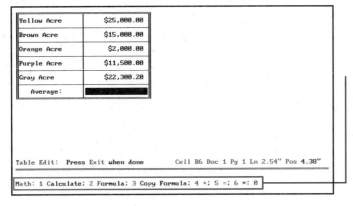

WordPerfect
displays the Math
menu.

4. Make a selection from the Math menu's options:

Select Calculate (**1**) to calculate the cells.

Select Formula (**2**) to enter a formula within a cell.

Select Copy Formula (**3**) to copy a formula from one cell to another.

Select + (**4**) to insert a subtotal of numbers.

Select = (**5**) to insert a total of numbers.

Select * (**6**) to insert a grand total of numbers.

For this example, select Formula (**2**).

5. To calculate an average, type the following as a formula:

B1+B2+B3+B4+B5/5

6. Press ⏎Enter.

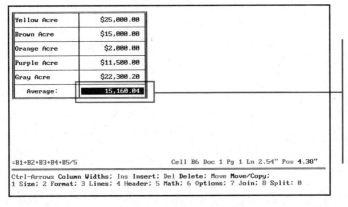

When you press
⏎Enter, Word-
Perfect adds cells
B1 through B5,
divides the total
by 5, and displays
the answer in
cell B6.

Notice that when the cursor is in cell B6, the formula is displayed at the lower left corner of the screen, regardless of whether the table editor is activated.

7. Press ⎣F7⎦ (Exit) and save the table.

Summary

14

In this chapter, you learned about WordPerfect's Table feature. Despite its substantial power, the Table feature is easy to use. You learned to create the table structure, enter and modify text within the table, modify the table structure, and change the format of cells within the table.

Specifically, you learned the following key information about WordPerfect:

■ When you create a table, a group of empty boxes, called cells, forms a grid on-screen. A cell is the intersection of a column and a row.

■ To create a table structure, move the cursor to the left margin, select Columns/Table (Alt-F7), and choose **Tables** (**2**). Select **Create** (**1**) and enter a value for the number of columns and a value for the number of rows.

■ Use WordPerfect's table editor to define and change a table's structure and cell format. Keep in mind that you cannot enter or edit text while the table editor is active.

■ With the table editor, you can insert and delete rows and columns, join and split cells, change the grid lines, and shade rows. You can also change the cell format.

■ Use the math capabilities with the Table feature to perform basic math operations and enter simple formulas that reference cells. To access the math capabilities from within a table, position the cursor within the cell in which you want to enter a formula, select Columns/Table (Alt-F7), choose **Math** (**5**), and make a selection from the Math menu.

In the next chapter, you learn how to customize many aspects of WordPerfect to meet your needs.

Customizing WordPerfect

After you use WordPerfect for a while, you may find that some of the program's default (initial startup) settings are not the best ones for your particular applications. For example, perhaps the default margin settings do not work with your letterhead, or perhaps you prefer your text to be ragged right instead of justified.

You can customize many aspects of the WordPerfect program to meet your needs. Among the options you can choose as the new default features of the program are a left-handed mouse, a customized screen display, a customized environment, designated initial settings, an alternative keyboard layout, and specified locations for files.

This chapter describes in detail some of the more common ways you can customize WordPerfect. Many of the other customizing options are only summarized in this chapter. For more detailed information about those options, refer to Que's *Using WordPerfect 5.1,* Special Edition.

<table>
<tr><td colspan="2">Key Terms in This Chapter</td></tr>
<tr><td>Backups</td><td>Copies of your working files.</td></tr>
<tr><td>Cursor speed</td><td>In WordPerfect, the speed at which a character repeats when you hold down a key.</td></tr>
<tr><td>Units of measure</td><td>The segments (such as inches) of measurements used for margins, tabs, and other features.</td></tr>
</table>

15

Accessing the Setup Menu

You can use the Setup menu at any time to customize the program.

To access the Setup menu, press Shift-F1 to activate the Setup command.

Access the **F**ile pull-down menu and select Se**t**up to display the Setup menu options.

If you pressed Shift-F1, this Setup menu is displayed.

```
Setup

      1 - Mouse

      2 - Display

      3 - Environment

      4 - Initial Settings

      5 - Keyboard Layout

      6 - Location of Files




    Selection: 0
```

By changing the default settings within this menu, you can select the way many of WordPerfect's features work. The choices you make are the new start-up defaults; they affect all documents until you use this menu again to change them.

Many settings can be overridden for a specific document. You can make setting changes that affect the current document only by using the options on the Format and Font menus.

Each of the choices on the Setup menu is described in the text that follows.

Customizing the Mouse

15

Use the **Mouse (1)** option on the Setup menu to tell WordPerfect which kind of mouse you are using and to change some of the defaults WordPerfect uses to interact with your mouse. Among the changes you can make are changing the mouse to a left-handed operation.

To customize the mouse, follow these steps:

1. Press ⬆Shift F1 to activate the Setup command.

   ▭ Access the **File** pull-down menu and select **Setup**.

2. Select **Mouse (1)**.

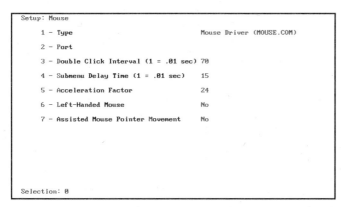

The Setup: Mouse menu appears.

3. Select an item and enter the appropriate information as described in the following text.

4. Press F7 (Exit) to leave the Setup menu and return to your document.

Use the Mouse menu to designate the following options:

- *Type:* Use this option to tell WordPerfect which type of mouse you are using with the program. For specific steps, see the text that follows.

- *Port:* Use this option to specify the port to which a serial mouse is connected.

- *Double Click Interval:* Specify the time interval between clicks of a double-click with this option. If you find that WordPerfect treats what you intend to be double clicks as single clicks, increase the double-click interval.

- *Submenu Delay Time:* By default, WordPerfect displays a pop-out menu if the pointer rests on the main menu selection for 0.15 seconds. If menus "pop out" when you don't want them to, increase the delay time; if you find yourself waiting for the menu to appear, decrease the delay time.

- *Acceleration Factor:* Use this option to determine how sensitive the mouse pointer is to physical movements of the mouse. Set a higher number to make the mouse move farther or "livelier." Set a lower number to decrease how far the pointer moves—to make the mouse more sluggish.

- *Left-Handed Mouse:* Change the mouse to left-handed operation with this option. For specific steps, see the text that follows.

- *Assisted Mouse Pointer Movement:* By default, the mouse pointer remains at its location on the editing screen when you pull down a menu or display a menu at the bottom of the screen. Use this option to have the mouse pointer move to the menu.

Designating Which Type of Mouse You Are Using

WordPerfect must know which type of mouse you are using with the program. You can give WordPerfect this information by following these steps:

1. Press ⇧Shift F1 to activate the Setup command.

   🖱 Access the File pull-down menu and select Setup.

2. Select Mouse (1).

3. Select Type (1).

   The Setup: Mouse Type menu appears.

4. Use the cursor keys or mouse to highlight the mouse you use.

5. Choose Select (**1**).

   The Setup: Mouse menu reappears.

6. If you have a serial mouse, choose Auto-select (**1**) and select which COM port is being used.

   Or

   If you do not have a serial mouse, choose Port (**2**) and press the number corresponding to the port you use for your mouse.

7. Press F7 (Exit) to return to the editing screen.

Changing the Mouse to Left-Handed Operation

The mouse is designed to be put on the right side of the keyboard. If you are left-handed, or if you are simply more comfortable with the mouse on the left, follow these steps to change the mouse to left-handed operation:

1. Press ⇧Shift F1 to activate the Setup command.

   Access the File pull-down menu and select Setup.

2. Select Mouse (**1**).

3. Select Left-Handed Mouse (**6**).

4. At the prompt, select Yes.

5. Press F7 (Exit) to return to the editing screen.

Adjusting the Screen Display

The Display (**2**) option on the Setup menu controls many aspects of WordPerfect's screen display. For instance, you can change the color of normal text and various text attributes (if you have a color monitor), specify whether the current file name is displayed on the status line, and select how menus and columns are shown on-screen.

To adjust the screen display, follow these steps:

1. Press ⇧Shift F1 to activate the Setup command.

   Access the File pull-down menu and select Setup.

2. Select Display (**2**).

The Setup: Display menu appears.

```
Setup: Display

     1 - Colors/Fonts/Attributes

     2 - Graphics Screen Type      VGA 640x480 16 Color

     3 - Text Screen Type          Auto Selected

     4 - Menu Options

     5 - View Document Options

     6 - Edit-Screen Options




Selection: 0
```

15

3. Select an item and enter the appropriate information as described in the following text.

4. Press F7 (Exit) to leave the Setup menu and return to your document.

Use the Display menu to change the following options:

- *Colors/Fonts/Attributes:* The choices displayed when you select this option depend on your monitor and hardware. For specific steps about using this option, see the text that follows.

- *Graphics Screen Type:* WordPerfect automatically adjusts to your monitor and graphics card. If, for example, you have more than one monitor attached, you can use this option to switch the display type. Simply select this option, and then select a screen driver from the list.

- *Text Screen Type:* If you have a monitor with special fonts or that can display more than the standard number of columns or rows of text, use this option to select the appropriate driver.

- *Menu Options:* You select a menu choice by pressing a number or letter. Use this option to choose how the letter options (*mnemonics*) display. Then choose size and appearance attributes from the menu.

- *View Document Options:* If you have a high-resolution (EGA or VGA) color monitor, text (and bold characters) in View Document appears in colors used in the text-editing screen, and graphic images are displayed in color. You can change these defaults. These options have no effect on monochrome or CGA color monitors.

- *Edit-Screen Options:* Use these options to customize the display of the editing screens. For specifics, see the text later in this section.

Changing the Display Colors

Use the **Colors/Fonts/Attributes (1)** option to control the colors and fonts that represent text attributes. The procedure will vary depending on what type of video adaptor you have.

If you have a VGA/EGA adaptor, follow these steps to adjust the screen colors:

1. Press ⬆Shift F1 to activate the Setup command.

   ▭ Access the File pull-down menu and select Setup.

2. Select Display (2).

3. Choose Colors/Fonts/Attribute (1).

   The screen that appears differs depending on what kind of video display you have.

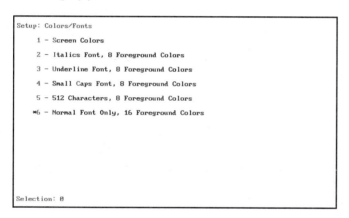

```
Setup: Colors/Fonts

    1 - Screen Colors

    2 - Italics Font, 8 Foreground Colors

    3 - Underline Font, 8 Foreground Colors

    4 - Small Caps Font, 8 Foreground Colors

    5 - 512 Characters, 8 Foreground Colors

  *6 - Normal Font Only, 16 Foreground Colors




Selection: 0
```

This Setup: Colors/Fonts menu appears if you have a VGA/ EGA adaptor.

4. Choose Screen Colors (1).

```
Setup: Colors          A B C D E F G H I J K L M N O P
                       A B C D E F G   I J   M
Attribute              Foreground  Background   Sample
Normal                     A           H        Sample
Blocked                    H           A        Sample
Underline                  A           D        Sample
Strikeout                  A           F        Sample
Bold                       E           H        Sample
Double Underline           B           D        Sample
Redline                    E           H        Sample
Shadow                     B           H        Sample
Italics                    A           C        Sample
Small Caps                 E           D        Sample
Outline                    F           D        Sample
Subscript                  E           H        Sample
Superscript                F           H        Sample
Fine Print                 A           F        Sample
Small Print                H           F        Sample
Large Print                E           A        Sample
Very Large Print           D           A        Sample
Extra Large Print          H           A        Sample
Bold & Underline           P           H
Other Combinations         A           G        Sample

Switch documents; Move to copy settings    Doc 1
```

The Setup: Colors menu is displayed.

5. Use the arrow keys or mouse to highlight each foreground and background color you want to change and press the appropriate letter from the list at the top of the screen.

   A sample of the attribute appears in the right-hand column.

6. Press F7 (Exit) twice to return to your document.

Setting Edit-Screen Options

To customize the display of the editing screen, follow these steps:

1. Press ⬆Shift F1 to activate the Setup command.

   ▭ Access the **File** pull-down menu and select Setup.

2. Select **D**isplay (2).

3. Choose **E**dit-Screen Options (6).

The Setup: Edit-Screen Options menu is displayed.

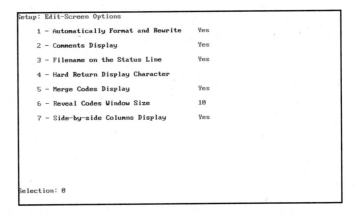

```
Setup: Edit-Screen Options

        1 - Automatically Format and Rewrite    Yes

        2 - Comments Display                     Yes

        3 - Filename on the Status Line          Yes

        4 - Hard Return Display Character

        5 - Merge Codes Display                  Yes

        6 - Reveal Codes Window Size             10

        7 - Side-by-side Columns Display         Yes




Selection: 0
```

4. Choose an option, as described in the text that follows.

5. Press F7 (Exit) to return to the editing screen.

The options on the Setup: Edit-Screen Options menu are described in the following text:

- *Automatically Format and Rewrite:* By default, WordPerfect automatically reformats text and rewrites the screen as you edit. Most users probably want this feature turned on. If you turn off this feature, the editing process is generally faster and WordPerfect reformats line-by-line as you move the cursor down.

- *Comments Display:* Use this option to turn off the display of document comments. Then, only a **[Comment]** code is visible in Reveal Codes.

- *Filename on the Status Line:* By default, WordPerfect displays the name of the current document on the status line at the bottom of the screen (after you've named the document). Use this option to turn off the display of the file name.

- *Hard Return Display Character:* Use this option to display hard returns on the editing screen. You can designate any character to represent the hard return.

- *Merge Codes Display:* Use this option to turn off the display of merge codes on the editing screen. Even when this option is turned off, the merge codes appear in Reveal Codes.

- *Reveal Codes Window Size:* Use this option to change the default size (10 lines) of the Reveal Codes window.

- *Side-by-side Columns Display:* By default, WordPerfect displays columns side-by-side. You can use this option to change to a single-column display. For specific steps, see "Displaying a Single Column" in Chapter 13.

15

Customizing the Environment

Among the *environment* options, WordPerfect lets you set backup options, turn beeps on and off, vary the cursor speed, set document summary options, customize the List Files display, turn Fast Save on and off, set hyphenation options, set units of measure, and choose an alternate keyboard.

To change the environment options, follow these steps:

1. Press ⧆Shift F1 to activate the Setup command.

   ▭ Access the File pull-down menu and select Setup.

2. Select Environment (3).

```
Setup: Environment

     1 - Backup Options

     2 - Beep Options

     3 - Cursor Speed                    50 cps

     4 - Document Management/Summary

     5 - Fast Save (unformatted)         Yes

     6 - Hyphenation                     External Dictionary/Rules

     7 - Prompt for Hyphenation          When Required

     8 - Units of Measure

     9 - Alternate Keyboard              No
              (F1 - Help, Esc - Cancel, F3 - Repeat)



Selection: 0
```

The Setup: Environment menu is displayed.

3. Select an item and enter the appropriate information as described in the following text.

4. Press F7 (Exit) to leave the Setup menu and return to your document.

Use the Environment menu to change the following options:

- *Backup Options:* Select from Timed or Automatic backups. See specific steps in the text that follows.

- *Beep Options:* You can tell WordPerfect under what circumstances you want the program to beep. You can have the program beep whenever it encounters an error, whenever hyphenation is called for, and whenever a Search operation fails.

- *Cursor Speed:* Change the rate at which a character repeats. See specific steps in the text that follows.

- *Document Management/Summary:* Use this option to have WordPerfect prompt you to enter document summary information the first time you save a document. You can also use this option to designate a default of long or short file names for the List Files screen. In addition, you can designate a document type to appear as the default when you create a document summary.

- *Fast Save:* Turn on Fast Save to save files quickly. Fast-saved files are not formatted, and you cannot print a fast-saved file from disk. See specific steps in the following text.

- *Hyphenation:* Use this option to choose between dictionary-based and rule-based hyphenation.

- *Prompt for Hyphenation:* Use this option to tell WordPerfect when and if to prompt you when hyphenation is turned on.

- *Units of Measure:* Choose this option to change the measurements used in screen displays and in the status line. For more information about changing the unit of measurement, see Chapter 4.

- *Alternate Keyboard:* Choose this option to remap the function of the Esc, F1 and F3 keys. To further customize your keyboard, choose Keyboard Layout (5) from the Setup menu, as described later in this chapter.

Setting Automatic Backups

WordPerfect's Setup menu offers two automatic backup features: Timed Backup and Original Backup. Before you request automatic backups, make sure that you have enough disk space for the original and edited versions of the file, especially if you are using a dual floppy disk system.

If you select the Timed Backup option, at specified intervals, WordPerfect automatically saves the document displayed on-screen. If you have documents in both windows (Doc 1 and Doc 2), only the active document is backed up. WordPerfect creates backup files called WP{WP}.BK1 (for Doc 1) and WP{WP}.BK2 (for Doc 2). These backup files are only temporary. When you exit WordPerfect properly, the temporary backup files are deleted. Therefore, you must save your work manually even if you choose this option.

Timed Backup is useful in emergency situations. For example, if a power failure occurs, you can retrieve the backup files from the disk when you restart WordPerfect.

If you set the Original Backup option, WordPerfect saves both the original file and the edited version. The original document is renamed with the extension .BK!. For example, the original LETTER.JLS becomes LETTER.BK!. Each time you edit and save the file, the .BK! file is replaced with the last version. Note that with the Original Backup feature turned on, WordPerfect assigns the same backup name to two files if they share the same name but have different extensions. A backup of either LETTER.JLS or LETTER.RMJ, for example, would become LETTER.BK!.

To select an automatic backup option, follow these steps:

1. Press `⇧Shift` `F1` to activate the Setup command.

   ▭ Access the File pull-down menu and select Setup.

2. Select Environment (3).

3. Select Backup Options (1).

```
Setup: Backup

     Timed backup files are deleted when you exit WP normally.  If you
     have a power or machine failure, you will find the backup file in the
     backup directory indicated in Setup: Location of Files.

          Backup Directory

     1 - Timed Document Backup              Yes
         Minutes Between Backups            30

     Original backup will save the original document with a .BK! extension
     whenever you replace it during a Save or Exit.

     2 - Original Document Backup           No




Selection: 0
```

The Setup: Backup menu is displayed.

4. To select timed backups, select Timed Document Backup (**1**), press
   Y, type the interval between backups (in minutes) and then press
   ⏎Enter.

   Or

   To select original document backups, select Original Document
   Backup (**2**), and then press Y.

5. Press F7 (Exit) to leave the Setup menu and return to your
   document.

To retrieve a backup file, you first rename the file. Then you can press Retrieve
(Shift-F10), or you can use the Retrieve option from the List Files menu.

15

Setting the Cursor Speed

When you hold down a key and don't release it, the key repeats its character.
The rate at which the character repeats is called the cursor speed.

To change the cursor speed, follow these steps:

1. Press ⬆Shift F1 to activate the Setup command.

   ▭ Access the File pull-down menu and select Setup.

2. Select Environment (**3**).

3. Select Cursor Speed (**3**).

4. Press a number from 1 to 5 to choose the cursor speed from the menu
   at the bottom of the screen.

To return the
speed to 10
characters per
second, select
Normal (**6**).

```
Setup: Environment

     1 - Backup Options

     2 - Beep Options

     3 - Cursor Speed                         50 cps

     4 - Document Management/Summary

     5 - Fast Save (unformatted)              Yes

     6 - Hyphenation                          External Dictionary/Rules

     7 - Prompt for Hyphenation               When Required

     8 - Units of Measure

     9 - Alternate Keyboard                   No
           (F1 - Help, Esc - Cancel, F3 - Repeat)



Characters Per Second: 1 15; 2 20; 3 30; 4 40; 5 50; 6 Normal: 0
```

5. Press F7 (Exit) to leave the Setup menu and return to your
   document.

378

Using Fast Save

You can turn on Fast Save to save files quickly. Fast-saved files are not format-ted, and you cannot print a fast-saved file from disk. Instead, you must retrieve the document to the screen and then print. Unless you have long files, turn off Fast Save so that files are saved and formatted.

To turn Fast Save on or off, follow these steps:

1. Press ⬥Shift F1 to display the Setup menu.

   Access the File pull-down menu and select Setup.

2. Select Environment (3).

3. Select Fast Save (5).

4. Select Yes to turn on Fast Save or No to turn it off.

5. Press F7 (Exit) to leave the Setup menu and return to your document.

15

Selecting Initial Settings

With the Initial Settings menu in Setup, you can—for all your documents—change the date format, change many default format settings with initial codes, and set the repeat value.

To change initial settings, follow these steps:

1. Press ⬥Shift F1 to activate the Setup command.

   Access the File pull-down menu and select Setup.

2. Select Initial Settings (4).

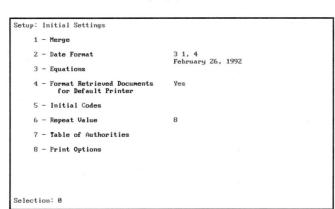

```
Setup: Initial Settings

    1 - Merge

    2 - Date Format              3 1, 4
                                 February 26, 1992
    3 - Equations

    4 - Format Retrieved Documents   Yes
          for Default Printer

    5 - Initial Codes

    6 - Repeat Value             8

    7 - Table of Authorities

    8 - Print Options




Selection: 0
```

The Setup: Initial Settings screen appears.

3. Select an item from the menu, as described in the text that follows, and enter the desired information.

4. Press [F7] (Exit) to leave the Setup menu and return to your document.

Use the Initial Settings menu to change the following options:

*   *Merge:* You can use WordPerfect files or DOS text files as secondary files during a merge operation. If you use DOS text files, use this option to specify what ASCII characters serve as the field and record delimiters in the text files.

*   *Date Format:* Specify how the date and time appear with this option. The date formats you select from are identical to those used by Date Format on the Date/Outline screen. When you set the formats in Setup, the formats are used as defaults.

*   *Equations:* Use this option to specify how equations are printed, how equations are aligned in equation boxes, and what keyboard definition is activated when you enter the equation editor.

*   *Format Retrieved Documents for Default Printer:* When WordPerfect retrieves a file, the program normally formats the document for the currently selected printer. If you want, you can specify that Word-Perfect format all retrieved documents for the printer in effect at the time the document was saved.

*   *Initial Codes:* When you choose this option, WordPerfect displays an editing screen with Reveal Codes turned on. Choose formatting commands and change the values you want; these codes become the default for all future documents.

    For example, to turn off justification, press Format (Shift-F8), select Line (1), choose Justification (3), and select Left. Or, to change the alignment character, press Format (Shift-F8), select Other (4), choose Decimal/Align Character (3), type a new alignment character, and press Enter twice.

*   *Repeat Value:* Change the default value of the Repeat function with this option.

*   *Table of Authorities:* Specify the default formatting for tables of authorities with this option.

*   *Print Options:* You can change the defaults for some of the print time options so that the options affect all documents printed subsequently. You can also change some options not available on the Print menu.

15

Assigning a Keyboard Layout

WordPerfect assigns a specific key to each of the program's features. For instance, the F3 function key is assigned to the Help feature, and the Alt-F4 key combination is assigned to the Block feature. Several other useful keyboard definitions are supplied with the program. You can edit these definitions for your particular needs or create your own definitions.

Selecting a Keyboard Definition

To select a keyboard definition, follow these steps:

1. Press ⬆Shift F1 to activate the Setup command.

   🖱 Access the **F**ile pull-down menu and select Se**t**up.

2. Select **K**eyboard Layout (**5**).

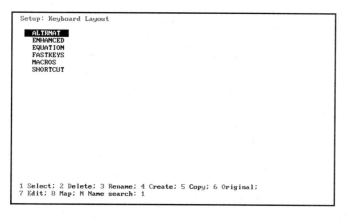

Six keyboard definitions are supplied with WordPerfect.

```
Setup: Keyboard Layout
  ALTRNAT
  ENHANCED
  EQUATION
  FASTKEYS
  MACROS
  SHORTCUT




1 Select; 2 Delete; 3 Rename; 4 Create; 5 Copy; 6 Original;
7 Edit; 8 Map; N Name search: 1
```

Options on the Keyboard Layout screen let you select, delete, edit, or rename the highlighted key definition; create a new definition; view key assignments (map); or restore the keyboard to its original definition.

3. Move the cursor to the definition you want and choose **S**elect (**1**).

   The alternative definition remains in effect until you switch back to WordPerfect's default keyboard.

4. Press F7 (Exit) to leave the Setup menu and return to your document.

15

The ALTRNAT keyboard definition moves the Help key (F3) to F1, moves Cancel (F1) to the Esc key, and moves the Esc key to F3. The ENHANCED keyboard definition assigns keys available only on the enhanced (101-key keyboard, such as Shift-F11 and Ctrl-F12. The EQUATION keyboard remaps the keyboard for use in the equation editor. The FASTKEYS keyboard definition assigns a list of WordPerfect fast keys (Ctrl-letter key combinations to activate certain commands). The MACROS keyboard definition assigns useful macros to Alt- and Ctrl-key combinations. And the SHORTCUT keyboard definition assigns some common multi-keystroke combinations to Alt-key and Ctrl-key combination.

Returning to the Original Keyboard

To return to WordPerfect's original keyboard, follow these steps:

1. Press `⇧Shift` `F1` to activate the Setup command.

   ⌨ Access the File pull-down menu and select Setup.

2. Select Keyboard Layout (5).

3. Choose Original (6).

4. Press `F7` (Exit) to leave the Setup menu and return to your document.

An alternate method is simply to press Ctrl-6 from the editing screen.

Editing a Keyboard Definition

To edit a keyboard definition, follow these steps:

1. Press `⇧Shift` `F1` to activate the Setup command.

   ⌨ Access the File pull-down menu and select Setup.

2. Select Keyboard Layout (5).

3. Move the cursor to the definition you want—ALTERNAT, in this example—and choose Edit (7).

```
Keyboard: Edit

  Name: ALTRNAT

  Key            Action           Description

  F1             {Help}           Help
  F3             {Esc}            Esc
  Esc            {Cancel}         Cancel




  1 Action; 2 Dscrptn; 3 Original; 4 Create; 5 Move; Macro; 6 Save; 7 Retrieve;
```

The Keyboard:
Edit menu for the
ALTERNAT
keyboard is
displayed.

15

4. Choose an option from the menu at the bottom of the screen.

   With the Edit options, you can change the action of an existing key, change a description displayed on the Keyboard: Edit screen, restore a key definition to its unmodified definition, create a new key definition, reassign an existing definition to a different key, save a key definition as a macro, or retrieve an existing macro file into a key definition.

5. Press [F7] (Exit) to leave the Setup menu and return to your document.

Some keys (such as the Cancel, Esc, and arrow keys) require you to press Ctrl-V before you can enter them as part of a definition. For example, you normally use the down-arrow key to move the cursor down one line in the Key Edit screen. If you want to enter the down-arrow key as part of a key definition, you must press Ctrl-V and then the down-arrow key to enter a {Down} code.

Specifying the Location of Files

With the Location of Files option, you can store different types of files in separate directories. To manage program and other special files, you can select separate subdirectories for the following files: backup, keyboard/macro, thesaurus/dictionaries/hyphenation, printer, style library (enter a file name), graphics, documents, and spreadsheet.

To specify a subdirectory for files, follow these steps:

1. Press [⇧Shift] [F1] to activate the Setup command.

   ⌨ Access the File pull-down menu and select Setup.

383

```
Setup: Location of Files

     1 - Backup Files

     2 - Keyboard/Macro Files          C:\WP51

     3 - Thesaurus/Spell/Hyphenation
                           Main         C:\WP51
                           Supplementary C:\WP51

     4 - Printer Files                 C:\WP51

     5 - Style Files
                 Library Filename

     6 - Graphic Files                 C:\WP51

     7 - Documents                     C:\WP51

     8 - Spreadsheet Files


Selection: 0
```

The Setup: Location of Files screen is displayed.

15

2. Select Location of Files (6).

3. Select the file type from the menu, type the drive and directory name, and press `⏎Enter`.

4. Press `F7` (Exit) to leave the Setup menu and return to your document.

Summary

In this chapter, you learned to customize many aspects of the WordPerfect program to meet your needs. You learned that you can choose to customize the mouse, the screen display, the environment, initial settings, an alternative keyboard layout, and the particular location of files.

Specifically, you learned the following key information about WordPerfect:

■ Use the Setup menu to customize WordPerfect. To access the Setup menu, select Shift-F1.

■ Use the Mouse (1) option on the Setup menu to tell WordPerfect which kind of mouse you are using and to change some of the defaults WordPerfect uses to interact with your mouse.

■ The Display (2) option on the Setup menu controls many aspects of WordPerfect's screen display.

■ Among the settings you can change with the Environment (3) option, WordPerfect lets you set backup options, turn beeps on and off, vary the cursor speed, set document summary options, customize the List Files display, turn Fast Save on and off, set hyphenation options, set units of measure, and choose an alternate keyboard.

■ With the Initial Settings (4) option in Setup, you can—for all your documents—change the date format, change many default format settings with initial codes, and set the repeat value.

■ Several other useful keyboard definitions are supplied with the program. You can edit these definitions for your particular needs or create your own definitions. Use the **Keyboard Layout** (5) option to customize the keyboard.

■ With the Location of Files (6) option, you can store different types of files in separate directories.

In the next chapter, you learn to create special characters and type equations.

15

Using Special Characters and Typing Equations

16

In your documents, you may need to create special characters or type equations. WordPerfect has features that enable you to create a variety of special characters as well as superscripts and subscripts. And with WordPerfect's equation editor, you can create mathematical expressions with complex structures and a number of symbols.

Key Terms in This Chapter

Superscript	A number or letter written immediately above, or above and to the right or left of, another character.
Subscript	A number or letter written immediately below, or below and to the right or left of, another character.
Equation editor	A WordPerfect feature that lets you create complex equations which contain characters and symbols that are not included in the printer's font.
Keyword	An alphabetic description of a command, a symbol, or a Greek letter. For example, *bold* is the keyword for the BOLD command.
Symbol	Any item that is neither a number nor a character from the Latin alphabet. Examples of symbols include arrows, brackets, and Greek letters.
Variable	Any group of alphabetic characters or numbers that begins with an alphabetic character, and that the equation editor does not recognize as a reserved keyword.
Number	Any nonnegative integer (such as 0, 1, or 2) that is followed by a noninteger (such as a symbol, a space, a period, or an alphabetic character).
Command	A word with a reserved meaning to the equation editor. Each command has a specific syntax that governs its use.
Function	A set of alphabetic characters recognized by the equation editor as a standard mathematical function name, such as *sin, cos, tan,* and *log*.

Creating Special Characters

In most documents, only one character appears in a space. For special characters, you may want two characters to print in the same space, such as è or ç. You can use WordPerfect's Compose and Overstrike features to create special characters. Note that special characters are not displayed on the editing screen. To see them, you must use View Document or print.

Using Compose

With the Compose feature, you can insert one of WordPerfect's more than 1,700 special characters or combine two characters. (See Appendix P of the WordPerfect manual for a list of available character sets.)

To insert one of WordPerfect's special characters, follow these steps:

1. Press ⌊Ctrl⌋⌊2⌋ or ⌊Ctrl⌋⌊V⌋. If you press ⌊Ctrl⌋⌊V⌋, WordPerfect displays the prompt Key =.

   ▭ Access the Font pull-down menu and select Characters.

2. Type the number of the character set, type a comma, and then type the number of the character.

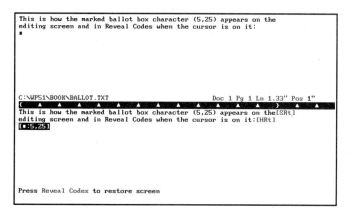

```
This is how the marked ballot box character (5,25) appears on the
editing screen and in Reveal Codes when the cursor is on it:
■




C:\WP51\BOOK\BALLOT.TXT                      Doc 1 Pg 1 Ln 1.33" Pos 1"
[    ▲    ▲    ▲    ▲    ▲    ▲    ▲    ▲    ▲    )    ▲
This is how the marked ballot box character (5,25) appears on the[SRt]
editing screen and in Reveal Codes when the cursor is on it:[HRt]
[■:5,25]




Press Reveal Codes to restore screen
```

For example, to create a marked ballot box character, type **5,25**.

3. Press ⌊⏎Enter⌋.

To combine two characters, follow these steps:

1. Press ⌊Ctrl⌋⌊2⌋ or ⌊Ctrl⌋⌊V⌋. If you press ⌊Ctrl⌋⌊V⌋, WordPerfect displays the prompt Key =.

   ▭ Access the Font pull-down menu and select Characters.

2. Type the first character and then type the second character.

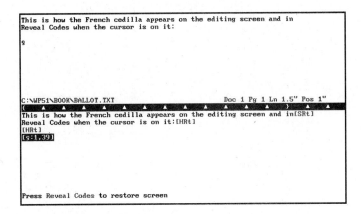

For example, to create a French cedilla (ç), type **c** and then type a comma (,).

16

Note: The characters that you can combine in WordPerfect are built into the program. That is, you cannot combine just any characters—only those that are part of the built-in set. For a complete list of characters, print the file CHARACTR.DOC (located on the WordPerfect Conversion disk) or any printer with graphics capability.

Using Overstrike

Overstrike is another feature you can use for creating special characters. To create special characters with Overstrike—for example, to create an *r* with a macron (overbar)—follow these steps:

1. Move the cursor to the place where you want to create an overstrike character.

2. Press ⬆Shift F8 to activate the Format command, select **O**ther (**4**), and choose **O**verstrike (**5**).

   ⌨ Access the **L**ayout menu, select **O**ther, and choose **O**verstrike (**5**).

3. Select **C**reate (**1**).

4. At the [Ovrstk] prompt, type each character (or attribute) that you want to appear in the character position.

```
Format: Other

   1 - Advance

   2 - Conditional End of Page

   3 - Decimal/Align Character       .
       Thousands' Separator          ,

   4 - Language                     US

   5 - Overstrike

   6 - Printer Functions

   7 - Underline - Spaces          Yes
                  Tabs             No

   8 - Border Options

   9 - End Centering/Alignment


1 Create; 2 Edit: 0
```

The Format:
Other menu
appears.

16

```
Format: Other

   1 - Advance

   2 - Conditional End of Page

   3 - Decimal/Align Character       .
       Thousands' Separator          ,

   4 - Language                     US

   5 - Overstrike

   6 - Printer Functions

   7 - Underline - Spaces          Yes
                  Tabs             No

   8 - Border Options

   9 - End Centering/Alignment


Ovrstk    ▪r
```

For example, to
create an *r* with a
macron (overbar),
press Ctrl V,
type **1,8**, press
↵Enter, and then
type r.

5. Press ↵Enter.

6. Press F7 (Exit) to return to the document.

As you type, you can see the characters and codes. When you return to the
document, however, only the last character you've entered is visible. All the
characters you enter are printed in the same character position. To review the
codes and characters, use the Reveal Codes screen. To edit a character created
with Overstrike, follow the preceding steps, but select **Edit (2)** rather than
Create (1) in Step 3. WordPerfect searches backward from the cursor position
and displays the first overstrike character it encounters.

Using Superscripts and Subscripts

Superscript and subscript are font attributes accessed through the Font menu. A *superscript* is a number or letter written immediately above, or above and to the right or left of, another character (for example, $E=mc^2$). A *subscript* is a distinguishing symbol written immediately below, or below and to the right or left of, another character (for example, H_2SO_4).

To create a superscript or subscript character, follow these steps:

1. Press Ctrl F8 to activate the Font command, and select Size (**1**).

   ⌨ Access the Font pull-down menu.

WordPerfect displays an attribute menu.

```
E = mc
```

```
1 Suprscpt; 2 Subscpt; 3 Fine; 4 Small; 5 Large; 6 Vry Large; 7 Ext Large; 0
```

2. Select either Suprscpt (**1**) or Subscpt (**2**).
3. Type the superscript or subscript character(s).
4. To return to the normal font, press → to move the cursor one character to the right, past the hidden attribute-off code.

The shifted characters look normal on-screen but are printed above or below the character baseline.

$$E = mc^2$$

$$H_2SO_4$$

The exact spacing depends on your printer's capabilities, and some printers may not be capable of printing superscripts or subscripts. The characters also are printed in small type, if your printer can print small type.

If the text to be superscripted or subscripted is already typed, first mark the text as a block and then complete the preceding steps.

Typing Equations

WordPerfect has a built-in equation editor for creating mathematical expressions with complex structures using a large variety of symbols. Although you can create equations with WordPerfect's normal text editor (along with WordPerfect's formatting and positioning features as well as its character sets), using the equation editor is less tedious and gives you more versatility. The equation editor automatically positions, sizes, and aligns the elements in mathematical expressions, such as complex ratios, built-up fractions, and multilevel subscripts and superscripts.

The equation editor has its own screen, editing features, and command syntax. Each equation occupies its own graphics box, which can be aligned, sized, and placed in the document just as any other graphics box. (Refer to Chapter 18 for more information about WordPerfect graphics.) The equation editor creates the equation file that forms the contents of the box. With the equation editor, managing equations in a document is similar to managing figures. WordPerfect can print as graphics any characters you use in an equation, whether or not those characters are part of the printer's fonts, as long as the printer is capable of printing graphics. You therefore can create equations that use virtually any character or mathematical symbol.

To access the equation editor screen, use the following procedure:

1. Press [Alt] [F9] to activate the Graphics command, select Equation (6), and choose Create (1).

16

393

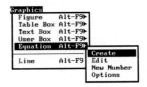

Access the Graphics pull-down menu, select Equation, and choose Create.

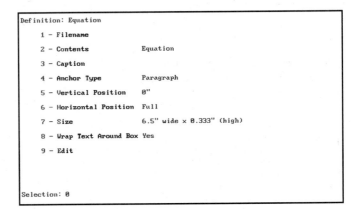

WordPerfect displays the Definition: Equation menu.

16

2. Select Edit (9).

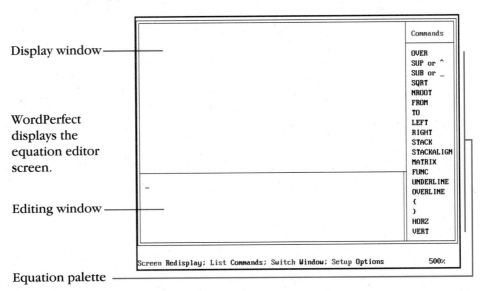

Display window —

WordPerfect displays the equation editor screen.

Editing window —

Equation palette —

You can create entries by typing from the keyboard. Your entries appear in the Editing Window, which is used to develop the equation with WordPerfect's equation commands and symbols. You can also enter commands and symbols into the Editing Window by selecting them from the Equation Palette. The resulting equation appears in the Display Window (the top window) when you press Screen (Ctrl-F3).

You cannot edit the equation in the Display Window; you must perform all editing in the Editing Window. The Editing Window is active when a double bar appears at its right side.

You access the Equation Palette by pressing List (F5). The name of the menu appears at the top of the Palette, and a reverse-video highlighted bar appears. (The default menu is Commands.) Use the arrow keys or mouse to move the bar up and down. Scroll to the bottom of the list by using the down-arrow key.

The Equation Palette contains eight menus: Commands, Large, Symbols, Greek, Arrows, Sets, Other, and Functions. You can scroll these menus up or down by pressing PgUp or PgDn while the equation editor is active. When you select an item from the Palette menus, the equation editor automatically inserts a space before and after the item.

16

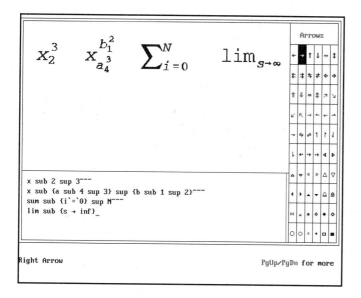

Here are some examples of mathematical expressions you can produce with the equation editor.

Using the Mouse in the Equation Editor

You can use the mouse in the equation editor to select items from the equation editor's menus and the Equation Palette. For example, instead of pressing the Screen (Ctrl-F3) key to display an equation, you can move the mouse pointer to Screen in the menu at the bottom of the equation editor screen, and then click the left mouse button.

To access the Equation Palette with the mouse, click List on the menu at the bottom of the equation editor. To scroll through the Palette menus, click PgUp or PgDn at the bottom right of the screen.

In the Equation Palette, you can select an item by placing the mouse pointer over the item and double-clicking the left button.

You also can move among the three equation editor windows by clicking the desired window.

16

Creating an Equation in the Editing Window

To create the simple equation ax + b = y, follow these steps:

1. Press [Alt] [F9] to activate the Graphics command, select Equation (6), and then select Create (1).

   ⌐ Access the Graphics pull-down menu, select Equation, and then select Create.

   The Definition: Equation menu is displayed.

2. Press Edit (9) to start the equation editor.

3. Type the following:

   ax~+~b~=~y

4. Press [Ctrl] [F3] (Screen).

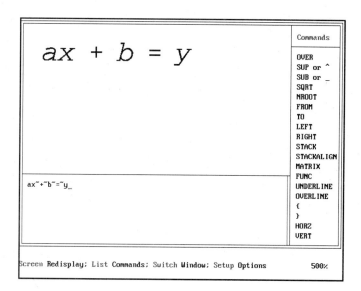

The equation is shown in the Display Window.

Note: Pressing the space bar in the equation editor does not insert a space in the equation. The space only enhances the readability of the text in the Editing Window. The ~ (tilde) is the equation editor's symbol for a space that will appear in the printed equation. The ~ symbol will not be printed.

Using Commands To Create Equations

You can use the commands in the Commands menu to accomplish the same type of formatting available in the normal text editor. For example, you can create bold, italic, and underline characters within an equation. With the Commands menu, you can also create equations that contain subscripts, superscripts, symbols for integration and summation, complicated fractions, and many sizes of vertical lines, parentheses, brackets, and braces. The text that follows introduces you to some of these features.

Note that you must include a space before and after each command. If you type the command, press the space bar before and after it to insert the necessary spaces. If you choose the commands from the Commands menu, WordPerfect automatically enters a space before and after each command.

Note also that WordPerfect treats all alphabetic characters (except Greek letters) as variables and italicizes them. The exceptions to this rule are the reserved commands such as BOLD and the functions contained in the Equation Palette.

Creating Subscripts and Superscripts

Subscripts and superscripts are created with the SUB and SUP commands. You can type the commands in any mixture of uppercase or lowercase letters. In addition, you can use the underscore (_) as an abbreviation for the SUB command, and the caret (^) as an abbreviation for the SUP command.

Suppose that you want to produce the simple expression x_2, which contains a subscript. Type either of the following expressions into the Editing Window:

    x sub 2~~~

or

    x_2~~~

Suppose that you want to produce the simple expression x^3, which contains a superscript. Type either of the following expressions into the Editing Window:

    x sup 3~~~

or

    x^3~~~

To produce an expression that simultaneously uses subscripts and superscripts (one directly over the other), type the subscript before the superscript. For example, type either of the following:

    x sub 2 sup 3

or

    x_2^3

Using the INT, SUM, FROM, and TO Commands

You can produce integrals and summations by using the keywords INT and SUM or by selecting the appropriate symbols from the Large menu in the Palette. You can insert the symbols, rather than the keywords, into the Editing Window by pressing Ctrl-Enter instead of Enter.

16

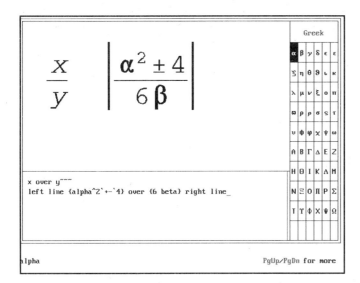

One simple and a more complex expression are shown in the equation editor.

Using Functions in the Equation Editor

You can use the Functions menu on the Equation Palette to enter functions in the equation editor. Keep in mind the following rules when you enter functions:

- You must separate a function from any variable that comes before and after the function. Separate the function by entering a space, pressing Enter, or entering a symbol such as a brace.

- When you enter a function from the Equation Palette, WordPerfect automatically inserts a space before and after the function, and displays the function in lowercase. If you instead type a function, you should type it in lowercase because that is the normal mathematical practice.

Note that functions, unlike other alphabetic characters entered in the equation editor, are automatically formatted in the base (nonitalic) font. If you want to italicize a command, you can use the ITAL command.

Suppose that you want to enter the following expression:

A`tan`theta~+~B~~~

Keep in mind that functions are often separated by thin spaces from the rest of the expression. The reverse-accent character (`) represents the thin space.

To enter the sin function first in regular typeface and then in italic, type the following expression:

sin~ital{sin}

The preceding expressions are shown here in the equation editor.

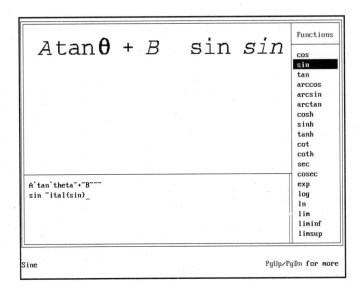

Positioning and Sizing Equations

The standard type of equation box has no box lines and is positioned from margin to margin. WordPerfect lets you adjust the border, position, and size of the printed equation.

To create a special box that does not have the default equation editor box characteristics, follow these steps:

1. Press Alt F9 to activate the Graphics command, select Figure (1), and then select Create (1).

    Access the Graphics pull-down menu, select Figure (1), and then select Create (1).

    WordPerfect displays the Definition: Figure menu.

2. Specify the box contents to be an equation by selecting Contents (2) and then Equation (4).

3. Select Edit (9) to load the equation editor.

4. Enter the equations you want.

5. Press [F7] (Exit) to return to the editing screen.

The equations appear in a special box.

To create a special equation box without a border, follow these steps:

1. Press [Alt] [F9] to activate the Graphics command and select Figure (**1**).

   ⌨ Access the Graphics pull-down menu and select Figure (**1**).

2. Select Options (**4**).

   The Options: Figure menu is displayed.

3. Select Border Style (**1**) and select None for the Left, Right, Top, and Bottom borders.

4. Press [F7] (Exit) to return to the editing screen.

Now you can go into the equation editor and type equations. The equations will appear in the default figure size and position—smaller than the equation box and on the right side of the page. The equations will appear without a border.

To adjust the position of elements in the equation, use the HORZ and VERT commands in the Editing Window.

The syntax of HORZ is

   HORZ n

The syntax of VERT is

   VERT n

n is the number of 0.012" (1200ths of an inch) to move in a relative direction to the right for HORZ and up for VERT. To move to the left or down, you must make n a negative number.

Managing Equation Files

Because an equation box is a type of graphics box, an equation is saved or retrieved when the document containing it is saved or retrieved using the normal WordPerfect Save (F10) and Retrieve (Shift-F10) features. However, you also can save and retrieve an equation as a separate file, independent of the document containing the equation.

Saving an Equation as a Separate File

To save an equation as a separate file, follow these steps:

1. While in the equation editor, press F10 (Save).

   WordPerfect prompts you for a file name.

2. Type a file name (including the drive and directory if different from the one displayed) and press ⏎Enter.

Retrieving an Equation File

There are three ways to retrieve an equation previously saved as a separate file:

- Press Retrieve (Shift-F10) while in the equation editor. At the prompt, type the file name and press Enter.
- Press Retrieve (Shift-F10) while in the equation editor. Then press List (F5). When the highlight bar is over the file name, press **Retrieve** (**1**).
- Enter the file name under the Filename (**1**) heading on the Definition: Equation menu. This is the only way to retrieve an equation file while not in the equation editor.

Saving Equation Files in a Graphics Directory

You may find it convenient to save equation files in a separate directory. To specify a default directory for equation files, follow these steps:

1. Press ⚬Shift F1 to access the Setup menu.

   ▱ Access the File pull-down menu and select Setup.

2. Select Location of Files (6).

3. Select Graphics (6).

4. Type a path name for a graphics directory and press ⏎Enter.

5. Press F7 (Exit) to return to the editing screen.

If you press Save (F10) while in the Equation Editor, WordPerfect will prompt you to save your equation file in that directory.

Printing Equations

WordPerfect is initially set to print all equations as graphics (without using the printer's fonts). When WordPerfect prints equations as graphics, it tries to emulate one of three fonts: Helvetica, Times Roman, or Courier. WordPerfect will use the one that is closest to the base font.

Equations created in the equation editor are printed in the initial base font for the document unless there is a font-change code preceding the equation. If there is a font-change code, all subsequent equations are printed in that font.

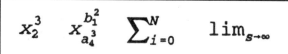

Here are some examples of printed equations.

16

Summary

In this chapter, you learned to create special characters using WordPerfect's Compose and Overstrike features. You learned to create a variety of special characters as well as superscripts and subscripts. You also learned to use WordPerfect's equation editor to create mathematical expressions with complex structures and a number of symbols.

Specifically, you learned the following key information about WordPerfect:

- Use WordPerfect's Compose and Overstrike features to create special characters.

- To insert one of WordPerfect's special characters using the Compose feature, press Ctrl-2 or Ctrl-V, type the number of the character set, type a comma, and then type the number of the character. Finally, press Enter.

- To combine two characters using the Compose feature, press Ctrl-2 or Ctrl-V, type the first character, and then type the second character.

- To create special characters with Overstrike, select Format (Shift-F8), select **Other** (**4**), choose **Overstrike** (**5**), and select **Create** (**1**). At the [Ovrstk] prompt, type each character (or attribute) that you want to appear in the character position. Then press Enter.

- To create a superscript or subscript character, select Font (Ctrl-F8) and choose **Size** (**1**). Select either **Suprscpt** (**1**) or **Subscpt** (**2**), and then type the superscript or subscript character(s). To return to the normal font, press the right-arrow key to move the cursor one character to the right, past the hidden attribute-off code.

- Use WordPerfect's built-in equation editor to create mathematical expressions with complex structures using a large variety of symbols.

- To access the equation editor screen, select Graphics (Alt-F9), choose Equation (6), and select Create (1). Then choose Edit (9).

- Use the commands in the Commands menu to create equations that contain subscripts, superscripts, symbols for integration and summation, complicated fractions, and many sizes of vertical lines, parentheses, brackets, and braces.

- Use the Functions menu on the Equation Palette to enter functions in the equation editor.

- To save an equation as a separate file, while in the equation editor, select Save (F10). Type a file name and press Enter.

- From the equation editor, to retrieve an equation previously saved as a separate file, select Retrieve (Shift-F10), type the file name, and press Enter.

- From the editing screen, to retrieve an equation previously saved as a separate file, enter the file name under the Filename (1) heading on the Definition: Equation menu.

In the next chapter, you are introduced to WordPerfect's referencing features. You will learn how to create a number of referencing tools, such as footnotes and a table of contents, which supplement the main document.

16

Referencing

When you create a formal document, you often need to develop the manuscript through a number of drafts. Moreover, the document may need to include elements other than the main text, such as footnotes, an index, or a table of contents. WordPerfect has a number of referencing tools to help you develop a manuscript and create the related elements.

As you develop your manuscript, you will find WordPerfect's Outline, Paragraph Numbering, and Line Numbering features valuable for getting the project organized, and you will find these features convenient when conferring with others about particular passages. The Document Comment feature is handy for making notes to yourself about items that need further research. And you can use WordPerfect's Footnote and Endnote feature to help you enter and keep track of reference information. As the manuscript evolves, you may want to use WordPerfect's date and time code to enter the current date on each draft.

This chapter covers WordPerfect's basic referencing tools and introduces some of the more advanced referencing features. Although the specifics of using the advanced features are beyond the scope of this book, you learn how to access the features for creating a list, an index, a table of contents, and a table of authorities. You also become acquainted with WordPerfect's features for creating automatic references, creating a master document, and comparing documents.

Key Terms in This Chapter

Document comments   Notes and reminders that you can type into a WordPerfect file. The comments appear on-screen but are not printed.

Master document   A WordPerfect file containing codes that reference and combine a number of sub-document files. The master document file for a dissertation, for example, might combine subdocument files, such as a title page, table of contents, list of tables, and the body text.

17

Creating Footnotes and Endnotes

Footnotes and endnotes provide a simple, standard way of referencing sources as well as offering the reader additional parenthetical information. Footnotes appear at the bottom or foot of the page; endnotes are grouped at the end of the document. (Some authors group endnotes at the end of each chapter or section.) Both types of notes are marked in the text by a number or character you specify.

Typing a Footnote or an Endnote

Suppose that you want to add a footnote to this example.

```
In Charles Dickens's story of Nicholas Nickleby, one of the
villains is Mr. Wackford Squeers:

    Mr. Squeers's appearance was not prepossessing.  He had but
    one eye, and the popular prejudice runs in favour of two....
    The blank side of his face was much wrinkled and puckered up,
    which gave him a very sinister appearance, especially when he
    smiled, at which times his expression bordered closely on the
    villainous....  He wore...a suit of scholastic black, but his
    coat sleeves being a great deal too long, and his trousers a
    great deal too short, he appeared ill at ease in his clothes,
    and as if he were in a perpetual state of astonishment at
    finding himself so respectable.



C:\WP51\BOOK\FOOTNOTE.TXT                        Doc 1 Pg 1 Ln 3" Pos 4.6"
```

To create a footnote or an endnote, follow these steps:

1. Move the cursor to the place where you want to insert a note number.

2. Press [Ctrl] [F7] to activate the Footnote command, and choose Footnote (**1**) or Endnote (**2**).

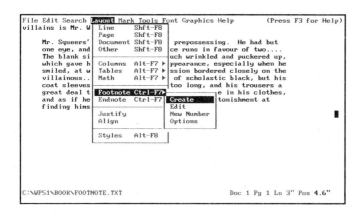

Access the Layout pull-down menu and choose Footnote or Endnote.

3. Select Create (**1**) to create a footnote or an endnote.

   An editing screen appears with the cursor immediately to the right of the current footnote or endnote number.

4. Enter the text for the footnote or endnote, using all the normal editing and function keys. You also can spell check the note.

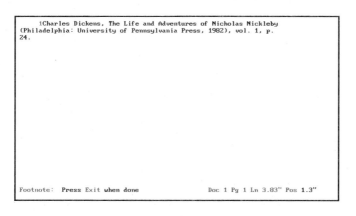

Here, the text of a footnote has been typed.

17

5. After you type the text, press [F7] (Exit) to return to the document.

WordPerfect inserts a code that includes the first 50 characters of the note. You can view the code and partial text with Reveal Codes (Alt-F3, or F11 on an Enhanced Keyboard). To see how the note will appear when printed, use View Document (press Shift-F7, and then press 6).

17

This page shows a printed footnote.

```
In Charles Dickens's story of Nicholas Nickleby, one of the
villains is Mr. Wackford Squeers:

    Mr. Squeers's appearance was not prepossessing.  He had but
    one eye, and the popular prejudice runs in favour of two....
    The blank side of his face was much wrinkled and puckered up,
    which gave him a very sinister appearance, especially when he
    smiled, at which times his expression bordered closely on the
    villainous....  He wore...a suit of scholastic black, but his
    coat sleeves being a great deal too long, and his trousers a
    great deal too short, he appeared ill at ease in his clothes,
    and as if he were in a perpetual state of astonishment at
    finding himself so respectable.[1]
```

```
                    _____
                    [1]Charles Dickens, The Life and Adventures of Nicholas Nickleby
                    (Philadelphia: University of Pennsylvania Press, 1982), vol. 1, p.
                    24.
```

Editing a Footnote or an Endnote

To edit a footnote or an endnote, follow these steps:

1. Press `Ctrl` `F7` to activate the Footnote command, select Footnote (1) or Endnote (2), and choose Edit (2).

   Access the Layout pull-down menu, select Footnote or Endnote, and choose Edit.

   WordPerfect displays the `Footnote number?` prompt (or `Endnote number?` prompt) as well as the number of the note that immediately follows the cursor.

2. Press `Enter` if the number is correct; or type the number of the footnote or endnote you want to edit, and then press `Enter`.

3. Edit the text.

4. Press `F7` (Exit) to return to the document.

Deleting a Footnote or an Endnote

17

Because the entire note (number and text) is in one code, you can delete the note in the same way you delete any other WordPerfect code. To delete a footnote or an endnote, follow these steps:

1. Move the cursor under the note number you want to delete.

2. Press `Del`.

   If the Reveal Codes window is not open, WordPerfect displays a prompt similar to the following:

   `Delete [Footnote:1]? No (Yes)`

3. Select Yes to confirm the deletion.

Alternatively, you can press Reveal Codes (Alt-F3 or F11), place the cursor on the note code, and press Del. WordPerfect automatically renumbers the other notes.

Positioning and Generating Endnotes

Unlike footnotes, which are printed at the bottom of the page on which you create them, endnotes are placed together at the end of the document or at any location you specify. If you want to place endnotes in a location other than the end of the document, you enter an endnote placement code. When WordPerfect encounters this code, the program collects all the endnotes between the code and the beginning of the document (or the previous endnote placement code).

To position endnotes in a place other than the end of the document, follow these steps:

1. Move the cursor to the place where you want to compile the endnotes.

2. Press `Ctrl` `F7` to activate the Footnote command, and select Endnote Placement (3).

    ⌐◻ Access the Layout pull-down menu, choose Endnote, and select Placement.

    WordPerfect displays this prompt:

    ```
    Restart endnote numbering? Yes (No)
    ```

3. Select Yes or press `↵Enter` to restart numbering with 1. Select No if you do not want to restart at 1.

To generate the endnotes, complete these steps:

1. Press `Alt` `F5` to activate the Mark Text command, and select Generate (6).

    ⌐◻ Access the Mark pull-down menu and select Generate.

2. Select Generate Tables, Indexes, Cross-References, etc. (5).

3. At the prompt, select Yes.

To print endnotes on a separate page, press Ctrl-Enter to insert a hard page code before the endnote placement code.

Selecting a Format for Footnotes and Endnotes

If you don't like the format WordPerfect has chosen for footnotes and endnotes, you can change the numbering style, placement, and format with the following steps:

1. Press `Home`, `Home`, `↑` to move the cursor to the beginning of the document.

2. Press ⌨Ctrl⌨ ⌨F7⌨ to activate the Footnote command, and select Footnote (**1**) or Endnote (**2**).

   ▭ Access the Layout pull-down menu and choose Footnote or Endnote.

3. Select Options (**4**) to display the Footnote Options menu (or Endnote Options menu).

```
Footnote Options

    1 - Spacing Within Footnotes        1
             Between Footnotes          0.167"

    2 - Amount of Note to Keep Together  0.5"

    3 - Style for Number in Text        [SUPRSCPT][Note Num][suprscpt]

    4 - Style for Number in Note                 [SUPRSCPT][Note Num][suprscpt

    5 - Footnote Numbering Method        Numbers

    6 - Start Footnote Numbers each Page No

    7 - Line Separating Text and Footnotes 2-inch Line

    8 - Print Continued Message          No

    9 - Footnotes at Bottom of Page      Yes


Selection: 0
```

This is the Footnote Options menu.

4. Select the options you want to change, and enter the needed information.

5. Press ⌨F7⌨ (Exit) to return to the document.

Using a Date and Time Code

WordPerfect can check your computer's clock and insert the current date and time into a document. Additionally, the program can insert a code that up-dates the date and time automatically every time you retrieve the document.

Note: WordPerfect cannot insert the correct date and time unless your computer's clock is set correctly. Check the instruction manual for your computer to learn how to reset the clock.

413

Inserting a Date and Time Code

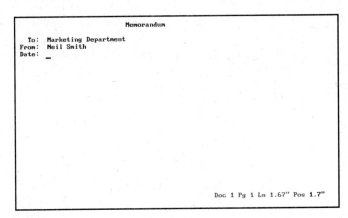

Suppose that you want to insert a date code in this example.

To insert a date and time code, follow these steps:

1. Move the cursor to the place where you want to insert the code.

2. Press ⬆Shift F5 to activate the Date/Outline command, and select Date Text (**1**) or Date Code (**2**).

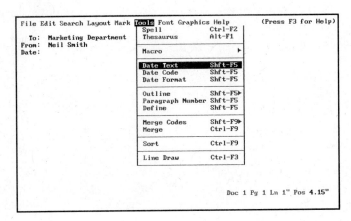

Access the Tools pull-down menu and select Date Text or Date Code.

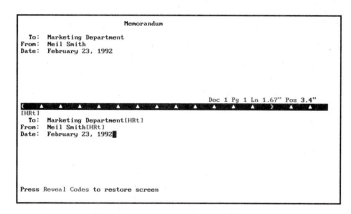

If you select Date Text (**1**) from the Date/Outline menu, WordPerfect inserts the current date into the document. WordPerfect immediately displays the current date— for example, February 23, 1992.

If you have set the Date/Time format to include the time, the current time is included also—for example, February 23, 1992, 10:32 am. This date and time information is text you can edit. The information is not updated the next time you retrieve or print the document.

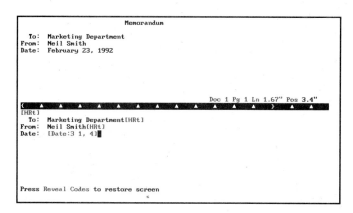

If you select Date Code (**2**) from the Date/Outline menu, WordPerfect inserts the current date and a date code into the document.

If you have set the Date/Time format to include the time, the current time is inserted also. The date code updates the date and time information each time you retrieve or print the document.

17

Setting the Format for Date and Time

To set the format for the date and time, follow these steps:

1. Press ⇧Shift F5 to activate the Date/Outline command, and select Date Format (3).

   ▭ Access the Tools pull-down menu and select Date Format.

WordPerfect displays the Date Format menu.

```
Date Format

    Character     Meaning
        1         Day of the Month
        2         Month (number)
        3         Month (word)
        4         Year (all four digits)
        5         Year (last two digits)
        6         Day of the Week (word)
        7         Hour (24-hour clock)
        8         Hour (12-hour clock)
        9         Minute
        0         am / pm
       %,$        Used before a number, will:
                      Pad numbers less than 10 with a leading zero or space
                      Abbreviate the month or day of the week

    Examples:  3 1, 4        = December 25, 1984
               %6 %3 1, 4    = Tue Dec 25, 1984
               %2/%1/5 (6)   = 01/01/85 (Tuesday)
               $2/$1/5 (%6)  =  1/ 1/85 (Tue)
               8:90          = 10:55am

Date format: 3 1, 4
```

2. Enter new options.
3. Press F7 (Exit) twice to return to the document.

The options on the Date Format menu establish the format that WordPerfect uses to print the date and time. You can mix format numbers with any text you want to print. For example, in Reveal Codes, your text and codes might appear as the following:

    Today's date is **[Date:3 1, 4]**, and the time is **[8:9 0]**.

With this combination of text and codes, WordPerfect displays something similar to the following:

    Today's date is February 23, 1992, and the time is
    12:47 pm.

To print just the first three characters of the names for months and day of the week, type a percent sign (%) before the appropriate code. For example, you can enter the following:

    %3. 1, 4 (%6)

Using this date format, WordPerfect displays the following:

    Feb. 23, 1992 (Sun)

Outlining and Numbering Paragraphs

With WordPerfect's Outline feature, you can create an outline and generate
outline numbers automatically. If you prefer to enter numbers manually, you
can use WordPerfect's Paragraph Numbering feature instead. Paragraph numbering is convenient when you have few numbers and a large amount of text.

Creating an Outline

If you want to title the outline, follow these steps:

1. Press ⬆Shift F6 to activate the Center command.

   ⌨ Access the Layout pull-down menu, select Align, and choose
   Center.

2. Type the title and press ↵Enter.

To turn on the Outline feature, complete these steps:

1. Move the cursor to the place where you want the outline to begin.

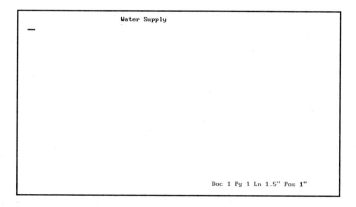

In this example,
you want to begin
the outline just
under the cen-
tered heading.

2. Press ⬆Shift F5 to activate the Date/Outline command, and select
   Outline (4).

417

```
┌Tools────────────────────────────┐
│ Spell          Ctrl-F2          │
│ Thesaurus      Alt-F1           │
│                                 │
│ Macro                     ▶     │
│                                 │
│ Date Text      Shft-F5          │
│ Date Code      Shft-F5          │
│ Date Format    Shft-F5          │
│                                 │
│ Outline        Shft-F5▶┌────────────────┐
│ Paragraph Number Shft-F5│ On            │
│ Define         Shft-F5 │ Off            │
│                        │               │
│ Merge Codes    Shft-F9 │ Move Family   │
│ Merge          Ctrl-F9 │ Copy Family   │
│                        │ Delete Family │
│ Sort           Ctrl-F9 └────────────────┘
│                                 │
│ Line Draw      Ctrl-F3          │
└─────────────────────────────────┘
```

⬓ Access the Tools pull-down menu and choose Outline.

3. Select On (**1**).

The Outline indicator appears at the bottom left corner of the screen.

While Outline is visible on-screen, the Enter and Tab keys perform special functions. Each time you press Enter, you create a new outline number. Within a line, each time you press Tab, you create a different level number.

To generate outline numbers automatically (with the Outline feature turned on), use this procedure:

1. Press ⏎Enter to insert the first number in the outline (I. in Outline style). The default numbering style is Outline: uppercase Roman numerals for level one, uppercase letters for level two, Arabic numbers for level three, continuing with different characters up to eight levels.

2. Press F4 (Indent) to position the cursor.

3. Type the text for the first outline entry.

   If the text is long, the lines wrap underneath the indent.

4. Press ⏎Enter. WordPerfect moves the cursor to the next line and automatically enters the next number. If you want, you can press ⏎Enter again to insert a blank line and move the number down.

5. Press Tab⇥ to move to the next (lower) outline level.

   The number follows and changes to the next level number (A. in Outline style).

6. Press F4 (Indent) again.

7. Type the text for the entry.

17

418

```
                        Water Supply


      I.    Water Supply Requirements
            A.    Population Trends













      Outline                              Doc 1 Pg 1 Ln 1.83" Pos 3.7"
```

Repeat these steps to complete the outline. If you press Tab too many times, you can move back one level by pressing Margin Release (Shift-Tab).

To turn off the Outline feature, follow these steps:

1. Position the cursor after the outline in the text.

2. Press ⇧Shift F5 (Date/Outline) and select Outline (4).

   ⌨ Access the **Tools** pull-down menu and choose **Outline**.

```
                        Water Supply


      I.    Water Supply Requirements
            A.    Population Trends
            B.    Per Capita Consumption
            C.    Design Flaws
            D.    Summary of Projected Water Supply Requirements for the
                  Years 1990 Through 1995

      II.   The Present Water System and Recommended Requirements
            A.    The Raw Water Collection System
                  1.    The Present System
                  2.    Recommended Improvements
            B.    The Pumping Station
                  1.    The Present Pumping Station
                  2.    Recommended Improvements
                        a.    Pump Number 1
                        b.    Pump Number 2
                        c.    Pump Number 3
                        d.    Pump Number 4_

      1 Date Text; 2 Date Code; 3 Date Format; 4 Outline; 5 Para Num; 6 Define: 0
```

Here, the cursor is positioned at the end of the outline and the menu is displayed at the bottom of the screen.

3. Select Off (2).

17

Editing an Outline

You can edit an outline by changing the text within the numbered entries, changing the level numbers of entries, deleting the numbers, adding numbered entries, deleting entries, moving entries, and adding unnumbered entries. Use Enter, Tab, Indent (F4), and Margin Release (Shift-Tab) to make adjustments in numbering levels, as described in the preceding section.

When you add, delete, or move numbered entries, WordPerfect automatically renumbers the entries for you. To redisplay the screen with the correct numbers, move the cursor through the document, or press Screen (Ctrl-F3) and select **Rewrite (3)**.

Numbering Paragraphs

Paragraph numbering differs from outlining because you must insert numbers manually. And unlike the Outline feature, the Paragraph Numbering feature enables you to choose the level number, regardless of the cursor position. You can edit numbered entries (or paragraphs) by using the same techniques for editing an outline. When you add or delete an entry number, WordPerfect automatically renumbers the remaining sections.

To number an entry or paragraph, follow these steps:

1. Position the cursor at the left margin of the line where you want to begin the entry. If you want the number to appear at the left margin, continue with Step 2. If you want the number to appear in a different location, press Tab to move the cursor to a different level of numbering.

2. Press ⬆Shift F5 to activate the Date/Outline command, and choose **Para Num (5)**.

   ⌨ Access the **T**ools pull-down menu and choose **P**aragraph Number.

```
I.   Design Guidelines

     A.   Consistency

          Establish a format for your publication and stick with
          it.  Decide on the features and formats you will use.

     B.   Clarity

          A page should not be confusing.  Can you look at the page
          and immediately know where to begin reading?

     C.   Emphasis

          Put important ideas first.




Paragraph Level (Press Enter for Automatic):
```

WordPerfect prompts you to enter the paragraph level.

3. At the prompt, press ⏎Enter to have WordPerfect insert the number that corresponds to the level at the cursor position. Or type the level number you want to assign, and then press ⏎Enter.

4. Press F4 (Indent).

5. Type the text for the entry or paragraph.

Changing the Numbering Style

Outline levels are determined by tab stops and by the style of numbering selected. The default numbering style is Outline, but you can specify a different style.

To change the numbering style, follow these steps:

1. Place the cursor at the beginning of the outline.

2. Press ⇧Shift F5 to activate the Date/Outline command, and select Define (6).

   ⌐▭ Access the Tools pull-down menu and choose Define.

```
Paragraph Number Definition

          1 - Starting Paragraph Number              1
                 (in legal style)
                                                  Levels
                                      1    2    3    4    5    6    7    8
          2 - Paragraph               1.   a.   i.   (1)  (a)  (i)  1)   a)
          3 - Outline                 I.   A.   1.   a.   (1)  (a)  i)   a)
          4 - Legal (1.1.1)           1    .1   .1   .1   .1   .1   .1   .1
          5 - Bullets                 •    o    -    ■    *    +    ·    x
          6 - User-defined

          Current Definition          I.   A.   1.   a.   (1)  (a)  i)   a)
          Attach Previous Level       No   No   No   No   No   No   No

          7 - Enter Inserts Paragraph Number           Yes

          8 - Automatically Adjust to Current Level     Yes

          9 - Outline Style Name


          Selection: 0
```

WordPerfect displays the Paragraph Number Definition menu.

3. Choose from the selection of predefined numbering styles (options 2 through 5 on the menu).

    If you want to create your own style, choose User-defined (6); the cursor moves to the Current Definition line. Then type a level number, press ⏎Enter to move to the next level, and press F7 (Exit) when you have completed your numbering definition.

4. After you specify the numbering style, press F7 (Exit) twice to return to the document.

5. Press Ctrl F3 to activate the Screen command, and select Rewrite (3) to display the document with the new numbering style.

Numbering Lines

In addition to numbering paragraphs, WordPerfect can number the lines in a document. With line numbering, you can refer easily to a particular clause in a legal document or to a specific passage in a manuscript. For instance, you can cite a passage by referring to page 11, line 26.

When you number lines in WordPerfect, the body text as well as the footnotes and endnotes are numbered; headers and footers are not numbered. Numbers are not displayed on-screen but appear when you print the document or use View Document.

Turning On Automatic Line Numbering

To turn on automatic line numbering, follow these steps:

1. Move the cursor to the place where you want line numbering to begin (usually at the beginning of the document).

2. Press ⟨⇧Shift⟩ ⟨F8⟩ to activate the Format command, and select Line (1).

    ▭ Access the Layout pull-down menu and choose Line.

3. Select Line Numbering (5).

4. Select Yes to turn on line numbering.

```
Format: Line Numbering

     1 - Count Blank Lines                     Yes

     2 - Number Every n Lines, where n is      1

     3 - Position of Number from Left Edge     0.6"

     4 - Starting Number                       1

     5 - Restart Numbering on Each Page        Yes




Selection: 0
```

WordPerfect displays the Format: Line Numbering menu.

17

5. If you want to accept the default line-numbering settings, press ⟨↵Enter⟩. Otherwise, select the option you want to change, and then enter the desired modification.

6. Press ⟨F7⟩ (Exit) to return to the editing screen.

Selecting Line Numbering Options

When you turn on the Line Numbering feature, you can change how the lines are numbered with the following options:

*   Select Count Blank Lines (1) to specify whether blank lines are numbered. To count blank lines, select Yes; to exclude blank lines from line numbering, select No.

*   Choose Number Every n Lines (2) to specify at what intervals you want line numbers printed. For instance, select this option, type 5, and press Enter to print numbers only every 5 lines (on lines 5, 10, 15, and so on).

- Select **P**osition of Number from Left Edge (**3**) to change the default position where line numbers are printed. By default, line numbers are printed six-tenths of an inch from the left edge. To change that distance, select this option, type a measurement (from the left edge of the page), and press Enter.

- Select **S**tarting Number (**4**) to specify the beginning number for line numbering. Use this option to continue numbers for a document containing text in another disk file, or to restart line numbering in a file in which you previously used line numbering.

- Choose **R**estart Numbering on Each Page (**5**) to specify whether you want line numbers to restart on each page. Select **Y**es to restart line numbering on each page; select **N**o to number lines consecutively throughout the document. Continuous numbering is helpful when pages are not numbered.

Displaying Line Numbers

17

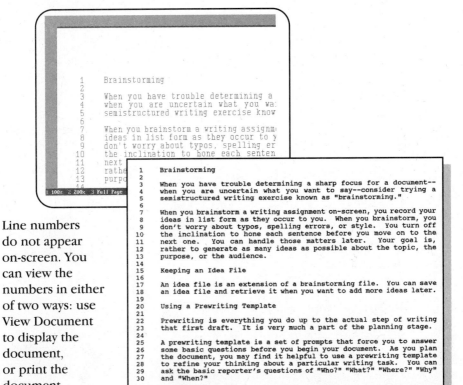

Line numbers do not appear on-screen. You can view the numbers in either of two ways: use View Document to display the document, or print the document.

424

Turning Off Automatic Line Numbering

To turn off automatic line numbering after a numbered section, follow these steps:

1. Move the cursor to the line where you want numbering to stop.
2. Press ⬆Shift F8 (Format) and select Line (1).

    🖙 Access the Layout pull-down menu and choose Line.
3. Select Line Numbering (5).
4. Select No to turn off line numbering.
5. Press F7 (Exit) to return to the document.

To remove all line numbering from a document, you must delete the code that was inserted when you turned on the feature. To delete the code, follow these steps:

1. Press Alt F3 or F11 to activate Reveal Codes.

    🖙 Access the Edit pull-down menu and select Reveal Codes.
2. Move the cursor to the **[Ln Num:On]** code.
3. Press Del.
4. Press Alt F3 or F11 to return to the editing screen.

    🖙 Access the Edit pull-down menu and select Reveal Codes.

Using Document Comments

You can insert notes and reminders called *comments* into a document. Document comments are useful for reminding you of what you had in mind during a particular writing session. The comments are displayed on-screen only; they are not printed. If you want to print the comments, however, you can do so by first converting them to text.

17

Creating a Comment

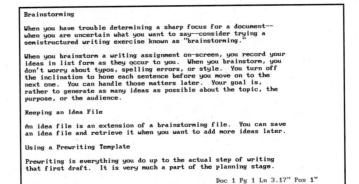

Suppose that you want to add a comment to this document.

To create a document comment, complete these steps:

1. Move the cursor to the place where you want to insert the comment.

2. Press Ctrl F5 to activate the Text In/Out command, select Comment (4), and choose Create (1).

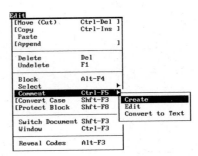

Access the Edit pull-down menu, select Comment, and choose Create.

WordPerfect places the cursor in the Document Comment editing box.

3. In the comment box, type the text of your comment. You can use bold or underline to emphasize text within the box.

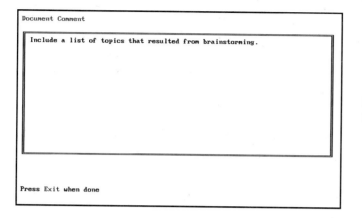

```
Document Comment

┌─────────────────────────────────────────────────────────┐
│ Include a list of topics that resulted from brainstorming. │
│                                                           │
│                                                           │
│                                                           │
│                                                           │
└─────────────────────────────────────────────────────────┘

Press Exit when done
```

Here, a comment has been typed.

4. Press F7 (Exit) to return to the document.

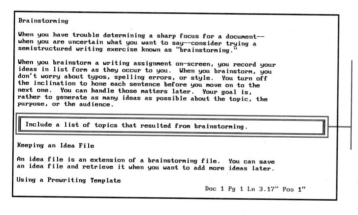

```
Brainstorming

When you have trouble determining a sharp focus for a document--
when you are uncertain what you want to say--consider trying a
semistructured writing exercise known as "brainstorming."

When you brainstorm a writing assignment on-screen, you record your
ideas in list form as they occur to you.  When you brainstorm, you
don't worry about typos, spelling errors, or style.  You turn off
the inclination to hone each sentence before you move on to the
next one.  You can handle those matters later.  Your goal is,
rather to generate as many ideas as possible about the topic, the
purpose, or the audience.

┌─────────────────────────────────────────────────────────┐
│ Include a list of topics that resulted from brainstorming. │
└─────────────────────────────────────────────────────────┘
Keeping an Idea File

An idea file is an extension of a brainstorming file.  You can save
an idea file and retrieve it when you want to add more ideas later.

Using a Prewriting Template
                                    Doc 1 Pg 1 Ln 3.17" Pos 1"
```

The document comment appears on-screen within a double-ruled box in the middle of the text.

Editing a Comment

To edit a document comment, follow these steps:

1. Position the cursor after the comment to be edited.

2. Press Ctrl F5 to activate the Text In/Out command, select Comment (4), and choose Edit (2).

   Access the Edit pull-down menu, choose Comment, and select Edit.

   WordPerfect searches backward from the cursor, displays the first comment found, and places the cursor at the beginning of the comment text.

427

3. Edit the comment, using the normal editing keys.

4. Press [F7] (Exit) to return to the document.

If no comment is found, the message `* Not found *` appears at the bottom of the screen.

Converting Comments to Text

If you want to print document comments, you first must convert them to text. To change a comment to text, follow these steps:

1. Position the cursor after the comment to be converted.

2. Press [Ctrl][F5] to activate the Text In/Out command, select Comment (4), and choose Convert to Text (3).

   ⌐⊙ Access the Edit pull-down menu, select Comment, and choose Convert to Text.

WordPerfect searches backward from the cursor and converts the first comment found.

Converting Text to Comments

To change text to a comment, follow these steps:

1. Highlight the block of text to be changed to a comment by using [Alt][F4] or [F12] to activate the Block command; or highlight the block by dragging the mouse.

2. Press [Ctrl][F5] to activate the Text In/Out command.

3. When WordPerfect displays the prompt `Create a comment?`, select Yes.

WordPerfect places the marked text inside a comment box. Note that some formatting codes may be lost during this process.

Using Other Referencing Features

When you create a document, especially a lengthy one, you often need to include supplementary reference material. For example, when you create a book, manual, or research report, you may need to include lists of figures and tables, a table of contents, and an index. When you create a legal document, you may want to include a table of legal citations. WordPerfect has built-in features to make the preparation of these materials easier. In addition, WordPerfect offers three other features that are handy in preparing reference materials: Automatic Reference, Master Document, and Document Compare.

Although the specifics of these referencing features are beyond the scope of this book, this section introduces you to the kinds of reference materials you can create with WordPerfect. For detailed instructions on creating these materials, refer to Que's *Using WordPerfect 5.1*, Special Edition.

You use Mark Text (Alt-F5) to control the creation of reference materials. Alternatively, you can use the options on the **Mark** pull-down menu to identify the items that you want to incorporate into a list, a table of contents, an index, or a table of authorities. You use this menu also to specify the format and style of these special sections of your document and to generate the references where they need to be included.

Whether you are creating a table of contents, a list, an index, or a table of authorities, you follow the same set of procedures:

- Mark the entries you want to include in the table of contents, list, index, or table of authorities. You can mark the entries as you create the document, or you can go back later and mark them.

- Select the type of reference list you want to create, and then define the style for the reference list. For example, you might select a table of contents and choose a particular style for the page numbers.

- Generate the reference list at the appropriate place in the document.

Table of Contents

The Mark Text (Alt-F5) command or **Mark** pull-down menu is the starting point for creating the supplementary reference materials you need. Whether you are creating a table of contents, a list, an index, or a table of authorities, you follow the same basic procedures. This section describes the process for creating a table of contents.

When you create a table of contents, you generally use text taken directly from the document—for example, chapter headings. To mark entries for a table of contents, follow these steps:

1. Highlight the entry by using Alt F4 or F12 to activate the Block command, or by dragging the mouse.

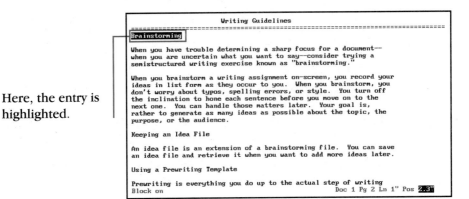

Here, the entry is highlighted.

2. Press Alt F5 to activate the Mark Text command, and select ToC (**1**).

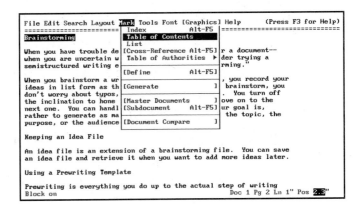

Access the Mark pull-down menu and select Table of Contents.

3. At the ToC Level: prompt, press 1 and then press ↵Enter.

Repeat the preceding steps to mark each entry for the table of contents.

After marking all the entries, you position the cursor where you want the reference list to appear. Generally, a table of contents is included as part of a document's front matter. You then select the type of reference list and define the style elements. Follow these steps:

1. Position the cursor where you want the table of contents to appear.

```
                    Writing Guidelines
================================================================
-

================================================================
Brainstorming

When you have trouble determining a sharp focus for a document--
when you are uncertain what you want to say--consider trying a
semistructured writing exercise known as "brainstorming."

When you brainstorm a writing assignment on-screen, you record your
ideas in list form as they occur to you.  When you brainstorm, you
don't worry about typos, spelling errors, or style.  You turn off
the inclination to hone each sentence before you move on to the
next one.  You can handle those matters later.  Your goal is,
rather to generate as many ideas as possible about the topic, the
purpose, or the audience.

Keeping an Idea File

An idea file is an extension of a brainstorming file.  You can save
an idea file and retrieve it when you want to add more ideas later.
C:\WP51\BOOK\BRAIN.TXT                   Doc 1 Pg 2 Ln 1" Pos 1"
```

In this example, the cursor is positioned at the top of the second page.

2. To select the type of reference list, press [Alt] [F5] (Mark Text) and choose **D**efine (**5**).

   ⌨ Access the **M**ark pull-down menu and select **D**efine.

```
Mark Text: Define

    1 - Define Table of Contents

    2 - Define List

    3 - Define Index

    4 - Define Table of Authorities

    5 - Edit Table of Authorities Full Form
```

The Mark Text: Define options are displayed.

3. Select Define Table of **C**ontents (**1**).

```
Table of Contents Definition

    1 - Number of Levels          1

    2 - Display Last Level in     No
        Wrapped Format

    3 - Page Numbering - Level 1  Flush right with leader
                         Level 2
                         Level 3
                         Level 4
                         Level 5
```

The Table of Contents Defini-tion screen appears.

4. Define the numbering style for the table of contents.

To generate the table of contents, follow these steps:

1. Press [Alt] [F5] to activate the Mark Text command, and select **G**enerate (**6**).

   ⌨ Access the **M**ark pull-down menu and select **G**enerate.

17

431

```
Mark Text: Generate

   1 - Remove Redline Markings and Strikeout Text from Document

   2 - Compare Screen and Disk Documents and Add Redline and Strikeout

   3 - Expand Master Document

   4 - Condense Master Document

   5 - Generate Tables, Indexes, Cross-References, etc.
```

The Mark Text: Generate screen appears.

2. Select Generate Tables, Indexes, Cross-References, etc. (5) to generate the table of contents.

3. At the Existing tables, lists, and indexes will be replaced prompt, select Yes.

17

This table of contents is generated at the beginning of the document, following the title page.

```
                        Writing Guidelines
==============================================================================
                         Table of Contents

Brainstorming. . . . . . . . . . . . . . . . . . . .      3

Keeping an Idea File . . . . . . . . . . . . . . .       7

Using a Prewriting Template. . . . . . . . . . . . .      9

Freewriting. . . . . . . . . . . . . . . . . . . .      11

Using a Prewriting Template. . . . . . . . . . . .      13

Planning Documents . . . . . . . . . . . . . . . . .    15

==============================================================================
Brainstorming

When you have trouble determining a sharp focus for a document--
when you are uncertain what you want to say--consider trying a
semistructured writing exercise known as "brainstorming."

C:\WP51\BOOK\BRAIN.TXT                           Doc 1 Pg 3 Ln 1" Pos 1"
```

Index

WordPerfect's Index feature creates an alphabetical list of index headings and subheadings (called *entries*) for a document. You can generate an index only at the end of a document.

```
Exercises
     brainstorming  3
     idea file  7
     prewriting template  11

Freewriting  9









C:\WP51\BOOK\INDEX.TXT                        Doc 1 Pg 1 Ln 1.83" Pos 1.4"
```

Table of Authorities

```
                  TABLE OF AUTHORITIES
                    Decisions--State

Farhadi v. Anavian, 321 Misc.2d 194, 345 N.Y.S.2d
     229 (Sup. Ct., N.Y. County 1981) . . . . . . . . . . . . 4

Goodbody v. Ingalls, 198 N.Y. 307, 114 N.E. 124
     (1908) . . . . . . . . . . . . . . . . . . . . . . . . . 3

Jumbville v. Soc. of Elysian Masters, 114
     Misc.2d 245, 127 N.Y.S.2d 125 (Sup.
     Ct., N.Y. County 1984) . . . . . . . . . . . . . . . . . 3

Thimsley v. Blankwort, 329 A.D.2d 157, 157
     N.Y.S.2d 115 (1st Dept. 1983) . . . . . . . . . . . . . 3

                   Decisions--Federal

Marshall v. Taney, 37 U.S. 146 (1807) . . . . . . . . . . . . 3

U.S. v. Royall, 57 U.S. 427 (1837) . . . . . . . . . . . . 1,2

                       Statutes

New York Penal Law, $2106(c) . . . . . . . . . . . . . . . . 4

                    Other Authorities

Blackstone, Commentaries, p. 98 . . . . . . . . . . . . . . . 4

Savonarola, Report on Medieval Survivals in
     Those Areas of the United States Formerly
     Under the Dominion of Great Britain (1805),
     p. 1,317 . . . . . . . . . . . . . . . . . . . . . . . . 5
```

A table of authorities is a list of court cases, rules of court, statutes, agency opinions, and miscellaneous authorities mentioned in a document. Typically, each type of authority is assigned its own section in the table. Within each section, the citations are listed alphabetically, with page references.

17

List

```
                  LIST OF EXHIBITS

          Page numbers record first mention of
             each exhibit in this affidavit

Exhibit A. . . . . . . . . . . . . . . . . . . . . . . . . .1
Exhibit B. . . . . . . . . . . . . . . . . . . . . . . . . .2
Exhibit C. . . . . . . . . . . . . . . . . . . . . . . . . .2
Exhibit D. . . . . . . . . . . . . . . . . . . . . . . . . .3
Exhibit E. . . . . . . . . . . . . . . . . . . . . . . . . .3




C:\WP51\BOOK\LIST.TXT              Doc 1 Pg 1 Ln 2.5" Pos 7.5"
```

If your document contains figures, tables, maps, and other illustrations, you can list these resources in a reference table. Usually, a list appears on a page by itself following the table of contents. You can create up to nine lists per document.

Automatic Cross Reference

You use
WordPerfect's
Automatic Refer-
ence feature to
reference page
numbers, foot-
note numbers,
section numbers,
endnote num-
bers, and graphics
box numbers. If
you make
changes, the
references are
renumbered
automatically.

```
Brainstorming

When you have trouble determining a sharp focus for a document--
when you are uncertain what you want to say--consider trying a
semistructured writing exercise known as "brainstorming."

When you brainstorm a writing assignment on-screen, you record your
ideas in list form as they occur to you.  When you brainstorm, you
don't worry about typos, spelling errors, or style.  You turn off
the inclination to hone each sentence before you move on to the
next one.  You can handle those matters later.  Your goal is,
rather to generate as many ideas as possible about the topic, the
purpose, or the audience.  See the discussion of planning documents
on page 9.

Keeping an Idea File

An idea file is an extension of a brainstorming file.  You can save
an idea file and retrieve it when you want to add more ideas later.

Using a Prewriting Template

Prewriting is everything you do up to the actual step of writing
that first draft.  It is very much a part of the planning stage.
C:\WP51\BOOK\AUTOREF.TXT                      Doc 1 Pg 1 Ln 3.17" Pos 2"
```

17

Master Document

A master document contains information that enables you to easily combine
several subdocuments into a whole, as well as break them apart. Combining
subdocuments into a master document allows you to maintain the individual
subdocument files and to pull them together in the master document so that
you can generate indexes, tables of contents, and so on for the combined
documents.

The master
document file
contains codes
that reference the
subdocument
files. Each
subdocument
contains the text
for a particular
section of the
total document.

```
Subdoc: TITLE

Subdoc: ABSTRACT

================================================================

Subdoc: ACKNOWL

================================================================

Subdoc: CHAP1

Subdoc: CHAP2

C:\WP51\BOOK\MASTER.DOC                        Doc 1 Pg 3 Ln 1" Pos 1"
```

Document Compare

With the Document Compare feature, you can compare the new version of a document with an old version.

```
In the old days, writers had to stop editing days before a document
was due and start combing through the main text to prepare the
document references. One of WordPerfect 5.1's handiest features is
that it speeds up that process. One of WordPerfect 5.1's handiest
features is that it speeds up the process of assembling document
references. With a little foresight and planning, you can work on
a document right down to a few hours before a deadline, confident
that as your main text changes, the document references will keep
right up with it.

This chapter shows you how to create lists, tables of contents,
tables of authorities, and indexes. You also learn to use
automatic cross-referencing, which lets you change the structure of
your document and automatically maintain accurate references to
footnotes, pages, and sections. which lets you change the
structure of your document and automatically maintain accurate
references to certain spots in a document. Finally, you learn to
use the Document Compare feature so that you can show someone else
what was omitted from, you learn to use the Document Compare
feature so that you can see what was omitted from, or added to, a
document, without having to mark all those changes yourself.
```

Sections of the on-screen document that don't exist in the disk file are redlined. Text that exists in the disk file but not in the on-screen document is copied to the on-screen document and marked with strikeout.

Summary

This chapter introduced many of WordPerfect's referencing tools for developing a manuscript. You explored WordPerfect's features for creating footnotes and endnotes, inserting the current date and time in a document, generating outlines and paragraph numbers, numbering lines, and inserting document comments. You also learned about additional reference materials you can create with WordPerfect, including a table of contents, an index, a table of authorities, and a list of figures or tables. Finally, you were introduced to the Automatic Cross Reference, Master Document, and Document Compare features.

Specifically, you learned the following key information about WordPerfect:

- Footnotes appear at the bottom or foot of each page; endnotes are grouped at the end of a section or the end of the document.

- To create a footnote or an endnote, select Footnote (Ctrl-F7), and choose Footnote (**1**) or Endnote (**2**). Then select Create (**1**), and enter the text for the footnote or endnote.

- To edit a footnote or an endnote, select Footnote (Ctrl-F7), and choose Footnote (**1**) or Endnote (**2**). Then choose Edit (**2**), type the number of the note, and edit the text.

17

- To generate endnotes, select Mark Text (Alt-F5) and choose **Generate** (**6**). Then select **Generate Tables, Indexes, Cross-References, etc. (5)** and select **Yes**.

- To change the numbering style, placement, and format for footnotes and endnotes, select Footnote (Ctrl-F7), choose **Footnote** (**1**) or **Endnote** (**2**), and select **Options** (**4**).

- To insert a date and time code, select Date/Outline (Shift-F5), and choose either Date **Text** (**1**) or Date **Code** (**2**).

- To turn on the Outline feature, select Date/Outline (Shift-F5) and choose **Outline** (**4**). Then select **On** (**1**).

- Paragraph numbering differs from outlining because you must insert numbers manually. To number an entry or paragraph, select Date/Outline (Shift-F5) and choose **Para Num** (**5**).

- To change the numbering style of an outline, select Date/Outline (Shift-F5), choose **Define** (**6**), and make a selection from the list of predefined numbering styles.

- WordPerfect can number the lines in a document, but you cannot see the numbers on-screen; the numbers appear only when you print the document or use View Document. To turn on automatic line numbering, select Format (Shift-F8), choose **Line** (**1**), select Line **Numbering** (**5**), and choose **Yes**.

- Document comments are useful for reminding you of what you had in mind during a particular writing session. Comments are displayed on-screen; they are not printed. To create a document comment, select Text In/Out (Ctrl-F5), choose **Comment** (**4**), and select **Create** (**1**). In the comment box, type the text of your comment.

- To edit a document comment, select Text In/Out (Ctrl-F5), choose **Comment** (**4**), and select **Edit** (**2**). Then edit the comment.

- To print document comments, you must convert them to text. To change a comment to text, select Text In/Out (Ctrl-F5), choose **Comment** (**4**), and select **Convert to Text** (**3**).

- To change text to a comment, highlight the block, select Text In/Out (Ctrl-F5), and choose **Yes**.

- To mark entries for a table of contents, highlight the entry, select Mark Text (Alt-F5), choose **ToC** (**1**), and type **1**.

- To select the type of reference list and define the style elements for a table of contents, select Mark Text (Alt-F5), choose **Define** (**5**), select **Define Table of Contents** (**1**), and define the numbering style.

17

- To generate a table of contents, select Mark Text (Alt-F5) and choose **Generate (6)**. Then select **Generate Tables, Indexes, Cross-References, etc. (5)**.

- WordPerfect's Index feature creates an alphabetical list of index headings and subheadings (called entries) for a document.

- A table of authorities is a list of court cases, rules of court, statutes, agency opinions, and miscellaneous authorities mentioned in a document.

- If your document contains figures, tables, maps, and other illustrations, you can list these resources in a reference table using the List Reference feature.

- You can use WordPerfect's Automatic Cross Reference feature to reference page numbers, footnote numbers, section numbers, endnote numbers, and graphics box numbers.

- A master document contains information that enables you to easily combine several subdocuments into a whole.

- With the Document Compare feature, you can compare the new version of a document with an old version.

In the next chapter, you will learn about WordPerfect's graphics capabilities.

17

Creating Graphics

With WordPerfect's Graphics feature, you can enhance the appearance of a document with graphics boxes and lines. You can use five types of boxes: figure, table, text, user-defined, and equation.

As you create the boxes, you can insert text; graphics installed on your hard disk from the PTR Program/Graphics disks; or graphics, charts, and graphs created with external programs, such as Harvard Graphics, PC Paintbrush, DrawPerfect, and 1-2-3. If you prefer, you can create an empty box and enter text or graphics later. Graphics boxes can be placed in the body of a document as well as in headers, footers, and endnotes.

Border —

Horizontal line —

Graphics box
with imported —
clip-art image

Vertical line —

Text wrapped
around a box —

Text box

Here is an example of a publication created with WordPerfect. Notice the variety of graphics used in this page.

18

Key Terms in This Chapter

Graphics box   A box defined to hold a figure, a table, text, user-defined elements, or an equation, and to have certain characteristics, such as border style and caption style.

Box contents   The contents of a graphics box, such as an imported clip-art figure, statistical data, text, a photograph, or an equation.

Offset   A short distance established as a boundary to avoid the collision of two elements, such as a graphics image and a box.

Bit-mapped image   An image composed of dots.

Creating Graphics Boxes

To create a graphics box, you must complete these basic procedures:

- Choose the type of box you want.
- Determine the appearance of the box.
- Create the box and define its contents.

Each of these procedures is described in the text that follows.

18

Choosing the Box Type

Each of WordPerfect's five box types has a default definition. The definition includes the border of the box, the inside and outside border space, the caption-numbering method and style, the minimum offset, and the box shading. You can use the default box definitions, or you can define your own. Defining boxes gives you a consistent set of boxes to use in your documents. Although anything you put in one type of box can be put in any other type, you may want to reserve each type of box for a specific use. For instance, you might place clip art in figure boxes, statistical data in table boxes, text in text boxes, photographs (which you paste in later) in user-defined boxes, and mathematical formulas in equation boxes.

Figure 1: A figure created with WordPerfect's default figure options. The WordPerfect graphic CNTRCT-2.WPG is included in the box.

Figure box

Table I: A WordPerfect table box, using default options. The table inside the table box was created with WordPerfect's Table feature.

STAFF MEETING TIMES
July 1990

	Dept. A	Dept. B
Week 1	9:00	10:00
Week 2	10:00	3:00
Week 3	9:00	10:00
Week 4	3:00	1:30

Table box

1: A WordPerfect user-defined box, using default options for style. The WordPerfect graphic MAILBAG.WPG is included.

User-defined box

The new features of WordPerfect 5.1 make life easier for the user. while minimizing retraining costs for the organization.

1: This is WordPerfect's default text box, with a file retrieved.

Text box

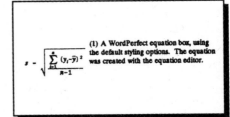

(1) A WordPerfect equation box, using the default styling options. The equation was created with the equation editor.

Equation box

To choose the type of box you want to create, follow this procedure:

1. Press ⌊Alt⌋ ⌊F9⌋ to activate the Graphics command.

The Graphics menu is displayed at the bottom of the screen.

Access the Graphics pull-down menu.

2. Select one of these box types:

     Figure (1)

     Table Box (2)

     Text Box (3)

     User Box (4)

     Equation (6)

WordPerfect then displays a menu similar to the following:

    Figure: 1 Create; 2 Edit; 3 New Number; 4 Options: 0

The first word of this menu will vary depending on what type of box you have selected.

If you are using the **Graphics** pull-down menu, selecting each of the box types from that menu displays a pop-out menu showing the preceding options.

18

443

Changing the Box Options

After you choose the box type, you can change the default options that determine how the box should look. If you want to change the options, you should do so before creating the box. Among the options you can change are the border styles, the spacing between the border and contents, the style and position of the caption, and the box shading.

To change the appearance of a box, follow this procedure:

1. Choose Options (4).

   ▭ Select Options from the pop-out menu.

The Options:
Figure screen
is displayed.

```
Options: Figure

    1 - Border Style
            Left                                Single
            Right                               Single
            Top                                 Single
            Bottom                              Single
    2 - Outside Border Space
            Left                                0.167"
            Right                               0.167"
            Top                                 0.167"
            Bottom                              0.167"
    3 - Inside Border Space
            Left                                0"
            Right                               0"
            Top                                 0"
            Bottom                              0"
    4 - First Level Numbering Method            Numbers
    5 - Second Level Numbering Method           Off
    6 - Caption Number Style                    [BOLD]Figure 1[bold]
    7 - Position of Caption                     Below box, Outside borders
    8 - Minimum Offset from Paragraph           0"
    9 - Gray Shading (% of black)               0%

Selection: 0
```

2. Select the options you want to change and enter the necessary information.

3. Press F7 (Exit) to return to the document.

You can choose any (or all) of nine options to determine the appearance of the box.

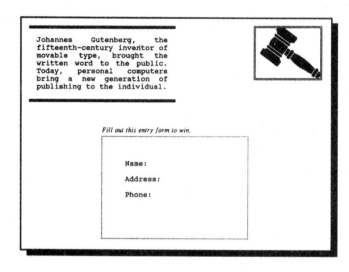

To specify a border for each side of the box, select **B**order Style (**1**) and choose a border (none, single, double, dashed, dotted, thick, or extra thick).

- To change the space between the border of the box and the text, select **O**utside Border Space (**2**) and type a distance for each of the sides.

- To change the space between the border and the contents of the box, choose **I**nside Border Space (**3**) and type a distance for each of the sides.

- To select the numbering for the caption, choose **F**irst Level Numbering Method (**4**) and indicate your choice (off, numbers, letters, or Roman numerals).

  WordPerfect automatically numbers the caption for the box. However, this option determines only the numbering style; you must add the caption when you create the box.

- If you want two levels of numbering for the caption, select **S**econd Level Numbering Method (**5**) and indicate your choice. If you choose letters or Roman numerals, they print in lowercase.

- To specify the text for the caption number, select **C**aption Number Style (**6**) and type the text you want. For example, type **Figure 1.2**. Press 1 to include first-level numbering; press 2 to include second-level numbering.

  You can include formatting codes within the caption number style. Keep in mind that this option defines only the caption number style; you must add the caption when you create the box.

18

To specify where the caption appears, select **P**osition of Caption (**7**) and choose whether to place the caption above or below the box, as well as outside or inside the border.

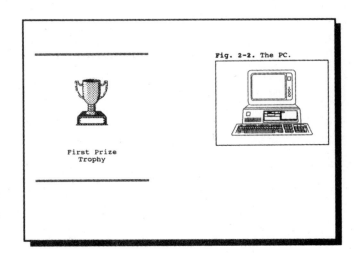

• To set the minimum paragraph offset, select **Minimum Offset from Paragraph** (**8**) and type the minimum offset.

A paragraph-type box is offset from the top of a paragraph by the amount you specify. If the paragraph falls at the end of the page, the box may not fit. This option specifies how much the offset can be reduced to fit the box on the page.

18

To add a gray shade to the box, select **Gray Shading** (% of black) (**9**) and type a percentage from 1 to 100. Zero percent shading is white; 100 percent shading is black.

When you change any of the options, WordPerfect inserts into the document a code for the new box appearance. All boxes of this type will have the same appearance until you change the options again.

Creating the Box and Defining Its Contents

After you choose the type of box and select the options you want, you can create the box. Note that if you create the box without first choosing options, WordPerfect uses the default box settings. When you create a box, you specify the type of box, its contents, the text for the caption, the placement on the page, and the size of the box.

To create a graphics box, follow this procedure:

1. Move the cursor to the place where you want the box to appear. If you have changed the options, be sure that the cursor is below the options code.

2. Press Alt F9 to activate the Graphics command, and select a box type.

   ▣ Access the Graphics pull-down menu and choose the box type you want to create.

3. Choose Create (1).

18

```
Definition: Figure

     1 - Filename

     2 - Contents            Empty

     3 - Caption

     4 - Anchor Type         Paragraph

     5 - Vertical Position   0"

     6 - Horizontal Position Right

     7 - Size                3.25" wide x 3.25" (high)

     8 - Wrap Text Around Box Yes

     9 - Edit



Selection: 0
```

The Definition: Figure screen is displayed.

4. Select the options you want and enter the changes, or press ↵Enter to accept the default definitions.

   The options you can choose are the same for all box types; only the menu heading varies.

5. Press F7 (Exit) to return to the document.

447

Only an outline appears on-screen. To view the document as it will appear when printed, use View Document.

You can specify the following options on the Definition menu:

- Select Filename (**1**) if you want to import a file (for instance, a text or graphics file). Then type the name of the file and press Enter. WordPerfect inserts the file into the box. To create an empty box and enter the contents later, leave this option blank. In subsequent sections, you learn how to import a graphics image and add text to the box.

- Select Contents (**2**) to tell WordPerfect what type of material the box should contain. The box can contain a graphics image, a block of text, or an equation. Usually, when you retrieve a file into the box by using Filename (**1**), WordPerfect automatically fills in the Contents option.

- Choose Caption (**3**) to add a caption to the box. An editing screen appears with the caption number displayed in the style you set when you specified the box options. You can delete, change, or add text to the caption number. Captions conform to the width of the current box.

- Select Anchor Type (**4**) to specify the way you want the box to be anchored. A paragraph-type box stays with the paragraph to which it is assigned. If the paragraph moves, the box moves. A page-type box is anchored to the page and stays in that position regardless of any editing changes. If you choose a page-type box, WordPerfect prompts you to indicate whether you want the box to appear on the current page or whether you want to skip some pages before inserting the box. A character-type box is treated as a character and wraps with the line of text to which the box is anchored.

- Choose Vertical Position (**5**) to specify the vertical alignment of the box. The type of box determines the placement options. For a paragraph-type box, enter the offset from the top of the paragraph. For a page-type box, choose one of five types of alignment: full page, top, center, bottom, or set position (enter an exact position). For a character-type box, choose to align the text with the top, center, or bottom of the box. Or choose Baseline (**4**) to align the last line of text in the box with the line of text where the character-type box is located.

- Select Horizontal Position (**6**) to specify where the box is positioned horizontally. Again, the type of box determines the placement options. For a paragraph-type box, choose to align the box with the left or right

18

margin, to center it between the margins, or to extend it from margin to margin. For a page-type box, choose to align the box with the margins or the columns (left, right, center, or from the left to the right margin or column); or use Set Position (3) to enter an exact location. A character-type box is aligned vertically only.

- Choose Size (7) to select the size of the box. You can enter the width or height, or both. If you enter only the width or height, WordPerfect calculates the other dimension. The Auto Both (4) option (the default setting) calculates both the height and width automatically.

- Select Wrap Text Around Box (8) if you want the text to wrap automatically around the box. If you want text to flow through the box, select this option and change the default from Yes to No.

- Choose Edit (9) to insert text in the box or to edit a graphics image retrieved into the box. When an editing screen appears, either type the text or edit the image.

Importing a Graphics Image

WordPerfect's PTR/Graphics disks contain clip-art files (with a WPG extension) you can import. Check your WordPerfect manual to review the other types of file formats you can import into WordPerfect.

Suppose that you want to import the image of a printer from the WordPerfect PTR/Graphics disks. Follow these steps to import the image:

1. Move the cursor to the place in the document where you want the image to appear.

2. Press Alt F9 to activate the Graphics command, and select a box type. For this example, choose Figure (1).

    Access the Graphics pull-down menu and choose Figure.

3. Choose Create (1) to display the Definition menu.

    The Definition: Figure screen is displayed.

4. Select Filename (1).

5. Type the name of the graphics file and press ↵Enter.

6. Press F7 (Exit).

18

For example, to
import the file
that contains
the image of a
printer, type
printr-3.wpg and
press ⏎Enter.

```
Definition: Figure

        1 - Filename            PRINTR-3.WPG

        2 - Contents            Graphic

        3 - Caption

        4 - Anchor Type         Paragraph

        5 - Vertical Position   0"

        6 - Horizontal Position Right

        7 - Size                3.25" wide x 2.35" (high)

        8 - Wrap Text Around Box Yes

        9 - Edit



Selection: 0
```

18

WordPerfect
returns to the
document.

```
Johannes Gutenberg, the fif-          ┌FIG 1─────────────
teenth-century inventor of mov-
able type, brought the written
word to the public, and thus is
responsible for publishing as it
has been known for five hundred
years.  In the last quarter
century, Gutenberg's metal type
has been replaced by electronic
typesetting—faster, more
flexible, but still very
expensive, and still only part
of the complex process of pub-
lishing.  Today, personal com-
puters bring a new generation of
publishing to the individual.
The technology is called "desktop publishing," and it represents a
whole new approach to a very old art.

Desktop publishing starts with a personal computer.  Your high-
powered computer, along with the right software, gives you all the
tools you need to design and publish a variety of printed materials
at your own desk.  Write a press release or create a simple
letterhead with a word processing program like WordPerfect for IBM
C:\WP51\BOOK\COLUMN.TXT                        Doc 1 Pg 1 Ln 3.83" Pos 1"
```

7. To display an outline of the image, position the cursor after the box.

8. To view the document as it will appear when printed, press ⇧Shift F7
   (Print) and select **V**iew Document (6).

   ▭ Access the **F**ile pull-down menu, choose **P**rint, and select **V**iew
   Document (6).

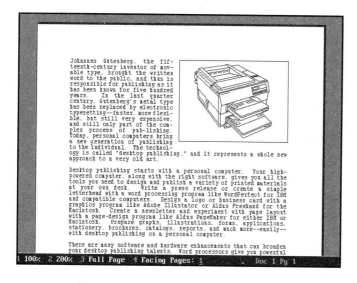

Here is the document in View Document mode.

9. Press ⬚F7⬚ (Exit) to return to the editing screen.

Note: If you do not specify the box size, WordPerfect calculates an initial box size based on the space remaining on the page. When you import a graphics image, WordPerfect adjusts the proportions of the box to suit the image. You can modify the size of the box at any time.

Entering Text into a Box

When you create a box, you can fill it with text by specifying on the Definition screen the name of an existing text file. If, however, you prefer to type text directly into the box, you can do that as you create the box, or you can go back later and type the text into an empty box.

To enter text directly into a box, follow these steps:

1. Press ⬚Alt⬚⬚F9⬚ to activate the Graphics command, and select Text Box (3).

   ⬚ Access the Graphics pull-down menu and choose Text Box.

2. To enter text as you create the box, select Create (1). To enter text into an empty existing box, select Edit (2), type the box number, and press ⬚↵Enter⬚.

3. From the Definition menu, select Edit (9).

   A screen for entering text appears.

4. Type the text, using any of WordPerfect's text-formatting features.

```
On this screen, you can enter
any text you want to include
in a graphics text box.




Box:  Press Exit when done, Graphics to rotate text        Ln 0.333" Pos 2.3"
```

Here, the text for
the box has been
typed.

5. Press [Alt][F9] (Graphics) if you want to rotate the text, and select a
   degree of rotation: 0, 90, 180, or 270.

6. Press [F7] (Exit) twice to return to the document.

18 Editing Boxes and Images

You can edit both the box and the image within it. You can edit the box, for
instance, by changing the numbering or type of box. If you import a graphics
file into a box, you can edit the image by moving, scaling, rotating, mirroring,
or inverting it.

Editing a Graphics Box

Box numbering begins with 1 (or I or A) at the beginning of the document
and continues consecutively through the document. You can change the
numbering, for example, when you begin a new chapter. To change a box
number, follow these steps:

1. Position the cursor before the box you want to renumber.

2. Press [Alt][F9] to activate the Graphics command, and select the type of
   box you want to renumber.

   ⌐⌐ Access the Graphics pull-down menu and select the type of box.

3. Choose New Number (3), type the new number, and press [↵Enter].

   If you are using two-level numbering, enter a new number for each
   level (for example, type 3e).

4. To see the change, position the cursor after the newly numbered box.

To change the box type, follow these steps:

1. Press ⌊Alt⌋⌊F9⌋ (Graphics) and select the type of box to be changed.

   ▭ Access the **G**raphics pull-down menu and select the type of box to be changed.

2. Select **E**dit (**2**).

3. Type the number of the box to be changed and press ⌊↵Enter⌋.

4. Press ⌊Alt⌋⌊F9⌋ (Graphics) and select a new box type.

5. Press ⌊F7⌋ (Exit) to return to the document.

6. To display the change on-screen, position the cursor after the box.

Editing a Graphics Image

If you import a graphics image into a box, you can edit the image by moving, scaling, rotating, mirroring, or inverting it.

To edit an imported graphics image, follow these steps:

1. Press ⌊Alt⌋⌊F9⌋ to activate the Graphics command, and select the type of box you want to edit.

   ▭ Access the **G**raphics pull-down menu and select the type of box.

2. Select **E**dit (**2**).

3. Type the box number and press ⌊↵Enter⌋.

4. Select **E**dit (**9**) from the Definition menu.

   The bottom of the screen shows the editing changes you can make to the image.

18

The graphics
image appears
on-screen.

Moving an Image

18

Use the arrow
keys to move the
graphics image.

454

Follow these steps to enter a precise measure of movement:

1. Select Move (1).

2. Type the horizontal distance to move, and then press ⏎Enter. Positive numbers move the image to the right; negative numbers move it to the left.

3. Type the vertical distance to move, and then press ⏎Enter. Positive numbers move the image up; negative numbers move it down.

Scaling an Image

Press PgUp to make the image larger, or press PgDn to make the image smaller.

Use the following steps to scale an image by a specified percentage:

1. Select Scale (2).

2. For Scale X, type the percentage to scale the image horizontally (from side to side) and press ⏎Enter.

3. For Scale Y, type the percentage to scale the image vertically (from top to bottom) and press ⏎Enter.

Note: To retain the proportions of the image, enter the same numbers for X and Y.

Rotating and Mirroring an Image

Press the minus sign (–) on the numeric keypad to rotate the image clockwise, or press the plus sign (+) to rotate the image counterclockwise.

18

Follow these steps to rotate an image by a specified amount:

1. Select Rotate (3).
2. Type the number of degrees to rotate the figure (positive numbers only), and then press ⏎Enter.
3. At the Mirror Image? prompt, select Yes if you want to mirror the image, or select No if you don't.

Inverting an Image

To invert an image, select Invert (4). WordPerfect redisplays the figure with each dot in its complementary color. For example, black-on-white becomes white-on-black. This feature works on only bit-mapped images.

Creating Graphics Lines

With WordPerfect, you can create vertical and horizontal graphics lines on the printed page. The lines can be shaded or black. You also can edit graphics lines.

To create graphics lines, follow these steps:

1. Position the cursor where you want to begin drawing a line.

2. Press ⌈Alt⌉⌈F9⌉ to activate the Graphics command, and select Line (5).

⊟⊐ Access the Graphics pull-down menu and select Line.

3. Choose Create Line: Horizontal (1) or Create Line: Vertical (2).

⊟⊐ Choose Create Horizontal or Create Vertical from the Line pop-out menu.

```
Graphics: Horizontal Line

    1 - Horizontal Position     Full

    2 - Vertical Position       Baseline

    3 - Length of Line

    4 - Width of Line           0.013"

    5 - Gray Shading (% of black) 100%
```

WordPerfect displays the Graphics: Horizontal Line menu.

```
Graphics: Vertical Line

    1 - Horizontal Position     Left Margin

    2 - Vertical Position       Full Page

    3 - Length of Line

    4 - Width of Line           0.013"

    5 - Gray Shading (% of black) 100%
```

Or WordPerfect displays the Graphics: Vertical Line menu.

4. If you want to change the defaults, choose options and enter the appropriate information.

18

5. Press F7 (Exit) to return to the editing screen.

From the Horizontal or Vertical Line menu, you can accept the defaults for the line or select from the following options:

*   For a horizontal line, choose **Horizontal Position (1)** to place the horizontal line against the left margin, against the right margin, centered between both margins, extending from the left to the right margin, or starting a specified distance from the left edge of the page.

    For a vertical line, you can position the line just outside the left or right margin, or between a specified column and the column immediately to the right. Or you can use **Set Position (4)** to enter a specific position measured from the left edge of the page.

*   For a vertical line, choose **Vertical Position (2)** to extend the vertical line from the top margin to the bottom margin (the default setting) or to place such a line against the top or bottom margin, centered between the top and bottom margins, or at a specified distance from the top of the page.

    For a horizontal line, you can choose **Baseline (1)**, which is the default setting, to establish the line at the current cursor position; or you can select **Set Position (2)** to specify an exact location.

*   Unless you have specified a horizontal position of Full or a vertical position of Full Page, choose **Length of Line (3)** to specify the length of the line. Depending on the placement of the line, WordPerfect may calculate the line length for you. The line length is calculated as the distance between the cursor and the left margin.

*   Select **Width of Line (4)** to define the thickness of the line.

*   Select **Gray Shading (% of black) (5)** to print the line shaded between 0% (white) and 100% (black).

You can edit a graphics line after you have created it, using the following procedure:

1. Position the cursor immediately after the line you want to edit.

2. Press Alt F9 (Graphics) and select **Line (5)**.

    ⌐⌐ Access the **Graphics** pull-down menu and select **Line**.

3. Select **Edit Line: Horizontal (3)** to edit a horizontal line, or select **Edit Line: Vertical (4)** to edit a vertical line.

    ⌐⌐ Select **Edit Horizontal** or **Edit Vertical** from the **Line** pop-out menu.

18

WordPerfect searches backward from the cursor position for an existing line; if no line is found, WordPerfect searches forward to the end of the document.

Depending on the type of line you specified to edit, WordPerfect displays the Graphics: Horizontal Line menu or the Graphics: Vertical Line menu.

4. To edit the line, select the options you want.

5. Press F7 (Exit) to return to the editing screen.

Keep in mind that text does not wrap around graphics lines. If you place a vertical or horizontal graphics line in the middle of text, the line will print over the text.

Using Line Draw

If you plan to edit your document, use the Graphics feature to draw lines and boxes so that the images don't change inadvertently as you edit. If you want, you can use the Line Draw feature to draw a line or box by simply moving the cursor. Keep in mind that lines and boxes drawn with Line Draw are composed of characters and are part of the text. You cannot type over them or around them without disturbing them.

18

To draw a line or box with Line Draw, complete these steps:

1. Press Ctrl F3 to activate the Screen command, and select Line Draw (2).

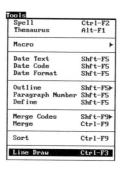

Access the Tools pull-down menu and select Line Draw.

A menu of line-
drawing options
is displayed.

```
1 |; 2 ||; 3 *; 4 Change; 5 Erase; 6 Move: 1                    Ln 1" Pos 1"
```

2. Select one of the following options:

    Choose **1** to draw a single line.

    Choose **2** to draw a double line.

    Choose **3** to draw a line of asterisks (****).

Choose **4** to
display a menu of
alternative line
styles, and then
select the one you
want.

```
1 ||; 2 ||; 3 ||; 4 |; 5 ■; 6 |; 7 |; 8 ■; 9 Other: 8
```

18

Select **5** to erase a line you have drawn.

Select **6** to move the cursor to a new location without drawing
a line.

3. Use the cursor keys to draw the line or box.

4. Press [F7] to quit Line Draw.

Summary

In this chapter, you learned to define various types of graphics boxes and to
import images into those boxes. You explored some of the options for each
type of box, such as border styles, caption styles, spacing between the border
and contents, and box shading. You learned that you can edit a graphics image
in WordPerfect by changing the size of the image or by rotating it. And you
learned about WordPerfect's capabilities for drawing lines to enhance a
document.

Specifically, you learned the following information about WordPerfect:

■ With WordPerfect's Graphics feature, you can enhance the appearance of a document with graphics boxes and lines. You can use five types of boxes: figure, table, text, user-defined, and equation.

■ To create a graphics box, choose the type of box you want, determine the appearance of the box, and create the box and define its contents.

■ To choose the type of box, select Graphics (Alt-F9), and choose one of the five box types.

■ To change the appearance of a box, select Graphics (Alt-F9), choose a box type, select **Options** (**4**), and choose the options you want to change.

■ To create a graphics box, select Graphics (Alt-F9), choose a box type, and select **Create** (**1**).

■ To import a graphics image, select Graphics (Alt-F9), choose a box type, and select **Create** (**1**). Then choose **Filename** (**1**) and type the name of the graphics file.

■ To enter text directly into a box, select Graphics (Alt-F9) and choose **Text Box** (**3**). To enter text as you create the box, select **Create** (**1**); or to enter text into an empty existing box, select **Edit** (**2**), type the box number, and press Enter. Then select **Edit** (**9**) and type the text.

■ To change a box number, select Graphics (Alt-F9), choose a box, select **New Number** (**3**), type the new number, and press Enter.

■ To change the box type, select Graphics (Alt-F9), choose a box type, select **Edit** (**2**), type the number of the box to be changed, and press Enter. Then select Graphics (Alt-F9) and choose a new box type.

■ If you import a graphics image into a box, you can edit the image by moving, scaling, rotating, mirroring, or inverting it.

■ To create graphics lines, select Graphics (Alt-F9) and choose **Line** (**5**). Then select **Create Line**: Horizontal (**1**) to create a horizontal line or select **Create Line**: Vertical (**2**) to create a vertical line.

■ Lines and boxes drawn with Line Draw are composed of characters and are part of the text. You cannot type over them or around them without disturbing them. To draw a line or box with Line Draw, select Screen (Ctrl-F3), choose Line Draw (**2**), select one of the options, and use the cursor keys to draw the line or box.

This chapter completes your introduction to WordPerfect.

18

Installing WordPerfect 5.1

If WordPerfect 5.1 is not already installed on your system, you must complete the installation procedure. WordPerfect 5.1 offers a number of installation options, including the Basic installation, the Custom installation (for installing WordPerfect to specific directories), and the Network installation (for installing WordPerfect for use on a network). This appendix shows you how to install WordPerfect to your hard disk in a standard manner, using the Basic installation option. You can use this procedure whether your copy of WordPerfect is on 5 1/4-inch or 3 1/2-inch disks. After you complete the installation, turn to Chapter 1, "Getting Started," for instructions on how to start WordPerfect. (That chapter also shows you how to exit the program.)

Part of the Basic installation includes installing one or more printers and selecting the one you want to use as your default printer. If you need to install a printer after you have installed the program, this text shows you how to install the new printer. You also learn how to select font cartridges and soft (downloadable) fonts for your printer, and how to select an initial (base) font. For instructions on selecting any printer you have installed, see Chapter 7, "Printing."

Making Backup Copies of Your Master Diskettes

Before you begin installing WordPerfect 5.1, you should make backup copies of your original program disks (your *master* disks). Store the master disks and the copies in safe, separate locations. The backup copies are important in case something happens to your master disks. Use the DOS DISKCOPY command to make the backup copies. Be sure to label each backup disk with the name of the master disk.

Follow these steps to make backup copies of your master disks:

1. Turn on the computer.
2. If prompted, type the current date and press ⏎Enter; then type the current time and press ⏎Enter.
3. At the C> prompt, type **diskcopy a: a:** and press ⏎Enter.
4. When DOS prompts you to insert a source disk, insert a WordPerfect master disk and press ⏎Enter.
5. When DOS prompts you to insert a target disk, insert a blank disk and press ⏎Enter.
6. When DOS displays the prompt Copy another disk (Y/N)?, press Y.
7. Repeat Steps 4 through 6 until you have made a copy of each master disk.
8. After you have copied all the master disks, press N at the Copy another disk (Y/N)? prompt.

Starting Install

To begin the installation to a hard disk system, follow these steps:

1. Place the Install/Learn/Utilities 1 disk into drive A and close the drive door.
2. To make sure that you are at the DOS A> prompt, type **a:** and press ⏎Enter.

A

3. Type **install** and press ⏎Enter.

   WordPerfect displays a welcome screen and asks whether you want to continue with the installation.

4. Select Yes.

5. At the prompt that asks whether you are installing to a hard disk, select Yes.

WordPerfect displays the Installation menu.

Selecting the Basic Installation

WordPerfect's Installation menu gives you a number of options for various kinds of installation. To select the standard type of installation, follow these steps:

1. Select Basic (1) to start the installation.

   WordPerfect displays a screen asking whether you want to install the Utility files.

2. Select Yes.

   You are then given the following instruction:

   ```
   Insert the Install/Learn/Utilities 1 master disk into
   A:\
   ```

3. Press ⏎Enter to continue with the installation.

4. Follow the screen prompts. At each prompt that asks whether you want to install particular files, select Yes. When you are prompted to place certain disks into drive A and press ⏎Enter, do so as directed.

   After you copy the WordPerfect files to your hard disk, the Install program next checks the CONFIG.SYS and AUTOEXEC.BAT files and alters them as needed to accommodate WordPerfect.

5. Select Yes to modify your CONFIG.SYS file as needed.

6. Select Yes to change the AUTOEXEC.BAT file so that you can run WordPerfect from any directory.

The next part of the installation process is to select printers.

A

Installing Printers

During this part of the installation, you install the printer drivers for each printer you want to use with WordPerfect. Note that the first printer that you install for WordPerfect becomes the default selected printer.

To install the printer(s) you will use with WordPerfect 5.1, follow these steps:

1. Place the disk labeled Printer 1 into drive A and press ⏎Enter to display a list of printer drivers.

2. To find the name of the printer you want to install, use the PgDn or PgUp keys, or press N (Name Search) and type the name of the printer you want. For example, press N, type **hp laserjet series II** to display the screen with that printer name, and press ⏎Enter.

3. After you locate the printer you want to install, type the number of the printer and press ⏎Enter. To install the HP LaserJet Series II printer, for example, type **17** and press ⏎Enter.

   The printer you choose in this step—that is, the first printer you choose during the installation—becomes the default selected printer.

4. When you are asked whether you want to install the printer, select Yes.

5. When you are asked whether you want to install the printer (ALL) files, select Yes to install these files; they are required to print your documents.

6. If you are prompted to insert another printer disk into the drive, do so and press ⏎Enter.

7. At the prompt asking whether you want to install another printer, select Yes if you want to do so, and then repeat Steps 2 through 6. If you don't want to install another printer, select No and continue with the steps that follow.

Completing the Installation

To complete the installation process, you need to enter your registration number, read any information that WordPerfect displays about printers you installed, exit Install, and reboot the system. Follow these steps:

1. At the prompt to enter your registration number, type the number found on the registration card in your WordPerfect binder, and then press ⏎Enter.

A

The Install program starts WordPerfect and automatically selects as the default the first printer you specified in the preceding steps from the ALL file. At this point, WordPerfect may display helpful information about the printers you have installed. Be sure to read this information. You can use ⌜⇧Shift⌝ ⌜PrtSc⌝ or ⌜PrtSc⌝ (on an Enhanced Keyboard) to copy this information to your printer.

2. To continue with the Install program, press any key.

   The final WordPerfect installation screen displays the names of README files that contain recent information on WordPerfect not included in the documentation. Make a note of these file names. You may want to retrieve these files into WordPerfect to read or print them later.

3. Press ⌜↵Enter⌝ to continue.

4. Remove the WordPerfect installation disk from drive A and reboot the computer by pressing ⌜Ctrl⌝ ⌜Alt⌝ ⌜Del⌝. You must reboot the computer in order to activate the changes in CONFIG.SYS and AUTOEXEC.BAT.

You are now ready to start WordPerfect. See Chapter 1, "Getting Started."

Installing a New Printer

In the course of using WordPerfect 5.1, you may acquire a new printer. If you have installed a group of printer drivers (that is, you copied the ALL files when you installed your printers) and you want to use a printer from that group, you can install a printer by using the Select Printer option on the Print menu. The first part of this section discusses how to install a printer with that option on the Print menu. If the printer driver for your new printer is not listed among those displayed through the Print menu, you must use the Install program to install your new printer. (See Chapter 7, "Printing," for instructions on selecting a printer after you have installed it.)

If your new printer is a laser printer, you may want to make some additional setting changes, either initially when you first get the printer, or later for some particular uses. For example, you may want to select certain font cartridges or soft (downloadable) fonts so that they are available for use. Or you may want to change the initial font set for your new printer.

A

Installing a New Printer with the Print Menu

Some offices have a variety of printers from the same manufacturer. For instance, an office may have an HP LaserJet and an HP LaserJet+. Later, an HP LaserJet Series II may be added to the office. When WordPerfect was initially installed and the printers were installed, the ALL file was copied to the disk. Now, to use the Series II printer, instead of using the Install program, you can simply use the Print menu to install the HP LaserJet Series II as an additional printer.

To install a new printer with the Print menu while running WordPerfect, follow these steps:

1. Press ⇧Shift F7 to activate the Print command.

   ▭ Access the File pull-down menu and select Print.

2. From the Print menu, choose Select Printer (S).

   Note: If your printer is listed, you do not need to install it. Press F7 (Exit) twice to return to the editing screen.

3. Select Additional Printers (2).

   If you see the message Printer files not found, you must use the Install program to install the printer files you will need.

4. Use PgUp or PgDn to move through the list of displayed printer drivers until you find the printer you want to install.

   If the printer you want to install is not listed, you must use the Install program, as described in the next procedure, to install the appropriate printer files.

5. Move the highlight bar to the printer you want to install, and choose Select (1).

6. Press ⏎Enter to accept the displayed name.

   WordPerfect displays information about the printer.

7. Press F7 (Exit) four times to return to the editing screen.

Installing a New Printer with the Install Program

To install a new printer with the Install program, start the Install program as described in the section "Starting Install." Then follow these steps:

1. From the Installation menu, select Printer (4).

2. At the prompt, place the Printer master disk in the disk drive.

A

3. Look through the list of printers to find your printer; then type the corresponding number for your printer and press ⏎Enter.

4. When you are asked whether you want to install the printer, select **Yes**.

5. When you are asked whether you want to install the printer (ALL) files, select **Yes** to install these files; they are required to print your documents.

6. If instructed, place the correct Printer disk into the disk drive and press ⏎Enter.

   Your new printer is installed for use by WordPerfect.

7. At the prompt asking whether you want to install another printer, select **Yes** to install another printer, or select **No** if you don't want to do so.

   WordPerfect displays information about the printers you have installed.

8. Press any key to complete the process.

9. Remove the Printer disk from drive A.

Selecting Font Cartridges and Soft Fonts

Most printers enable you to print in two or three different fonts that come built into the printer. However, many printers (especially laser printers) give you great printing flexibility by letting you use fonts that are not built into the printer. These fonts are stored either on your computer or in font cartridges that plug into the printer. The fonts stored on your computer are called *downloadable* fonts because they must be sent, or downloaded, to your printer before the printer can use them. (Downloadable fonts often are called soft fonts.)

WordPerfect enables you to take full advantage of font cartridges and downloadable fonts. You first, however, must purchase the font cartridges and downloadable fonts; they are not included with WordPerfect.

If you have purchased either type of additional font, you must tell WordPerfect that you have the fonts available. You do this after defining the printer by following these steps:

1. From the editing screen, press ⇧Shift F7 to activate the Print command.

   ⌨ Access the **File** pull-down menu and select **Print**.

A

2. Choose Select Printer (S).

3. Highlight the printer you want, and then select Edit (3).

4. From the Select Printer: Edit screen, select Cartridges and Fonts (4).

   WordPerfect displays the Select Printer: Cartridges and Fonts screen. Note that this screen will look slightly different for each printer.

Follow the instructions in the next sections to tell WordPerfect which font cartridges and soft (downloadable) fonts you are using.

Font Cartridges

To tell WordPerfect which font cartridges you are using, follow these steps:

1. From the Select Printer: Cartridges and Fonts screen, highlight the Cartridges line and press ↵Enter.

   WordPerfect displays a list of cartridges available for the printer.

2. Highlight the cartridge you will be using and press *. If you have another cartridge, highlight it and press *.

3. Press F7 (Exit) five times to return to the editing screen.

If you also will be using soft fonts, continue with the next section. Otherwise, move ahead to the section "Selecting an Initial Font."

Soft (Downloadable) Fonts

If you are using soft fonts, you must tell WordPerfect which fonts you are using. In addition, you must tell WordPerfect whether the soft fonts are always loaded in the printer or are simply available for loading when needed during a print job.

To tell WordPerfect which soft fonts you will be using, follow these steps:

1. From the Select Printer: Cartridges and Fonts screen, highlight the Soft Fonts line and press ↵Enter.

   WordPerfect displays a list of font families commonly used with the printer.

2. Highlight the family of fonts you will be using and press ↵Enter.

   WordPerfect displays a list of fonts available for use with the printer.

3. Mark every font you may ever use with a plus sign (+). In this step, you are telling WordPerfect that the marked fonts are available for use. Generally, you should mark every font you have available.

A

470

4. Decide which fonts you will be using frequently and mark each of those with an asterisk (*).

   These are the fonts you will send to the printer every day when you initialize the printer. After initialization, the fonts remain in the printer until you turn it off. Instructions for initializing the printer are contained in the last section of this appendix.

   You should mark only your most frequently used fonts for initialization because they use the memory available in your printer. The more memory you use, the slower your printer will operate, especially when printing graphics.

5. Press F7 (Exit) three times to return to the Select Printer: Edit screen.

   Now you must tell WordPerfect where the soft fonts are stored on your computer.

6. Select Path for Downloadable Fonts and Printer Command Files (6).

7. Type the name of the directory that contains your fonts and press ↵Enter. A recommended directory name is C:\WP51\FONTS.

8. Press F7 (Exit) three times to return to the editing screen.

Now you can move ahead to the next section, "Selecting an Initial Font." When you use soft fonts, you must also initialize your printer, as described in the final section of this chapter.

Selecting an Initial Font

When you define your printer, WordPerfect automatically selects one of the printer's fonts as its initial (or base) font. This font will automatically become the initial font for any document you create while this printer is selected. The initial font should be the font you use most frequently with this printer.

If the selected font is not the one you want, you can change it by following these steps:

1. From the editing screen, press ⇧Shift F7 to activate the Print command.

   ▭ Access the File pull-down menu and select Print.

2. Choose Select Printer (S).

3. Highlight the printer you want, and then select Edit (3).

4. Select Initial Base Font (5).

   WordPerfect displays a list of fonts currently available for the printer.

A

5. Highlight the font you will use most often with this printer, and then choose Select (1).

6. Press [F7] (Exit) three times to return to the editing screen.

Initializing Your Printer

The final step in preparing to use soft (downloadable) fonts is to send your most frequently used fonts to the printer so that they will be immediately available for use. This procedure is called *initializing* the printer. You must initialize the printer when you first turn it on or whenever the printer loses power.

To initialize your printer, follow these steps:

1. Make sure that the printer is turned on and that it is on-line with your computer.

2. From the editing screen, press [⇧Shift][F7] to activate the Print command.

   ⌨️ Access the File pull-down menu and select Print.

3. Check to be sure that the proper printer is selected.

4. Select Initialize Printer (7).

Depending on how many fonts you send to the printer, the initialization process could take anywhere from a few seconds to several minutes. After starting initialization, you can begin sending documents to the printer. They will print immediately after the initialization is completed.

A

B

Summary of WordPerfect 5.1 Commands

Keyboard Commands

Action	Keyboard	Pull-Down Menu or Mouse
Cursor Movement		
Up one line	↑	Point to new position and press left mouse button
Down one line; reformat existing text	↓	Point to new position and press left mouse button
Left one character	←	Point to new position and press left mouse button
Right one character	→	Point to new position and press left mouse button
Move right one word	Ctrl →	Point to new position and press left mouse button
Move left one word	Ctrl ←	Point to new position and press left mouse button
To right end of line	Home → or End	Point to new position and press left mouse button
To left edge of screen	Home ←	
Up one paragraph	Ctrl ↑	
Down one paragraph	Ctrl ↓	
To top of document	Home, Home, ↑	
To bottom of document	Home, Home, ↓	
To top of current page	PgUp	
To top of next page	PgDn	

B

474

Action	Keyboard	Pull-Down Menu or Mouse
To top of screen or preceding screen	`-` (Numeric keypad)	
To bottom of screen or next screen	`+` (Numeric keypad)	
To specific page	`Ctrl` `Home`, page #, `↵Enter`	
To specific character	`Ctrl` `Home`, character	
To top of page	`Ctrl` `Home`, `↑`	
To bottom of page	`Ctrl` `Home`, `↓`	
Editing		
Retrieve file	`⇧Shift` `F10`	**F**ile, **R**etrieve
Delete single character	`Del` or `←Backspace`	
Delete word to left	`Ctrl` `←Backspace`	
Delete word to right	`Home` `Del`	
Delete rest of line	`Ctrl` `End`	
Delete to end of page	`Ctrl` `PgDn`, **Y**es	
Delete sentence	`Ctrl` `F4`, **S**entence, **D**elete	**E**dit, **S**elect, **S**entence, **D**elete
Delete paragraph	`Ctrl` `F4`, **P**aragraph, **D**elete	**E**dit, **S**elect, **P**aragraph, **D**elete
Delete page	`Ctrl` `F4`, **P**age, **D**elete	**E**dit, **S**elect, **P**age, **D**elete
Restore deleted text	`F1`, **R**estore	**E**dit, **U**ndelete, **R**estore
Switch document	`⇧Shift` `F3`	**E**dit, **S**witch Document

B

475

Summary of WordPerfect 5.1 Commands

Action	Keyboard	Pull-Down Menu or Mouse
Split screen (window)	`Ctrl` `F3`, **Window**	**E**dit, **W**indow
Display hidden codes	`Alt` `F3` or `F11`	**E**dit, **R**eveal Codes
Save and continue	`F10`	**F**ile, **S**ave
Save and quit	`F7`, **Yes**	**F**ile, **E**xit, **Yes**
Blocks		
Define block	`Alt` `F4` or `F12`	Move mouse while pressing left button
Rehighlight block	`Alt` `F4`, `Ctrl` `Home`, `Ctrl` `Home`	
Move defined block	`Ctrl` `F4`, **Block**, **Move**; or `Ctrl` `Del`	**E**dit, **M**ove (Cut)
Copy defined block	`Ctrl` `F4`, **Block Copy**; or `Ctrl` `Ins`	**E**dit, **C**opy
Save defined block	`F10`	**F**ile, **S**ave
Print defined block	`⇧Shift` `F7`, **Yes**	**F**ile, **P**rint, **Yes**
Append defined block	`Ctrl` `F4`, **Block**, **Append**	**E**dit, **A**ppend, **To** **File**
Boldface defined block	`F6`	**F**ont, **A**ppearance, **B**old
Underline defined block	`F8`	**F**ont, **A**ppearance, **U**nderline
Center defined block	`⇧Shift` `F5`, **Yes**	**L**ayout, **A**lign, **Center**, **Yes**
Formatting Lines and Paragraphs		
Change left and right margins for current document only	`⇧Shift` `F8`, **Line** **Margins**	**L**ayout, **L**ine, **Margins**

B

476

Action	Keyboard	Pull-Down Menu or Mouse
Change left and right margins permanently	⇧Shift F1, Initial Settings, Initial Codes, ⇧Shift F8, Line, Margins	File, Setup, Initial Settings, Initial Codes, Layout, Line, Margins
Boldface	F5	Font, Appearance, Bold
Underline	F8	Font, Appearance, Underline
Change size of base font	Ctrl F8, Size	Font, Size
Change appearance of base font	Ctrl F8, Appearance	Font, Appearance
View tab stop settings	Ctrl F3, Window, 23, ↵Enter	Edit, Window, 23, ↵Enter
Change tab stops	⇧Shift F8, Line, Tab Set	Layout, Line, Tab Set
Indent text	Tab ⇥	
Indent paragraph	F4	Layout, Align, Indent-→
Indent paragraph from both margins	⇧Shift F4	Layout, Align, Indent-→-←
Create flush-right text	Alt F5	Layout, Align, Flush Right
Change line spacing	⇧Shift F8, Line, Line Spacing	Layout, Line, Line Spacing
Formatting Pages		
Change paper size	⇧Shift F8, Page, Paper Size/Type, Select	Layout, Page, Paper Size/Type, Select

B

Summary of WordPerfect 5.1 Commands

Action	Keyboard	Pull-Down Menu or Mouse
Change top and bottom margins	`Shift` `F8`, **Page**, **Margins Top/Bottom**	**Layout**, **Page**, **Margins Top/Bottom**
Center page (top to bottom)	`Shift` `F8`, **Page**, **Center Page (top to bottom)**, **Yes**	**Layout**, **Page**, **Center Page (top to bottom)**, **Yes**
Advance page	`Shift` `F8`, **Other**, **Advance**	**Layout**, **Other**, **Advance**
Create header	`Shift` `F8`, **Page**, **Headers, Header A** or **Header B**	**Layout**, **Page**, **Headers, Header A** or **Header B**
Create footer	`Shift` `F8`, **Page**, **Footers, Footer A** or **Footer B**	**Layout**, **Page**, **Footers, Footer A** or **Footer B**
Edit header	`Shift` `F8`, **Page**, **Headers, Header A** or **Header B, Edit**	**Layout**, **Page**, **Headers, Header A** or **Header B, Edit**
Edit footer	`Shift` `F8`, **Page**, **Footers, Footer A** or **Footer B, Edit**	**Layout**, **Page**, **Footers, Footer A** or **Footer B, Edit**
Proofreading		
Search forward for text	`F2`	**Search**, **Forward**
Search backward for text	`Shift` `F2`	**Search**, **Backward**
Search and replace text	`Alt` `F2`	**Search**, **Replace**
Check spelling of word, page, or document	`Ctrl` `F2`, **Word** or **Page** or **Document**	**Tools**, **Spell**, **Word** or **Page** or **Document**
Check spelling of defined block	`Ctrl` `F2`	**Tools**, **Spell**
Access thesaurus	`Alt` `F1`	**Tools**, **Thesaurus**

B

Action	Keyboard	Pull-Down Menu or Mouse
Printing		
Print single page	⇧Shift F7, Page	File, Print, Page
Print full document	⇧Shift F7, Full	File, Print, Full
Print selected pages	⇧Shift F7, Multiple Pages	File, Print, Multiple Pages
Print defined block	⇧Shift F7, Yes	File, Print, Yes
Print document on disk	⇧Shift F7, Document on Disk	File, Print, Document on Disk
Print document on disk from the List Files screen	F5, ↵Enter, highlight file, Print	File, List Files, ↵Enter, highlight file, Print
Control printing	⇧Shift F7, Control Printer	File, Print, Control Printer
View document	⇧Shift F7, View Document	File, Print, View Document
Managing Files		
List files	F5	File, List Files
Search for file name	F5, ↵Enter, Find, Name	File, List Files, ↵Enter, Find, Name
Create or edit document summary	⇧Shift F8, Document, Summary	Layout, Document, Summary
Macros		
Create macro	Ctrl F10	Tools, Macro, Define
Run descriptive macro	Alt F10, enter name	Tools, Macro, Execute, enter name
Edit macro	Ctrl F10, enter name, Edit	Tools, Macro, Define, enter name, Edit

B

Summary of WordPerfect 5.1 Commands

Action	Keyboard	Pull-Down Menu or Mouse
Merging Documents		
Select merge codes	`⇧Shift` `F9`	Tools, Merge Codes
Merge files	`Ctrl` `F9`, **Merge**, enter primary and secondary file names	Tools, **Merge**, enter primary and secondary file names
Sorting		
Sort	`Ctrl` `F9`, **Sort**	Tools, **Sort**
Paragraph sort	`Ctrl` `F9`, **Sort**, enter input and output, **Type**, **Paragraph**, **Perform Action**	Tools, **Sort**, enter input and output, **Type**, **Paragraph**, **Perform Action**
Line sort	`Ctrl` `F9`, **Sort**, enter input and output, **Type**, **Line**, **Perform Action**	Tools, **Sort**, enter input and output, **Type**, **Line**, **Perform Action**
Merge sort	`Ctrl` `F9`, **Sort**, enter input and output, **Type**, **Merge**, **Perform Action**	Tools, **Sort**, enter input and output, **Type**, **Merge**, **Perform Action**
Select sort order	`Ctrl` `F9`, **Sort**, enter input and output, **Order**	Tools, **Sort**, enter input and output, **Order**
Specify sort keys	`Ctrl` `F9`, **Sort**, enter input and output, **Keys**	Tools, **Sort**, enter input and output, **Keys**

B

Action	Keyboard	Pull-Down Menu or Mouse
Styles		
Create open style	Alt F8, **C**reate **N**ame, type name, ⏎Enter, **T**ype, **O**pen, **D**escription, type description, ⏎Enter, **C**odes, insert codes and text, F7 three times	**L**ayout, **S**tyles, **N**ame, type name, ⏎Enter, **T**ype, **O**pen, **D**escription, type description, ⏎Enter, **C**odes, insert codes and text, F7 three times
Create paired style	Alt F8, **C**reate, **N**ame, type name, ⏎Enter, **D**escription, type description, ⏎Enter, **C**odes, enter beginning codes, →, enter ending codes, F7, **E**nter; **H**rt, **O**ff, or Off/**O**n, F7 twice	**L**ayout, **S**tyles, **C**reate, **N**ame, type name, ⏎Enter, **D**escription, type description, ⏎Enter, **C**odes, enter beginning codes, →, enter ending codes, F7, **E**nter; **H**rt, **O**ff, or Off/**O**n, F7 twice
Use open style	Home, Home, Home, ↑, Alt F8 highlight style, **O**n, type text	Home, Home, Home, ↑, **L**ayout, **S**tyles, highlight style, **O**n, type text
Use paired style with existing text	Highlight block, Alt F8, highlight style, **O**n	Highlight block, **L**ayout, **S**tyles, highlight style, **O**n
Use paired style with text you are about to type	Alt F8, highlight style, **O**n, type text; ⏎Enter, or Alt F8 and **O**ff	**L**ayout, **S**tyles, highlight style, **O**n, type text; ⏎Enter, or **L**ayout, **S**tyles, and **O**ff
Edit style definition	Alt F8, highlight style, **E**dit, make changes, F7 twice	**L**ayout, **S**tyles, highlight style, **E**dit, make changes, F7 twice

B

Action	Keyboard	Pull-Down Menu or Mouse
Delete style definition	Alt F8, highlight style, Delete; Leaving Codes, Including Codes, or Definition Only	Layout, Styles, highlight style, Delete; Leaving Codes, Including Codes, or Definition Only
Save definitions to style	Alt F8, Save, type file name, ↵Enter, F7	Layout, Styles, Save type file name, ↵Enter, F7
Retrieve style library file	Alt F8, Retrieve, type file name, ↵Enter, Y or N, F7	Layout, Styles, Retrieve, type file name, ↵Enter, Y or N, F7
Update document with current style	Retrieve document, Alt F8, Update, F7, save document	Retrieve document, Layout Styles, Update, F7, save document
Specify default style library file	⇧Shift F1, Location of Files, Style Files, type file name, ↵Enter, F7	File, Setup, Location of Files, Style Files, type file name, ↵Enter, F7

Columns

Action	Keyboard	Pull-Down Menu or Mouse
Define newspaper-style columns	Alt F7, Columns, Define, Type, Newspaper, F7, On	Layout, Columns, Define, Type, Newspaper, F7, On
Display a single newspaper-style column	⇧Shift F1, Display, Edit-Screen Options, Side-by-side Columns Display, No	File, Setup, Display, Edit-Screen Options, Side-by Screen Options, Side-by-side Columns Display, No
Define parallel columns	Alt F7, Columns, Define, Type, Parallel or Parallel with Block Protect, F7, On	Layout, Columns, Define, Type, Parallel or Parallel with Block Protect, F7, On

B

482

Action	Keyboard	*Pull-Down Menu or Mouse*
Tables		
Create table structure	Alt F7, Tables, Create, enter column and row values, F7	Layout, Tables, Create, enter column and row values, F7
Customizing		
Access Setup menu	⇧Shift F1	File, Setup
Customize mouse	⇧Shift F1, Mouse, enter information, F7	File, Setup, Mouse, enter information, F7
Designate type of mouse	⇧Shift F1, Mouse, Type, highlight mouse, Select, Auto-select or Port, F7	File, Setup, Mouse, Type, highlight mouse, Select, Auto-select or Port, F7
Change mouse to left-hand operation	⇧Shift F1, Mouse, Left-Handed Mouse, Yes, F7	File, Setup, Mouse, Left-Handed Mouse, Yes, F7
Adjust screen display	⇧Shift F1, Display, enter information, F7	File, Setup, Display, enter information, F7
Change display colors	⇧Shift F1, Display, Colors/Fonts/ Attribute, Screen Colors, highlight color and press letter, F7 twice	File, Setup, Display, Colors/ Fonts/ Attribute, Screen Colors, highlight color and press letter, F7 twice
Customize display of editing screens	⇧Shift F1, Display, Edit-Screen Options, choose option, F7	File, Setup, Display, Edit-Screen Options, choose option, F7
Change environment options	⇧Shift F1, Environment, enter information, F7	File, Setup, Environment, enter information, F7

B

483

Pull-Down Menu or Action	Keyboard	Mouse
Select automatic backup	⇧Shift F1, **B**ackup Options, **T**imed Document Backup or **O**riginal Document Backup, F7	**F**ile, **S**etup, **E**nvironment, **B**ackup Options, **T**imed Document Backup or **O**riginal Document Backup, F7
Set cursor speed	⇧Shift F1, **E**nvironment, **C**ursor Speed, type number **1-5**, F7	**F**ile, **S**etup, **E**nvironment, **C**ursor Speed, type number **1-5**, F7
Use Fast Save	⇧Shift F1, **E**nvironment, **F**ast Save, **Y**es, F7	**F**ile, **S**etup, **E**nvironment, **F**ast Save, **Y**es, F7
Select units of measure	⇧Shift F1 **E**nvironment, **U**nits of Measure, **1**, enter units, **2**, enter units, F7	**F**ile, **S**etup, **E**nvironment, **U**nits of Measure, **1**, enter units, **2**, enter units, F7
Change initial settings	⇧Shift F1, **I**nitial Settings, enter information, F7	**F**ile, **S**etup, **I**nitial Settings, enter information, F7
Select a keyboard definition	⇧Shift F1, **K**eyboard Layout, highlight definition, **S**elect, F7	**F**ile, **S**etup, **K**eyboard Layout, highlight definition, **S**elect, F7
Return to original keyboard	⇧Shift F1, **K**eyboard Layout, **O**riginal, F7	**F**ile, **S**etup, **K**eyboard Layout, **O**riginal, F7
Edit keyboard definition	⇧Shift F1, **K**eyboard Layout, highlight definition, **E**dit, choose option, F7	**F**ile, **S**etup, **K**eyboard Layout, highlight definition, **E**dit, choose option, F7

B

Action	Keyboard	Pull-Down Menu or Mouse
Specify subdirectory for files	⇧Shift F1, Location of Files, select type, type drive and directory, ↵Enter, F7	File, Setup, Location of Files, select type, type drive and directory, ↵Enter, F7

Special Characters and Equations

Action	Keyboard	Pull-Down Menu or Mouse
Insert special character	Ctrl 2 or Ctrl V, type number of character set, type a comma, type number of character, ↵Enter	Font, Characters, type number of character set, type a comma, type number of character, ↵Enter
Combine two characters	Ctrl 2 or Ctrl V, type first character, type second character	Font, Characters, type first character, type second character
Create special character with Overstrike	⇧Shift F8, Other, Overstrike, Create, type each character, ↵Enter, F7	Layout, Other, Overstrike, Create, type each character, ↵Enter, F7
Create superscript or subscript	Ctrl F8, Size, Suprscpt or Subscpt, type characters, →	Font, Superscript or Subscript, type characters, →
Access equation editor	Alt F8, Equation, Create, Edit	Graphics, Equation, Create, Edit
Display equation in Display Window	Ctrl F3	Click Screen
Access Equation Palette	F5	Click List
Scroll through Palette menus	PgUp or PgDn	Click PgUp or PgDn
Save equation as separate file	F10, type file name, ↵Enter	F10, type file name, ↵Enter

B

485

Action	Keyboard	Pull-Down Menu or Mouse
Retrieve equation file	⬆Shift F10, type file name, ↵Enter	⬆Shift F10, type file name, ↵Enter
Save equation files in a graphics directory	⬆Shift F1, Location of Files, Graphics, type path, ↵Enter, F7	File, Setup, Location of Files, Graphics, type path, ↵Enter, F7

Referencing

Action	Keyboard	Pull-Down Menu or Mouse
Create footnote	Ctrl F7, Footnote, Create, type text, F7	Layout, Footnote, Create, type text, F7
Create endnote	Ctrl F7, Endnote, Create, type text, F7	Layout, Endnote, Create, type text, F7
Edit footnote	Ctrl F7, Footnote, Edit, enter number, make changes, F7	Layout, Footnote, Edit, enter number, make changes, F7
Edit endnote	Ctrl F7, Endnote, Edit, enter number, make changes, F7	Layout, Endnote, Edit, enter number, make changes, F7
Generate endnotes	Alt F5, Generate, Generate Tables, Indexes, Cross-References, etc., Yes	Mark, Generate, Generate Tables, Indexes, Cross-References, etc., Yes
Change footnote options	Ctrl F7, Footnote, Options	Layout, Footnote, Options
Change endnote options	Ctrl F7, Endnote, Options	Layout, Endnote, Options
Turn on outline	⬆Shift F5, Outline, On	Tools, Outline, On
Turn off outline	⬆Shift F5, Outline, Off	Tools, Outline, Off

B

Action	Keyboard	Pull-Down Menu or Mouse
Change numbering style	⇧Shift F5, **Define**, select style, F7, F7, Ctrl F3, **Rewrite**	**Tools, Define**, select style, F7, F7, Ctrl F3, **Rewrite**
Turn on automatic line numbering	⇧Shift F8, **Line**, Line **Numbering**, Yes, ↵Enter, F7	**Layout, Line**, Line **Numbering**, Yes, ↵Enter, F7
Turn off automatic line numbering	⇧Shift F8, **Line**, Line **Numbering**, No, F7	**Layout, Line**, Line **Numbering**, No, F7
Create a document comment	Ctrl F5, **Comment**, **Create**, type comment, F7	**Edit, Comment**, **Create**, type comment, F7
Edit a document comment	Ctrl F5, **Comment**, **Edit**, edit comment, F7	**Edit, Comment, Edit**, edit comment, F7
Convert a comment to text	Ctrl F5, **Comment**, **Convert to Text**	**Edit, Comment**, **Convert to Text**
Convert text to a comment	**Block** text, Ctrl F5, **Yes**	**Block** text, **Edit**, **Comment Create**, Yes
Mark a Table of Contents entry	**Block** text, Alt F5, **ToC**, 1, ↵Enter	**Block** text, **Mark**, **ToC**, 1, ↵Enter
Define the style for a Table of Contents	Ctrl F5, **Define**, **Table of Contents**	**Mark, Define, Table of Contents**
Generate a Table of Contents	Ctrl F5, **Generate**, **Generate Tables**, Indexes, Cross-References, etc., Yes	**Mark, Generate**, **Generate Tables**, Indexes, Cross-References, etc., Yes

B

Summary of WordPerfect 5.1 Commands

Action	Keyboard	Pull-Down Menu or Mouse
Graphics		
Select type of box	Alt F9, **F**igure or **T**able Box or Te**x**t Box or **U**ser Box or **E**quation	**G**raphics, **F**igure or **T**able Box or Te**x**t Box or **U**ser Box or **E**quation
Select box options	Alt F9, select box type, **O**ptions	**G**raphics, select box type, **O**ptions
Create graphics box	Alt F9, select box type, **C**reate	**G**raphics, select box type, **C**reate
Change box number	Alt F9, select box type, **N**ew Number, enter new number	**G**raphics, select box type, **N**ew Number, enter new number
Change box type	Alt F9, select old box type, **E**dit, enter number to change, Alt F9, select new box type, F7	**G**raphics, select old box type, **E**dit, enter number to change, Alt F9, select new box type, F7

B

Pull-Down Menu Commands

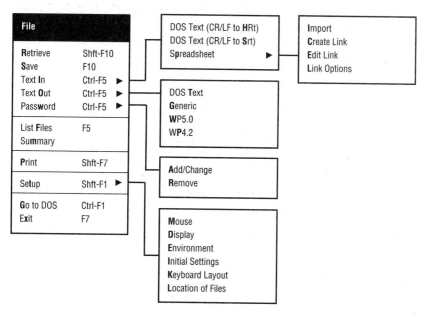

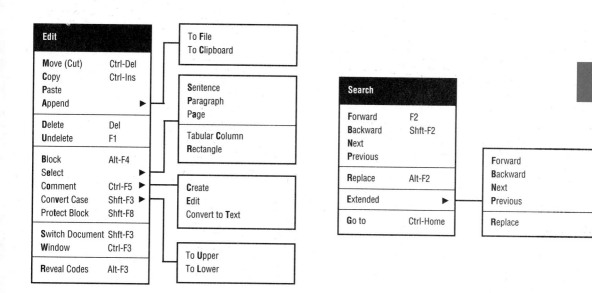

Summary of WordPerfect 5.1 Commands

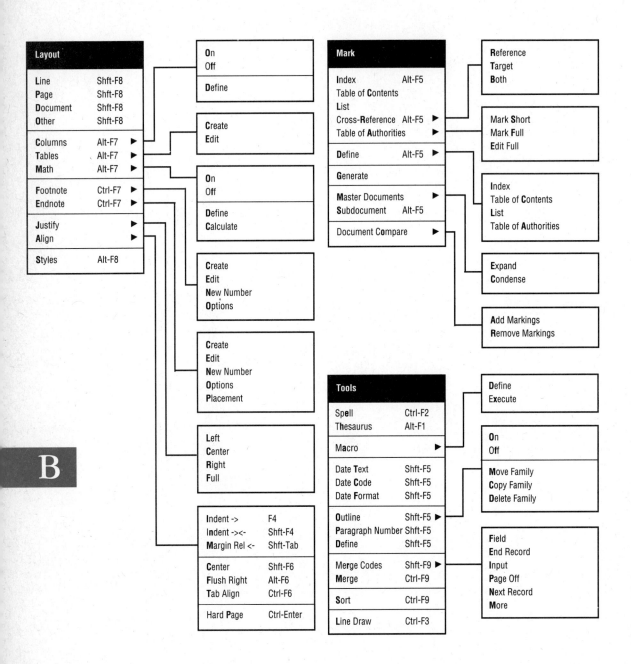

Layout

Line	Shft-F8
Page	Shft-F8
Document	Shft-F8
Other	Shft-F8
Columns	Alt-F7 ▶
Tables	Alt-F7 ▶
Math	Alt-F7 ▶
Footnote	Ctrl-F7 ▶
Endnote	Ctrl-F7 ▶
Justify	▶
Align	▶
Styles	Alt-F8

On
Off

Define

Create
Edit

On
Off

Define
Calculate

Create
Edit
New Number
Options

Create
Edit
New Number
Options
Placement

Left
Center
Right
Full

Indent ->	F4
Indent -><-	Shft-F4
Margin Rel <-	Shft-Tab
Center	Shft-F6
Flush Right	Alt-F6
Tab Align	Ctrl-F6
Hard Page	Ctrl-Enter

Mark

Index	Alt-F5
Table of Contents	
List	
Cross-Reference	Alt-F5 ▶
Table of Authorities	▶
Define	Alt-F5 ▶
Generate	
Master Documents	▶
Subdocument	Alt-F5
Document Compare	▶

Reference
Target
Both

Mark Short
Mark Full
Edit Full

Index
Table of Contents
List
Table of Authorities

Expand
Condense

Add Markings
Remove Markings

Tools

Spell	Ctrl-F2
Thesaurus	Alt-F1
Macro	▶
Date Text	Shft-F5
Date Code	Shft-F5
Date Format	Shft-F5
Outline	Shft-F5 ▶
Paragraph Number	Shft-F5
Define	Shft-F5
Merge Codes	Shft-F9 ▶
Merge	Ctrl-F9
Sort	Ctrl-F9
Line Draw	Ctrl-F3

Define
Execute

On
Off

Move Family
Copy Family
Delete Family

Field
End Record
Input
Page Off
Next Record
More

B

490

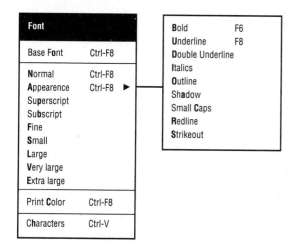

Font

Base Font	Ctrl-F8
Normal	Ctrl-F8
Appearence	Ctrl-F8 ▶
Superscript	
Subscript	
Fine	
Small	
Large	
Very large	
Extra large	
Print Color	Ctrl-F8
Characters	Ctrl-V

Bold	F6
Underline	F8
Double Underline	
Italics	
Outline	
Shadow	
Small Caps	
Redline	
Strikeout	

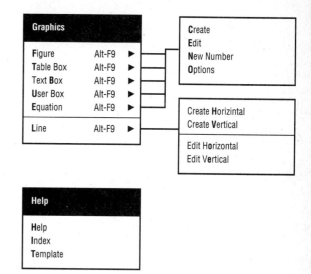

Graphics

Figure	Alt-F9 ▶
Table Box	Alt-F9 ▶
Text Box	Alt-F9 ▶
User Box	Alt-F9 ▶
Equation	Alt-F9 ▶
Line	Alt-F9 ▶

Create
Edit
New Number
Options

Create Horizintal
Create Vertical

Edit Horizontal
Edit Vertical

Help

Help
Index
Template

B

Index

Computer Books from Que Mean PC Performance!

Spreadsheets

1-2-3 Beyond the Basics	$24.95
1-2-3 for DOS Release 2.3 Quick Reference	$ 9.95
1-2-3 for DOS Release 2.3 QuickStart	$19.95
1-2-3 for DOS Release 3.1+ Quick Reference	$ 9.95
1-2-3 for DOS Release 3.1+ QuickStart	$19.95
1-2-3 for Windows Quick Reference	$ 9.95
1-2-3 for Windows QuickStart	$19.95
1-2-3 Personal Money Manager	$29.95
1-2-3 Power Macros	$39.95
1-2-3 Release 2.2 QueCards	$19.95
Easy 1-2-3	$19.95
Easy Excel	$19.95
Easy Quattro Pro	$19.95
Excel 3 for Windows QuickStart	$19.95
Excel for Windows Quick Reference	$ 9.95
Look Your Best with 1-2-3	$24.95
Quattro Pro 3 QuickStart	$19.95
Quattro Pro Quick Reference	$ 9.95
Using 1-2-3 for DOS Release 2.3, Special Edition	$29.95
Using 1-2-3 for Windows	$29.95
Using 1-2-3 for DOS Release 3.1+, Special Edition	$29.95
Using Excel 4 for Windows, Special Edition	$29.95
Using Quattro Pro 4, Special Edition	$27.95
Using Quattro Pro for Windows	$24.95
Using SuperCalc5, 2nd Edition	$29.95

Databases

dBASE III Plus Handbook, 2nd Edition	$24.95
dBASE IV 1.1 Quick Reference	$ 9.95
dBASE IV 1.1 QuickStart	$19.95
Introduction to Databases	$19.95
Paradox 3.5 Quick Reference	$ 9.95
Paradox Quick Reference, 2nd Edition	$ 9.95
Using AlphaFOUR	$24.95
Using Clipper, 3rd Edition	$29.95
Using DataEase	$24.95
Using dBASE IV	$29.95
Using FoxPro 2	$29.95
Using ORACLE	$29.95
Using Paradox 3.5, Special Edition	$29.95
Using Paradox for Windows	$26.95
Using Paradox, Special Edition	$29.95
Using PC-File	$24.95
Using R:BASE	$29.95

Business Applications

CheckFree Quick Reference	$ 9.95
Easy Quicken	$19.95
Microsoft Works Quick Reference	$ 9.95
Norton Utilities 6 Quick Reference	$ 9.95
PC Tools 7 Quick Reference	$ 9.95
Q&A 4 Database Techniques	$29.95
Q&A 4 Quick Reference	$ 9.95
Q&A 4 QuickStart	$19.95
Q&A 4 Que Cards	$19.95
Que's Computer User's Dictionary, 2nd Edition	$10.95
Que's Using Enable	$29.95
Quicken 5 Quick Reference	$ 9.95
SmartWare Tips, Tricks, and Traps, 2nd Edition	$26.95
Using DacEasy, 2nd Edition	$24.95
Using Microsoft Money	$19.95
Using Microsoft Works: IBM Version	$22.95
Using Microsoft Works for Windows, Special Edition	$24.95
Using MoneyCounts	$19.95
Using Pacioli 2000	$19.95
Using Norton Utilities 6	$24.95
Using PC Tools Deluxe 7	$24.95
Using PFS: First Choice	$22.95
Using PFS: WindowWorks	$24.95
Using Q&A 4	$27.95
Using Quicken 5	$19.95
Using Quicken for Windows	$19.95
Using Smart	$29.95
Using TimeLine	$24.95
Using TurboTax: 1992 Edition	$19.95

CAD

AutoCAD Quick Reference, 2nd Edition	$ 8.95
Using AutoCAD, 3rd Edition	$29.95

Word Processing

Easy WordPerfect	$19.95
Easy WordPerfect for Windows	$19.95
Look Your Best with WordPerfect 5.1	$24.95
Look Your Best with WordPerfect forWindows	$24.95
Microsoft Word Quick Reference	$ 9.95
Using Ami Pro	$24.95
Using LetterPerfect	$22.95
Using Microsoft Word 5.5: IBM Version, 2nd Edition	$24.95
Using MultiMate	$24.95
Using PC-Write	$22.95
Using Professional Write	$22.95
Using Professional Write Plus for Windows	$24.95
Using Word for Windows 2, Special Edition	$27.95
Using WordPerfect 5	$27.95
Using WordPerfect 5.1, Special Edition	$27.95
Using WordPerfect for Windows, Special Edition	$29.95
Using WordStar 7	$19.95
Using WordStar, 3rd Edition	$27.95
WordPerfect 5.1 Power Macros	$39.95
WordPerfect 5.1 QueCards	$19.95
WordPerfect 5.1 Quick Reference	$ 9.95
WordPerfect 5.1 QuickStart	$19.95
WordPerfect 5.1 Tips, Tricks, and Traps	$24.95
WordPerfect for Windows Power Pack	$39.95
WordPerfect for Windows Quick Reference	$ 9.95
WordPerfect for Windows Quick Start	$19.95
WordPerfect Power Pack	$39.95
WordPerfect Quick Reference	$ 9.95

Hardware/Systems

Batch File and Macros Quick Reference	$ 9.95
Computerizing Your Small Business	$19.95
DR DOS 6 Quick Reference	$ 9.95
Easy DOS	$19.95
Easy Windows	$19.95
Fastback Quick Reference	$ 8.95
Hard Disk Quick Reference	$ 8.95
Hard Disk Quick Reference, 1992 Edition	$ 9.95
Introduction to Hard Disk Management	$24.95
Introduction to Networking	$24.95
Introduction to PC Communications	$24.95
Introduction to Personal Computers, 2nd Edition	$19.95
Introduction to UNIX	$24.95
Laplink Quick Reference	$ 9.95
MS-DOS 5 Que Cards	$19.95
MS-DOS 5 Quick Reference	$ 9.95
MS-DOS 5 QuickStart	$19.95
MS-DOS Quick Reference	$ 8.95
MS-DOS QuickStart, 2nd Edition	$19.95
Networking Personal Computers, 3rd Edition	$24.95
Que's Computer Buyer's Guide, 1992 Edition	$14.95
Que's Guide to CompuServe	$12.95
Que's Guide to DataRecovery	$29.95
Que's Guide to XTree	$12.95
Que's MS-DOS User's Guide, Special Edition	$29.95
Que's PS/1 Book	$22.95
TurboCharging MS-DOS	$24.95
Upgrading and Repairing PCs	$29.95
Upgrading and Repairing PCs, 2nd Edition	$29.95
Upgrading to MS-DOS 5	$14.95
Using GeoWorks Pro	$24.95
Using Microsoft Windows 3, 2nd Edition	$24.95
Using MS-DOS 5	$24.95
Using Novell NetWare, 2nd Edition	$29.95
Using OS/2 2.0	$24.95
Using PC DOS, 3rd Edition	$27.95
Using Prodigy	$19.95
Using UNIX	$29.95
Using Windows 3.1	$26.95
Using Your Hard Disk	$29.95
Windows 3 Quick Reference	$ 8.95
Windows 3 QuickStart	$19.95
Windows 3.1 Quick Reference	$ 9.95
Windows 3.1 QuickStart	$19.95

Desktop Publishing/Graphics

CorelDRAW! Quick Reference	$ 8.95
Harvard Graphics 3 Quick Reference	$ 9.95
Harvard Graphics Quick Reference	$ 9.95
Que's Using Ventura Publisher	$29.95
Using DrawPerfect	$24.95
Using Freelance Plus	$24.95
Using Harvard Graphics 3	$29.95
Using Harvard Graphics for Windows	$24.95
Using Harvard Graphics, 2nd Edition	$24.95
Using Microsoft Publisher	$22.95
Using PageMaker 4 for Windows	$29.95
Using PFS: First Publisher, 2nd Edition	$24.95
Using PowerPoint	$24.95
Using Publish It!	$24.95

Macintosh/Apple II

Easy Macintosh	$19.95
HyperCard 2 QuickStart	$19.95
PageMaker 4 for the Mac Quick Reference	$ 9.95
The Big Mac Book, 2nd Edition	$29.95
The Little Mac Book	$12.95
QuarkXPress 3.1 Quick Reference	$ 9.95
Que's Big Mac Book, 3rd Edition	$29.95
Que's Little Mac Book, 2nd Edition	$12.95
Que's Mac Classic Book	$24.95
Que's Macintosh Multimedia Handbook	$24.95
System 7 Quick Reference	$ 9.95
Using 1-2-3 for the Mac	$24.95
Using AppleWorks, 3rd Edition	$24.95
Using Excel 3 for the Macintosh	$24.95
Using FileMaker Pro	$24.95
Using MacDraw Pro	$24.95
Using MacroMind Director	$29.95
Using MacWrite Pro	$24.95
Using Microsoft Word 5 for the Mac	$27.95
Using Microsoft Works: Macintosh Version, 2nd Edition	$24.95
Using Microsoft Works for the Mac	$24.95
Using PageMaker 4 for the Macintosh	$24.95
Using Quicken 3 for the Mac	$19.95
Using the Macintosh with System 7	$24.95
Using Word for the Mac, Special Edition	$24.95
Using WordPerfect 2 for the Mac	$24.95
Word for the Mac Quick Reference	$ 9.95

Programming/Technical

Borland C++ 3 By Example	$21.95
Borland C++ 3 Programmer's Reference	$29.95
C By Example	$21.95
C Programmer's Toolkit, 2nd Edition	$39.95
Clipper Programmer's Reference	$29.95
DOS Programmer's Reference, 3rd Edition	$29.95
FoxPro Programmer's Reference	$29.95
Network Programming in C	$49.95
Paradox Programmer's Reference	$29.95
Programming in Windows 3.1	$39.95
QBasic By Example	$21.95
Turbo Pascal 6 By Example	$21.95
Turbo Pascal 6 Programmer's Reference	$29.95
UNIX Programmer's Reference	$29.95
UNIX Shell Commands Quick Reference	$ 8.95
Using Assembly Language, 2nd Edition	$29.95
Using Assembly Language, 3rd Edition	$29.95
Using BASIC	$24.95
Using Borland C++	$29.95
Using Borland C++ 3, 2nd Edition	$29.95
Using C	$29.95
Using Microsoft C	$29.95
Using QBasic	$24.95
Using QuickBASIC 4	$24.95
Using QuickC for Windows	$29.95
Using Turbo Pascal 6, 2nd Edition	$29.95
Using Turbo Pascal for Windows	$29.95
Using Visual Basic	$29.95
Visual Basic by Example	$21.95
Visual Basic Programmer's Reference	$29.95
Windows 3.1 Programmer's Reference	$39.95

For More Information,
Call Toll Free!
1-800-428-5331

All prices and titles subject to change without notice.
Non-U.S. prices may be higher. Printed in the U.S.A.

Teach Yourself
with QuickStarts from Que!

Personal computing is easy when you're using Que!

**Using 1-2-3 for DOS Release 2.3,
Special Edition**
$29.95 USA
0-88022-727-8, 584 pp., 7³/₈ x 9¹/₄

**Using 1-2-3 for DOS Release 3.1+,
Special Edition**
$29.95 USA
0-88022-843-1, 584 pp., 7³/₈ x 9¹/₄

Using 1-2-3 for Windows
$29.95 USA
0-88022-724-9, 584 pp., 7³/₈ x 9¹/₄

Using 1-2-3/G
$29.95 USA
0-88022-549-7, 584 pp., 7³/₈ x 9¹/₄

Using AlphaFOUR
$24.95 USA
0-88022-890-3, 500 pp., 7³/₈ x 9¹/₄

Using AmiPro
$24.95 USA
0-88022-738-9, 584 pp., 7³/₈ x 9¹/₄

Using Assembly Language, 3rd Edition
$29.95 USA
0-88022-884-9, 900 pp., 7³/₈ x 9¹/₄

Using BASIC
$24.95 USA
0-88022-537-8, 584 pp., 7³/₈ x 9¹/₄

Using Borland C++, 2nd Edition
$29.95 USA
0-88022-901-2, 1,300 pp., 7³/₈ x 9¹/₄

Using C
$29.95 USA
0-88022-571-8, 950 pp., 7³/₈ x 9¹/₄

Using Clipper, 3rd Edition
$29.95 USA
0-88022-885-7, 750 pp., 7³/₈ x 9¹/₄

Using DacEasy, 2nd Edition
$24.95 USA
0-88022-510-6, 584 pp., 7³/₈ x 9¹/₄

Using DataEase
$24.95 USA
0-88022-465-7, 584 pp., 7³/₈ x 9¹/₄

Using dBASE IV
$24.95 USA
0-88022-551-3, 584 pp., 7³/₈ x 9¹/₄

**Using Excel 3 for Windows,
Special Edition**
$24.95 USA
0-88022-685-4, 584 pp., 7³/₈ x 9¹/₄

Using FoxPro 2
$24.95 USA
0-88022-703-6, 584 pp., 7³/₈ x 9¹/₄

Using Freelance Plus
$24.95 USA
0-88022-528-9, 584 pp., 7³/₈ x 9¹/₄

Using GeoWorks Ensemble
$24.95 USA
0-88022-748-6, 584 pp., 7³/₈ x 9¹/₄

Using Harvard Graphics 3
$24.95 USA
0-88022-735-4, 584 pp., 7³/₈ x 9¹/₄

Using Harvard Graphics for Windows
$24.95 USA
0-88022-755-9, 700 pp., 7³/₈ x 9¹/₄

Using LetterPoerfect
$24.95 USA
0-88022-667-6, 584 pp., 7³/₈ x 9¹/₄

Using Microsoft C
$24.95 USA
0-88022-809-1, 584 pp., 7³/₈ x 9¹/₄

Using Microsoft Money
$19.95 USA
0-88022-914-4, 400 pp., 7³/₈ x 9¹/₄

Using Microsoft Publisher
$22.95 USA
0-88022-915-2, 450 pp., 7³/₈ x 9¹/₄

**Using Microsoft Windows 3,
2nd Edition**
$24.95 USA
0-88022-509-2, 584 pp., 7³/₈ x 9¹/₄

**Using Microsoft Word 5.5: IBM
Version, 2nd Edition**
$24.95 USA
0-88022-642-0, 584 pp., 7³/₈ x 9¹/₄

**Using Microsoft Works for Windows,
Special Edition**
$24.95 USA
0-88022-757-5, 584 pp., 7³/₈ x 9¹/₄

Using Microsoft Works: IBM Version
$24.95 USA
0-88022-467-3, 584 pp., 7³/₈ x 9¹/₄

Using MoneyCounts
$24.95 USA
0-88022-696-X, 584 pp., 7³/₈ x 9¹/₄

Using MS-DOS 5
$24.95 USA
0-88022-668-4, 584 pp., 7³/₈ x 9¹/₄

Using Norton Utilities 6
$24.95 USA
0-88022-861-X, 584 pp., 7³/₈ x 9¹/₄

Using Novell NetWare, 2nd Edition
$24.95 USA
0-88022-756-7, 584 pp., 7³/₈ x 9¹/₄

Using ORACLE
$24.95 USA
0-88022-506-8, 584 pp., 7³/₈ x 9¹/₄

Using OS/2 2.0
$24.95 USA
0-88022-863-6, 584 pp., 7³/₈ x 9¹/₄

Using Pacioli 2000
$24.95 USA
0-88022-780-X, 584 pp., 7³/₈ x 9¹/₄

Using PageMaker 4 for Windows
$24.95 USA
0-88022-607-2, 584 pp., 7³/₈ x 9¹/₄

Using Paradox 4, Special Edition
$29.95 USA
0-88022-822-9, 900 pp., 7³/₈ x 9¹/₄

**Using Paradox for Windows,
Special Edition**
$29.95 USA
0-88022-823-7, 750 pp., 7³/₈ x 9¹/₄

Using PC DOS, 3rd Edition
$24.95 USA
0-88022-409-3, 584 pp., 7³/₈ x 9¹/₄

Using PC Tools 7
$24.95 USA
0-88022-733-8, 584 pp., 7³/₈ x 9¹/₄

Using PC-File
$24.95 USA
0-88022-695-1, 584 pp., 7³/₈ x 9¹/₄

Using PC-Write
$24.95 USA
0-88022-654-4, 584 pp., 7³/₈ x 9¹/₄

Using PFS: First Choice
$24.95 USA
0-88022-454-1, 584 pp., 7³/₈ x 9¹/₄

**Using PFS: First Publisher,
2nd Edition**
$24.95 USA
0-88022-591-2, 584 pp., 7³/₈ x 9¹/₄

Using PFS: WindowWorks
$24.95 USA
0-88022-751-6, 584 pp., 7³/₈ x 9¹/₄

Using PowerPoint
$24.95 USA
0-88022-698-6, 584 pp., 7³/₈ x 9¹/₄

Using Prodigy
$24.95 USA
0-88022-658-7, 584 pp., 7³/₈ x 9¹/₄

Using Professional Write
$24.95 USA
0-88022-490-8, 584 pp., 7³/₈ x 9¹/₄

**Using Professional Write Plus for
Windows**
$24.95 USA
0-88022-754-0, 584 pp., 7³/₈ x 9¹/₄

Using Publish It!
$24.95 USA
0-88022-660-9, 584 pp., 7³/₈ x 9¹/₄

Using Q&A 4
$24.95 USA
0-88022-643-9, 584 pp., 7³/₈ x 9¹/₄

Using QBasic
$24.95 USA
0-88022-713-3, 584 pp., 7³/₈ x 9¹/₄

Using Quattro Pro 3, Special Edition
$24.95 USA
0-88022-721-4, 584 pp., 7³/₈ x 9¹/₄

**Using Quattro Pro for Windows,
Special Edition**
$27.95 USA
0-88022-889-X, 900 pp., 7³/₈ x 9¹/₄

Using Quick BASIC 4
$24.95 USA
0-88022-378-2, 713 pp., 7³/₈ x 9¹/₄

Using QuickC for Windows
$29.95 USA
0-88022-810-5, 584 pp., 7³/₈ x 9¹/₄

Using Quicken 5
$19.95 USA
0-88022-888-1, 550 pp., 7³/₈ x 9¹/₄

Using Quicken for Windows
$19.95 USA
0-88022-907-1, 550 pp., 7³/₈ x 9¹/₄

Using R:BASE
$24.95 USA
0-88022-603-X, 584 pp., 7³/₈ x 9¹/₄

Using Smart
$24.95 USA
0-88022-229-8, 584 pp., 7³/₈ x 9¹/₄

Using SuperCalc5, 2nd Edition
$24.95 USA
0-88022-404-5, 584 pp., 7³/₈ x 9¹/₄

Using TimeLine
$24.95 USA
0-88022-602-1, 584 pp., 7³/₈ x 9¹/₄

**Using Turbo Pascal 6,
2nd Edition**
$29.95 USA
0-88022-700-1, 800 pp., 7³/₈ x 9¹/₄

Using Turbo Pascal for Windows
$29.95 USA
0-88022-806-7, 584 pp., 7³/₈ x 9¹/₄

**Using Turbo Tax: 1992 Edition Tax
Advice & Planning**
$24.95 USA
0-88022-839-3, 584 pp., 7³/₈ x 9¹/₄

Using UNIX
$29.95 USA
0-88022-519-X, 584 pp., 7³/₈ x 9¹/₄

Using Visual Basic
$29.95 USA
0-88022-763-X, 584 pp., 7³/₈ x 9¹/₄

Using Windows 3.1
$27.95 USA
0-88022-731-1, 584 pp., 7³/₈ x 9¹/₄

**Using Word for Windows 2,
Special Edition**
$27.95 USA
0-88022-832-6, 584 pp., 7³/₈ x 9¹/₄

Using WordPerfect 5
$27.95 USA
0-88022-351-0, 584 pp., 7³/₈ x 9¹/₄

Using WordPerfect 5.1, Special Edition
$27.95 USA
0-88022-554-8, 584 pp., 7³/₈ x 9¹/₄

Using WordStar 7
$19.95 USA
0-88022-909-8, 550 pp., 7³/₈ x 9¹/₄

Using Your Hard Disk
$29.95 USA
0-88022-583-1, 584 pp., 7³/₈ x 9¹/₄

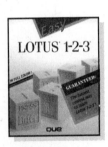
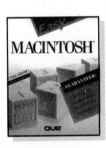